Richard Greene was born in 196[...]  [...]
Oxford, taking a doctorate in 1[...]
professor of English at the Univers[...]
of two volumes of poetry and a biog[...]
eighteenth-century poet Mary L[...] (with Ann
Messenger) of an edition of Leapor's works. He edited *The Selected
Letters of Edith Sitwell*, and is the author of a biography of Sitwell.

Praise for *Graham Greene: A Life in Letters*

'Richard Greene has done a masterly job in producing this book,
not for scholars but for the general reader, for fans of Graham
Greene and for people, like me, who just love poking their noses
into other people's correspondence. *A Life in Letters* . . .
simultaneously broadens our understanding of this remarkable
man and, at long last, liberates his posthumous image from the
Norman Sherry stranglehold'
Alexander Waugh, *Sunday Telegraph*

'A fascinating new book which sheds light on that great writer'
Richard Ingrams, *Independent*

'Richard Greene has made a judicious selection that gives a more
balanced portrait of the man than most biographical and critical
studies'
David Lodge, *Guardian*

'An exemplary collection of his letters'
Spectator

'Impeccably edited'
Tablet

'Highly addictive and has oodles of old-school swagger and
improbable panache'
Kevin Barry, *Irish Times*

...He studied at Christ Church,
... and is now an associate
... University of Toronto. He is the author
... biographical and critical study of the
... eacon and editor (with Ann...

GRAHAM GREENE

A Life in Letters

Edited by Richard Greene

ABACUS

First published in Great Britain in 2007 by Little, Brown
This paperback edition published in 2008 by Abacus
Reprinted 2011, 2012

A CIP catalogue record for this book
is available from the British Library.

ISBN 978-0-349-11914-4

Typeset in Goudy by M Rules
Printed and bound in Great Britain by
Clays Ltd, St Ives plc

Papers used by Abacus are from well-managed forests
and other responsible sources.

MIX
Paper from
responsible sources
FSC® C104740

Abacus
An imprint of
Little, Brown Book Group
100 Victoria Embankment
London EC4Y 0DY

An Hachette UK Company
www.hachette.co.uk

www.littlebrown.co.uk

In memory of
Amanda Saunders (née Dennys)
1945–2007

Contents

Over the Border: *The Letters of Graham Greene* ix

1 The Early Years 1

2 The Man Within 31

3 The Power and the Glory 77

4 The Heart of the Matter 111

5 The End of the Affair 165

6 A Burnt-Out Case 230

7 The Comedians 268

8 The Honorary Consul 294

9 The Human Factor 336

10 The Last Word 387

Abbreviations 424
Acknowledgements and Sources 426
Appendix: The Comma and the Applecart 428
Index 433

Over the Border

THE LETTERS OF GRAHAM GREENE

'I was present once at a premature cremation', says Aunt Augusta to Henry Pulling, a retired bank manager who has lost the ability to be surprised.[1] And perhaps we believe that we know all we are going to know about Graham Greene, that he has indeed been apprehended by the memoirists and biographers who pursued him. But a journey through his letters – which have never before been brought together in one volume – reveals him as a fugitive from our inquiries, a most wanted man who has slipped over the border just when we thought to seize him.

It is hard to imagine that the greater part of what Graham Greene wrote in his life remains unpublished. Greene once guessed that he wrote about two thousand letters each year. Some have simply vanished, but many thousands have recently come to light, some in dusty filing cabinets, others in out-of-the-way archives. One extremely important collection of letters to his son, wife and mother was recently discovered inside a hollow book. The sum of all these discoveries is to make Graham Greene a stranger to us again.

Graham Greene's personal letters are written with the wit and passion that made him a great novelist. He records suffering, articulates longing and recounts absurdity. His sense of place mingles vibrancy and horror. While an intelligence officer in Sierra Leone in 1942, he described for his mother the small but ubiquitous movements of decay in the city where he would set *The Heart of the Matter*:

---

1 *Travels with My Aunt* (Harmondsworth: Penguin, 1971), 10. Unless otherwise indicated, Greene's works will be cited in the Penguin editions.

Freetown always looks its best from the water. On shore after the rain the plague of house flies has come back to my part. And at night there are far too many objects flying and crawling for my liking. Wherever one wants to put one's hand suddenly, to turn on a switch or what not, there always seems to be a gigantic spider. Whenever one kills something which has flopped on the floor the ants come out and get to work, stripping the corpse and then heaving and pushing the skeleton towards the door. Last night I counted a slow procession of four black hearselike corpses: you couldn't see the ants underneath. And I never get quite used to seeing a vulture sitting complacently on my roof as I come home.   (p. 114)

'Simply crazy about flying' (p. 58), he visited Scandinavia, Russia, Kenya, the Congo, Cuba, Paraguay, Panama and other countries where his stories are set. He recounts long journeys by mule in Mexico and by paddle steamer along the river Momboyo, as well as a dive-bombing mission in Vietnam. In 1967 he visited the Sinai after the Six Day War, only to be caught in a sudden clash: 'For more than two and a half hours in the sun I had to lie with my companion & our driver on the side of a sand dune with artillery (anti-tank guns), mortars, & small arms fire. Alas. I'd only had lemonade for two days – I could have done with a whisky. As we were within a hundred yards of the Israelite artillery who didn't know we were there & which was the Egyptian objective, I really thought I'd had my last game of roulette.' (p. 292) Restless by temperament, he yearned for excitement, but he also believed that something essential about life is revealed in privation, and his travels did not serve merely as a painted backdrop to the stories but were necessary to the work of imagining human reality; he wrote of Sierra Leone: 'Here you could love human beings nearly as God loved them, knowing the worst'.[2]

In a formal exchange of letters in 1948, he debated with V. S. Pritchett and Elizabeth Bowen the writer's obligations to the state: 'I met a farmer at lunch the other day who was employing two lunatics; what fine workers they were, he said; and how loyal. But of

2 *The Heart of the Matter*, 26.

course they were loyal; they were like the conditioned beings of the brave new world. Disloyalty is our privilege.' (p. 151)

Graham Greene is a hard man simply to agree with. His political 'positions' shifted again and again as circumstances altered, and in no small part because he insisted that he wanted to be on the side of victims and that victims change[3] – which explains some part of his intellectual history. More fundamental still is Greene's rejection of closed doctrines, including Marxism and, eventually, the Catholic belief in Infallibility. For him, knowledge and belief came in fragments, and they could always fall apart.

Greene tended to the mid-left politically, but took very different views of socialist governments in Mexico, the Soviet Union, Czechoslovakia, Poland, Cuba, Nicaragua, Chile and China, and of insurgencies in Malaya, Vietnam, Kenya, Haiti and El Salvador. Those differences of view were usually shaped by detailed knowledge of situations on the ground. For example, as a vigorous supporter of Israel, he rejected the conventionally pro-Arab views of the European left as uninformed. Of course, Greene had a contrary turn of mind, and some of his decisions are hard to fathom: he refused to visit the Soviet Union during the Brezhnev years because of its treatment of dissidents but sympathised with his old colleague Kim Philby, whose treachery caused many deaths and strengthened the hand of the KGB. Greene's letters from the defector were passed on to MI6 and he made no secret of their communications, so there can be nothing unconsidered in the remark: 'To me he was a good and loyal friend.' (p. 401) Loyalty was hardly Philby's strength, but Greene regarded loyalty to individuals – what he called 'the human factor' – as more important than an allegiance to a state or an idea. He took a black or white view of friend or foe: that the enemy of an enemy of his own (for example, someone echoing his antipathy to America) must be of necessity a friend. He could not really understand that others can fail to hold this view.[4]

There is an important paradox here. Although he investigated and poured time and effort into fighting many specific injustices and often

3 'The Virtue of Disloyalty', *Reflections*, ed. Judith Adamson, 269.
4 An observation by the novelist's son Francis Greene.

introduced impassioned debate into his novels, Graham Greene was not in the final sense a political writer: he could not trust the notion of an impersonal public good that must underlie a coherent political vision. He wrote in 1948: 'In our hearts there is a ruthless dictator, ready to contemplate the misery of a thousand strangers if it will ensure the happiness of the few we love.'[5] Oppression, persecution and poverty make the human heart observable in the writings of Graham Greene, yet the ultimate drama is not that of the masses but of individual men and women.

Many letters in this book discuss problems in the craft of writing. Graham Greene at one time earned a living as an editor and publisher, and he took great pleasure in the fine details of editing – he brought to his work a novelist's eye and was, for example, willing to chastise one of his discoveries, Mervyn Peake, over the manuscript of *Titus Groan*: 'I'm going to be mercilessly frank – I was very disappointed in a lot of it & frequently wanted to wring your neck because it seemed to me you were spoiling a first-class book by laziness.' He said he could not publish it without cuts of ten thousand words of adjectives and prolix dialogue. He ended by cheerfully offering to meet the author in a duel, preferably 'over whisky glasses in a bar'. (p. 130) Many letters in this book describe his own dealings with publishers, editors and agents. In the late 1920s, we glimpse a young author gleeful at the acceptance of his first novel, while in 1969 we see the established man of letters who will hold his own publisher's feet to the fire. In the midst of a simmering dispute over money, the Viking Press proposed that Greene change the title of *Travels with My Aunt* to something more saleable. He cabled his agent: 'Would rather change publisher than title. Graham Greene'. (p. 302) And a year later, he did so.

In his letters, Greene, an astute and passionate reader, frequently offers opinions on who is worth reading. A lover of good story-telling above all, he much preferred Arthur Conan Doyle to the grand figures of Bloomsbury: 'I can reread him as I find myself unable to reread Virginia Woolf and Forster, but then I am not a literary man.' (p. 369) Although an admirer of *Dubliners*, Greene, like Roddy Doyle, thought Joyce's *Ulysses* one of the most overrated classics and a 'big bore'. (p. 288) His own canon of modern fiction, which was decidedly international, included R. K. Narayan, the outstanding Indian novelist whom he discovered and promoted in the 1930s. Throughout his career, Narayan relied on Greene to edit his manuscripts, and he even accepted the suggestion that he drop most of the syllables from his name so that elderly librarians would have no trouble ordering his books. Greene also promoted the careers of Muriel Spark and Brian Moore, whom he regarded as the finest novelists of a younger generation. Among the treasures of this volume are his letters to Evelyn Waugh and to Auberon Waugh. No one was better qualified than Greene to judge the merits of fiction, and in his view the finest work of the finest novelist of his time was *Brideshead Revisited* – a novel that has been routinely savaged by lesser critics.

Many readers of this book will want to understand something new about Greene's own writing. In some letters, he explains his intentions for the novels as he either collaborates or disputes with scriptwriters seeking to bring his work to the stage or to the cinema. He answered the letters of many fans who wanted to understand more clearly what they had just read. Greene was never certain whether he would be able to finish any book he had begun or, having finished it, whether it ought to be published. He consistently denigrated his own accomplishments, as when he advised the publisher Peter Owen about translations of Shusaku Endo's novel *Silence*: 'I still think it very sad that his best book about the Jesuit missionaries never had more than a paperback publication in England. Perhaps one day you could revive it in hardback. A marvellous book – so much better than my own *Power and the Glory*.' (p. 323) A disturbing study of martyrdom in seventeenth-century Japan, *Silence* is a masterpiece, but Endo could hardly have written it without serving an apprenticeship to Graham Greene.

Greene's misgivings about his work gave way occasionally to rejoicing, as when he suddenly conceived the plot of *The Third Man*. He wrote in a love letter (of which there are many in this book) to Catherine Walston:

> I believe I've got a book coming. I feel so excited that I spell out your name in full carefully sticking my tongue between my teeth to

pronounce it right. The act of creation's awfully odd & inexplicable like falling in love. A lock of hair touches one's eyes in a plane with East Anglia under snow, & one is in love . . . I walked all up Piccadilly & back, went back in a gent's in Brick Street, & suddenly in the gent's, I saw the three characters, the beginning, the middle & the end, & in some ways all the ideas I had – the first sentence of the thriller about the dead Harry who wasn't dead, the risen-from-the dead story, & the one the other day in the train – all seem to come together. I hope to God it lasts. (p. 146)

For Greene, the moments of inspiration actually counted for less than the years of unfailing effort – often thousands of words per day in his early career and afterwards a daily minimum of five hundred. His labours amounted to a new book almost every year into old age. And, of course, he delighted in praise; in 1949, he told Catherine Walston about a bevy of graduate students in Paris writing on his work: '. . . commonsense tells me it's all a joke that will soon pass. But I wish you could see the joke too. I'd love to preen my feathers in front of you.' (p. 163)

It is redundant in writing of a human being to say that he was flawed and that on occasion he caused grief. Some of Greene's biographers have imputed to him, without other evidence, all the moral flaws to be found in his characters. Indeed, his situation has been like that of Dame Muriel Spark, who observed: 'There's a lot of people think they can take my books and analyse me from them. On that principle Agatha Christie would be a serial killer.'[6] Graham Greene was a man of decency and courage; he chronicled the suffering of the world's most oppressed people and devoted his life to writing books that enriched the lives of millions. Readers may be surprised at just how ready he was to make other people's problems his own, including John Sutro's nervous breakdowns, Mervyn Peake's disability from Parkinson's Disease, the penury of the wives of the Soviet dissidents Daniel and Sinyavsky, and the incarceration and torture of the Baptiste brothers in Haiti. He gave away much of what he earned, often with a discretion and grace that removed all sense of patronage. He wrote to Marie Biche, his

6 *Scotsman* (6 March 2004).

French agent: 'we have been friends for nearly thirty years & I know how much you've done for me during that time, so be reasonable & do something – which will hurt you – to please me. I'm scared of your reaction & afraid you'll disappoint me, but please say Yes & allow me this year for Christmas to give you instead of a classic shirt from the Faubourg unsuitable for country wear, allow me – I ask it with trembling voice – to give you a small car – Volkswagen or what you like.' (p. 346–7) His kindness to this particular friend continued to the end; when her health failed, he gave her the use of his Paris flat, and she remained there until her death from cancer.

While much has been said of the 'sliver of ice' in the novelist's heart, there is another dimension, very private, here documented for the first time. His immediate concern for those in trouble or in grief is reflected throughout this book, as in his comments to a Russian friend whose husband had recently leapt to his death from the balcony of their apartment: 'I don't believe myself that death is the end of everything . . . Personally even when I doubt I go on praying at night my own kind of prayers. Why not try at night talking to your husband and telling him all you think. Who knows whether he mightn't be able to hear you and now with a mind unclouded?' (p. 367) Greene's compassion was remarkable in that it was combined with a steady gaze. In the Congo, in 1959, he was confronted with ravages of leprosy, which left behind burnt-out cases by the thousand:

> A nice leper brought me back through the forest carrying a dish of eggs – bad lesions on the face & one eye nearly gone, but chattered cheerfully in French. In spite of modern drugs there are still some horrors: an old man cheerily waving goodbye with hands & feet, but without fingers or toes. Half one hut was in complete darkness – one could just make out an enamel pot. My black companion called & one heard movements. Presently an old woman crawled into the half light like a dog out of a kennel – no fingers or toes or eyes of course & she couldn't even raise her head.   (p. 242)

Greene's views on religion and the possibility of an afterlife are an important theme in his letters. A Catholic convert, he disputed Church teaching and was repelled by the liturgical reforms of

Vatican II. He was pleased to discover that Pope Paul VI read his novels, but despised Pope John Paul II as an ecclesiastical version of Ronald Reagan. In old age, he spoke of himself as a 'Catholic agnostic' (p. 409) and took nothing at face value. It is hard to imagine a more ironic reversal than for one of the great Catholic writers of the century to dispute the validity of a spiritual experience described by one of its most distinguished sceptics. When the philosopher A. J. Ayer choked on a piece of smoked salmon and claimed a near-death experience, Greene wrote to Jocelyn Rickards: 'How does he know that the experience he had during those four minutes was not an experience he had immediately his heart began to beat again and before he became fully conscious? I don't see that there is any proof there of the memory existing for a while after death. Do get him to explain that.' (p. 404) In Greene's lexicon, doubt is not the same as disbelief – his mind gnawed at any kind of certainty including atheism. He claims, for example, that his encounter with the stigmatic Padre Pio in 1949 'introduced a *doubt* in my *disbelief*'.[7] Caught between orthodoxies, Greene positioned himself just inside the church door: 'I respect their belief and sometimes share it.' (p. 407)

Most of the letters in this book are written close to the events they describe, and letters surviving from his youth add to our sense of his relations with his family and closest friends. At nineteen, he asked his ten-year-old sister Elisabeth:

Have you ever noticed how useful numbers are in filling up a letter? Take the tip the next time you write to anyone. If you can't think of anything to say just write something like this, 'I hope you are in the best of health, myself I am somewhat

$$7x - 59\,q^2b = \frac{10 \times 16^2\,4^4}{9^3 \times 25_q} + 10_3 - \frac{\lambda qb}{ady}\,,$$

You can go on like this for a long time.   (p. 7)

How silly this is, and how far from the bleak young man he described in his memoir *A Sort of Life* and later in *Ways of Escape*, which were

7 *Articles of Faith*, 132.

written, it seems, when he had forgotten some of the vitality of his younger self and could remember only sadness. An enormous amount of family correspondence has only recently become available, so it is possible, at last, to see Greene as a son, a brother, a nephew, a father, an uncle and a grandfather. It is poignant to hear him speaking to his daughter from a leproserie:

> Look after yourself, dearest Carol. I so want you to have a happy life.
>   All love from your wandering but loving
>   Daddy   (p. 240)

Or to hear him address one of his young grandsons: 'I know that life for you at this stage is not very easy (it's not all that easy at my stage!), but I do want you to feel that you can write to me in confidence & if there is any way that I can help I'll do my best. We are too alike to remain strangers!' (p. 384) This is a man rarely revealed in the formal biographies.

The letters of Graham Greene offer another 'sort of life'. A conventional biography moves in straight lines, while a life in letters makes its points gradually and sometimes by backward glances. However, a life in letters has a crucial advantage over a conventional biography: it is chiefly in the subject's own voice and in his words. The editor has a hand in creating this effect by including certain letters, dropping others and offering opinions in the notes, but this book intends to clear the stage and to give the life back to its subject. Since letters are usually written in a single draft and many letters in this book were actually dictated, the prose is conversational, at times near to table-talk, but the effect is compelling, the exercise of a unique voice.

No work of scholarship can be the final authority on Graham Greene. He himself would tell curious interviewers to read his novels if they wished to understand him. His laconic 'I am my books'[8] contains much truth. And a collection of letters that makes their author better known also confirms a sense of mystery. At best, it marks the boundaries of character, opinion and experience, but it cannot finally explain away the strangeness of a life: 'I called out to her as she went

8 Cloetta, 45.

by, "Aunt Augusta," but she didn't answer to the name; there was no sign that she even heard me. They danced on in their tireless passion into the shadows.'[9]

A SORT OF CHRONOLOGY

Henry Graham Greene was born in Berkhamsted near London on 2 October 1904. His parents, Charles Henry Greene and Marion Raymond Greene, were cousins, both descended from the brewing family of Bury St Edmunds, which in another branch included the novelist Christopher Isherwood. Graham came as the fourth child; his siblings were Alice Marion or 'Molly' (1896–1963), the handsome and feckless Herbert (1898–1968), Raymond (1901–82), who became a notable physician and mountaineer, Hugh (1910–87), the future Director General of the BBC, and Elisabeth (1914–99), eventually the novelist's secretary and his confidante. Charles Greene's brother Edward, a rich coffee merchant, also lived in Berkhamsted, and his six children were close in age to their cousins. Surrounded by books and companions, Graham's earliest years seem to have been happy; they were, perhaps, not unlike those of his brother Raymond, who remarked, 'I saw nothing horrible in the woodshed, perhaps because we had no woodshed.'[10]

Charles Greene was a master and, from 1910, the headmaster of Berkhamsted School, which began, Graham wrote later, 'just beyond my father's study, through a green baize door'.[11] His father's views were characterised by a 'rather noble old Liberalism' (p. 123) and, while many of the masters quietly ignored his example, he promoted humane principles: 'What an advanced man my father was as Headmaster of Berkhamsted. No prefects or fagging there.' (p. 386)

Graham's contemporaries at the school included Peter Quennell, later a well-known man of letters, and the journalist Claud Cockburn. Another of his friends, Arthur Mayo, recalled that Graham was a

9 *Travels with My Aunt*, 269.
10 *Moments of Being: The Random Recollections of Raymond Greene* (London, 1974), ix.
11 *A Sort of Life*, 46.

friendly and outgoing boy, with an impressive loyalty to the victims of bullying.[12] As the child of the headmaster, however, Graham was eventually caught between his school-friends and his father. By thirteen, he was a boarder and felt himself a Judas in St John's House. When he was fourteen and fifteen, he was tormented by a sometime friend named Lionel Carter and betrayed to Carter by another friend, Augustus Wheeler. He was haunted by these events and was surprised at the banality of an encounter with Wheeler in Malaya in 1950: 'And instead of saying "What hell you made my life 30 years ago," one arranged to meet for drinks!' (p. 183)

Greene's first volume of autobiography, *A Sort of Life* (1971), records his unhappiness as a student – episodes of truancy, self-mutilation by means of a pen-knife and attempts to poison, then drown, himself. After eight terms as a boarder, he ran off to Berkhamsted Common, where he planned to conceal himself as 'an invisible watcher, a spy on all that went on', but was apprehended after two hours by his sister Molly.[13] His parents accepted his protest and allowed him to live at home again – that is, on their side of the green baize door.

Sensing in him something like the mental illnesses that had afflicted both of his grandfathers, his parents sent him, when he was sixteen, for a six-month course of treatment with a psychoanalyst 'of no known school' named Kenneth Richmond in London. Trained by Maurice Nicoll, a sometime Jungian and the main commentator on Ouspensky's and Gurdjieff's works, Richmond was himself a spiritualist and became a leading light in the Society for Psychical Research. With Richmond, Graham began the lifelong habit of recording dreams in a diary: 'My experience bears out the fact that one dreams at least four or five times a night when once one has disciplined oneself to have a pencil and paper beside one in bed!' (p. 358) Dreams are recounted in most of his novels, and are sometimes crucial to the plots. He made selections from the diaries, which were published posthumously as *A World of My Own* (1992).

---

12 Information from Hilary Rost, Mayo's daughter (see p. 316).
13 *A Sort of Life*, 65–6.

Greene enjoyed his time in the Richmonds' house immensely, meeting their literary friends, among them Walter de la Mare. At the end of the course, Richmond recommended that Greene be encouraged in his desire to write.

Psychoanalysis, however, did not banish his illness. Greene claimed that in the autumn of 1923 he began to play Russian roulette with a gun of Raymond's that was kept in a corner-cupboard in their bedroom. Raymond, however, doubted the story, since the gun, which actually belonged to a cousin who had brought it back from the war, was stored without bullets, even though Graham said they were there in a cardboard box.[14] Whether the episode is factual or symbolic hardly matters – it explains with great aptness a key pattern of boredom and risk-taking that characterised Greene's life. Many years later, after he had received lengthy treatment from a distinguished psychiatrist named Eric Strauss, Greene described himself as a manic-depressive.[15] Also known as bipolar illness, manic depression involves mood swings from elation, expansiveness or irritability to despair. Symptoms can appear in adolescence, as occurred in his case. The disease can lead to suicidal depressions, drinking, risk-taking, thrill-seeking, promiscuity and a desire to seduce and be seduced.[16] Such tendencies can manifest in a person who is otherwise responsible, loving and ethical. The disorder, which is hardly culpable, may have caused Greene to rush into ill-advised relationships and to be unsettled throughout his life, constantly seeking 'Ways of Escape' – the title he gave to his second volume of memoirs (1980), in which he also wrote: 'Writing is a form of therapy; sometimes I wonder how all those who do not write, compose or paint can manage to escape the madness, the melancholia, the panic fear which is inherent in the human situation.' [p. xiii].

14 *A Sort of Life*, 92; information from Raymond's son, Oliver Greene, relying on an account by his mother, Eleanor Greene; see also Mockler, viii and 214.

15 See Amory, 502 and 560; *A Sort of Life*, 92.

16 For an authoritative description of this illness, see, for example, *Diagnostic and Statistical Manual of Mental Disorders*, 4th ed. (DSM-IV-TR), which notes, ironically for these purposes, that those who suffer bipolar disorder may write many letters (357). I am grateful to Karl Orend for his observations on bipolar disorder among writers.

In Michaelmas term 1922, Graham went up to Balliol College, Oxford, to read history. His tutor, Kenneth Bell, was an old student of his father's. Among Graham's contemporaries at the university were Harold Acton, John Sutro, John Betjeman and Anthony Powell. Although they later became very close, Graham Greene and Evelyn Waugh moved in separate circles at university – Graham's being heterosexual. Writing to Waugh in 1964, he recalled: 'For a considerable period of my time at Oxford I lived in a general haze of drink. I've never drunk so much in my life since!' (p. 270) Through those years he thought of himself as a poet, and his first book, *Babbling April* (1925), was a collection of verse that in later years he would not willingly mention. On one occasion he was invited with other young poets of Oxford to read on the BBC: 'We sat in a kind of sumptuous drawing room, with beautiful armchairs & sofas, & each in turn had to get up & recite in front of a beautiful blue draped box on a table. I felt like Harold swearing on the saint's bones.' (p. 9)

In the spring of 1925, as he was approaching the end of his degree, Greene fell in love with the fervently Catholic Vivienne Dayrell-Browning. At one point he described his passion for her, with greater accuracy than he intended, as 'monomania'.[17] For the next two years he courted her, mainly in an outpouring of hundreds of letters, and they were married in October 1927. There is no doubt that they were fond of each other, but neither was ready for this step. Graham was managing the impulses of his as yet undiagnosed condition and would quickly be guilty of repeated infidelities. Vivien (as she then began to spell her name) affected an extreme girlishness, was uneasy about sex and could be both priggish and sentimental. Their marriage had some periods of happiness, but Graham became deeply absorbed in his writing and would often go abroad. Vivien developed interests in Victorian furniture and antique doll's houses. The couple had two children, Lucy Caroline (b. 1933) and Francis (b. 1936). The marriage effectively came to an end in 1939, but a formal separation did not occur until 1947.

As part of his courtship of Vivien, Graham adopted her religion.

17 Letter to Vivienne Dayrell-Browning, December 1925, at the Harry Ransom Center, Austin, Texas.

While working for the *Nottingham Journal* in early 1926, he was received into the Roman Catholic Church. Within twenty years, there would be no more famous layman in the Church, but Catholicism was always a struggle for him – he tended to believe most easily when he was in love, for example, with Vivien in the 1920s or with Catherine Walston in the late 1940s. At other times, belief was difficult, as when he was writing *A Burnt-Out Case*. He wrote to Catherine Walston in 1961: 'I feel as though I've come to the end of a long rope with *A Burnt-Out Case* & that I'll probably never succeed in getting any *further* from the Church. It's like, when one was younger, taking a long walk in the country & at a certain tree or a certain gate or the top of one more hill one stopped & thought "Now I must start returning home."' (p. 255) In old age, Graham Greene kept 'one foot in the Catholic Church' (p. 409) identifying with ecclesiastical dissidents such as Hans Küng and the Liberation Theologians in Latin America.

Working as a sub-editor on *The Times*, Greene enjoyed his first literary success in 1929 with *The Man Within*. His publishers, William Heinemann and Doubleday, Doran, made an arrangement for him to write full-time with an annual advance of six hundred pounds for three years. The novels *The Name of Action* (1930) and *Rumour at Nightfall* (1931) – turned out in quick succession – were badly written, and a biography of the notorious seventeenth-century Earl of Rochester was rejected at the beginning of 1932 as obscene. As it turned out, his publishers had paid for his apprenticeship. Living with Vivien in a cottage in the village of Chipping Campden, Greene wrote the first of his mature novels, *Stamboul Train*, with bankruptcy looming. When the book appeared at the end of 1932, it was a bestseller and established him as a bankable author. His next novel, *It's a Battlefield* (1934), the most political of his early works, failed to sell but still won him the praise of V. S. Pritchett, Ezra Pound and Ford Madox Ford.[18]

Graham Greene belonged to the last generation that could think of the world as containing unexplored places. His childhood reading included many stories of Victorian travellers. When he was fourteen,

18 *Ways of Escape*, 28.

he wrote to the explorer William S. Bruce, criticising his book *Polar Exploration*, and wished fervently to visit the South Pole himself.[19] As a young man, he undertook many journeys, including particularly reckless ones to Ireland in 1923 and the Ruhr in 1924. Even his early works often incorporate distant settings; for example, *The Name of Action* has Germany for its background, and *Stamboul Train* sets key events at Subotica on the border of Hungary and Serbia. Research for *England Made Me* (1935) brought him to Denmark and Sweden in the summer of 1933. He visited Paris frequently and was there to report on the aftermath of the Stavisky riots of 1934. In May of that year he visited Latvia and Estonia, a trip that would eventually influence the writing of *Our Man in Havana*.

Greene's most dangerous journey came at the beginning of 1935. Accompanied by his beautiful and intrepid young cousin Barbara Greene (later Countess Strachwitz) and their carriers, he undertook the jungle trek through Sierra Leone and Liberia described in *Journey Without Maps* (1936). He had literally no idea of what lay before him: 'The whole trip gets more & more fantastic every day; at last I've managed to get a fairly large scale map; most of it blank white with dotted lines showing the probable course of rivers!' (p. 68) He wrote of Liberia, as he might have written of most of his destinations: 'There seemed to be a seediness about the place you couldn't get to the same extent elsewhere, and seediness has a very deep appeal . . . It seems to satisfy, temporarily, the sense of nostalgia for something lost'.[20] That nostalgia nearly killed him, as he contracted fever, treated it with quinine and whisky, and survived only by luck (and perhaps thanks to Barbara), but he was surprised by what happened when the fever was at its worst: 'I had discovered in myself a passionate interest in living. I had always assumed before, as a matter of course, that death was desirable'.[21]

Confident of making a living with his pen, in 1935 he rented, and a year later purchased, a large house at Clapham Common – a source

19 Marie-Françoise Allain, *The Other Man: Conversations with Graham Greene*, trans. Guido Waldman (London: The Bodley Head, 1981), 31; hereafter cited as Allain. I am very disappointed that Greene's letter to Bruce seems not to have survived.

20 *Journey Without Maps*, 19.

21 *Journey Without Maps*, 213.

of particular pride to Vivien, who filled it with costly antiques. His standing as an author and reviewer was by now such that he was able to convince Hamish Hamilton to publish *Swami and Friends* (1935), the first novel of the distinguished Indian writer R. K. Narayan. Throughout his career, Narayan was venerated by critics but ignored by readers in Britain. In the years to come, Greene would cajole and badger agents and publishers to make sure that Narayan's works were published and promoted as they deserved.

Part of Greene's own success was that he could produce books that appealed to the popular market. He had become expert in writing thrillers, among them *A Gun for Sale* (1936) and *The Confidential Agent* (1939). One of his most admired novels, *Brighton Rock* (1938), began in the seediness of racetracks as a murder story, but 'turned round and bit me' (p. 88) as a reflection on good and evil and the chances of clemency: 'You can't conceive, my child, nor can I or anyone the . . . appalling . . . strangeness of the mercy of God'.[22]

In early 1938 Greene visited Mexico to report on the persecution of the Catholic Church in the states of Chiapas and Tabasco. Leaving behind him in England a libel case brought by Twentieth Century Fox and Shirley Temple for his review of *Wee Willie Winkie* in the short-lived magazine *Night and Day* (in which he described the child star as having 'a certain adroit coquetry which appealed to middle-aged men'),[23] Greene found Mexico a desperate and unpleasant country, and it seems he could not abide Mexicans. As the years passed, this view reversed itself; Greene visited Latin America and the Caribbean many times, setting several of his most important books there. *Lawless Roads* (1939) is an observant but dyspeptic work that honours the courage of a people he does not like. Greene's most admired novel, *The Power and the Glory* (1940), also set in Mexico's 'atmosphere of desertion', describes the martyrdom of a whisky priest. Pursuing an idea 'of frightening difficulty & hazard' (p. 95), Greene crystallised for the first time the dialogue between Catholic and communist belief central

22 *Brighton Rock*, 246. Few sentences have had such a grip on the modern imagination. For example, it is quoted in the violent soliloquy of President Bartlet in the 'Two Cathedrals' episode of *The West Wing*, a television series influenced by Graham Greene's fiction.

23 *Ways of Escape*, 46.

to many of his subsequent works: '"We agree about a lot of things," the priest said, idly dealing out his cards. "We have facts, too, we don't try to alter – that the world's unhappy whether you are rich or poor – unless you are a saint, and there aren't many of those."'[24]

The coming of the war marked the end of Greene's marriage. He began a serious affair with a stage designer named Dorothy Glover, which continued into the late 1940s. With Vivien and the children evacuated to the country, Greene went into the Ministry of Information, working in the nights as a fire warden, often alongside Dorothy. In October 1940, the house at Clapham Common was bombed. Although saddened by the destruction, he was also relieved of a financial burden, and the end of the house seemed to promise his release from a domestic life he found unbearably claustrophobic. He confided his marriage problems to his sister Elisabeth: 'I always used to laugh at emotional situations and feel they couldn't any of them beat toothache. One lives and learns.' (p. 120)

In 1941, Elisabeth, who had herself joined the Secret Intelligence Service at the start of the war, recruited him, and he was sent back to Sierra Leone as an MI6 officer – a lonely, out-of-the-way posting. There, he gathered many of the impressions that would shape *The Heart of the Matter* (1948). While not searching cargo ships and vaguely keeping track of the Vichy forces in French Guinea, he wrote *The Ministry of Fear* (1943), the best of his thrillers, a work that evoked with terrible clarity the atmosphere of wartime London, a setting he would describe again in *The End of the Affair* (1951). Personal news reached him by cable, first that he had won the Hawthornden Prize for *The Power and the Glory*, then that his father had died – of diabetic complications. In Sierra Leone, he remarked: 'I've had an odd life when I come to think of it. Useless and sometimes miserable, but bizarre and on the whole not boring.' (p. 113)

Greene returned to London in March 1943. He worked under the Soviet agent Kim Philby in the Iberian section of MI6, in St Albans. His relationship with Philby was warm – Philby had great charm and was a convivial and deep drinker—and survived his defection to the Soviet Union in 1963. Nonetheless, in June 1944 Greene left

24 *The Power and the Glory*, 1945.

the service because of Philby's efforts to gain control of counter-intelligence against the Soviets. Greene says that it appeared then that Philby was motivated by personal ambition (see p. 354). Whether he privately suspected Philby of being a Soviet infiltrator may never be known. In later years, Greene occasionally took on assignments for the service in a collegial fashion – he was never again in their employ – but seems not to have been an important figure in the field of intelligence. His usual contact with MI6 was Elisabeth's husband, Rodney Dennys, a senior intelligence officer who gave up that career in 1957 largely because of his dissatisfaction with the ongoing internal investigation into the possibility of a larger Soviet spy network within MI6. Dennys opted for a scholarly life in the College of Arms, where he eventually became Arundel Herald Extraordinary, but remained informally in touch with MI6. He actually knew Philby much better than Greene did and was unforgiving, having personally trained some of the intelligence officers for whose deaths Philby was directly responsible.[25]

Between 1944 and 1948, Greene worked at the publisher Eyre & Spottiswoode, having been a director of the firm for several years before that. He was responsible for the fiction list, bringing to the firm such authors as Mervyn Peake, R. K. Narayan and François Mauriac. He left after a conflict with the managing director, Douglas Jerrold, and a row with Anthony Powell, whom he accused of writing a 'a bloody boring book' (p. 162).

Greene's life underwent a revolution in 1946. Catherine Walston (1916–78), the American wife of the Labour politician, later peer, Harry Walston, approached him to be her godfather as she was being received into the Catholic Church. They began a passionate, some-times frantic, affair, which lasted more than a decade, coinciding with the worst period of Greene's bipolar illness. The general outlines of *The End of the Affair* (1951), in which an author becomes involved with the wife of a civil servant, were inspired by this relationship; however, the major characters have obvious differences from Graham Greene and Catherine and Harry Walston.

In early 1947, Greene took a holiday with Catherine in Ireland, during which he wrote part of *The Heart of the Matter* (1948), the book

25 Information from Amanda Saunders, Louise Dennys and Nicholas Dennys.

so well received that he became a perennial, though disappointed, candidate for the Nobel Prize (always claiming, however, that he was in very good company). It also ensured that he became a Catholic celebrity. His friend, the poet Edith Sitwell, had remarked in 1945: 'What a great priest you would have made. But you are better as you are.'[26] When *The Heart of the Matter* was published, she wrote to a friend, 'Have you read Graham Greene's new book? It may prevent me from committing suicide!!'[27] But Greene had to deal with more than the accolades of fellow writers; he was beset by troubled clergymen and devout neurotics looking for answers he was not qualified to give. In the meantime, his private life was in disarray. Finally separated from Vivien, who refused, on religious grounds, to allow a divorce, he found that Catherine, though willing to conduct an affair, would not marry him for fear of losing her children, and that Dorothy simply would not let him go. On several occasions he came near to suicide: 'Perhaps the ban on killing oneself is only during the first three years of a policy.' (p. 141)

For many years an influential film reviewer, he had worked as a scriptwriter for the producer Alexander Korda in the late 1930s. In the late 1940s he had his greatest success in the cinema. With Terence Rattigan, he co-wrote the script of *Brighton Rock* (1947). He then worked with Korda and the director Carol Reed – both close friends in this period – as the scriptwriter for *The Fallen Idol* (1948) and the great classic *The Third Man* (1949). Greene preferred the film of *The Third Man* to the novella published in 1950, and although he wrote scripts for *Loser Takes All* (1956), *St Joan* (1957), *Our Man in Havana* (1960) and *The Comedians* (1967), none of these achieved the same standard. Many of Greene's stories were made into films by other scriptwriters – some of the results pleased him, but some, notably *The Man Within* (1947) and *The Quiet American* (1957), he regarded as abominations.

The 1950s saw Greene's greatest success as a playwright, beginning with *The Living Room* in 1952, which embodied his frustration with Catholic marriage doctrine. His most admired play, *The Potting Shed*, about a family torn apart by the memory of an apparent miracle, was

---

26 Greene sometimes wondered if Sitwell had actually made this often-quoted remark. It can be found in a letter of Sitwell's to Greene now deposited at Georgetown University.
27 Edith Sitwell, letter to David Horner, 1 June 1948, Harry Ransom Center, Austin, Texas.

presented in different versions in New York in 1957 and London in 1958. *The Complaisant Lover* was first performed in 1959. His last major play, *Carving a Statue* (1964), was a failure that Greene rather harshly blamed on the acting of Sir Ralph Richardson, who had earlier turned in one of the great performances in British cinema as the butler Baines in *The Fallen Idol*, and another very strong performance as 'C' in *Our Man in Havana*.

From the late 1940s, Greene chose to live near the Walstons. He first took a flat in St. James's Street, and when they moved, he moved too – to Albany, an elegant and quiet enclave just yards from Piccadilly, which had in the nineteenth century numbered among its residents Lord Byron, William Gladstone and 'Monk' Lewis. He also had a small house in Anacapri where he did much of his writing. However, he spent long periods outside Europe. At the end of 1950 he visited Malaya, where his brother Hugh was in charge of psychological warfare against the Communist insurgency. His reasons for going there were not poetic: 'Nature doesn't really interest me – except in so far as it may contain an ambush – that is, something human.' (p. 182) He later commented on war reporters' habit of subtly congratulating themselves on their own courage: 'I think when one is dealing with horrors one should write very coldly. Otherwise it reads like hidden boasting – "just see what a brave chap I am to have voluntarily put myself in the way of such experiences." To adapt Wordsworth, horror should be remembered in tranquillity.' (p. 345)

He went on to Vietnam in the first of four winter sojourns that led to the writing of *The Quiet American* (1955). From the 1950s until the end of his life, Greene criticised the Americans for meddling in Vietnam, Haiti and Latin America. In particular, he enjoyed creating 'incidents' that would expose the silliness of the McCarran Internal Security Act (1950), which was meant to keep members of dangerous organisations out of the country. That act was opposed by many Americans, including President Harry Truman, whose veto Congress overrode. Having briefly been a member of the Communist Party at Oxford, Greene repeatedly dared American officials to refuse him visas. The anti-American habit of mind was deeply ingrained and can be detected in his writings from the 1930s, when his knowledge of the country came chiefly from books and films. Indeed, several of his literary heroes – James, Pound and Eliot – had abandoned their supposedly uncultured homeland for Europe. The prejudice sometimes pushed him into untenable positions, as when, in his later years, he asserted moral equivalence between the superpowers and, occasionally, a preference for the Soviets (see p. 296).

In 1953 Greene reported on the Mau Mau rebellion in Kenya, but, like his trip to Malaya, this journey did not result in a novel. He made his first trip to Haiti in 1954, with Peter and Natasha Brook and the novelist Truman Capote, who Greene thought had 'an odd psychic quality about him' – he told Greene's fortune with spectacular inaccuracy (see p. 210). They attended a voodoo ceremony, which included 'a procession carrying fuel & food & dishes & a live hen. The man carrying the hen swung it like a censer, & then would dash to this & that member of the congregation & plaster his face & body with the live bird . . . More interminable prayers & then the bird's feet were cracked off like cheese biscuits & the attendant put the live bird's head in his mouth & bit it off' (p. 209).

In the following year, Greene travelled to Alberta with his twenty-one-year-old daughter, Lucy Caroline. With his backing, she bought a ranch, which he visited often, writing portions of *Our Man in Havana* there: 'It's a strange feeling looking round at the country, hill & valley & stream, & knowing that Lucy is the owner. It makes one feel there's some point in writing books after all.' (p. 223) She married in Canada and had two sons, Andrew and Jonathan Bourget.

By the mid-fifties, there was little reason for Greene to hope for marriage from Catherine Walston. He began a relationship with the recently widowed Swedish actress Anita Björk. He found himself very much in love but Stockholm was dull, and his sense of humour shocked the Swedes. Short of asking Anita to abandon her career and live elsewhere, there was no hope of marriage or any other satisfying arrangement between them. By the end of the decade, Greene was in a profound depression and went so far as to seek electric-shock therapy from Dr Eric Strauss, who suggested instead that he write about his childhood. So, on doctor's orders, he began his volume of autobiography, *A Sort of Life*, which did not actually appear until 1971.[28]

Around 1958, Greene also started a novel about school life, but

28 Allain, 15.

found the subject so grim that he abandoned it in favour of leprosy.[29]
He visited the Congo in early 1959, spending most of his time at a lep-
roserie in Yonda in the company of Dr Michel Lechat and a group of
Belgian missionaries. The novel that came from this experience, *A
Burnt-Out Case*, was published at the beginning of 1961. Evelyn
Waugh wrote: 'It is the first time Graham has come out as specifically
faithless – pray God it is a mood, but it strikes deeper and colder.'[30]
However, other Catholics thought well of it, among them Edith
Sitwell, who described it as a 'holy book'.[31]

Greene met Yvonne Cloetta in Cameroon in March 1959.
Although for the sake of their children she did not divorce her husband, she became Greene's de facto spouse for the next thirty-two
years. An elegant and thoughtful woman, her temperament was more
cheerful and moderate than those of Greene's earlier loves. Her influence seems to have coincided with a quieting of the cycles of manic
depression and the beginning of a happier phase in the novelist's life.
Nonetheless, Greene defended his right to be melancholy: 'Does anybody really want to change a little? A complete change, I suppose, one
could accept, but not a small change – otherwise one would be losing
one's thing.' (p. 315)

Greene was always cagey about money, but in the early 1960s he
was swindled by a financial adviser named Thomas Roe. After a long
dispute, Greene squared things with the Inland Revenue at the beginning of 1966 by moving to Antibes, in the south of France. At just the
moment one branch of the government was forcing him abroad,
Downing Street was approving him as a Companion of Honour.
Greene was actually glad to be nearer to Cloetta. Much of the rest of
his life was spent in Paris, Antibes and Anacapri. He returned occasionally to England to see his family, to do business and, somewhat
reluctantly, to collect medals and doctorates.

In 1963 and 1965 Greene returned to Haiti to observe the homicidal regime of President François 'Papa Doc' Duvalier, whose gang of
national police thugs, the Tonton Macoutes, had kept him in power by

torturing and killing his supposed opponents. Once Greene's Haitian novel *The Comedians* was published in 1966, 'Papa Doc' developed a very personal hatred for its author, threatening him with death – much to Greene's pleasure, since it was the only novel that he deliberately wrote to effect political change – by drawing the world's attention to the plight of the Haitians. Greene's main guide in Haiti was another man despised by the regime, the journalist Bernard Diederich, a New Zealander who also organised many of Greene's journeys to Cuba, the Dominican Republic, Panama and Nicaragua.

By now in his mid-sixties, Greene opened new territory in his fiction with *Travels with My Aunt* (1969), a subtle work about old age and death. He felt the novel was much underrated by publishers and critics, many of whom thought it merely funny – which it is, too. Part of that novel was set in South America, and from 1968 he made a series of visits to Paraguay, Argentina and Chile that would also provide the background for *The Honorary Consul* (1973), a work that returned to the problems of faith and tyranny that had preoccupied him since *The Power and the Glory*. In the summer of 1973 he visited the farm in the Transvaal of the novelist Etienne Leroux, a journey that brought into focus the questions of apartheid addressed in *The Human Factor* (1978). That novel draws a portrait of a defector, whose actions, if not his motives, resemble Philby's.

In July 1976, Greene took the first of a series of journeys through Spain and Portugal with his friend the literary scholar and priest Leopoldo Durán, who wrote a memoir of him. Out of their travels came *Monsignor Quixote* (1982), a work that considers age, death and illusion with the lightness of touch and the gentleness Greene had first demonstrated in *Travels with My Aunt*. He may have learned that particular set of narrative skills from many years of reading R. K. Narayan.

Greene made his first visit to Panama in December 1976 as the guest of the charismatic, anti-American head of government, General Omar Torrijos. He became particularly close to 'Chuchu', a member of the General's bodyguard who happened to hold a doctorate from the Sorbonne. Torrijos took Greene (to his great delight) along with him as a member of the Panamanian delegation to Washington for the 7 September 1977 signing of the Panama Canal Treaty, an event attended by several South American despots who, in their own countries, would gladly have made the novelist disappear. After Torrijos's death in an airplane crash in 1981, Greene wrote *Getting to Know the General* (1984), a memoir of Torrijos, Chuchu, and a country that became dangerous for him under the rule of Manuel Noriega.

A difficult and unproductive time for Graham Greene began in 1979, when he was treated for intestinal cancer. Although he was cured, more troubles were pressing on him. Yvonne's daughter Martine was caught in a child-custody dispute with a former husband whose underworld connections seemed to shield him from the law. Martine, her parents and Greene were all threatened with violence. Described in a pamphlet he wrote called *J'Accuse* (1982), the conflict took five years to resolve and, by the end of it, Greene had finally become an old man. In his last decade he produced just one novel, *The Captain and the Enemy* (1988) – an enigmatic and technically perfect book whose first paragraph, about a boy being won in a game of backgammon, is unforgettable. In this book, Greene finally brought school life into his fiction and introduced, very obliquely, memories of the psychoanalyst Kenneth Richmond and his wife Zoë.[32]

Greene took three trips to the Soviet Union in 1986 and 1987, where he visited again with Kim Philby. The novelist's fame in Russia was considerable. At one point Greene met a cosmonaut, B. I. Gretchko, who had spent three months in orbit: 'He presented me with his marked copy of a Penguin of *Our Man in Havana* which he had taken with him into space!' (p. 392)

Greene maintained through these years a wide range of political contacts in Latin America and a heavy correspondence throughout the world. In December 1989 he was hospitalised with an illness eventually diagnosed as leukaemia. The following summer he bought a flat in Vevey, Switzerland, the country where his daughter, Lucy Caroline, and Martine Cloetta were both living. As his illness advanced, his wits remained sharp, though he suffered some loss of memory. His daughter recalls that he looked on his own death with great curiosity as to what, if anything, lay ahead. It was, for him, another journey without maps. He died on 3 April 1991.

32 See West, 246–7.

SOURCES AND ORGANISATION

The material available for this selection is vast – one collection alone fills seventeen linear feet of files, and there are others nearly as large. An edition of the complete letters would take several decades to complete and would be valuable for scholars but otherwise forbidding and essentially unreadable. In this volume, I have chosen a substantial group of letters that are engaging to read and that reveal Greene's personal, literary, religious and political concerns over a period of seventy years. The book is arranged on chronological lines, with chapters divided mainly according to his major works.

With so much material at hand, it has not been necessary to include in this volume Greene's many letters to the editors of newspapers and magazines – these are already available in an excellent edition by Christopher Hawtree, *Yours etc.* (1989). Likewise, I have omitted Greene's letters to the bookseller David Lowe available in *Dear David, Dear Graham: A Bibliophilic Correspondence* (1989). I have, however, included Greene's contributions to the important book *Why Do I Write?* (1948), which had little circulation and now is largely forgotten.

The Graham Greene literary estate has given me complete freedom in preparing this book. As is well known, the Greene archives at Georgetown University were subject to various restrictions. All but one of those have now been lifted. The letters Greene wrote to Yvonne Cloetta, who died in 2001, remain, by her instruction, under an embargo during the lifetime of Jacques Cloetta. Some have found their way into print, but this is a violation of the arrangement made when they were sold. The full publication of those letters will have to wait. Her experiences with Graham Greene are admirably described in her interviews with Marie-François Allain, *In Search of a Beginning* (2004).

From the 1950s, Greene's correspondence was so burdensome that he dictated letters onto dictabelts, which were then sent to his secretary, who kept stocks of signed letterhead. Where letters were produced by a secretary listening to tapes, accidental features have limited authority. In this volume, I have retained a minimal style of punctuation but adjusted it where necessary. Some very long paragraphs have been divided. Errors resulting from faulty transcription of the dictabelts are noted where they occur, but otherwise I have corrected obvious errors silently. Some addresses and postscripts have been deleted and, where the source is a carbon copy, the signature is added – both types of emendation occurring silently. I have added all necessary punctuation to telegrams and regularised the presentation of titles of books and articles.

THE EARLY YEARS

TO MARION GREENE

In the late spring of 1921, Graham suffered an emotional collapse, and from July he undertook a six-month course of psychoanalysis with Kenneth Richmond at his home in London.[1] During his treatment, he took a brief holiday with his aunt Eva – she was going to Lisbon to meet her husband, Edward Greene, who ran a coffee business in Brazil. Graham describes some of the characters on the ship with a skill astonishing in a sixteen-year-old.

R.M.S.P. 'Avon' | Sat. Sep. 3. 1921

Dear Mumma,

We are having another glorious day; the Bay of Biscay not fulfilling its reputation. I've been having a most energetic day, with deck tennis and bowls etc. and am getting back a sea-side appetite. We've got a most amusing table. There's a large fat profiteer, who had the title, probably nominal, of captain during the war. He has practically no chin, the fat of his neck [?] drowning it in one colossal 'bulge'. He has cultivated a critical twist downwards to his mouth, and snorts at every dish. Having ordered three bottles of champagne at dinner, he snorted and 'peeved' for ten minutes until at last the waiter realised his dreadful mistake. He'd brought him champagne – but, in ice! No good! Besides the admiring chorus of his Spanish wife, he has an attendant satellite in the person of a little, old

1 *A Sort of Life*, 64–76; NS 1: 92.

gentleman who does nothing but flatter him. We have also a very thin, silent dour Scotchman, who interjects a meaningless joke about every quarter of an hour.

The Irish clergyman who shares my cabin comes fully up to expectations. In answer to a remark about the amount of food they give us, he answered 'Yes, keep your stomach full, and then, if you are sea-sick you'll be quite all right!' When he was at a University (Manchester, I believe he said) De Valera took him in mathematics. Nothing evil can be said of De V. for 'he is a devout man, a good layman.'[2]

Father Roach comes from the South, from Tipperary and, though he has no desire for a republic, is very indignant at the idea of the Northern Parliament.

Altogether there's an amusing ship load and, of course, there was an invasion of French people at Cherbourg. I had never dreamed of such a wonderful harbour as C. We got quite far in, so that we could see a lot of the forts.

Tomorrow we get to Vigo, and hope to go ashore for a few hours. But it's rather uncertain, as we have not got a Spanish visa on our passports. We also pass close into Corunna, and will probably be able to land at Leixoes.

It will seem funny coming back as we will be quite a large party, six in fact.

Aunt Eva sends her love to all,
   love from
      Graham

Graham and his aunt visited the grave of General Sir John Moore (1761–1809), a distant relative and a hero of the Napoleonic wars. He was killed in the retreat to La Coruña and buried, according to the poet Charles Wolfe, 'darkly at dead of night, the sods with our bayonets turning'.

2 With negotiations for the Anglo-Irish Treaty about to begin, Eamon de Valera (1882–1975) had recently been declared President of the Republic of Ireland. Graham undertook a reckless journey to Ireland in 1923, and wrote of Dublin in the aftermath of civil war: 'It is like that most nightmarish of dreams, when one finds oneself in some ordinary and accustomed place, yet with a constant fear at the heart that something terrible, unknown and unpreventable is about to happen.' ('Impressions of Dublin', *Weekly Westminster Gazette*, 25 August 1923, reprinted in *Reflections*, 1–4).

Graham revisited the grave sixty years later when he was planning
Monsignor Quixote.[3]

TO MARION GREENE

*Here, Graham describes a service at Westminster Abbey on 17 October
1921, during which the American Chief-of-Staff General John Pershing
(1860–1948) laid the Congressional Medal of Honor on the tomb of the
unknown warrior. The ceremony was attended by Prime Minister Lloyd
George (1863–1945), Winston Churchill (1874–1965), then Colonial
Secretary, and Earl Haig (1861–1928), who had commanded the British
Expeditionary Force.*

Tuesday [18 October 1921] | At 15 Devonshire Terrace W.2

Dear Mumma,

Thanks very much for the foolscap, and letter. I'm afraid the story
is no use for a magazine. It's much too short. I've sent it in for the
school competition. Yesterday Aunt Eva came to see Mr Richmond
about Ave;[4] to-day in the distance, while reading in the gardens, I
saw Raymond's friend Crompton,[5] and two other people, doing
experiments of some kind.

Yesterday I went to the American ceremony. I got into the Abbey
for the service, but as far as the actual service went, I should have
preferred being outside, as I was too far away to see anything, but a
glimpse of Winston Churchill's head, and to hear anything but a
monotonous drone. I had a dreadful man next me, who expatiated to
me the whole time on the League of Nations and insisted on reading
a long poem on its ideals, written by a friend of his. But it was worth
being bored by the service because of the waiting period beforehand.

3 *Getting to Know the General*, 10.

4 Graham's cousin Ave began psychoanalysis with Kenneth Richmond near the end
of 1921.

5 Raymond Greene (1901–82), Graham's brother who was studying medicine. He
would become famous for an attempt on Mount Everest in 1933. His friend Crompton
has not been identified.

The Abbey itself lighted up brilliantly, but outside the door nothing but a great bank of mist, with now and again a vague steel helmeted figure appearing, only to disappear again. The whole time the most glorious music from the organ, with the American band outside, clashing in at intervals. Then the feeling of expectancy through the whole people, the minds of everyone on tip-toe. It got back the whole atmosphere of the war, of the endless memorial services; I'd never realised before how we had got away from the death feeling.

But when Pershing and the rest arrived, there was a ghastly anti-climax, people standing up on the seats, and peering over other people's shoulders, the whole dramatic effect lost, and the service did nothing to restore it. I rushed out afterwards and managed to get a good view of the inspection, Pershing and Haig and a lot of other generals whom I didn't recognise. I'd never realised what a militarist face Haig had got before. As bad as Hindenburg. Lloyd George, before the inspection, drove off amidst very feeble cheers, and a great deal of laughter and chaff. I got another good view of the others driving off, Pershing amidst great enthusiasm, but Haig in practically silence. Altogether it was quite worth seeing.

Love to all,

Graham

TO MARION GREENE

15 Devonshire Terrace | W.2. | Tuesday [25 October 1921]

Dear Mumma,

I hear you are going to stay a week-end with Aunt N.,[6] but I suppose you won't have room for any books. If you should have room to spare could you bring my Warner and Martin? (History) If Mrs O'Grady would ask Guest,[7] he'd get it from my locker in the library. But don't trouble about finding room, if it's at all difficult, because it's

6 Marion Greene's sister Nora (d. 1971), known within the family as 'Aunt Nono'.
7 Mrs O'Grady was the wife of a master at Berkhamsted School. Eric Guest, a close friend of Graham's, later became a magistrate.

not necessary. It is so to speak a 'luxury'. Tell Hugh, if he would like to send me our stamp swops, I'd try and exchange them for a few we haven't got at Stanley Gibbons.[8] Of course, as most of them are very common, we'd only get a few for them. It's just as he likes.[9] If he wants to, he must also send me Stanley Gibbons' address. I expect you'd have room for them, as they are only in a small sort of notebook, which would take up no room at all. But again, if it's any bother don't.

I hope to see Walter de la Mare[10] soon. Mrs. Richmond has promised to ask him to tea, before I go. I hope soon to blossom into the Saturday *Westminster*. 'The Creation of Beauty. A study in sublimation,' by H. Graham Greene. Ahem! Ahem! Mr. Richmond is going to thrust it before the Editor's eyes, and thinks he'll accept it. The cold weather at last! It is a gloriously sharp, raw day today.

Love to all,

Graham

P.S. Hugh will find S. G.'s address on the stamp catalogues. I remember passing the shop a day or two ago, but I forget where.

TO MARION GREENE

Graham went up to Balliol College, Oxford, in the autumn of 1922. He had an appetite for pranks and helped to launch a candidate for the general election on 15 November.

Oxford Union Society [c. 12 November 1922]

Dear Mumma,

There've been great excitements here lately. Armistice night was on the whole a rather wet show after the first exhilaration had worn

---

8 A philatelic shop.

9 Stamp collecting figures in a number of Graham's books, notably *The Heart of the Matter*.

10 The poet Walter de la Mare (1873–1956) was a friend of the Richmonds. Through him, Graham met Naomi Royde-Smith, the literary editor of the *Weekly Westminster Gazette*, who published a number of his early works but not 'The Creation of Beauty'.

off. There was football with tin trays down the High, & with a
bucket up St. Giles's, where I cut my ankle on it, getting it wedged
in the bucket & tripping up on it. Last night was a much better
organised show. There was a bogus candidate, Jorrocks, up, & a
bogus committee room, from which he made speeches in a mask.
The townees imagined that he was a real candidate, & there were
several scrimmages as a consequence, with the Liberal element in
the crowd. I enclose a Jorrocks pamphlet . . .

*The campaign pamphlet proclaimed: 'Old Wine in Old Bottles! A Plague on
Promises! Personality Pays! . . . Ask the Returning Officer where to put
your X for Jorrocks The Independent Independent! Only Triangular
Candidate for Oxford.'*

TO ELISABETH GREENE

Balliol College | Oxford [March 1923?]

Dear Elisabeth,

I hope you haven't got this. You hadn't last holidays. It's not as
good as *Peacock Pie*,[11] but some of them are quite good. Are you
having a birthday party? Is Hugh still spotty? Have you & Katherine
acted any more plays? I think you might act one of Kipling's *Just So*
stories, & let Hugh take part in 'How the Leopard got his Spots,' or
write a modern musical comedy & call it 'Spot & Carry One,' or an
ancient play of the brave & wicked 'Hugh the Rash,' or a puzzle play
called 'Spot the' no, that's quite enough plays.
    Love from
    Graham

11 A volume of poems for children by Walter de la Mare.

TO ELISABETH GREENE

Balliol College, | Oxford [March 1924]

Dear Elisabeth,

Here is a little memento of this auspicious, nay, may I say epoch making, occasion. For the first time you leave the single state (no, not to enter into matrimony, but into double figures). Double figures! What a thought is there! To think of the time that must elapse before you leave them. To be exact, if my mathematics does not fail me, ninety years. Did I say ninety years? Yes, ninety years. Though there's always a trick about these numbers somewhere. For instance, the other day I was adding up the number of days between the first of March & the fourth. One from four, I said to myself, leaves three. Why, I learned that on my mother's lap, I added (to myself). It was the first thing that my baby lips learned to lisp, I continued. But, would you believe it, I was wrong! There are not three days between. In the same way I have an awful suspicion that in some queer way you will only remain in double figures for eighty-nine years. Think of that! As the Americans say, it won't be no freight train. Only eighty-nine years!

Have you ever noticed how useful numbers are in filling up a letter? Take the tip the next time you write to anyone. If you can't think of anything to say just write something like this, 'I hope you are in the best of health, myself I am somewhat

$$7x - 59 \, q^2 b = \frac{10 \times 16^2 \, 4^4}{9^3 \times 25_q} + 10_3 - \frac{\lambda q b}{a d y}. \quad \text{[12]}$$

You can go on like this for a long time. Then they may think you are very deep, or they may think you are mad, & then *they* won't write to you again, or else they'll try & work it out, & then I am quite sure you'll never have to write to *them* for a second time.

Of course, it may not look as if this little lecture has anything to do with your birthday, but it has really. Only it's very subtle, & very, oh so very, deep. You'll probably not understand it till you get into

[12] The equation, meant to be meaningless, is also, to a degree, illegible.

treble years, though of course if it's only a question of eighty-nine – I wish you'd consult a mathematician about it, or 'teacher' or somebody & set my mind at rest. As Mr Leslie Henson[13] sang

> '*O I'm so very n-n-n-n-nervous,*
> *I'm not myself to-day.*'

O, the last line doesn't mean that at all. Don't be ridiculous. You are very rude. Even if you are in double figures, you needn't say that kind of thing.

What's that? You didn't. Then that thin & tenuous whisper that seemed just now to float mockingly round my head, tickling the back of my nose into a sneeze, cannot have been you at all. If it was Hugh, sock him one on the point of the jaw.

The enclosed letter is for Mumma, the book for you. Don't muddle the two up, & keep the letter yourself & give the book to Mumma.

    Love & happy returns
    from Graham

TO HUGH GREENE

On 22 January 1925, Graham, along with other young poets from Oxford, Harold Acton, Brian Howard, Joseph Macleod, Patrick Monkhouse and A. L. Rowse, read poems on the BBC.

                    Balliol College, | Oxford [23 January 1925]

Dear Hugh,

Many thanks for the P.O.[14] You may as well throw the other books away. Congratulations on being moved up. Don't work too hard!!

I went & had tea at Aunt N's yesterday. I enjoyed the broadcasting

---

13 A well-known comedian and music hall entertainer.
14 Postal order.

very much, though I felt extremely nervous. People in Oxford seem to have heard very clearly, did you? I read a thing, which has just been accepted by the *Weekly Westminster*. I'm rather glad, as their rate of pay has gone up. We sat in a kind of sumptuous drawing room, with beautiful armchairs & sofas, & each in turn had to get up & recite in front of a beautiful blue draped box on a table. I felt like Harold swearing on the saint's bones. Now I've got to set to work & snatch a guinea from the *Oxford Chronicle* for a humorous account of it,[15] but I don't know how to be humorous. Here's a cig-card for Elisabeth.

Love,
Graham

P.S. The B.B.C. got very nervous, when Bryan Howard started on his naked lady. They say they have to be very careful indeed.

TO——

This letter appears in the papers at the Huntington Library of Patrick Balfour (Lord Kinross), a gossip writer and friend of Evelyn Waugh. The addressee is unidentified.

Balliol College, | Oxford [1925?]

Dear ——,

Perhaps it would be best to let out any ill-feeling there may be in a properly arranged fight in some agreed place, now that you are cooler. Not pokers of course. All lethal weapons must be excluded, as I should be so sorry if my young life (or even yours) came to an untimely end.

Yours affectionately,
Graham Greene

15 'Poetry by Wireless', *Oxford Chronicle* (30 January 1925); reprinted in *Reflections*, 14–16.

TO VIVIENNE DAYRELL-BROWNING
(LATER VIVIEN GREENE)

In an issue of Oxford Outlook, *Graham referred slightingly to 'worship' of the Virgin Mary. He received a letter from Vivienne Dayrell-Browning (later she altered the spelling of her first name), a Catholic convert who was Basil Blackwell's private secretary, telling him that Mary was not worshipped but venerated, the technical term being 'hyperdulia'.*[16] *According to her recently discovered birth certificate, Dayrell-Browning was born in 1904 (not 1905) in Rhodesia; she died in 2003 at the age of ninety-nine. Her childhood was excruciating. Her father had an affair; her mother left him and required her at the age of fifteen to write a letter, ending their relationship.*[17] *By the time Graham encountered her, Vivien had developed into a brilliant, complex and slightly eccentric young woman, ruled by a bitter mother. Doubtful about men and marriage, she hesitated as Graham flirted. Their courtship ought to have demonstrated that they were not suited to each other; nonetheless, they were married on 15 October 1927.*

Junior Common Room | Balliol College | Oxford [March 1925]

Dear Miss Dayrell,

I most sincerely apologise. I'm afraid any excuses will sound very lame. But I wrote the article in a frightful hurry, & without preconceiving it, as the paper was already in press. At the same time I was feeling intensely fed up with things, & wanted to be as offensive all round as I could. One forgets that *The Outlook* is read by other than undergraduates, whose thick hides challenge attacks of every description.

I really am very sorry. Will you forgive me, & come & have tea with me as a sign of forgiveness?

Yours sincerely,
    Graham Greene

16 *A Sort of Life*, 118.
17 NS 1:475.

TO AMY LOWELL

Along with Ezra Pound, with whom she fell out, Amy Lowell (1874–1925)
was a leading Imagist poet. She planned a reading tour of England to follow
the publication of her biography of Keats in February 1925. Graham's
interest in her work was probably matched by a mischievous desire to bring
a cigar-smoking lesbian to the university.

Balliol College, | Oxford. [c. 1 March 1925]

Dear Miss Lowell,

I am writing on behalf of The Ordinary, the University Literary
Club, to ask whether you could possibly be so good as to pay us a
visit, when you are in England. If you would be so kind, perhaps you
would let me know a date that would be convenient for you?

Yours sincerely,

Graham Greene

(Sec.)

Lowell accepted for 29 April, but cancelled because of illness. She died of a
stroke on 12 May.

TO VIVIENNE DAYRELL-BROWNING
(LATER VIVIEN GREENE)

29 Museum Road [n.d.]

Dear Miss Dayrell,

Splendid. Do you mind keeping me company in disreputability?
Respectability I have left behind at my Summertown digs, & I dare
not fetch it, since my land lady believes I am at home, & would be
horribly annoyed to find I'd merely changed my digs.

The cinema with me has reached mania. I average four times a
week. Every now & then I catch myself talking of live wires & the
game kid, who could overdraw two dollars out of a Wisconsin
County Bank, & was as quick as a Kentucky sausage.

Will seven o'clock at the George suit you?

I will pray for Skyscrapers & Sixshooters, for Black Jake of Dead Man's Gulch, & the Man with the Broken Finger Nail.

Yours,

   Graham Greene

TO VIVIENNE DAYRELL-BROWNING
(LATER VIVIEN GREENE)

Balliol College | Oxford | Tues. 26 May | 11.10 p.m.

It must be rather fun collecting Souls, Vivienne. Like postage stamps. Last addition to collection Undergraduate Versifier, a common kind. Fair specimen, but badly sentimentalised. Colouring rather faded. Will exchange for Empire Exhibition Special Stamp, or ninepence in cash.

I wish you weren't so futilely far off. I don't mean the mile & a half between Magdalen Street & Thorncliffe Rd. Or I wish I weren't in love with you. I've always enjoyed it before, even when I thought I was being miserable. So I could stand outside & write jangly verse & say to myself 'That's a good idea. That's how I feel.' But I don't know how I feel now. I enjoyed this evening marvellously, but now I've got back I feel you are just as far away as ever, & that it's just as hopeless that you will ever be more than mildly interested in that blasted non-existent soul of mine. This letter will help you to analyse the specimen won't it?

What it all comes to, I suppose, is that I've never really been in love before, only suggested myself into a state of mild excitement in which I could draw fifteen bob out of the *Westminster* for a piece of verse. I can't do that now though. I can't think nearly clear enough to fit anything into a metre. You wouldn't expect me to write verse when I was blind drunk would you? All this is 'absurd.' Of course it is to you. You can't sympathise I suppose, any more than I can with the excitement & scurry of ants. Though how you can expect to know anyone's mind or soul or anything, when you are so far off, I don't know.

I don't know why I'm being so heavy & horrid, when really I'm frightfully grateful to you for to-night. If you ask me to, I won't say a single serious thing, when I next see you. I won't even talk about you, if you ask me not to. It's wonderful what you put up with. With love (which you won't understand[18]).

Graham

The blot is not carefully arranged to show desperation, but my thumb slipped.

Do send me the snapshot you half said you would. Nine days! If you do, I'll even discuss the Budget or the latest books with you. G.

TO A. D. PETERS

On 1 May 1925, Basil Blackwell published Graham's first book, a collection of poems. He had also finished a novel called 'Anthony Sant'. Although Blackwell rejected it, the literary agent A. D. Peters liked it and tried, unsuccessfully, to find a publisher. In his last term at Oxford, Graham accepted a position in China with the British American Tobacco Company but resigned after a period of training.

The School House | Berkhamsted [c. June 1925]

Dear Mr. Peters,

I must confess to a horrid crime. Being rather bored & not knowing how long I shall remain in England, as I am running for a post in China, I sent the volume of verse altered & revised, under the title of *Babbling April*, to Blackwell, who published it last month. Alas! I went & contracted for first refusal of my next two books, & sent the revised A.S. to him. I wrote yesterday asking him to come to a decision, & will write again today enclosing your letter, & asking him to let me know within a week. In any case, I shall be free of my contract I think by August, as I shall have a long poem ready for him by then. I have just started on a new novel,

18 This word is blotted.

which I think will [illeg.] than the A.S. If I may, I will send it you, when finished.

    Yours sincerely,
      Graham Greene

TO WALTER DE LA MARE

29. Thorncliffe Rd. | Oxford [1925]

Dear Mr. de la Mare,

    I hope it will not be presumptuous of me to send you this, my first book. I expect you've forgotten who I am, unless you remember our strawberry tea at Berkhamsted.

    Yours sincerely,
      Graham Greene

TO VIVIENNE DAYRELL-BROWNING
(LATER VIVIEN GREENE)

Vivien had written, 'Do you know you've had a letter every day this week? I shall appoint myself chairman of a Committee empowered to look into the matter & draw up a report.'

[2 June 1925]

On behalf of the shareholders of this Company I should like to state that we are fully satisfied with the management of the Chairman & Board, & would like the business of the Company carried on in the future on the same lines, which have proved so eminently satisfactory in the past. I should like to move a vote of very sincere thanks to, & confidence in, the Chairman & Directors of this Company.

    I can't say this in the Board Room, but the Chairman is the most wonderful person in the world.

    You darling!

TO VIVIENNE DAYRELL-BROWNING
(LATER VIVIEN GREENE)

On Friday, 20 June 1925, Graham and Vivien said a 'final goodbye' by the river at Wolvercote. However, the courtship resumed shortly after.

The School House | Berkhamsted | 10 a.m. Mon. [22 June 1925]

I haven't written before. I haven't had much time, except in nearly four hours of ghastly train journey, & anyway I hoped I might be able to write a bit cheerfuller this morning. I'm sorry if I can't. Your letter was lovely.

You were quite right about saying goodbye outside Oxford. I couldn't have stood the bus journey back. And it is of value to have been the first person you've kissed. But it doesn't make me feel a bit pleased with myself. It only makes me wonder how somebody like you can exist, who's willing to do something you don't want to do, just because a friend of yours is so mundane that he can't do without it. And even if I can't say as much, I can say that I've never kissed anyone I've wanted to really badly before, or held off for so long, for fear of offence. You are so precious that I'm afraid of doing or saying any thing which might prevent me seeing you.

Now I'm writing a horrid depressing sort of letter, which will come just when you've got nice & cheerful again, & giving a free lift to your shoulders & saying 'Well at last, he's over.' You see, our depressions are so different. You feel melancholy, because you think you may not see a friend again. I'm depressed, because I love you so frightfully, & even though I do see you again several times, I shan't be able to feel that you are there, living in the same place, & that I can always ring you up at any moment & hear your voice, even if it's an angry or a bored voice. It's all so silly that I should love someone, whom I should want to marry, whatever conditions she might choose to make, but just the someone who wouldn't marry me on any conditions. It's bad luck at the least. [. . .]

TO A. D. PETERS

Graham completed 'Anthony Sant' by November 1924, but revised it for
submission to publishers. Of this novel he wrote: 'The subject, like so many
first novels, was childhood and unhappiness. . . . By a mistaken application
of the Mendelian theory I told the story of a black child born of white par-
ents – a throwback to some remote ancestor. . . . There followed in my novel
a hushed-up childhood and a lonely colour-barred life at school, but to me
even then the end seemed badly botched, and I can see that it was strangely
optimistic for one of my temperament. I made the young man find a kind of
content by joining a ship at Cardiff as a Negro deckhand, so escaping from
the middle class and his sense of being an outsider.'[19]

Balliol College | Oxford [c. June 1925]

Dear Mr. Peters,

Many thanks for your letter. I've been at work on 'Anthony Sant'.
I found a lot of small things I wanted to alter in the first chapter,
mostly in the way of terribly banal adjectives.

I've got Ch. IV properly sorted now, so that there's no break in
the narrative; I've also eliminated all the first persons.

I'm just beginning on the last chapter. Do you think the public
must have Anthony settling down somewhere with a woman? My
idea now is so to alter the character of the prostitute, as to make her
return to the old trade not particularly unpleasant to a soft hearted
reader. A. would then recover not only from his attempted suicide,
but also a little of his sense of humour. The whole drift of the story
hitherto has been in the difficulty of reconciling his colour with his
civilised sex instincts. Now he will find a perfectly happy
compromise by cutting out any idea of the 'love instinct.' And he'll
be left in the stoke hold of a ship, finding happiness in physical
fatigue, & in mixing with a medley of nationalities, where his
colour does not give him any inferiority complex, & where he is
completely cut off from his family & caste. The idea would wind up
with a description of the furnaces etc. conveying the feeling that

this in its way is like the forest, which he has been aiming at in his dreams.[20]

It sounds very crude put like this, but I think it could be worked out all right, & seems to me more plausible than a sexually happy ending. Do you think it might go down all right?

Then there'd be quite a number of titles one might have. What about 'Escape', 'The Joyful Compromise', or 'Open Sea'?

Yours sincerely,

Graham Greene

P. S. I hope I may have the chance of seeing you in the vac.

TO A. D. PETERS

Following the failure of the Germans to pay war indemnities, the French attempted to set up a 'Revolver Republic' in the occupied Ruhr in 1922. They assembled a loose army of German separatists, thugs recruited from brothels and French prisons, to assist the collaborators. Graham persuaded the Count von Bernstorff at the German embassy to finance a trip in the spring of 1924 for himself, his cousin Edward Greene (called 'Tooter') and Claud Cockburn, so they could write articles on the crisis from the German perspective. While there, the three conceived a novel after the manner of John Buchan, but nothing came of it.[21] A year later, Graham made another attempt at the thriller. He returned to the subject in The Name of Action *(1930).*

The School House | Berkhamsted [1925]

Dear Mr. Peters,

I enclose the first 20,000 (circa) words of the 'shocker' in the hope that you may be able to serialise it. Is it necessary to give a synopsis of the whole plot? Once again I do not like the title, but at

---

20 This idea reappears in *A Burnt-Out Case* (1960), in which the main character, Querry, yearns for a place of peace named Pendélé deep in the jungle.

21 *A Sort of Life*, 100–5.

present I have been unable to think of anything else. There is another point also. Try as I would I could not introduce a love interest before, at the very earliest, Ch. VI. Will this militate against its being taken as a serial? I expect you will find the whole story rather derivative, though the main theme of the German Separatists has, I think, not yet been taken in this type of fiction.

Re Anthony Sant's title. What do you think of 'Crouching Dust' from Blunden's lines (I quote from memory)

> '*And all my hopes shall with my body soon*
> *Be but as crouching dust & wind-blown sand.*'?[22]

Yours very sincerely
    Graham Greene

P.S. Let me know if you require a synopsis of the rest of this story.

TO VIVIENNE DAYRELL-BROWNING
(LATER VIVIEN GREENE)

37 Smith St. | Chelsea, S.W. | Aug. 7 [1925]. 6.30 p.m.

Darling,

I got your second lovely letter when I got back from work this evening. It was lovely, but it made me feel the most utter beast that ever was, because you talked about looking forward to my letter, & I know that you'll have got two rotten ones. I ought never to have sent them, especially the last. I tell you that I don't want to give you pain, & then I go & write like that. But, my darling, it *is* true, only sometimes I can't help whining.

Darling, it's wonderful when the person one loves most in the world encourages one in what one loves next best (even though far less).

---

22 From Blunden's poem 'The Giant Puffball'. The exact wording is: 'And all my hopes must with my body soon / Be but as crouching dust and wind-blown sand.'

I've never met so complete a companion as you. Those winter evenings you describe seem to me the only thing worth having. It's companionship with you that I want & just that sort of companionship. You see somehow I feel as if you've pushed me through a door, so that some things, as you say, do seem a bit trivial & second rate now. What I long for is a quite original marriage with you, companionship & companionship only, all that Winter evenings part, & to have someone worth fighting for. And you would go on holidays, when you liked, & see your mother when you liked, & I should share your companionship. I shouldn't grumble if it was a less share than your mother had. You could work too if you wanted to. There'd be no domestic tying down, & you'd always keep your ideal of celibacy, & you could help me to keep the same ideal. I didn't know six months ago that I should ever want to keep that ideal, but as I say you've shoved me through a door. And besides having some of the Winter evenings with me, as well as having some with your mother, we should have our own adventures together. Because sometimes, when I'd been good, you'd come for a holiday with me, & we should have that night train journey across Europe. Do you remember talking about it?

And the whole thing would be an adventure finer than the ordinary marriage, because it would be two, not merely fighting for each other, but for a shared ideal. Darling, it sounds fantastic, but the fantastic is often wildly practical, as when Columbus put out from Spain. And I remember you wrote once that you did love me, though it wasn't in a way I understood, but, darling, it's a way I do understand, & it's the final because there's no reason why it should ever end, which is very different to the other. I wish to God (& I mean that literally) that this dream could come true. You talked about how pleasant it would be to round off our friendship properly. Then you meant making a clean break, & leaving no ragged ends, but suppose God *did* make us come together, & the rounding off was as I've imagined, & that he brought us together, in order to strike out together across this new country. For it would be new country, & perhaps even the kind of promised land to which people have really been aiming, though they didn't know it, & they'll follow us in. This is still another thing I could not have believed six months ago, that I should write a kind of religious letter. But I can't help it. I've been wanting to say this for a long time now. O my dear, if you only made it true – this 'monastic marriage' – then it would be goodbye to business in China, & there'd be something more than money in the future.

I can't write anymore. Lots of love (& can't you believe that it's *not* love, just because you are beautiful?)

Graham

Graham was a man of strong appetites, often made utterly unmanageable by bipolar illness. His offer of a 'monastic marriage' was doomed from the start. His sexual life was conducted mainly outside the marriage; he was involved in many brief liaisons, sometimes with prostitutes, and he had several long relationships.

TO VIVIENNE DAYRELL-BROWNING (LATER VIVIEN GREENE)

With Vivien travelling on the Continent, Graham headed north for a job as tutor at Ambervale, Ashover, near Chesterfield. He was now anxious for a career that would allow him to remain in England.

At St. Pancras | 1.10 p.m | Monday [24 August 1925]

O my darling, you've forgotten all about me. My guardian angel's gone fast asleep. First of all the glass of your frame breaks, then comes the taxi accident, & just now I've found I've lost my ticket to Stretton & will have to get another. O my dear, I hope you'll send it back quickly. I'm feeling so nervous of my future 'charge.' I wonder when I shall hear from you, my dear love.

I've just been to see the Editor of the Lit. Supp.[23] A charming man. I'm to send him a card for books I want & he'll try & send me some of them. I hit on a good stunt quite by accident. He said 'If I

23 Bruce Richmond (1871–1964) gave Graham three biographies to review: *Sir Thomas More* and *Sir Thomas Gresham* (3 December 1925) and *A Short Life of William Pitt* (7 January 1926).

asked you to do a front page leader on anything you liked, what would you do?' I said the first thing that came into my head 'The Prose of the Restoration.' He was fearfully pleased, because he said that he had no specialist in that, & that someone he knew was publishing a book on Rochester soon. So I hope to get that. If I start doing a column or two in the *Lit. Supp.* it won't be a bad start. And, my darling, he said there was an unrivalled opportunity on *The Times* just now. He said if I get on next year, I'd have a chance of doing leaders on home politics at once, & there was no reason why I shouldn't leap into a good salary, a very good salary. [. . .]

TO VIVIENNE DAYRELL-BROWNING
(LATER VIVIEN GREENE)

Graham here proposes an engagement which is no engagement. A further concession, he announces his decision to become a Catholic. A decade later, in Mexico, he would discover some of the emotional aspect of his faith as he studied the progress of a persecution.[24] *By that time, his marriage was very much in decay.*

The Golden Cross [Oxford] | 8.45 a.m. | Weds. Sept. 16 '25

My darling love, thank you so much for the dear cinema note. It stayed under my pillow all through the night & slept when I did, which wasn't very much.

My very dearest sweetest heart. I wrote to you before the Capitol proposing a Marriage, which the world would not call a Marriage. Darling heart, can't we have an Engagement, which the World would not call an Engagement. I would not ask that that one in fifty chance should be increased. I would wait until I was settled & then ask you whether you'd marry me, & I should be neither surprised nor angry, if you said No. And of course at any time you could write & say that you didn't want to see me again. In fact, darling, really there'd be no Engagement at all. I should still be fighting for a one in

24 *Ways of Escape*, 58–60.

fifty chance. *But*, darling, & this is a big *but*, it would make it so much easier for us to see each other. You could come for a week-end occasionally to Berkhamsted without feeling shy & out of place, &, my own darling, that would be lovely. I think you'd like my family a lot, my own love, & they'd adore you. And no one could object to things like the Thorncliffe Rd. plan. And, darling heart, I give you my word of honour that I would not build a single brick upon it.

My dear sweet love, I seem to be always asking of you, & never giving. I wish to God I could give anything, which would make you even happier than you are. But I've got good precedents for asking, haven't I, & being a persistent worry to you. 'Ask & it shall be given.' 'Knock & it shall be opened.' Dearest heart, I've but little hope that you'll agree, but one in a million, when it means an easier sight of you, is worth a struggle.

O my darling heart, I wish we could have wiped out everyone else for an hour or two last night, so that I could have got just one star. My dear, dear one.

Now, I've got to fill up the time somehow, between now & 3.10. O dear, I hope I don't have to wait a long time at Bletchley.

Darling one, here's a secret between us two. It's my turn to be shy now of speaking. I couldn't tell you out aloud [*sic*] last night, even in the dark. Directly I know that I'm going to be settled somewhere for a few months on end, I'm going to get instruction & become a Catholic, if they'll have me.

My own dear heart. I've reached the end of my paper, & this hotel doesn't seem to stock any. Goodbye, dear heart, for a little, & do keep my nursery hug safe for me, my own. I'm feeling rather grey this morning, but last night, oh my darling, I wanted you badly. I heard one o'clock strike & I woke up again at 4, silly me. My darling I love you so.

Your own Graham

[*At the end is a large star indicating a kiss.*]

TO VIVIENNE DAYRELL-BROWNING
(LATER VIVIEN GREENE)

Working on The Nottingham Journal *from November 1925 until the beginning of March 1926, Graham took religious instruction from Father George Trollope (d. 1933), a former actor, a 'stout cheerful man who loved the smell of greasepaint and the applause at a curtain-fall'.[25] After an initial unease, he developed a fondness and respect for Father Trollope, who later became a monk. On 26 February 1926, Graham was received into the Roman Catholic Church.*

Fri. Nov. 13 [1925]

Dear love, just another line before I go out to tea, which I will add to at the office, if I get the chance.

My reception was most friendly, no questions asked, & times fixed for instruction. This Father Trollope did not it appears become an R.C. himself, till he was 25, & he looks no more than 40. I was not struck by him. He was a little gross in appearance, & there was also a most trashy novel from Boots library, lying in his room. However he was very pleasant.

There's a most marvellous fog here to-day, my love. It makes walking a thrilling adventure. I've never been in such a fog before in my life. If I stretch out my walking stick in front of me, the ferrule is half lost in obscurity. Coming back I twice lost my way, & ran into a cyclist, to our mutual surprise. Stepping off a pavement to cross to the other side becomes a wild & fantastic adventure, like sailing into the Atlantic to find New York, with no chart or compass. Once where the breadth of the road was greater than the normal, I found myself back on the same pavement, as I started, having slowly swerved in my course across the road. I've got to sally out now & find my little Editor to give him some tea. If you never hear from me again, you will know that somewhere I am moving round in little plaintive circles, looking for a pavement.

25 *A Sort of Life*, 119.

TO VIVIENNE DAYRELL-BROWNING
(LATER VIVIEN GREENE)

Mon. 3:30 [7 December 1925]

Darling, I'm writing again, not because I've got anything to say, but because I've got to.

I want you so terribly.

I tried to read a novel, but every sentence nearly reminded me of you. Phrases that you'd used. Small points of character.

It's when this comes on me, this wanting, that I almost wish I'd never answered that first letter. I didn't know it was possible to want someone so badly.

And yet it would be so horribly ungrateful to say that I wished it had never happened. You have been so good to me, my darling. Sometimes the whole of my mind & my brain & even my body seems tired out with it, when you aren't with me. And I want to sleep & sleep & sleep, & forget all about you & everything. And then I almost wish I was in China, only I've never got the courage to take anything to its logical conclusion.

And now I'm writing to you gloomily, worrying you, when I want more than anything else that you should be always happy. It's all so tortuous & paradoxical.

Often I've half made up my mind that I wasn't strong enough to cling to so flimsy & crazy a hope. Once I even got as far as a letter to end it, pretending I'd found that I didn't love you after all, so as to prevent you writing to me, being rude & unpleasant. And then I couldn't post it.

Darling I love you. I love you. I love you. I've never loved anybody before as I love you, & I never shall again. I should be careful not to be a fool twice.

Oh my darling one that sounds horrid, what I've just written.

Darling, you must try & not let yourself be worried by this. It's only a selfish desire to get relief by talking, not caring about the unfortunate person, who has to listen. To-morrow I shall be better I expect. Things will not seem quite so empty. I'm probably tired & peevish.

Darling, I've got nothing to say & yet I daren't stop. I feel there's something awful in sealing up the envelope, not being able to add to this. I feel as if I must go on talking, talking, talking to you hard, until I've got back control. Chatter, chatter, chatter, chatter. On & on &on.

You were so lovely on the platform & in the firelight & coming out of No. 23 this morning. You were so lovely all the time. For Goodness sake! Talk, darling. The only two methods I've had to fight emptiness I can't use since I've loved you. I suppose in time I shall discover a new & proper way of doing it.

Don't you ever wonder, in moods, now & again, what the use of going on is? Religion doesn't answer it. One can believe in every point of the Catholic faith, & yet at times like this hate the initiator of it all, of life I mean. Justice can be just as hateful as injustice, more so often enough, because injustice puts us on a level with the wielder of it, whilst justice is more hateful because it emphasizes our own inferiority.

[. . .]

VIVIENNE DAYRELL-BROWNING
(LATER VIVIEN GREENE)

In support of striking coal miners, the Trades Union Congress called a general strike, which lasted from 3 to 12 May 1926. The government, fearing the worst, made preparations against a revolutionary uprising. Most of the country's newspapers were unable to publish, but The Times, *which Graham had joined in March as a sub-editor, printed and distributed a reduced edition.*[26]

11.30 a.m. | May 6. Thurs. 1926

No letter from you to-day, darling. I hope I get one to-morrow. I've *written* every day, but I don't suppose you've got them.

Great triumph! Last night we got off a properly printed four page paper, with one machine working. The only paper in London to do it. The strikers are getting nasty though. Last night about 9.30 they set us on fire with the help of some petrol & a squirt, but we got it out all right, almost before the brigade arrived. We had a bit of trouble about 1.30 this morning. The police seemed to have disappeared & we had to carry parcels of papers to private cars lined up along Victoria St. to carry them into the country, Oxford, Margate, Bournemouth, Dover etc. There was a bit of a scrimmage then. I didn't get hurt at all, but one man got slight concussion from a blow on the head from his own parcel – they tripped him up & got hold of it – & another had his jaw cut & there were a number of bruises.

Later the police arrived in greater force & they were held at a distance, but they'd already tampered with some of the cars. The ridiculous thing is that most are our own men, who were awfully decent, cheerful & contented, when one had met in the canteen etc. They didn't want to strike, but now they've struck they've entirely changed, & of course no filth is bad enough to describe us & our parentage. We are trying to produce a five page paper to-night. But either there'll be no trouble at all or else last night's fire & scrimmage will be a mild opening. It's all very exciting.

[. . .]

TO VIVIENNE DAYRELL-BROWNING
(LATER VIVIEN GREENE)

Friday. 12.15 p.m. | May 7th 1926

[. . .]

Last night & this morning (!) were fearfully disappointing after the previous excitements. We'd got properly organized for trouble this time. The 20 of us who are acting as 'storm troops' were divided into two parties. One party escorted a car round from Queen Victoria St. into the square, & then after it was loaded escorted it as far as Blackfriars Bridge, whilst the other party loaded. Then for the next car the two parties changed places & so on. We had a doctor ready to deal with casualties & about 1 a.m. a dozen M.P.s came round from the Commons to join in the fight – but the rioters never showed their faces, & they had to content themselves with talking to the peaceful pickets. Darling, you talk as if I was labour. I'm not. I'm really conservative now – especially after labour tried to burn us all.

[. . .]

TO VIVIENNE DAYRELL-BROWNING
(LATER VIVIEN GREENE)

On 5 October 1926 Graham underwent an appendectomy in Westminster Hospital. During his recovery he witnessed deaths in the ward.

Wednesday | Oct. 13, 1926

[. . .]

We had an awful to-do yesterday evening – the first time I've ever been in a room when someone dies. Do you remember the small boy with the broken leg on the opposite side of the room? He had an operation yesterday afternoon apparently perfectly all right. In fact about six his mother & father came in to see him, & he spoke to them & they went off happily. Then about 8 the house surgeon on his round seemed to find his breathing almost non-existent. There was half an hour's rush & scurry round his bed with oxygen apparatuses, an undignified scrambling for the tail end of his life & he was gone. Absolutely unexpected. No one thought he was in any danger. Of course they rigged a screen up round the poor little devil's bed, but the terrible thing was when the mother turned up about 8.45. I've never seen any one with all their self-control gone before. She had to be supported in & she was calling out things at the top of her voice – what made it worse it was the sort of things people say on the cinema & which one had fondly imagined real life was free of – sentimental hackneyed things. 'Why did you go without saying goodbye to your mother?' & 'Royston, Royston' (the ridiculous name seemed to make it worse), & 'What shall I do without him?' 'Sister, sister, don't tell me we're parted.' All in a sort of scream. It was ghastly lying in bed listening to it. Then they half carried her out.

I'm afraid we're going to have another death in the ward to-day. An emergency case was brought in yesterday evening before they found the child was going out. An old man of about 76, who'd been in a motor accident, head fractured, one hand smashed & both legs. I don't think they expected him to last through the night. He's quite quiet though. I shall be glad to get away – it's all very morbid.

Are people who write entirely & absolutely selfish, darling? Even though in a way I hated it yesterday evening – one half of me was saying how lucky it was – added experience – & I kept on catching myself trying to memorise details – Sister's face, the faces of the other men in the ward. And I felt quite excited aesthetically. It made one rather disgusted with oneself.

[. . .]

The Death Register of Westminster Hospital records that Royston Walker, aged nine, died on 12 October 1926 in Chadwick Ward, as did Thomas Lowe, seventy-six, on the following day. (Information from Robert Baker; see also A Sort of Life, *133–5)*

TO HERBERT GREENE

Handsome and charming when young, Herbert Greene spent most of his life between jobs. Despite annoyance with his alcoholic brother's impositions on their parents, Graham liked Herbert and in later years provided him and his wife Audrey with an allowance. Graham modelled a number of characters on him, notably Anthony Farrant in England Made Me *(1935) and Hands in the unfinished novel 'The Other Side of the Border' (c. 1936).*

Nov. 13 [1928]. | 8 Heathcroft, | Hampstead Way, N.W.11.

Dear Herbert,

This is to wish you & Audrey a happy Christmas. How does the farm go? I do hope it's a success. I hear you had a bad disappointment over a splendid crop of mealies.

V. & I took our summer holiday in Devonshire at Lynton & had lovely weather in July, bathing every day. We got another scrap of holiday last month & went to Wells & Glastonbury. Having done England this year we have hopes, if we can get a holiday in the spring, of going to Corsica next year. But the General Election is likely to get in the way.

We are going down to Crowborough[27] for Christmas Eve & Christmas Day – all I can get – to take the place of Raymond & Charlotte[28] who won't be there this year.

Life goes on peaceably. I've written another novel, but I don't suppose it will be taken any more than the others. I haven't yet seen Janet, except in photographs.[29]

I'm sending under a separate cover the Centenary *Spectator*. It has 188 pages of reading matter, so that you'll have quantity if not quality.

V. sends her love to you both. I hope Audrey's fit again.

Ever yours,
Graham

TO HUGH GREENE

8 Heathcroft, | Hampstead Way, | N.W. 11.[December 1928?]

Dear Hugh,

I have sent off your book under another cover. I can't say that we are enthusiastic over the idea of learning anything by heart; we arrive jaded & way-worn for lunch on Christmas Eve which leaves little time. Unless of course you give us silent parts or such speeches as 'My lady, the carriage waits.'

If you fell back on a form of charade what about taking a situation, say the murder of a greengrocer or some other bloodthirsty situation, & do it in parody of various authors, making the actors[30] guess the authors. Shakespeare – you know the way the dear old

27 Following retirement from Berkhamsted School, Charles and Marion Greene made their home in Crowborough, Sussex.

28 Charlotte was Raymond Greene's first wife.

29 Probably a reference to their sister Molly's daughter.

30 The word 'authors' appears here.

Bard has with death scenes, 'Enter the Duke. Sound the sennets & take up the corpse' sort of touch with the usual panegyric. 'He was the noblest tradesman of them all.' Etc.

J. M. Barrie. Elisabeth in pantaloons tripping. 'Now he belongs to the fairies.'

Galsworthy. Should the murderer be blackballed by his club? Honour of an English soldier touch.

Edgar Wallace?

Georg Kaiser on one of the 'modernists'. You know the kind of thing. Everyone is very triangular & talks geometrical nonsense.

Love.

Graham

One hand-sketched play-bill survives from 'Grand Guignol Theatre' for 'The Ape-Man' by Graham Greene, a skit set on a wintry island off the coast of Norway, with the part of Olaf played by Graham, Grethe his wife by Vivienne, Frida his daughter, a moron, by Elisabeth, and a Sailor by Hugh.

2

THE MAN WITHIN

TO MARION GREENE

Graham's first published novel was The Man Within, *a work about smugglers set against the Lewes Assizes in the nineteenth century. It was accepted first by Charles Evans, chairman of Heinemann, and later by the American publisher George Doran. Although he retained an affection for the book, Graham said in 1980 that if he had been the publisher's reader, 'I would have turned it down unhesitatingly.'*[1]

The Times | [7 January 1929]

Dear Mumma,

Great news! Doubleday, Doran & Co. have taken the book. £50 in advance of royalties & ten percent on all copies. They've promised to send it to the Book Society of America & if they take it as their book for the month (very unlikely of course) it sells about 80,000 copies straight away. It's coming out in England in May. Evans this morning read me a letter from Clemence Dane in which she said that she liked the book immensely & that I was 'a born writer' & she thought perhaps a born dramatist too, as there was a fine play to be got out of the novel![2] Evans sent me to an agent he recommended who's going to see if he can do anything about dramatising it! Evans was very sweet again & told me that I must

1 *Ways of Escape*, 14.
2 Clemence Dane (Winifred Ashton), 1888–1965, novelist and playwright. Graham first met her through Kenneth Richmond in 1921 (West, 13).

get started on the next book as not more than a year should elapse between the two! I've got to go & see Doran, the American publisher, at the Savoy Hotel, as he's on a visit to England. We still haven't found a title. The m.s. is going to be sent to Tennyson Jesse[3] as apparently she has a flair for such. 'Flight' has too much of a Lindbergh suggestion. My latest idea is 'The Man Within' & quotation from Sir Thomas Browne 'There's another man within me that's angry with me.' We had lunch this morning at Montagu Sq.

    With much love to both in haste,
      Graham

TO RAYMOND GREENE

            8 Heathcroft, | Hampstead Way, | N.W. 11.
                   [postmark: 13 January 1929]

Dear Raymond,

    How sweet of Charlotte & you to write. I hope you are better & Charlotte well. We should love to come down for a week-end. The difficulty is to get one. Flu' & colds are rampant at the office. Awful fate! I'm terribly afraid that I'm going to succeed Leslie-Smith as Court sub-editor, he being removed to more exalted regions. A hellish job without the compensations of hell, save I hope a 'rise'. However nothing is settled.

    It's certainly fun about the book. I hoped that one day one might be taken but never in wildest dreams so to be received with open arms & told that in five years I should be at the head of the profession!! £80 in advance of royalties – £50 in America & £30 in England – & the possibility of a dramatisation. And the funniest part of the absurd, joyful situation is that the book is quite terribly second-rate.

    I went and saw my American publisher at the Savoy. He was a darling. What one has always imagined the Virginian gentleman of

3 F. Tennyson Jesse, 1888–1958, novelist and crime writer.

old family to be like. Tall & courteous with a little white imperial & advice as to exercising the 'abdominal muscles'.

I've been told that I've got to have another novel ready within a year; great fun & great sense of importance!

Love to Charlotte & you

from both of us,

Graham

TO CHRISTOPHER ISHERWOOD

The novelist Christopher Isherwood (1904–86), descended from the brewing Greenes of Bury St Edmunds, was Graham Greene's distant cousin. His first novel All the Conspirators *was published by Jonathan Cape on 18 May 1928.*

8 Heathcroft, | Hampstead Way, | N.W. 11. | April 15 [1929?]

Dear Christopher,

Will you forgive these terribly tardy congratulations on your fine novel & implicitly, therefore, my terribly tardy reading of it? I only wish I had been still reviewing when it appeared that I might have aided, if by no more than a tin whistle, to have trumpeted its praise. It is a far finer book than I believed that any of our generation could produce. I have but just finished it & must praise or burst.

Yours with admiration & envy,

Graham Greene

TO HUGH GREENE

Hampstead Heath, | *Broiling gently.* May 22 [1929]

Dear Hugh,

You set me a terrible task. I know what I should get & if you would like to give me the money & thus save yourself wearing perplexity – But your lines of liking I do not know any longer. For instance do you care at all for literary criticism – if so there is nothing better than *Avowals* by George Moore (Heinemann, 10/6). Or do you like biography – *François Villon* by D. B. Wyndham Lewis is good (Gerald Howe, 12/6?). Or travel in weird places *The Magic Island* (Seabrooke, about 12/6, publisher I'm not sure of) is an interesting work telling of black magic & Voodoo worship in Haiti.[4] Did you like *A Path to Rome*? Belloc's *The Voyage of the Nona*, a bit of everything, travel, sailing, criticism, a medley, is good & can be got in Constable's charming 3/6 series. Of novels I have read few that I like better than Joseph Hergesheimer's *Tampico*, scene Mexico.[5] Do you like Aldous Huxley? You ought to try him – *Mortal Coils* Phoenix Library, 3/6, is a good introduction to him. Or *Chrome Yellow* if you don't mind a novel without a plot.

The town sounds lovely.[6] If the novel proves a best seller we must visit you. Next month we go to a Musicale in Mayfair! given by my American publisher, which necessitates the buying of tails, alas! Write again of your experiences & how life is with you.

Love,

Graham

TO HUGH GREENE

8 Heathcroft. | Hampstead Way N.W.11 [28 June 1929]

Dear Hugh,

So many thanks for your letter. I'm very glad you liked the book. It's selling fairly well & gone into a second impression. I've had very

---

4 Greene's interest in Haiti began more thirty years before he wrote *The Comedians* (1966).

5 This novel about American oilmen in Mexico, published in 1926, probably influenced *The Power and the Glory*. It opens in a seaport, and its main character, Bradier, is a brutal business man with a capacity for personal loyalty; like the whisky priest, he excites both sympathy and revulsion in the reader. At the end of the book, Bradier is a self-described 'fugitive'. It is worth noting, however, that the novel is not theological and that Bradier survives his ordeal.

6 The letter is addressed to Hugh Greene in Marburg an der Lahn. After leaving Oxford in 1933, Hugh worked as a journalist in Germany until 1939. As a first-hand observer, he kept Graham informed about the Nazis.

good reviews so far in *The Times, Times Lit Supp., Sunday Times, Bystander, Piccadilly* (with photo!), *Spectator* & *Daily Telegraph.* The provincial papers have been inclined to sniff. We went to a terribly grand party at the American publishers the day before publication, with people like the Duchess of Devonshire, Rudyard Kipling etc. floating about. We drank a lot of champagne & felt happy.

[. . .]

TO RAYMOND GREENE

8 Heathcroft, | Hampstead Way, | N.W. 11.
[postmark: 3 July 1929]

Dear Raymond,

[. . .] The book continues to sell well – about 5,000 have gone & Heinemann hope to keep it going through the autumn & are optimistic of 15,000–20,000. What a joke! How is the world fooled! But most amusing of all – I lunched with my managing director yesterday & he is preparing to give me a fixed yearly salary, in advance of royalties, of say six hundred in order that I may do nothing but write. No binding conditions. Just a book when I feel like it!

Summer in England & winter in the South of France seem within reach. He has to discuss the plan with Doran of USA & I hear their decision next week. Apparently they did this for many years with H. M. Tomlinson until he became a best seller with *Gallion's Reach.*[7]

How is your throat? Have you yet had your operation? We are very sad that Charlotte didn't come & see us as she half promised. Love to you & her from both of us,

Graham

P.S. First editions have gone up to 15/-!

7 Henry Major Tomlinson (1873–1958) often wrote about the sea. His novel *Gallion's Reach* (1927) was a success in Britain and America. Greene's arrangement lasted for three years and was not a simple salary. As a series of large advances against royalties, Greene's debt was not paid off until the publication of *Brighton Rock* in 1938. (St John, 295).

TO GLENWAY WESCOTT

*An American expatriate, Glenway Wescott (1901–87) established himself
as one of the most promising talents of the 1920s with his second novel* The
Grandmothers *(1927), set in the midwest. He wrote to congratulate
Graham Greene on* The Man Within.

8, Heathcroft, | Hampstead Way, | N.W.11. | October 11 [1929]

Dear Mr Wescott,

Thank you very much indeed for your kind & generous letter.
Your praise is particularly valuable to me as I both know & admire
your work. Hitherto I have been haunted by the ominous silence of
all those whose opinion I respect, while listening to a chorus of
praise from those whose ideas & beliefs I have always despised.

Are you ever in London? Because I should very much like to meet
you.

Yours sincerely,
    Graham Greene

TO HUGH GREENE

8 Heathcroft, | Hampstead Way, N.W. 11 [23 January 1930]

Dear Hugh,

What a bore! That O.U.D.S. is *Macbeth*, I mean. I don't care for
the Bard when he's being all Bardic. And all the Scotch business. I
always feel it was written at the command of Queen Victoria. The
Bard at Balmoral. 'This castle hath a pleasant seat.' And Bertie –
OUR PRINCE – acting Macbeth at private theatricals in kilts. His
mother – the dear Queen – so liked to see his knees.

However, how I do ramble on. I suppose it's because I'm feeling so
autumnal. Youth gone. Garrulous. Yes, but then Donne is such a
comfort isn't he? 'No Spring nor Summer's beauty hath such grace,
As I have seen in one Autumnal face.'[8] – however, as I was saying,

8 The opening of 'Elegy IX. The Autumnal'.

would you be a dear & get us two seats for the first night if possible, the Wednesday if not? Somewhere central between the second & sixth row of stalls? Directly tickets are available? Then let me know how much & on my honour you shall have a cheque by return of post.

Of course, easily the best talkie to date seems to me to be *Atlantic*. Wonderful & quite throbbing. *Hallelujah* is also good, but not to my mind comparable.[9] And of course it puzzles me that you like *Java Head*[10] better than 'Tampico.' A very good book, I grant, but rather encrusted.

Oh yes, & that reminds me. If the sea is reasonably low I go to Coblenz to-morrow.

Yesterday we went & had lunch & tea at the Windmill Press, Heinemann's works in Surrey. A wonderful building, & they just let us choose a book each to take away with us.

Love,
   Graham

TO MARION GREENE

The Name of Action, Graham's second published novel, is set in Trier. With the manuscript nearly complete, he headed for Germany, hoping to reinvigorate his impressions of the country.

8. Heathcroft | Hampstead Way. N.W.11 [2 February 1930]

Dearest Mumma,

We so much enjoyed having you & Da to tea the other day.

I got back from Germany on Tuesday morning. Going I spent the night in the train between Ostend & Cologne. After Cologne, where I changed, the sun rose just as the train came alongside the Rhine, the water becoming the colour of this paper.[11] There was also

9 Two films from 1929, *Atlantic* told the story of the *Titanic*, and *Hallelujah* portrayed a bad gambler becoming a good preacher.
10 An earlier novel by Joseph Hergesheimer.
11 Cream.

a ruined castle on a hill at the exact psychological moment, the whole affair being too like a stage back cloth for words. I spent one night at Coblenz, explored in the morning & evening, & in the afternoon walked across the river & out into the country behind Ehrenbreitstein.[12] The French have gone now. It was apparently Carnival time, & all the hotels were having masked balls, females in masks & fancy dress disappearing coyly into lighted doorways from round dark corners.

After Mass next day I took the train to Trier, a lovely journey following the Moselle. Trier of course was beautiful, & I spent the night there. It's the loveliest place I've ever been to; it has a curious emotional effect on me every time I see it. I think it must have been my home in a previous incarnation. I had to drag myself away in the morning to Luxembourg. I had lunch there & came back by a night boat from Dunkirque. It was an awful crossing. I've never heard such wind. Every time a wave hit the boat it was like a collision & the whole boat shook. I wasn't ill though.

[. . .]

TO MARION GREENE

The Name of Action *was published on* 6 October 1930. *Reviews were negative and sales bad.*

8 Heathcroft. | Hampstead Way. | N.W. 11 | October 20 [1930]

Dearest Mumma,

Many thanks for your card. I hope Michael Sadleir[13] will prove quotable. So far *The Times* is the only valuable review I've had. All very depressing. *The Oxford Mail*'s (C.F. I presume is Fenby,[14] the editor) is the most understanding review, I think, I've ever had, but it cuts no ice. I'm getting tired of kind friends who tell me they like

12 A fortress built *c.* 1000 on a cliff overlooking the Rhine at Coblenz.
13 Michael Sadleir (1888–1957) was a novelist and bibliographer.
14 Charles Fenby (1905–74), a friend of Raymond Greene's, was editor of the *Oxford Mail* 1928–40.

this, but of course they much prefer the other!! *The Man Within*, I'm convinced, is a moderately bad book, while this, I'm equally certain, is a moderately good one. I don't agree with you about Elizabeth in the other. I don't think she's a character at all, but a sentimental complex. But though I sez it as shouldn't I think Anne-Marie Demassener quite adorable!

There was a painted old woman I used to see occasionally wandering about Oxford, rather a revolting spectacle. I used to wonder who she was. Now she's suddenly cropped up in the form of Lady Ottoline Morrell & invited us to tea. It appears that Aldous Huxley recommended her to read *The Man Within*! The bugbear again! I'm beginning to hate the sound of it!

[. . .]

The literary hostess Lady Ottoline Morrell (1873–1938) became a friend and supporter of Graham in the early years of his career. Sometimes cruelly drawn, her portrait appears in novels by D. H. Lawrence, Aldous Huxley and Evelyn Waugh. Graham modelled the sympathetic character of Lady Caroline in It's a Battlefield *(1934) on her.*[15]

TO HUGH GREENE

at The British Library | Nov. 15 [1930]

Dear Hugh,

Forgive a. these tardy good wishes & b. the pencil. I have practically speaking no money & therefore can send you no present. I hope by Christmas that I shall be better off & be able to give you two in one. You find me, as it were, deeply engaged working on my magnum opus, 'Strephon: The Life of the Second Earl of Rochester' – that is to say I am waiting in patience while half a dozen books of varying shades of indecency are brought to me. I've forgotten my ink so I can't go on with my third novel – now 1/7th [?] done!

[. . .]

15 *Ways of Escape*, 28.

TO DENYSE CLAIROUIN

'Writing a novel is a little like putting a message into a bottle and flinging it into the sea – unexpected friends or enemies retrieve it.'[16] *So Graham wrote of his friendship with Denyse Clairouin, his first translator and then his agent in France. Her translation of* The Man Within *under the title* L'homme et lui-même *was published by Plon in the* Roseau d'or *series, edited by the Neo-Thomist philosopher Jacques Maritain (1882–1973), who decided to cut some sexual references.*

Clairouin's fate was a sad one: 'when the war was over I learned how she had worked in occupied France for the British Secret Service. In 1942 in Freetown, where I was working for the same service, I received news from London that a suspected spy, a Swiss businessman, was travelling to Lisbon in a Portuguese liner. While he queued up at the purser's for passport control, I sat in my one-man office typing out, as quickly as I could with one finger, the addresses in the notebook which he had been unwise enough to leave in his cabin. Suddenly, among all the names that meant nothing to me, I saw the name and address of Denyse. From that moment I feared for her safety, but it was not until the war was over that I learned she had died after torture in a German concentration camp.'[17]

8 Heathcroft, Hampstead Way, | N.W. 11. | Friday [March 1931]

Dear Mlle Clairouin,

Your letter makes me feel very guilty, as if I had been selling the fort to the enemy. The fact is that I received what I thought a most courteous letter from Maritain the day after I wrote to Plon & you, & the consciousness that I had written very differently of him in the heat of the moment made me conscience-stricken. Also I assumed (perhaps wrongly?) that he is *the* Jacques Maritain, for whose work as a Catholic philosopher I have the greatest admiration. I, therefore, while asking him to reconsider the passages you suggested, *think* (I have no copy of the letter) that I left the decision with him. But I insisted on the inclusion of a note. How difficult it is to be fair & to

16 *Ways of Escape*, 14.
17 *Ways of Escape*, 15.

see clearly with all the Channel between. Now I feel that I have betrayed *you*, & that my letter may mean that your work (just as much as mine) will be tampered with, & I am not insincere when I say that yours has probably the greater value. However my insistence on the note may save all, as I will now write to Plon & withdraw that demand altogether if the five important passages are restored.

I feel that I have muddled the position & owe you many apologies. My excuse is that my nerves are in pieces at the moment as the result of writing against time, at the same moment as letting a flat & seeing to a removal into the country.

Our address after March 30 will be 'Little Orchard', Chipping Campden, Gloucestershire. I hope that you'll let me meet you in town or in the country when you are over here.[18]

I admire tremendously your phrase 'flesh haunting hating man' & regret exceedingly the weak courtesy of my rejoinder.

Sincerely yours,

Graham Greene

TO DENYSE CLAROUIN

Little Orchard, | Campden | Glos. | April 25, 1931

Dear Mlle Clairouin,

I received yesterday from Plon a copy of *L'Homme et Lui-Même*. The appearance is really very attractive, & they had (I suppose with tact) removed the label which called me the Stevenson of the Soul! I haven't yet more than dipped into the translation, but what I have read makes me much prefer the book in French.

I was amused to read in a review in the *Lit. Supp.* this week of one of Maritain's books several sentences which seem to fit in with your picture of the 'flesh haunted hating man.' They speak of a general impression 'of a powerful nature powerfully suppressed . . ., an excessive tension of soul: not a liberation of the mind . . . but a

18 Graham and Vivien rented for £1 per week a house without electricity and inhabited by rats (*A Sort of Life*, 145–6).

strained attitude.'[19] Which is the same thing in *Times* rather
pompous English!

    Yours sincerely,

      Graham Greene

TO HUGH GREENE

Rumour at Nightfall was published by Heinemann in November 1931. *In
retrospect, Graham remarked of this novel and its predecessor: 'Both books
are of a badness beyond the power of criticism properly to evoke – the prose
flat and stilted and in the case of* Rumour at Nightfall *pretentious (the
young writer had obviously been reading again and alas! admiring Conrad's
worst novel* The Arrow of Gold), *the characterization non-existent.'*[20]
*Indeed, his disgust with these novels was such that he left several letters
instructing his heirs not to reprint them.*[21]

        Little Orchard, | Campden, | November 15 [1931]

Dear Hugh,

    [. . .]

    How splendid that Headington is doing well. I doubt if my book
is. A good & longish review in *The Telegraph*, a short & bad review
in the *New Statesman*, a short & meant-to-be-good review in
Everyman, a good review in the *Nottingham Guardian* are all so far. I
may be going up to town with a half-day ticket on Thursday for a
cocktail party at my American publishers. There's trouble in New
York, as they are trying to cut out two pages as 'impious' & showing
'a lack of knowledge of the Catholic faith'! They don't know I'm a
Catholic! There's nothing like a fight to cure depression!

    Love,

      G.

19 John Middleton Murry accused Maritain of sharply dividing mankind into his
party and the devil's (*TLS*, 23 April 1931).

20 *Ways of Escape*, 15.

21 *A Sort of Life*, 140–1. The letters, which I have examined, are in the possession of
Francis Greene.

TO LADY OTTOLINE MORRELL

Little Orchard, | Campden, | Glos. | Nov. 19 [1931]

Dear Lady Ottoline,

Your encouraging letter was a joy to receive, especially at this moment. I think myself the book to be my best, but I seem doomed to please no one after *The Man Within*. It has been out nearly three weeks & has received only three reviews. The *Lit. Supp.* which has always before been both kind & prompt remains grimly silent; one does not expect anything from *The Observer*, but *The Sunday Times* seems to have abandoned me. After praising extravagantly my first book, it never reviewed my second at all & looks like ignoring this one. Altogether I am feeling depressed. Books are a labour to write & a hell to publish; why does one do it? The grim spectre of a return to journalism looms on the horizon.

This catalogue of woes is a poor return for a letter which was the bright spot in my week. You have certainly understood the *motif*. Even Caveda was meant to be a kind of third part of a more than Siamese twin.

My wife sends her regards.

Yours very sincerely,
Graham Greene

TO LADY OTTOLINE MORRELL

Little Orchard | Campden | Glos. | December 17 [1931]

Dear Lady Ottoline,

It was very nice of you to write & I found your letter very encouraging. The wave of depression at the book's failure has passed, now that the next one is forming in the mind. 'Rochester' I have just got packed off to Kenneth Bell,[22] of Balliol, to be vetted for historical blunders, & I believe it's coming out in April. It's not the

---

22 Kenneth Bell had been Graham's tutor.

book it ought to have been, as I was writing against time. It will be amusing to be reviewed by a new set of people for a change!

I wish I could have been in town to-day. I miss Thursday teas!

Thank you very much again for writing.

Yours very sincerely,
Graham Greene

As it turned out, he was not 'writing against time'. Rejected by Heinemann owing to its sexual content, Lord Rochester's Monkey *was not published until September* 1974.

TO R. N. GREEN-ARMYTAGE

'The reviewing of novels at the beginning of the thirties was at a far lower critical level than it has ever been since. Gerald Gould, a bad poet, and Ralph Strauss, a bad novelist, divided the Sunday forum between them. One was not elated by their praise nor cast down by their criticism . . .'[23] The last sentence need not be believed, as Greene certainly resented Gould's mixed review of Rumour at Nightfall *(Observer,* 13 December 1931*). Writing to Vivien's maternal uncle, a lawyer and sometime poet in Bath, he takes a run at Gould for his praise of Guenther Birkenfeld's* A Room in Berlin, *and at a more substantial target, the diplomat, biographer and diarist Harold Nicolson (*1886–1968*), who had raved over Lady Eleanor Smith's now-forgotten* Flamenco, *a novel about gypsies.*

As from Little Orchard | Campden | Glos. |
December 26 [1931?]

Dear Uncle Bob,

A thousand thanks for my share in your exquisite present. The second poem I already knew & admired: indeed I had a cutting from the Westminster ragged & worn in my copy of *The Veil*.[24] To have it in beautiful print is a delight.

23 *A Sort of Life*, 145.

24 Greene treasured his copy of de la Mare's poems inscribed by the poet 'Christmas 1921'. The librarians at Boston College have found in its pages fragile clippings of two more poems by de la Mare, 'Horse in a Field' and 'The Strange Spirit'.

I'm in the last desperate throes of the final revision of a life of Rochester which is to come out in the spring: on January 1, I have to begin another novel for the autumn. The life of a novelist, alas, is not all beans & bacon. Apropos of which my Ballade *against* Certain Reviewers.

'Ugly but beautiful,' the critic said,*
   'A masterpiece of incest, poverty,
Life in a German slum,' but then I read
   The agonising scene in chapter three
   When 'little Anna' leaves her family
To go with baby out into the rain,
   And sin so nobly & incessantly:
I have mistaken Gould for gold again.

True, Mr. Nicolson must earn his bread,
   And Lady Eleanor may know a gypsy,
But can't he go & boil his head
   Rather than call her Borrow[25] in epitome?[x]
   'Another Fielding, Smollett, Dostoievski' –
They never tire of taking names in vain,
   Describing Herr von X; I read so hopefully –
I have mistaken Gould for gold again.

Are critics, when they go upstairs to bed,
   Ever affrighted by the fantasy,
At a dark corner, of the mighty dead,
   Whose names they've dealt in so dishonourably?
   No, if a hand stretch out, more probably
It's that of Mr Ernest Potts,[26] whose 'Drain,'
   'Ugly & beautiful' was lent to me:
I have mistaken Gould for gold again.

25 George Borrow (1803–81) was an English novelist who often wrote about Gypsies.
26 An invented author.

Prince of the Pen, your masterpiece I flie,
   Hearing the unbalanced praises of some men,
Who laud C's plot & W's poetry.
   I have mistaken Gould for gold again.

*A favourite expression of Mr G. . .ld G. . .ld, who used it in particular in describing *A Room in Berlin*.

x of 'Flamenco' Mr H. . .ld N. . .n said 'It is impossible to get more out of a novel than out of this.'

Ever yours,
Graham

TO HUGH GREENE

Little Orchard, | Campden, | Glos. [20 July 1932]

Dear Hugh,

We should love to have you, *but*
                         Frankly! –
                                        we are on the verge of bankruptcy, & we had someone to stay last week, whom we didn't want to see nearly so much as you, & we can't afford to put you up for four nights; we have been trying since we lost £250 a year to make p.g.s[27] the rule at 2/6 a night, but it's difficult. <u>But *do come for two nights*</u>, if you can manage to stay a day longer at Crowborough & go to R.[28] a day earlier. One can manage two nights without increasing housekeeping.

Love
   G.

27 Paying guests.
28 Raymond.

TO HUGH GREENE

[7 November 1932]

Dear Hugh,

Many thanks for your letter. We were given an unexpected lift
into Oxford last Friday, but found you were away. We tried to go to
Wedding Rehearsal[29] but times were wrong & we had to go to *Love on
Wheels*[30] – which was just seeable in spite of Hulbert & the
caricature of Clair.[31]

Do come over some time.

Metro-Goldwyn-Mayer, Universal, & R.K.O. all seem biting at
Stamboul Train.

We are dreaming of a flat in Oxford if we get rich. We looked at
one the other day in Broad St., but it was too large.

Love

G.

TO HUGH GREENE

Little Orchard, | Campden, | Glos. | Nov. 30 [1932]

Dear Hugh,

Stamboul Train is not appearing till the 8th. On Monday Priestley
appeared at Heinemann's and said that if it was published as it stood
he would bring an action for libel. He remained adamant and I had a
frantic day on the phone arranging for alterations. 13,000 copies
were all printed and bound and they all have to be unstitched and
some pages printed over again.

Yours in exhaustion,

Graham.

---

29 A film in which a young marquis endeavours not to marry.

30 A musical starring Jack Hulbert.

31 René Clair (1898–1981) was a French director known for witty and stylish productions. Greene found 'happy lyrical absurdity' in his work (*Journey Without Maps*,
33).

J. B. Priestley (1894–1984) spotted a portrait of himself in the character of Quin Savory, a popular novelist. Greene was forced to rewrite offending passages at the last minute, dictating revisions in a phone booth.[32] He came to admire Priestley for his wartime broadcasts but never for his books.

TO DENYSE CLAIROUIN

Little Orchard, | Campden, | Glos. | January 27 [1933]

Dear Denyse Clairouin,

But I should be terribly pleased if you translated 'The End of the Party'. I send it in its most portable form. Don't trouble to return this copy.

Yes, 'S.T.'[33] has done well. A week ago it had turned 15,000. It's all rather dull because it all goes to pay the yawning deficit of Heinemann on the last book. So I have no hope of a holiday in Burgundy this year.

I do hope you are successful with S.T. But how I wish it was *Rumour at Nightfall*, which obstinately in spite of publishers & public I so much prefer. You heard I expect how J. B. Priestley sabotaged S.T. at the last moment with a threatened libel action, costing Heinemann £400!

Yours sincerely,

Graham Greene

TO MARIE ADELAIDE BELLOC LOWNDES

Best known for her crime novels, Marie Lowndes (1868–1947) was the sister of Hilaire Belloc. Her husband, Frederick Lowndes, was a staff writer on The Times, *where Graham had met him.*

---

32 *A Sort of Life*, 155.
33 *Stamboul Train*.

Little Orchard, | Campden, | Glos. | April 4 [1933]

Dear Mrs. Belloc Lowndes,

So many thanks for your letter. I'm glad you liked *Stamboul Train*:
I've never been more uncertain of a book. It was nice of you to send
me the cutting which I had not seen. The book seems to be doing as
well in America as one can expect: it came out the very week when
the banks were closed.

We've been down here in the country for the last two years & are
now struggling to find a flat in Oxford for a year. Do come & see us if
you are ever near. Everybody seems to turn up in the Cotswolds at
least once a year. Do please remember me to your husband.

Yours very sincerely,
Graham Greene

TO R. N. GREEN-ARMYTAGE

*During a holiday in Wales, Vivien learned of the death of her very forceful
mother, Muriel Dayrell-Browning, who had suffered an embolism following
a broken leg.*[34]

at Sea beach, | Horton, | Pontcynon, | Swansea, |
May 23 [1933]

Dear Uncle Bob,

I'm so sorry about this. It came as a terrible shock. Unfortunately
we left Campden early yesterday morning before your first wire, &
both wires were delivered together to us here just after tea.

Vivienne, actually, was terribly upset, & the worst of it is that she's
going to have a baby. She was bent on going up to town for the
funeral; I was a little worried – three journeys of over five hours each
within about four days, so I telephoned through last night to Uncle
Vivian & explained matters.[35] He said that she should certainly not

34 NS 1: 476.
35 Vivian Green-Armytage was a gynaecologist and obstetrician.

come up; it was useless to try & persuade her last night, so I waited till this morning, when I got a local doctor to see her & advise her. He said if she did travel up, she would probably feel too sick to attend the funeral. That & Uncle Vivian's advice have persuaded her.

I do hope you feel I've not done wrong over this. If we had been at Campden it would have been very different; I didn't like to bring pressure on her, for the reason that her mother & I did not care for each other & it looked as if I was carrying the feud on after her death; so I left it to the doctors. But if I had always been as fond of her mother as you all are I should have felt exactly the same. I shall come up as Vivien's representative by a train on Thursday morning & will go straight to Golders Green. I'll be catching an evening train home, as I don't want to leave her alone for the night. I expect I shall see you at Golders Green.

With all my sympathy,
yours affectionately,
Graham Greene

TO MARIE BELLOC LOWNDES

Little Orchard, | Campden, | Glos. | June 17 [1933]

Dear Mrs Belloc Lowndes,

How nice it is of you to remember us. I should be delighted to come to your party on Thursday. Alas! as we are moving to a flat in Oxford the next day, my wife has to be in Oxford laying the ground for our furniture. You may be amused to hear, too, that we are going to have a child in December, so she cannot leap from one spot to another with any celerity. May I enlist your kind heart in the cause of this book, *Love on the Dole*? I had it for review the other day[36] & was so deeply impressed by it that I wrote to the author, a thing I have never done before. He is a man of 29, who has had a terrible life on

36 The review of Walter Greenwood's *Love on the Dole* appeared in the *Spectator* (30 June 1933).

the dole & off it in Salford, & now works at 30/- a week. But the book is brilliant. Do read it & encourage others to read it.

    Yours very sincerely,
      Graham Greene

TO VIVIEN GREENE

Graham was planning a new novel, later entitled England Made Me, *based on the story of Ivar Kreuger, a Swedish tycoon whose vast wealth was founded on the production of matches. He shot himself just as he was about to be revealed as a swindler. With Hugh, Graham took a trip that included Oslo, Gothenburg, Stockholm and Copenhagen. They returned on 7 September.*

Strand Hotel | Göteborg | August 18 [1933] | 8.20 a.m.

Darling love, I'm almost glad you couldn't come. Such a crossing. Not very rough, but a soft slow regular undulation for 30 hours on end which seemed much worse than the Channel. Though quite all right as long as one lay down. Yesterday by the time I'd dressed & shaved, I had to go back to bed; Hugh didn't get up till the evening. Driven by the sporting spirit of the Wufflies I got up & had lunch (so as not to lose a bet), but then retired again till after tea. No supper. But by the evening I was getting used to it.

    As for the 'jolly girls' – Ursula, the younger, very healthy & managing & girl-guidish . . . she was on the look-out for us at the barrier at Victoria & pounced; there was no avoiding them. The elder sister is quite tolerable but with a bad skin. They've just departed with their mother in a car;[37] O darling such a lovely railway station where we took their luggage; beautiful plain modern brick with lovely proportions, & behind every buffer on every platform a little flower garden.

37 Graham and Hugh conducted a 'harmless flirtation' with the daughters, sixteen and twenty years old, of an English writer named Schelling. Once, when Hugh and Ursula were slow returning from a walk, the mother thought they had drowned in a canal. Later in Stockholm, Graham got his faced slapped by the elder sister in the same circumstances as Loo slapped Anthony's in *England Made Me* (*Ways of Escape*, 30; see NS 1: 488).

Hugh & I went & saw Mae West in *She Done Him Wrong* – an absolutely perfect film. The nineteeish atmosphere beautifully caught; showing up '[illeg]'s' spurious literary period air. A completely original film in photography, acting, integrity: no sentiment to mar the amoral story. You must see it if you get a chance.

[. . .]

TO IAN PARSONS, CHATTO & WINDUS

Ian Parsons (1906–80) was a partner in the firm of Chatto & Windus and went on to become chairman of Chatto, The Bodley Head and Jonathan Cape. His offer of a job to Graham presented the novelist with a dilemma.

9 Woodstock Close, | Woodstock Rd., | Oxford. |
Oct. 11 [1933]

Dear Parsons,

Very reluctantly, because I've always wanted to be in a publishing office, I must lose the chance. If I had been living in London, I could have gone gently on with my own work of an evening, but as it is my evening would be spent in getting home. I have still half a year's lease to run here, and as my wife is having a baby in December, I feel rather tied. It was very nice indeed of you to give me the chance which if I'd been in London I should have leapt at.

You spoke of an apprentice job being the one really vacant. I don't know if it would be any good putting in a word for a brother of mine who has just gone down from Oxford and is anxious to get into a publisher's? He was at a German university for a time and speaks German well. At Oxford he took a second in Honour Mods. and just missed a first in English. Edmund Blunden was his tutor and speaks highly of his work. His name is Hugh Greene, and his home is Incents, Crowborough, Sussex. But I daresay you've got dozens of apprentices to choose from.

Yours ever,
Graham Greene

The beginning of 1933 had seen Graham with a bestseller in Stamboul
Train, *but he was still deeply in debt to Heinemann, so his decision to earn
his living solely as a writer was a risky one. He was, however, able to rely
on a modest income as a reviewer for the* Spectator, *of which he became literary editor at the beginning of the war.*

TO HUGH GREENE

9 Woodstock Close, | Woodstock Rd., | Oxford. |
Feb. 28 [1934]

Dear Hugh,

Many thanks for your letter and thousands of congratulations on
your job.[38] I wonder what salary you are getting. Nine guineas a
week? I've heard nothing more from Cameron, and I didn't have a
chance to pump him at dinner, but I imagine that now you will have
small interest in the F.I.[39] How beautifully dramatic that you should
have got so good a job a few days before your time ran out.

If I see Peter Fleming[40] I'll show him the photo!

I've just been in bed with a bad cold and am overwhelmed with
acres of work. I seem to have gatecrashed into the highbrow citadels
with the new book, and have got the new Eliot to write an article on
for *Life and Letters.*[41] Cape are publishing *The Old School* in the
summer, paying me an editorial fee of £30.[42]

38 A trial position in the Berlin office of the *Daily Telegraph* (Tracey, 36).

39 Graham's friend Alan Charles Cameron (1893–1952), the husband of Elizabeth
Bowen, was one of the founders of the British Film Institute.

40 The essayist and travel writer Peter Fleming (1907–71) shared with Graham a long
association with the *Spectator.* His younger brother was the Bond-creator Ian Fleming.

41 Graham's review of *After Strange Gods* appeared in the April issue. In it, he makes
a memorable, if uncharacteristic, claim for the superiority of moral over aesthetic criticism: 'To be a Catholic (in Mr Eliot's case an Anglo-Catholic) is to believe in the
Devil, and why, if the Devil exists, should he not work through contemporary literature, it is hard to understand.' Twenty years later he found himself at the wrong end
of such an argument when the Holy Office sought to suppress *The Power and the
Glory* (see pp. 203–6).

42 Greene edited this book of memoirs of school life, to which prominent authors
including Auden, Powell and Greenwood contributed. In his own essay on

Paris was extraordinarily interesting, though I failed to see a riot. I have now become passionately addicted to flying. I have never enjoyed a breakfast more than the one I had over the Channel. I got a 25% reduction from Imperial Airways which made the price about 5/- more expensive than 2nd class Dover–Calais.

I rejoice over the news about D.

In haste,

    Graham

[*Note on the envelope*: 'Father Bede is critically ill, so I can do nothing about intros yet.']⁴³

TO VIVIEN GREENE

9 Woodstock Close : Woodstock Road : Oxford |
Tuesday [early 1934]

Darling best dearest most adored Puss Willow. I do hope you are having a nice time & seeing plenty of people & things. Your Wuffle misses you.

I did arrears of letters this morning & this afternoon went to the bumper [?] programme: it was lovely, especially *Birds in Spring* which I hadn't seen, & *The Three Little Pigs*. (Did I tell you that with Anna Sten there was a *Silly Symphony* called *The China Shop* with the most lovely colouring I've yet seen). *Whither Germany* was quite good, & *The Mayor of Hell* very seeable. A small boy beside me burst into loud sobs when a boy dies in a Reformatory.⁴⁴ When I got back, I

Berkhamsted (247–56), he said the book was an effort to understand why a man 'should feel more loyal to a school which is paid to teach than to a butcher who is paid to feed him'.

43 Bede Jarrett (1881–1934) was Prior Provincial of the English Province of the Dominicans 1916–32 and a well-known preacher and author; he had had a strong influence on Vivien.

44 *Birds in Spring*, *The Three Little Pigs* and *The China Shop*, were all Disney cartoons, to which Greene had a mild addiction (see p. 114). Ukrainian-born Anna Sten (1908–93) starred in *Nana*, released in February 1934. *Whither Germany*, written by Bertolt Brecht, was a melodrama concerned with unemployment in Germany; it was banned under the Nazis. In *The Mayor of Hell*, James Cagney is a former gangster who becomes a reforming administrator in a prison.

played the gramophone, did my minimum, & read this long (&
rather dull) Graves novel, which has suddenly descended on me at
the last minute.[45]

I'm so disappointed about tomorrow, but as Mary[46] is playing
hostess & hasn't told me where or when we are to have lunch, it's
useless trying to fix a meeting. I'd so much rather have lunch with
you. If by any chance you found yourself by the entrance to the Café
Royal between 12.15 & 12.30, we might snatch a cocktail together.
I'll be there on the chance, but don't put yourself out at all if you
aren't in the neighbourhood.

Dear love, I so love & adore you. I'm going down on the chance
of finding R. & E. in.[47]

All my love,

Tyg.

P.S. Dr S.'s Bill has come in. He's only charged 17.6.6. Isn't that a
lovely surprise?![48]

TO DENYSE CLAIROUIN

*The Stavisky affair nearly brought down France's Third Republic. A
swindler named Sacha Stavisky had been found dead in Chamonix and it
was not clear whether he had killed himself or been murdered by the police.*

45 Graham's mixed review of *I, Claudius*, praising the character but not the prose style,
appeared in the *Spectator* (4 May 1934).

46 Probably, Graham's American literary agent Mary Leonard (later Pritchett).
Graham's devotion to her deserves notice. Mitch Douglas of International Creative
Management recalls that after she had retired and Graham had retained Monica
McCall, he continued to pay her a separate commission: 'I know this for a fact because
I personally processed the checks. When Mary died after I joined the firm in 1974,
Greene insisted on continuing to pay her Estate a commission. However, Mary's
Estate lawyers begged him not to do that, as Mary left her Estate to around 17 entities,
and the division and processing of checks would be an extraordinary task. Therefore,
Greene asked if Mary had a church. She did. He decided to pay the church a com-
mission in Mary's memory.' (E-mail to RG, 6 January 2006).

47 Raymond and Eleanor at 10 Holywell Street in Oxford.

48 Dr Shorrocks had attended the protracted delivery of Lucy Caroline on
28 December 1933.

The Right claimed that he had been killed to hide corruption in the Socialist government. On 6 February 1934, one hundred thousand royalist and fascist demonstrators fought a pitched battle with police at Place de la Concorde. Graham flew to Paris to report on the General Strike called for Monday, 12 February. He and Clairouin drove about Paris looking for signs of trouble; in the end, he wrote his article for the Spectator *(16 February 1934; Reflections 30–3) without seeing blood.*

9 Woodstock Close, | Woodstock Rd., | Oxford. |
March 6 [1934]

Dear Denyse – May I?

I don't know what you will think of my rudeness in not having written before to thank you for your kindness to me in Paris, but I no sooner got home to a vile London fog than I had to go to bed with the worst cold & throat that I've had for years.

I so enjoyed myself, even though I missed a riot. Please don't show Mlle Bertillon this article; I had to suit my opinions to my market![49] After I left the Updegraffs[50] on the Monday night I went for a long walk & found a most interesting spot up by Belleville where I could watch the police searching people. But as you see I had precious little to make an article out of!

Yours ever,
Graham Greene

---

49 Graham described her: 'The middle-aged, fanatical rather bandy legged woman, Mlle B, who had given me so dubious an invitation [to protest against the Communists], turned out to be one of the leaders of the National Front which now claims 50,000 members. . . .' Suzanne Bertillon was a well-known journalist who had reported on the famine in the Ukraine; an anti-Soviet, she supported calls for Franco-German friendship and in 1935 wrote a famous article on whether Hitler would write a second volume of *Mein Kampf*.

50 Probably the American novelist, poet and translator Allan Updegraff (1883–1965). He was a friend of Sinclair Lewis and Upton Sinclair and lived for many years in Paris.

TO HUGH GREENE

9 Woodstock Close, | Woodstock Rd., | Oxford. |
March 11 [1934]

Dear Hugh,

Many thanks for your letter. Don't hurry to repay me; I'm not in urgent need.

About that address: I told Mumma about it & I imagined she'd tell you. When I was in Paris I met at Denyse Clairouin's this strange, fanatical, I should say sexually abnormal, Mlle Bertillon, a niece of the man who invented finger prints.[51] She is one of the leaders of a new French party – a revolutionary central [?] party & was the woman whom Denyse had promised to get some Munich introductions from. I said that you were in Berlin & she suggested that you should meet this woman, who is apparently an Austrian journalist.

I enclose a sheet from Arthur Rogers' latest catalogue. Is this the Byron book you wanted?

Isn't it maddening that Lapland is off? I'm just turning over in mind, but have said nothing to V. yet, about Moscow, not an Intourist trip but an individual one. If Nordahl Grieg is still there, it might be amusing.[52]

I suspect but don't know that the book is not going very well, though I have never before had so good a press: a really respectable press from people whom I respect. Indeed I really seem to have been promoted to the sixth form! In the new *Life & Letters* which comes out at the end of this month I believe Calder-Marshall[53] is doing a

---

51 She later wrote a biography of Alphonse Bertillon, pioneer of various forensic techniques including fingerprints and mugshots; he had been a witness in the Dreyfus trial.

52 The Norwegian poet, journalist and dramatist Nordahl Grieg (1902–43) surprised Greene with a visit to Chipping Campden in 1931. The two struck up a warm friendship, described in *Ways of Escape*, 18–22. He lived for a time in Moscow and during the war joined the RAF. He was shot down over Berlin in 1943.

53 The novelist and biographer Arthur Calder-Marshall (1908–92) was an important and insightful early critic of Graham Greene's fiction. Regrettably, he was the originator of the term 'Greeneland'.

fine review of it; I am doing (an unsigned) review of T.S. Eliot's new book.

There are various things brewing about which I went up to town the other day (seeing *The Country Wife*[54] – a really good production): Marge Tidy[55] is progressing not at all badly with the dramatisation of *The Man Within* (what is more amusing she is showing symptoms of nymphomania); there is talk of Knoblock[56] dramatising *The Name of Action*; & the B.B.C. are talking about special short stories for broadcasting – I met Ackerley, of *Hindoo Holiday*,[57] there – & of course the ubiquitous Felix[58] tried to push his way to the fore.

Did you hear that General Aspinall-Oglander, the Gallipoli historian,[59] wanted to dramatise *The Man Within*? You can read all about him as Colonel Aspinall in *Gallipoli Memories*.[60] It was all too funny for words; there was to be a happy ending, Elizabeth coming to life again just as the curtain fell.

I've become simply crazy about flying. I never want to go in a boat again.

Love,

Graham

54 William Wycherley's comedy (1675) was playing at the Ambassadors Theatre in London.

55 Not identified. Conceivably, Noël Margaret Tidy, who wrote on massage and physiotherapy.

56 Edward Knoblock (1874–1945), an American playwright who lived for many years in London and was a friend of Arnold Bennett and Edith Sitwell.

57 J. R. Ackerley (1896–1967) was a poet and memoirist, who worked as a producer with the BBC from 1928. He became the literary editor of the *Listener* in 1935 and spent twenty-four years in that job, exercising wide influence over the literary scene (ODNB).

58 Graham is probably referring to his cousin Felix Greene (1909–85), who worked with the BBC. He became notorious for his botched reporting of the huge famine in China in 1959–61 following Mao's Great Leap Forward and for an obsequious interview with Chou En-lai. Journalists often refer to him mistakenly as the brother of Graham and Hugh.

59 The abundantly named Brigadier General Cecil Faber Aspinall-Oglander was the author of *Military Operations, Gallipoli* (1929). He generally wrote on naval subjects and may have regarded smugglers as falling under his nautical expertise.

60 A book by Sir Compton Mackenzie, published in 1929.

TO HUGH GREENE

9 Woodstock Close, | Oxford. | March 18 [1934]

Dear Hugh,

I enclose a card with a note on the back for B. I think it's the best way. You could leave it at his house with one of your own. Tell him that you were at Oxford; he has a fondness for the place.[61]

I don't suppose I could afford to come through Berlin, much as I should like to. I'm pretty busy these days; I am starting fiction reviewing again for *The Spectator*. Derek[62] rang me up on Friday to ask me to write 1200 words on 'The Three Little Pigs', the book of the Silly Symphony, by to-morrow, which explains this hasty & jaded note.

Father Bede died yesterday, the priest who got you those introductions. He was the nicest & most intelligent man I ever knew. Raffalovitch too died the other day.[63]

I hope your girl has lots of money!

    Love,

      Graham

---

61 Count Albrecht von Bernstorff, who had provided the money for Graham's jaunt to the Ruhr in 1924, was in constant peril under Hitler. A public opponent of the Nazis, he was dismissed from the London embassy and retired to private life. During the war, he ran an escape route for Jews from Germany to Switzerland; he was shot by the Gestapo c. 23 April 1945. (*A Sort of Life*, 100–1; Knut Hansen, *Albrecht Graf von Bernstorff* [Frankfurt: Peter Lang, 1996]; see pp. 394–5).

62 Derek Verschoyle brought Greene into the *Spectator* as a reviewer, and Greene was his replacement as literary editor when he was called up for military service. Citing Diana Athill, Jeremy Lewis writes of Verschoyle: 'he kept a .22 rifle in the office in Gower Street, and would occasionally fling open his window and, his feet propped up on the desk, take pot shots at stray cats lurking in the garden or on the black-bricked wall beyond; but however unpopular he may have been with Bloomsbury cats, his con-vivial, heavy-drinking ways recommended him to his colleagues.' ('Grub Street Irregular', unpublished ms.)

63 Andre Sebastian Raffalovich was a member of a wealthy Russian banking family. As a young man, he wrote poetry and fiction and was involved in a number of liter-ary circles in London. He was received into the Catholic Church and contributed heavily to Church causes, including the construction of a new chapel at Downside Abbey. He visited Graham and Vivien at Chipping Campden, and NS suggests that he was the model for Mr Eckman in *Stamboul Train* (*The Times*, 24 February 1934; NS 1: 426).

TO VIVIEN GREENE

At the suggestion of the Norwegian poet Nordahl Grieg and Baroness Budberg, the mistress of H. G. Wells, Graham took a trip to eastern Europe.[64] *The Baltic countries lay in the sights of both the Soviet Union and Germany, who were intent on installing sympathetic governments. The Soviets had recently concluded non-aggression pacts with Finland, Estonia, Latvia and Lithuania. In March, Estonia declared martial law in order to purge Nazis from government posts, and it was expected that a major trial would reveal the extent of foreign infiltration. Immediately after Graham's departure from Latvia, Premier Ulmanis declared martial law to deal with Socialist and Nazi plots*[65] *– a de facto coup. The trip would later influence the writing of* Our Man in Havana *(see p. 403).*

As from Hotel Room, | Tallinn, | Estonia. | Thursday
[12 May 1934]

Dearest, dearest darling love – I've just got your letter. I might have had it yesterday but I seem to have gone to the wrong place – it's rather difficult when everything's written in Russian! This afternoon I go on to Tallinn. Darling, I love you so much. Do take care of yourself. I believe I remember what you mean about the play. I made a silly joke after something you said quite out of key with situation! It's not you are out of key with me one bit; you are like a juggler, I believe you could keep your Tyg & a score of Lucy's in the air at once; it was only I think due to my staleness of mind. I began to feel all fresh from the moment of playing, but not quite enough to avoid a stupid joke which meant nothing at all. I believe one more play & I could quite have dispensed with this holiday.

   Darling darling love. I do hope you are feeling well & that Lucy is allowing you to sleep. I don't wonder at her being thirsty in this weather. I am drinking all day – soft drinks mostly, as the wine is much more expensive than in England & the beer is not very good. I'm feeling terribly well & sunburnt & selfish, at having left you

64 See *Ways of Escape*, 19.
65 *New York Times*, 16 May 1934.

behind. I should be enjoying this so much more with you. One does get through a place terribly quickly by oneself. But Riga definitely rings a bell.[66]

One silly thing has happened. I lost my spectacles as soon as I got to Berlin. So I'm not reading much or going to cinemas. In a way it's a blessing because it will force me to go to the oculist as I ought to have done a year ago. According to my present plans I shall get back to London late on Friday week. That's to say about 9.30. So I shall come down on the Saturday before Whitsunday. I shall try to see an oculist on Saturday morning.

It's only a week since I left you but it seems at least a month to me. One has covered a lot of ground! I caught a glimpse of Goering in Berlin. And Berns. was most interesting. Yesterday I had a comic time which may make an article in itself with Colonel Sudakov.[67] I'm going to spend a night at Kovno on the way back to Berlin, but it sounds a one horse place.

[. . .]

Thursday 10 p.m.

O darling, this place is just too amusing to tintinnabulate, with its wall & towers Burgundian, with its minarets Turkish, with I should think its morals 20th century Mahommedan. I've been very lucky here. The train takes 10 hours to go the 100 miles from Riga, & as to fly only cost 25/- I flew, a pretty flight along the edge of the Baltic. My luck was to share a taxi to the aerodrome with the Vice-Consul at Tallinn.[68] I had tea with him when we arrived. A charming rather disappointed character, a Catholic who reads nothing but Henry James! I noticed when he unpacked his suitcase that he was carrying *The Ambassadors* with him. So we more or less fell into each other's

66 In the imagination.

67 *The Times* (20 October 1928) reported the expulsion of a Soviet military attaché named Sudakoff from Latvia. He and his secretary had been attempting to organise anti-constitutional groups. Presumably this is the same man.

68 Peter Leslie (d. 1971) had been an Anglican clergyman but became a Catholic, an arms dealer and a spy for the SIS as presumably those things were nearer heaven. Much later, he made a gift to Greene of his collection of Henry James first editions. See pp. 301–2 ; *Ways of Escape*, 55–6; and *Articles of Faith*, 165–79.

arms. He was also interested in Kovno. He has lived in Tallinn for
12 years with an interval when he was a commercial traveller in
armaments. I gave him dinner to-night and to-morrow I'm having
dinner with him. It's all amazingly cheap here. We had for dinner,
the two of us, 6 vodkas, a delicious hors d'oeuvres, 2 Vienna [*sic*]
schnitzel with fried potatoes, & two glasses of tea. Total bill in one
of the swell restaurants 3/6d.

I arrived too late to get to the Poste Restante, so am hoping for a
letter to-morrow. The great film on here is Ramon Novarro in 'Ben
Hur'.[69] Do you remember it in '26 & how you didn't wear your
specs?

Darling, I so love you. I've got such a lot of amusing things to tell
you. But I do wish we were having this time together, though *you*
might be a bit of a responsibility. The Vice-Consul was quite
astonished that I'd got here without knowing any languages.

Good night, dearest dearest heart, I'm going to bed early being
sleepy after the vodkas. I'm leaving the night life for Major Giffey to
show me. He is the standing joke here, as the hearty fellow, hard
drinker, man-about-Tallinn.[70]

The army is a sweet caricature of the English. They wear the same
uniform & it's such a shock to come round a corner & find them
playing marbles or photographing each other under the War
Memorial. All so like Gibraltar, one feels, & yet how different!

My love to Lucy. How splendid about her weight. Riga was
tropical in its heat. Here is lovely, but much cooler & fresher. I'm
feeling extremely well but that only makes me miss you the more.

Goodbye, dearest heart.

Your Tyg.

P.S. I hear nothing but bad reports of Kovno, dirty, dull & expensive,
so I may leave it out.

---

69 Ramon Novarro (1899–1968) played the lead in *Ben Hur* (1925), with its famously
huge cast of 125,000.

70 Major Giffey, a passport-control officer, was likely also engaged in espionage work
as Tallinn, 250 miles west of St. Petersburg, served as a 'listening-post' for the Soviet
Union (*Articles of Faith*, 165–79). Mockler (94) suggests that he is the model for the
poker-playing attaché in *England Made Me*.

TO MRS. KURATH[71]

9 Woodstock Close, | Woodstock Road, | Oxford. |
August 5. [1934?]

Dear Mrs Kurath,

Forgive my delay in answering your letter; I have been very busy finishing a novel; I don't suppose, as I see that is one of your questions, that it will come out before the new year.

My opinion of *Babbling April* is more or less unprintable: the sentimental emotionalism of adolescence slapped down on the page; useful for self-analysis but should never have been printed. I find myself mildly amused still by Page 4 et seq. and mildly approving of P.12 & 24. I continued to write verse for another year and a half, some of it a little better than this, but apart from a few things in weekly papers published no more. I have, thank God, written no more since 1927.

The Man Within was the third novel I completed, the first published. The first page was written, while recovering from appendicitis, in 1926, without any idea of continuing the story. It was merely the description of an image which had persisted in my brain for some weeks. I had been reading Lord Troubridge's (?)[72] history of smuggling, in which is printed a remarkable letter from an informer to the revenue officers, a particularly mean letter. This to the imagination represented, I suppose, a challenge to make such a character sympathetic. The book was not begun for a long while after the first page was written; then for about 18 months it was written rather irregularly, as I was working at the time on the staff of *The Times*.

I think this answers your questions. I look forward to seeing your article.

Yours sincerely,
Graham Greene

71 Unidentified. Her article appears not to have been published.

72 Greene's query. He is actually thinking of Lord Teignmouth's and Charles G. Harper's *The Smugglers*, 2 vols. (1923), 1: 42–5. A man who called himself 'Goring' explained in detail the activities of a Sussex gang and proposed the means to capture them: 'Do but take up some of the Servants, they will soon rout the Masters, for the Servants are all poor.'

TO HUGH GREENE

9 Woodstock Close | Woodstock Road | Oxford |
Aug. 18 [1934]

Dear Hugh,

I wish I could have seen you in town to-day, but I had to come up
on Thursday for a night to see about my Liberian project and can't
get away again so soon. This is the tenth letter I've had to write today and there are still two more to be done. Will you tell Barbara[73]
that alas I've found that air tickets to Amsterdam are over £8, more
than to Paris and more than I had to pay Copenhagen to London.

Is there any hope of seeing you here? Leslie, the nice Consul in
Tallinn, wrote to ask me for a line of intro. to you. He'll be passing
through Berlin while you are on holiday, so I suggested he might find
you on the way back to Esthonia. I've got to be in town one day of
the week beginning Aug. 27, in order to see Sir John Harris, of the
Anti-Slavery Soc. who's going to help me over Liberia.[74] Any
chance of seeing you that week? Otherwise do suggest a day and I'll
come up. Feeling horribly overworked, so would rather get bubonic
plague than write another novel for a year. It was nice seeing
Barbara on Thursday. Hope I wasn't too drunk. I found when I left
the Café that I was wearing a woman's brown belt and had my braces
in my pocket!

Charles Evans is enthusiastic over Liberia and has offered to pay
all my expenses in advance.

Give Mumma my love. I have been meaning to write for weeks,
but the bloody old nib, or rather typewriter has never been so hard
pressed. Why, I've even had to turn down a perfectly good offer from
a publisher to do a short story, to be published all by itself at first,

73 Hugh was staying with their cousin Barbara Greene at 4 Ormonde Gate in London.
74 Though now largely forgotten, Sir John Harris (1874–1940) was a man of rare qualities. An Evangelical Christian, he had investigated and testified about the horrors of
Leopold II's exploitation of the Congo. He then travelled the world, often at the risk
of his life, to report on enslavements of colonial peoples. From 1910 to 1940, he
acted as parliamentary secretary to the amalgamated Anti-Slavery and Aborigines'
Protection societies. He served a term in Parliament as a Liberal and was knighted in
1933. (ODNB)

swell as a daisy, in a limited edition at 15/-. Blast, I sprained my wrist on Thursday night putting the Editor of the Theatre World to bed and even typing is hurting.

The Old School went into a second impression this week-end, 1500 copies sold. Not bad for a joke of that kind.

Love,
  Graham

TO DENYSE CLAIROUIN

9 Woodstock Close | Woodstock Road | Oxford |
Nov. 22 [1934]

Dear Denyse,

  [. . .]

I've just finished a novel to be called *The Shipwrecked*,[75] but I don't think you'll be able to do anything with it, though, of course, I shall send you a copy. I enclose a short story. I'm afraid it will seem bad to you who are French. I'm working on another which Grayson are supposed to be publishing in a limited edition.[76] I'll send you a typescript when it's ready. Then on Jan. 5 I leave on the most absurd trip. I'm going to Liberia; Heinemann have contracted for a travel book.[77] I get off at Freetown, Sierra Leone, and try to make my way from the border at Pendembu to Monrovia by the jungle with carriers. As I can find no one silly enough to go with me,[78] and as I have never managed natives or been in the tropics, it's all rather silly. But I did want a rest from novels. France is very interested in Liberia, isn't she? I suppose there's no sort of investigating job to be picked up from your Colonial Office? Do you know anyone in French Guinea? I shall probably be stepping off at Conakry.

75 This title, which Greene preferred, was used for the American edition. It was re-titled *England Made Me* for the English market.

76 'The Bear Fell Free'.

77 *Journey Without Maps* was published in May 1936.

78 He travelled with his cousin Barbara Greene (later Countess Strachwitz), who bore the physical strains of the trek better than he did. Without her presence he would probably have died of fever. Her book about the journey is *Land Benighted* (1938).

Do tell me who the English woman is and why she's lecturing on me. I should love to hear what nonsense she talks.

I think the irony of an English author being continually censored in France is delicious. It quite atones for the cuts. Tell them I'm a Catholic. Perhaps one can do more if they are certain I'm inside the fold!

Remember me to the angelic Updegraffs.

   Ever yours,
   Graham

P.S. I was in Germany in October & feel too pessimistic for words. I wish the world could be rid of that nice, sentimental, abysmally stupid race.

TO HUGH GREENE

9 Woodstock Close | Woodstock Road | Oxford |
Nov. 26 [1934]

Dear Hugh,

I never wrote and thanked you for the cheque as I was frantically busy, finishing *The Shipwrecked*, doing a short story which is supposed to be coming out in a limited edition (!), and getting ready for Liberia. Now there's a slight calm before the storm, but my God what a storm – I've got to pay a small fortune in insurance.

What I'm really writing is to tell you amusing news about *The Man Within*. Ronald [sic] Ackland, the dramatist, and a young man called Roy Lockwood, who has been editing and assistant directing in various companies since he went down, have found a tame financier and they are going to do the Hecht Arthur stunt of film making on their own. They are proposing to start off with *The Man Within*. They can only afford to pay me £200, which is Godsend enough to me, but their object is to make a really first class film. I think the result may be very amusing. They've got apparently a very good camera man, the financier will put up as much money as they need, and they propose to get started directly I come home from

Liberia.[79] One really begins to feel as if one wants to come back more or less intact. Especially (another good joke) as someone's lecturing on me in Paris in April.

Did Barbara tell you I'd had a long letter from poor Ingeborg? written at five o'clock in the morning with a stump of pencil belonging to Mikael, Mikael with a high fever in one bed and herself feverish in another. Scandinavians are terribly Scandinavian. Apparently she arrived back from Moscow 'dirty, tired and full of longing' on Christmas Eve of all days to hear that night from Nils that he was in love with someone else. Now she's found work in a bookshop.[80]

Do you know anyone in England who owns a revolver? The consensus of opinion seems to be that one must have a revolver. My own feeling is that it would be more dangerous to me than to anyone else, and I certainly can't afford to buy one. An amusing result of this trip seems to be that one is likely to be offered the most amazing variety of jobs, varying from the most august to the most farcical, adoption by old Harris as his successor as Parliamentary Secretary to the Anti-Slavery Society. But this in confidence. I have to be stared at and my private life examined by a committee of philanthropists; I'm afraid I shan't get by this. On Wed. I have tea with Lady Simon.[81]

---

79 Rodney Ackland's and Roy Lockwood's plan to follow Ben Hecht and Charles MacArthur, whose independently produced *Crime Without Passion* had been released in August 1934, failed. Greene later sold the rights for a token sum to Ralph Keane, who had worked with him on a publicity film for Imperial Airways, because Keane was looking for an opportunity to make his first feature film. Unable to finance a production, Keane resold the rights to Sydney Box, who brought it to the screen in 1947 with an appalling script that represented torture with branding irons as part of the legal system in the nineteenth century. 'After the experience I added a clause to every film contract forbidding a resale to Mr. Box' (*Ways of Escape*, 14; Falk, 48).

80 Ingeborg was the girlfriend of Nils Lie, the Norwegian translator of *The Man Within*. Greene dedicated *It's a Battlefield* to them. She also worked in Russia as secretary to Nordahl Grieg.

81 Dame Kathleen Simon, later Viscountess Simon (1863/4–1955), an Irish campaigner against slavery. As a researcher, writer and lecturer, she worked closely with Sir John Harris and was comparably devoted to the cause. Her husband, Sir John Simon, later 1st Viscount Simon, was the Foreign Secretary (ODNB).

How are Helga[82] and the flat and you and the Grafin's maid?
Love,
    Graham.

P.S. The best I can get from the mean *Times* is a letter to all whom it
may concern that I may be doing a series of articles for them on
Liberia. The whole trip gets more & more fantastic every day; at last
I've managed to get a fairly [?] large scale map; most of it blank white
with dotted lines showing the probable course of rivers! I have to
take [illeg.] cases of food, & a book I've read on Sierra Leone says
cheerfully that several Europeans have recently gone across the
border but none of them have returned! This, of course, is not to be
repeated to the family!

TO R. K. NARAYAN

*R. K. Narayan's friend and former neighbour Kit Purna was studying at
Exeter College, Oxford, and had promised to find a publisher for Narayan's
first novel. After a series of rejections at precise six-week intervals, Narayan
told Purna to 'weight the manuscript with a stone and drown it in the
Thames'. Purna approached Greene in Oxford, and shortly after sent
Narayan a cable: 'Novel taken. Graham Greene responsible.'*[83]

        14 North Side, Clapham Common, S.W.4. | August 1 [1935]

Dear Mr Narayan Swami,

My friend Kit Purna[84] sent me your novel the other day to read,
and I should like to tell you as a fellow novelist how much I admired

---

82 Hugh had married his first wife Helga (née Guinness) 24 October 1934 in Chelsea
(Tracey, 47).

83 RKN, 110–11.

84 Purna's full name was Krishna Raghavendra Purna. He was born in Bangalore in 1911
and educated in Mysore. He came up to Exeter College in 1932 to prepare for a career
in the civil service; his record card notes that he was 'popular in his year'. An engaging
man and a hard drinker, he died in June 1948. (Information from John Madicott,
archivist of Exeter College; for further information see Susan Ram and N. Ram, *R. K.
Narayan: The Early Years 1906–1945* [New Delhi: Viking, 1996], esp. 143–5)

it. I took the liberty of sending it with a covering letter to a
publisher, Hamish Hamilton, and I have heard from him to-day that
he wishes to publish it. You couldn't, I think, have a better
publisher. His is a young firm with a very good literary reputation
and his connexion with the American publishers, Harper's, may
make it possible to find a publisher for it too in the U.S.A. He also
advertises well. With this book published too we may find it easier to
place your short stories, for some of which I felt an almost equal
admiration. It is a real joy to be of use to a new writer of your quality.

There are a few things I should like to ask you. Have you any
objection to a few alterations in the English? It's very good on the
whole, but at times the grammar and sense need tightening. Then it
will need a simpler and more taking title than the one you have
given it. Last as to terms. I am seeing Hamish Hamilton on Tuesday,
Aug. 6, to discuss them. You can rely on me to get you the best
possible terms, but with a first novel I'm afraid you won't get a large
advance on royalties. But if the advance has to be small, I hope and
believe that the book will sell well enough to earn you a satisfactory
amount in royalties.

Of course the proposed contract will be sent to you for your
approval and signature.

I hope this will be only the first of a long series of books.

I wonder if you have come across the books of my friend Dennis
Kincaid[85] in India?

Yours sincerely,

Graham Greene

TO R. K. NARAYAN

14 North Side, Clapham Common, S.W.4. | Aug. 23 [1935]

Dear Mr Narayan Swami,

Many thanks for your letter. The pleasure is all mine in having
read your book. I daresay the contract may already have reached

85 Dennis Kincaid (1905–37) was a novelist and historian of India.

you. Hamilton will pay 10% on the published price on all copies sold up to 2,000 and after that 12½%, with an advance of £20 on publication. These, I'm afraid, are not princely terms, but if this first book is a success you will be able to command better terms for your next book. He intends to publish it this autumn at 6/- as it's rather a short book. The title he wants to put on it is *Swami and Friends*. Another point (I consulted Purna on it): your name. Have you any objection to the Swami being left out and your being styled R. K. Narayan?[86] It's a silly thing to have to say, but in this country a name which it is difficult for the old ladies in libraries to remember materially affects a book's sales. I saw an excellent novel by a German completely fail because of the supposed difficulty of his name: Erik von Kuhnelt-Leddihn![87] But, of course, if R. K. Narayan is absurdly incorrect in Indian eyes, we won't dream of using it.

I have been through the book a second time, making a very few alterations in words (your style is admirable and I can promise you the alterations are verbal and negligible in number) and I enjoyed it at a second reading quite as much as I did at the first. I hope you will presently give me news of a second novel. When this one is published I hope we shall be able to do something with your short stories, though the market for good short stories here is absurdly limited.

I look forward one day not too far ahead to meeting you.

Yours sincerely,

Graham Greene

TO DENYSE CLAIROUIN

14 North Side, Clapham Common, S.W.4. | Oct. 25 [1935]

Dear Denyse,

Many thanks for your letter, dated Oct. 11 & for the cheque. I love that kind of letter!

---

86 His full name was longer than Greene knew: Rasipuram Krishnaswami Ayyar Naranayanaswami.

87 *The Gates of Hell: An Historical Novel of the Present Day*, trans. I. J. Collins (New York: Sheed & Ward, 1933). Greene reviewed it in the *Spectator* (15 December 1933).

By the way I suppose they sent you my last novel, *England Made Me?* Liberia won't be out till March or April. The title so far is 'Journey Without Maps'. Then I'm going to have ready for the spring a thriller, opus one of the works of Hilary Trench:[88] proposed title: 'A Gun for Sale.' This is in the *Stamboul Train* vein, only even more melodramatic!

If the riots come on, I'll be over. I want a few days holiday badly.

Yours in haste,

    Graham Greene

TO HUGH GREENE

14 North Side, Clapham Common, S.W.4. | Jan. 28 [1936]

Dear Hugh,

Many thanks for your letter. I believe I only thanked you both by proxy for the book token. I loved the account of the sexual detective; he would be of admirable use to me, so I hope he turns up.

I'm having sherry at the Camerons next week and will mention what you say, but I'm surprised. I thought you were permanently wedded to journalism. I'm getting deep into films, so deep that Grierson sounded me the other day on whether I should be interested in a producing job.[89] I hope he is picturing me as the head of the proposed B.B.C. Film Unit! I'm on a kind of advisory committee on television as it is! Altogether I seem to have cut into the racket at the right angle. Last night we were at quite an amusing party given for Lotte Reiniger[90] with a programme of trick films.

But I'm hellishly busy; two books of my own coming out in the next few months (great enthusiasm on Heinemann's part for the shocker)[91] and I'm doing things for three symposiums. I've never written so much in my life.

88 A pseudonym Graham had used since his student days. See p. 355.

89 John Grierson (1898–1972) was the central figure at the GPO Film Unit and was largely responsible for such films as *Night Mail* (1936).

90 Lotte Reiniger (1899–1981), German film director and scriptwriter.

91 *Journey Without Maps* and *A Gun for Sale*.

If Cameron says anything enlightening I'll let you know.

I suppose you get the news of Mumma. She seems to be making very good progress, but it must be the hell of a dull time, lying flat on the back with nothing to do. The operation too must have been pretty ghastly with only a local anaesthetic. I think I'd almost rather lose the sight of an eye.

Love,

  Graham

Did you see my sob stuff in the *Mail*? They suddenly rang up on lunch time & asked whether I'd go along that afternoon & do it: 15 guineas for about 700 words![92]

TO NANCY PEARN

H. R. Westwood, associate editor of The Fortnightly Review *and an admirer of Greene's film criticism, invited him to write an article on censorship for the magazine. Although no article appeared, the letter makes clear what his views are.*

14 North Side, Clapham Common, S.W.4. | April 10 [1936]

Dear Nancy,

Many thanks. I wonder if I could trouble your office to give Westwood a ring to say that I left for Dartmouth for ten days on Easter Monday and will give him a ring directly I return. I think an article could be made which would be by no means stale. I shouldn't hinge it on the *Peace Film*.[93] What I propose to do (if he commissions it) is really to go in to its constitution, its record of foolish acts, and its personnel. I should like to interview several of the censors, the old ladies and the retired colonels, and give their

92 'The People's Pilgrimage', an article about George V lying in state at Westminster Hall (*Daily Mail*, 23 January 1936; reprint, *Reflections*, 37–9).
93 *People of Britain* (also known as *Peace of Britain* and the *Peace Film*) was directed by Paul Rotha in 1936, with music composed by Benjamin Britten; it was a propaganda film urging people to work for peace.

views on films quite untouched up. Then there's the curious anomaly in their treatment of the big American companies and the small British companies: the question why they should allow the attractive, but wildly sexual and lascivious dance in the new Cantor film[94] and insist on cutting scenes from the G.P.O. film, *Citizens of the Future*, which was urging cleanliness and washing on the people! I think a really amusing article could be made, which would not need a topical peg.

Yours,
Graham

TO R. K. NARAYAN

The Royal Castle Hotel, | Dartmouth. | April 20 [1936].

Dear Narayan,

This is just a hasty note to say that Hamish Hamilton *hasn't* yet sent me your novel.[95] I'm away here on holiday, until the end of the week, but as soon as I get back to town I will phone him & let you know the result.

I doubt whether any more money will come due to you on *Swami*: it didn't, I think, sell very well, (you'll get the account of sales soon), but the next novel should earn you at least an equal advance. And should sell better. (I am assuming that it's equally good). Everyone to whom I show *Swami* is enthusiastic: I lent a copy to Malcolm Muggeridge[96] – you may have heard of him in connexion with the *Calcutta Statesman* – he is one of the most promising young writers here – & he was elated by it & said that he was writing a letter to the editor of the *Statesman* about it. I lent it a few days ago too to

94 *Strike Me Pink*, starring Eddie Cantor and Ethel Merman.

95 The manuscript of Narayan's second novel *The Bachelor of Arts*, in which the main character is named Chandran. Greene wrote highly appreciative introductions to editions of this novel appearing in 1937 and 1978 (see *Reflections* 55–7 and 299–302).

96 Malcolm Muggeridge (1903–90) had taken a position in 1934 as assistant editor of the *Calcutta Statesman*.

Margaret Wilson whose novels you may know & expect the same enthusiasm from her.[97]

Congratulations on the birth of your child. I am expecting a second one in September.

I still look forward to the day when your books bring you to England, so that we may meet. If you are writing to Purna do send mine & my wife's best wishes.

Yours sincerely,

Graham Greene

P.S. If all is well about the novel I'll get them to send a cheque as quickly as possible without waiting for your signature on the contract.

TO BASIL DEAN

Greene worked with the theatre and film producer Basil Dean (1888–1978) on a script of John Galsworthy's 'The First and the Last', a story '"peculiarly unsuited for film adaptation, as its whole point lay in a double suicide (forbidden by the censor), a burned confession and an innocent man's conviction for murder (forbidden by the great public)"'[98] The film was released in 1940 as Twenty-One Days, *with Laurence Olivier and Vivien Leigh playing the leads. At the time Greene promised never to write another screenplay.*

14 North Side, Clapham Common, S.W.4 [May? 1936]

Dear Basil Dean,

About *The First and the Last*: I should very much enjoy working on this with you. I think it has immense film possibilities. I don't,

---

97 Margaret Wilson (1882–1973) won the Pulitzer Prize for her novel *The Able McLaughlins* (1923). She also wrote extensively about India, where she had worked as a missionary. Her husband Colonel G. D. Turner was a prison inspector who had arranged for Greene to visit Wormwood Scrubs in preparation for writing *It's a Battlefield*. Colonel Turner's daughter by his first wife married the publisher Rupert Hart-Davis (Mockler, 701).

98 'My Worst Film', *Reflections*, 318. In this essay of 1987, Greene quotes his own comments on the film in a *Spectator* piece of January 1940.

frankly, like Berkman's[99] treatment at all: both the opening and the
ending seem to me wholly undramatic. I think I see, too, a way to
avoid the double suicide without in any way altering the characters.
I should be inclined to build up the elder brother into a figure of
more complete selfishness and self-righteousness, so that he could be
sacrificed at the end and leave a moderately happy ending for the
more sympathetic figures. I haven't worked out a treatment in detail
as I've been very busy this last week, and I should like first to see you
and find your reaction to my preliminary ideas. I feel strongly against
B's introduction of a second girl, and the whole party scene seems to
me so banal that it could only be saved by the dialogue – and should
a film need saving by its dialogue? It doesn't give a chance to the
director.

Then again the introduction of the actual murder, at any rate as
Berkman places it. One loses entirely the fine dramatic surprise of
Larry's confession and gains – a piece of action which one has seen
over and over again on the screen. But I think there's a way of
introducing the most dramatic part, the carrying of the body, after
the confession. The story anyway has got me!

Yours sincerely,

Graham Greene

TO R. K. NARAYAN

14 North Side | Clapham Common | SW4 | Aug. 19 [1936]

Dear Narayan,

A hasty note of congratulation. Pearn, Pollinger & Higham have
just telephoned to say that Nelson's want to publish 'Chandran', &
I've sent you off a cable to that effect. The terms & the contract
have to wait a short while until the managing director returns from
his holiday, but I think you may count at any rate on an advance of

99 Greene had worked with the screenwriter Edward O. Berkman on the film of *The
Green Cockatoo* (1937). Although he wrote respectfully of his collaborator, it is hard
to imagine Greene satisfied with a man who could write *Bedtime for Bonzo* (1951).

the same amount as last time. They wish me to write an introductory note: I hope you won't mind this. As for Nelson's, they are an older, larger & more old-fashioned firm than Hamish Hamilton. Until about two years ago they published little fiction, but recently they have been going ahead with this. L.A.G. Strong, whose work I expect you know, is their chief fiction advisor.[100]

I'm overjoyed about this. Nothing could be more depressing than your set-back, but now I feel it was all for the best. Nelson's is a firm which would be far readier to nurse talent than snatch-&-grab Hamilton. I hope to hear that you are on a new book. I corrected the proof of your story for *The Spectator* some weeks ago, so I hope it will soon appear.[101] I feel sure your star is in the ascendant now!

Ever yours,

Graham Greene

100 Leonard Alfred George Strong (1896-1958) was a well-known poet and novelist.
101 Narayan's 'A Breach of Promise' appeared in the *Spectator* (4 September 1936).

3

THE POWER AND THE GLORY

TO MARION GREENE

With Lucy (called 'Bear') in the care of her grandparents, Vivien gave birth to their second child, Francis, on 13 September 1936. Having recently completed the film treatment of the Galsworthy story, Graham was looking forward to the journey to Mexico that would lead him to write The Lawless Roads *(1939) and* The Power and the Glory *(1940).*

14 North Side. Clapham Common. | London. S.W. 4 |
August 29 [1936]

Dearest Mumma,

It's a long time since I've written, but I've been in a rather inert condition. My run-downness culminated about a week ago in a poisoned face, which swelled up in a most embarrassing way. Painful too, like continuous tooth-ache. The day before yesterday I couldn't stand it any longer and had a cut made by a doctor, and yesterday and today a good deal of the poison has been coming out. I think the swelling will be a lot down tomorrow, as I find I can get my toothbrush round this morning! Martha seems admirable, nice and a very competent cook. I only hope she'll stay. I feel it must be rather dull for her until we get a second girl. There's no chance now I'm afraid of having Bear back till the end of the month, I mean the end of Sept. We miss her a great deal.

When everything's settled down, I shall try to take a week's holiday. I've got to learn Spanish too [in] the next few months, for rather to my agent's surprise Sheed & Ward, the Catholic publishers, have accepted our terms, £500 advance on English language rights, for a Mexican book on the religious persecution, and D.V. I shall be going off in January. I shall go via New York to pick up introductions and information and try to arrange a lecture tour for later in the Catholic states.

I can't help hoping too that something might turn up from Hollywood when I'm actually in America. If I get across to Sonora in Mexico, where they had the Indian war in 1928, I shall be only about 300 miles from H.! I've just turned in the film treatment of the Galsworthy to Basil Dean. I expect we shall argue about it this coming week and then I'll have to set to work on the shooting script, a thing I've never done before. Every camera angle has to be described, each angle being a scene, the average film having about 550 scenes. A long business. I find it very tiring, as you have to visualise exactly the whole time, not merely what the person is doing, but from what angle you watch him doing it. Vivien is very well, except for a nasty stye, and Dr Pink is pleased with her. Can you let us know how one sets about national insurance for a foreign maid?

A *Gun* seems to have been doing pretty well.[1] I'm trying to follow up with another thriller, scene to be set at Brighton.

Our love to both of you,
    Graham

TO R. K. NARAYAN

14 North Side, Clapham Common, S.W.4 [September 1936]

Dear Narayan,

A hasty line to say that I have placed a second story for you with *The Spectator*: 'Gandhi's Meeting.'[2] Today I forwarded you a cheque from *The Spectator* by airmail for the first story. A copy of the paper went off to you a week ago. I feel sure your luck has turned now. I

---

1 The film rights of *A Gun for Sale* had brought in a windfall of $12,000 (NS 1: 585) and the book itself was selling well.
2 It appeared in the *Spectator* (11 September 1936).

spoke to David Higham[3] to-day on the phone about your book &
asked him to arrange for payment to be made on signing the
contract – so as not to wait for publication. I have to write a preface
of a thousand words, & I would welcome any information from you:
your age, etc. Your other short stories are now in the agent's hands.
Did you ever hear from *New Stories* or receive a copy of the paper
containing the story they printed – or at any rate accepted?

Hamilton tells me that he only sold 230 copies of 'Swami'. Never
mind: I think it is quite possible that we shall see this book revived.

[. . .]

TO HUGH GREENE

14 North Side, Clapham Common, S.W.4 | Oct. 31 [1936]

Dear Hugh,

I should dearly love to come, but I don't think it can be
managed – either from the point of view of work or finance. These
bloody boils have been going on for more than two months, four
days in seven painfully, & one has no certain feeling that one day
they will stop. At the moment I have them on me, all just broken –
the lip, the thigh & the scrotum – so they've ceased to hurt.

I may have to decide between Mexico & the literary editorship of a
new paper – if it gets all its finances by Christmas. A horrid decision.
I'd much rather have Mexico, but the L.E. would be worth £600 a year.

I have to decide too between buying this house or leaving next
year: the lease won't be renewed.

I had to see Hitchcock the other day about possible work for
G. B. A silly harmless clown. I shuddered at the things he told me
he was doing to Conrad's *Secret Agent*.[4]

---

3 David Higham had been a literary agent with the firm of Curtis, Brown but joined
with Laurence Pollinger and Nancy Pearn in 1935 to create the firm of Pearn,
Pollinger and Higham, which handled most of Greene's business.

4 Alfred Hitchcock's *Sabotage*, was released at the end of the year. Surprisingly, Greene
reviewed it enthusiastically: '. . . for the first time he has really "come off".' (*The
Spectator*, 11 December 1936)

The baby is crying, & I have ten books accumulated for review & this damned thriller to write.

I have broken with Doubleday's more or less, & have tried to buy back from them, without success, *Journey Without Maps*, which the Viking Press offered to take on. They, the V.P., are going to have my next book anyway, though D's keep on sending anxious cables.

Auden's new book of poems (I haven't had time to read it yet) looks very good.[5]

I had a painful purgatorial lunch yday with Grigson, Spender & Rosamond Lehmann, my mind clouded with aspirins. I hadn't met S. before: he struck me as having too much human kindness. A little soft.[6]

Love,

Graham

TO HUGH GREENE

In his reviews, Graham savaged the films of Alexander Korda (1893–1956), who decided to deal with his harshest critic by hiring him as a writer, so in late 1936 they began a close, if unlikely, friendship. Greene wrote the original story and scenario for The Green Cockatoo, *an initial foray into the world of homicidal racetrack gangs that would provide the material for* Brighton Rock. *This film, directed by William Cameron Menzies, with John Mills in the lead, was not actually released until 1940, when it was universally panned.[7]*

---

5 *Look Stranger!* had been released the week before. *Journey Without Maps* had contained an epigraph from Auden's 'Five Songs':

> 'O do you imagine,' said fearer to farer,
> 'That dusk will delay on your path to the pass,
> Your diligent looking discover the lacking
> Your footsteps feel from granite to grass?'

6 Greene was generally dismissive of the poet Stephen Spender (1909–95), whose best-known work figures in *The Heart of the Matter* (30) as part of Literary Louise's high-brow reading, 'A lovely poem about a pylon.' Geoffrey Grigson (1905–85), a poet and vituperative reviewer, was the editor of *New Verse*, the most influential poetry journal of the 1930s. The novelist Rosamond Lehmann (1901–90) had recently completed *The Weather in the Streets* (1936).

7 See Adamson, 27–8; Falk, 11–14.

14 North Side, Clapham Common, S.W.4 | Dec. 19 [1936]

Dear Hugh,

This is to wish you from both of us a cheerful Christmas. We are sending you a compilation which seems intelligent and amusing: forgive the thumbmarks on the jacket. We both wanted to read it before sending it.

Have you heard that I've got in with Korda. I had to write him an original film story in three weeks, for which he pays 175 down whether used or not. This runs to 12,000 words. I hear today all is O.K. Shooting to begin in Jan., so he now has to pay me a salary of 125 a week for 4 weeks to work on the film. With an option on my services for the same salary for 6 months. There is a typical Korda snag. The story is a fairly realistic low-life thriller about race gangs, the hero a stool-pigeon. Korda wishes me to write in a part for George Robey![8]

The other fly in the ointment is a libel action. I don't know whether you remember the drunk party at Freetown in *Journey Without Maps*. I called the drunk, whose real name was quite different, Pa Oakley. It now turns out that there is a Dr P. D. Oakley, head of the Sierra Leone Medical Service. The book's been withdrawn (luckily all but 200 copies have been sold), writs have been served, and he's out for damages! Anxious days.[9] This and Korda are delaying my Mexican trip. I shan't get out there now till the autumn.

I hope you have good news of Helga. We're having Christmas at home, so Crowborough will be very quiet this year. How is Graham?[10]

Love,
Graham

8 George Robey (1869–1954) was a famous music-hall comedian, specialising in panto dames. Through 1937, he appeared at the Prince of Wales theatre in a non-stop revue, performing sixteen times a day. (ODNB)
9 Pa Oakley appears on p. 50 of the first edition but disappears from later editions.
10 Hugh's infant son Graham Carleton Greene.

TO HUGH GREENE

14 North Side, Clapham Common, S.W.4 | Dec. 26 [1936]

Dear Hugh,

A thousand thanks for the Book Token. I collected a shelf-ful of books this Christmas. A very nice old edition of Gibbon in 12 volumes and the new Boswell from Vivien – oh and Bryant's anthology of Restoration letters, Frost's poems and Dylan Thomas's, and *Rare Poems of the 17th Century*, and the *Letters of Byron*.

I'm thick in scenario. Medium Shots and Insert Shots and Flash backs and the rest of the racket. Korda, I'm glad to say, has given up the Robey idea and seems to be leaving us alone. Casting is proving very different. Menzies finds lovely people with appallingly tough faces, but when they open their mouths they all have Oxford accents.

[. . .]

TO THE EARL OF IDDESLEIGH

Night and Day was one of the most impressive new magazines to appear in Britain between the wars. Writing to the Earl of Iddesleigh (1901–70) at the publisher Eyre & Spottiswoode, Greene names its prominent contributors and describes the audience it will appeal to.

[Night and Day] 21st May, 1937

Dear Lord Iddesleigh,

I am writing as Literary Editor of a new weekly *Night and Day* which is to appear for the first time on July 1st. Among its regular contributors will be Peter Fleming, David Garnett, Adrian Bell, Theodora Benson and Anthony Powell. Modelled to some extent on *The New Yorker*, it will be addressed to a sophisticated and literary public, and although its main appeal will be humorous, a section of the paper will be devoted to serious criticisms. Evelyn Waugh will contribute a page each week on recent books and another page will be given up to shorter notices.

I should be very glad, therefore, if you would add this paper to the list of those to which you regularly send your books for review.

Yours sincerely,

Graham Greene

The magazine folded after only six months. Already short of money, it was sued by the managers of the child-actor Shirley Temple over Greene's observation in a film review (28 October) that interest in her was exploitative: 'Her admirers – middle-aged men and clergymen – respond to her dubious coquetry, to the sight of her well-shaped and desirable little body, packed with enormous vitality, only because the safety curtain of story and dialogue drops between their intelligence and their desire.' The matter was settled on terms humiliating to Greene.[11] The Shirley Temple episode may have influenced Greene's portrayal of the whisky priest's sexually precocious daughter in The Power and the Glory: *'He was appalled by her maturity, as she whipped up a smile from her large and varied stock.' (p. 81)*

TO JOHN BETJEMAN

John Betjeman (1906–84) was a younger contemporary of Greene's at Oxford. He contributed five instalments of his 'Diary of Percy Progress' to Night and Day, *and Greene hoped that he would write on architecture as well.[12]*

Night and Day | 97 St. Martin's Lane | London WC2 |
19th August, 1937

Dear Betjeman,

Can I steal you for my end of the paper? I am starting a series under some such title as 'Those Stately Homes' to deal in an unserious manner with the big country houses, their architecture,

11 See *Ways of Escape*, 47–50.

12 See Bevis Hillier, 'The Graham Greene Betjeman Knew', *Spectator* (2 October 2004).

their interiors and their what-nots. Lancaster is opening the series with an article on Osborne House. I don't want to be too exclusively Victorian. Have you any ideas? The payment at my end of the paper, I am afraid, is rather smaller than in John's.[13] For an article of anything between 900 and 1,200 words, I could pay 4 or 5 guineas according to length. We would also, of course, pay any agreed expenses in getting the material. I very much hope you will do something for me.

Yours sincerely,
     Graham Greene

TO R. K. NARAYAN

Night and Day | 97 St. Martin's Lane | London WC2 |
Oct. 13 [1937]

Dear Narayan,

I have this moment finished reading the new novel & get off this hurried line. I shall be very much honoured by a dedication. I like the book very much indeed. I wasn't so immediately taken by it as I was with *Swami*, but like Chandran I feel I shall like it better with every reading. The ending I think is triumphantly successful. I think it may very well turn out to be your best book.

As a matter of policy I shall go through it making a few corrections before I pass it on to Higham for Nelson's.

I am frantically busy, & very overworked, so forgive this hasty line.

Yours,
     Graham Greene

Though admired by critics, Narayan's books did not sell. Like Hamish Hamilton after Swami and Friends, *Nelson retreated from him, and the new manuscript went to Macmillan which brought it out as* The Dark

---

13 John Marks, joint editor, with Greene, of *Night and Day*.

Room *in* 1938: '*I had the unique experience of having a new publisher for each book. One book, one publisher – and then perhaps he said to himself, "Hands off this writer."*'[14]

TO DAVID HIGHAM

On 7 January, Higham had sought Greene's opinion of the cartoonist and designer Osbert Lancaster (1908–86).

> 14 North Side, Clapham Common, S.W.4
> [*c.* 9 January 1938]

Dear David,

Osbert Lancaster is a charming creature with a heavy moustache looking like a miniature Guardsman. He wrote an admirable satirical description of a seaside place called *Progress at Pelvis Bay*. Like most amateurs his writing is not always reliable. He has a curious pompous style which is excellent when he is being funny, but is heavy when he's serious. He draws very good humorous pictures of a satirical kind. Don't hesitate to mention my name if you want to when writing to him.

I hope you have had good luck with Frere.[15] The other places I'm interested in are Paraguay – remains of old Jesuit missions, five revolutions or attempted revolutions since 1935, the totalitarian state transported to the centre of South America;[16] and Ecuador a

14 RKN, 114.

15 After service in the First World War and a stint of journalism in the early 1920s, A. S. Frere (1892–1984) took a job with F. N. Doubleday, who soon purchased William Heinemann Ltd. Frere was made a director of Heinemann in 1926 and managing director, under the chairmanship of Charles Evans, in 1932. He was guilty of some indiscretions, such as claiming at a party that his firm's leading author John Galsworthy went about erecting stiles to help lame dogs over them. Frere was an expert talent-spotter and his personal charm included a skill at tap-dancing (ODNB). He became Greene's most important literary adviser.

16 No such book was written, but Paraguay remained a fascination for Greene; he set the last section of *Travels with My Aunt* (1969) and much of *The Honorary Consul* (1973) there.

half unexplored country, opera bouffe politics, a purely Indian state. But I daresay we better not confuse the issue with these.

Yours,

Graham

TO HUGH GREENE

14 North Side | Clapham Common | SW4 [16 January 1938]

Dear Hugh,

Many thanks for your letter. It's as bad as that, is it? I haven't had time to read the thing. I envy you *The Thousand and One Nights*, which I shall give myself if I ever sell another film which doesn't look likely as the whole industry, except M.G.M., is dead. Mexico is looking very doubtful – Sheed has dropped it because he says the Church doesn't want it done any more (I think he's probably short of ready), and though Longman's are ready to take it on over here, I've still to find an American publisher. With fiction I've left Doubleday's and gone to the Viking, but they aren't exactly snatching at Mexico.

I had, too, what I thought was a good idea: me and Muggeridge combining in a fairly light book on the Palestine civil war, me coming from Syria and Transjordania with Arab introductions, he from Tel Aviv with Jewish. Then we'd meet at the Holy Sepulchre and begin to argue, each supporting the people he hadn't come across, idealistically, and being told by the other – 'But you should have seen the buggers'. He'd therefore be pro-Arab and me pro-Jew. A little light relief too at a military court-martial. M. was delighted with the idea, but we can't find a publisher to see the fun. They are all a bit scared of Muggeridge too. Did you read his Literary Pilgrimages in *Night and Day*? I thought they were admirable. Especially the one on Lawrence.

My damned novel is giving me worse hell than any other – I suppose because I've never been able to give it two months on end; my nerves as a consequence are in tatters, and I want to get out of this bloody country.

I'm glad you agree about S. T. The little bitch is going to cost me about £250 if I'm lucky. But see *Captain January*. That's her great film. The Fox people went round to Gaumont-British to try and get them to withdraw all tickets from me, thus breaking me as a critic, but G.B. told them to go to hell, and I'm popping up in *The Spectator* again in the Spring – and, my God, won't I go gunning.

Did you see Herbert's front page news story in the *Daily Worker*, Dec. 22. 'I Was A Secret Agent of Japan'. Claud Cockburn wrote it, paid him nothing and borrowed 5 s. The general line was: This story must be true, because Mr. Greene is a real 'pukka sahib', not a mere worker like you, dear reader. 'I felt it was time,' Mr Greene writes, 'to speak up, when the Empire of the Rising Sun laid fingers on the heritage of Princess Elizabeth.' I gather from the same source that the book is to be called 'Secret Agents in Spain'. There is a facsimile letter from a poor Captain Oko signing himself Arthur – I don't know why.

This letter now I come to look at its constipated and ungrammatical sentences looks just the sort of letter in which some silly little official would read things between the lines.[17] I mean my letter, not Capt. Oko's. So you might let me know if it arrives. Our love to you three. I hope Helga's having as easy a time as before.

    Love,
        Graham

From 1934, Herbert had been working with Japanese naval intelligence, and, like Wormold in Our Man in Havana, *feeding them bogus information – he was reporting to a Captain Oko, codenamed Arthur. The article was an advertisement for his book* Secret Agent in Spain. *Herbert did visit Spain, and Claud Cockburn says that Ernest Hemingway pointed to him in Madrid and said he was going to shoot that man because he was a spy. Cockburn recognised him and said, 'Don't shoot him, he's my headmaster's son.'[18]*

17 The letter is addressed to Berlin, where Hugh was a correspondent for the *Daily Telegraph*.
18 NS 1: 613–14

TO DAVID HIGHAM

14 North Side, Clapham Common, S.W.4 [17 January 1938?]

Dear David,

I'm sorry if I've been rather irritating and changeable over Mexico. The truth is I didn't want to do a book for Heinemann that they didn't really want. One would feel awfully uninterested oneself. So when I talked to Frere and found that really under the surface that was the position, I offered to drop the whole thing as far as they were concerned and if I did the book at all publish it through Longman's. With such a big amorphous overwritten scene as Mexico the only treatment, I'm convinced, is a particular one – in this case a religious. And Frere admitted that he hadn't the faintest idea how to sell a religious book. Why, they even have to sell the *Bible* as literature!!

So I think the thing to do is wait on Mary.[19] If she can't place the book soon, I'll give it up. If she can get £250 for it, then, I think I can manage on £200 from Longman's plus a definite commission from the *Tablet*. I think I'd better have a word with Burns too from that point of view.[20]

The novel in its last 5000 words has turned round and bit me (I've never had such a bother with a book: I suppose because I've never been able to concentrate on it for two months together), so I'm going off to a country pub, I hope, tomorrow evening to finish it. Frere proposes to publish in July – which sounds good to me. I've made him quite happy about the title which I'm convinced is a good one. I'll let you know immediately I get a cable from Mary.

Yours,

Graham

19 Mary Pritchett, Greene's American agent.
20 Tom Burns (1906–95) was a publisher with Longman's and a junior director of the Catholic magazine the *Tablet*, of which he served as editor from 1967 to 1982. He met Greene in 1929 and the two became lifelong friends. An account of their friendship and Burns's own memoir of Greene may be found in *Articles of Faith*, xiii–xxv and 146–50.

'Brighton Rock *I began in* 1937 *as a detective story and continued, I am
sometimes tempted to think, as an error of judgement . . . how was it that a
book which I had intended to be a simple detective story should have involved
a discussion, too obvious and open for a novel, of the distinction between
good-and-evil and right-and-wrong and the mystery of "the appalling
strangeness of the mercy of God" – a mystery that was to be the subject of
three more of my novels? The first fifty pages of* Brighton Rock *are all that
remain of the detective story . . .'*[21]

TO HUGH GREENE

14 North Side, Clapham Common, SW4 | Jan. 22 [1938]

Dear Hugh,

[. . .]

Mexico has suddenly come off after all. Longman's here, Viking in
America. I'm off with V. at a week's notice to New York on the
Normandie on the 29th; then I'm taking her to New Orleans; she's
finding her way home; I'm going to San Antonio, Texas, where
there's a mission college for Mexico, to get some dope, and then go
on down. Back middle of May. I wish you could meet me in Mexico
City. If a miracle should happen between now and April cable
Thomas Cook's.

[. . .]

TO RAYMOND GREENE

Shushan Airport | New Orleans, La. | Feb. 27 [1938]

Dear Raymond,

It's taken much longer getting away from America than I had
planned, but I'm off tomorrow & Vivien by boat on Monday. We
spent about nine days in New York, stopped a day in Charlottesville
to see the University of Virginia – a startlingly lovely place – & then

21 *Ways of Escape*, 58–60.

came here, a rather disappointing spot. We've escaped from the town itself to this airport on the edge of a lake.

I have suddenly realised that proofs of my novel will be waiting for me in Mexico, & I've left a blank space in M.S. for the official name – which would appear on a post mortem report – for a kind of heart disease which might kill from shock a man in the early forties, physically – apart from his heart – C3 with drink and smokes. Could you write it me on a card & post it to me c/o Thomas Cook's, Mexico City?

My love to Eleanor.

Yours,

Graham

P.S. Mexico's quite in the news here. Some chance of a Fascist outbreak.

C3 *was the lowest physical rating of conscripts in the First World War. In* Brighton Rock, *Hale's post-mortem shows that he died of cardiac thrombosis, although Ida suspects suicide or murder. The report also indicates that he possessed, as did Greene, an appendix scar and supernumerary nipples (*Brighton Rock *78–9; see also 371 below). Hale's other identity is Kolley Kibber, a name based on Colley Cibber, a poet and playwright ridiculed in* The Dunciad. *It is hard not to think that in this character, Greene intended a mocking portrait of himself as a creature of Grub Street and is playfully challenging the reader to find the clues and make the connection: 'You are Mr Kolley Kibber. I claim the Daily Messenger prize' (p. 5).*

TO NANCY PEARN

On his way to Mexico City, Greene met with General Saturnino Cedillo, who controlled the state of San Luis Potosí from his ranch at Las Palomas. Though not religious himself, Cedillo chose not to enforce anti-religious laws. Shortly afterwards, he openly rebelled against President Cárdenas, took to the mountains, and was shot by government soldiers.[22]

22 See *The Lawless Roads*, 42-61.

Hotel Canada [Mexico City] | March 11 [1938]

Dear Nancy,

I've arrived here rather late – detained by an interesting political character in San Luis Potosi. I'm off again to Vera Cruz in a day or two: there to Tabasco, & then a fortnight's ride by horse across T. & Chiapas to the road & the rail again. This should be interesting – almost untraveled [?] ground. Then I come back here to recuperate.

Listen! I enclose a story which I verily hope may have enough action for the *Strand*. The title can be changed. I have sent a small descriptive article to *The Spectator* called 'A Postcard from San Antonio' & told them if they don't want it to send it to you. It might do for *New Statesman* or *Time & Tide*. In a few days I am sending them another article – 'A Day at the General's' – with the same instructions.[23]

Mail address still Cook's [?].

Adios,
Graham

If anything should be printed – *proofs to my wife*.

TO ELIZABETH BOWEN

Graham spent five weeks in the country examining the effects of anti-religious laws in Chiapas and especially in Tabasco, where many priests had been imprisoned or executed. Here, he writes to his friend the novelist Elizabeth Bowen (1899–1973); he had been glad to find one of her novels in the home of a Norwegian family on whom he based the Fellowes family in The Power and the Glory.

---

23 Several of Greene's pieces about Mexico appeared in magazines, including 'A Day at the General's' in the *Spectator* (15 April 1938), 330–2. Most of this material was incorporated into *The Lawless Roads*. 'A Postcard from San Antonio' eventually appeared in *Modern Reading* No. 1, ed. Reginald Moore (London: Staples Books, 1941), 53–55.

Hotel Español | Ciudad Las Casas, Chis., Mex. | April 13 [1938]

Dear Elizabeth,

I can't resist writing to you a line of gratitude. About 9 days ago I got landed in a rather wretched village in Chiapas called Yajalon waiting for a guide & mules to bring me here. (Why do they call this stuff ink?) I was driven distracted by rats when I discovered in the house of a Norwegian, the widow of an American coffee planter, a copy of *The Hotel*, the only book of yours I hadn't read. – I must give up this ink. O, I've just discovered it's really for rubber stamps. So all of two nights, I was able to sit up & read by an electric torch & drink bad brandy & quite forget the rats. Your book was so infinitely more actual than the absurd situation. After I finished it I had to fall back on *Kristin Lavrandsdottir*[24] (the husband had belonged to the Book of the Month Club), but that didn't work at all – the rats beat 14th century Norway every time.

This is an awful & depressing country for anyone like myself who doesn't care for nature. And guides have a conviction – I haven't enough Spanish to share it – that 12 hours is a reasonable ride per day. Thank Goodness in San Cristobal one's back on the road again. I went to my first bootleg Mass today – in Northern Mexico & the capital some of the churches are open: no sanctus bell & the priest arriving in a natty motoring coat & a tweed cap, & the woman of the house immensely complacent.

I found a cable waiting for me in Mexico City asking me to agree to apologise to that little bitch Shirley Temple – so I suppose the case has now been settled with the maximum publicity. How I shall miss your dramatic criticisms.

Yours,

Graham

24 A novel by Sigrid Undset.

TO DENYSE CLAIROUIN

14 North Side: Clapham Common: SW4 | July 14 [1938]

Dear Denyse,

A hurried line. *The Spectator* has just rung me up to say would I cover the King's visit to Paris for them. I propose flying across on Monday & back on Wednesday. Could you possibly give me a bed? or if you can't, do you think the Golls[25] would (they mentioned a spare bed to me)? I'll get in touch with you when I arrive & perhaps you'd have some suggestions for where one might observe some bizarre celebrations.

Yours in great haste,
Graham

Graham's account of the visit opens with an instructive phonetic rendering of the British national anthem that appeared in Paris Soir: 'Godd saive aour grechieuss Kinng. Long laïve aour nobeul Kinng. Godd saive ze Kinng.'[26]

TO MARION GREENE

Hitler's demand to annex the Sudetenland led to a war panic in September 1938. Having recently taken on an expensive house in London, Graham was worried about the safety of his family and his ability to support them if he was called up for military service.

14 North Side: Clapham Common: SW4 | Sep. 27 [1938]

Dearest Mumma,

Don't worry too much about arrangements. Vivien, Lucy and Francis are going down with Eleanor[27] tomorrow afternoon, in case Parliament declares a state of emergency right away. Eleanor is

25 It is possible that Graham is referring to the French-German poet and anthologist Yvan Goll (1891–1950), who was associated with André Breton and the surrealists.
26 *Spectator*, 22 July 1938; *Reflections*, 69–72.
27 Raymond's wife.

seeing if she can get a room for Freda[28] near her cottage. In which case I shall send her by train. R. has suggested I should join him, but as long as old cook sticks I shall stay at home. Elisabeth too may join me, as she doesn't much relish being alone in her flat. I had to drag old cook almost by main force to be fitted for a gas mask yesterday. V., Freda and the children are being done this morning. We had an hour's wait in a queue. Nasty smelly things! Eleanor, I'm sure, will be able to keep the children for quite a long while so don't feel rushed. I should strongly advise you not to stay Wed. night in town, in case you weren't allowed to go back on Thursday. At some point it is obviously going to be impossible for adults to travel till the schools have been evacuated, and you might get caught.

Of course war may not come, but one has to organize on the assumption that it will.

I see things rather as follows: immediate conscription is certain. Therefore a. one may find oneself in the army with or without a commission. This means small earning power and only a small allowance. In that case one must make one's savings go as far and as long as possible. Under those circumstances I should feel very grateful if my family were boarded out either with Eleanor or you on some sharing basis: we'd contribute of course to rates, labour etc as well as board. And this house would be shut up or let.

b. one would find oneself in some ministry – of information or propaganda at a reasonable salary. In that case I should take as cheap lodging as possible in town or get someone to share expenses of this house, and find a cottage, perhaps at Campden for the children.

I imagine, as far as foreign maids are concerned, the Gov. will take that out of your hands. Their legations will see to their evacuation.

Anyway here's hoping for all of us.

Love,

Graham

28 A servant.

TO R. K. NARAYAN

14 North Side: Clapham Common: SW4 | Oct. 16 [1938]

Dear Narayan,

Just a line to wish every success to the new book.[29] I noticed an advertisement in one of the weeklies this week-end. I certainly shouldn't be despondent if I were you. Macmillan's are a very rich and influential firm & you have now at last hope of some continuity in the effort to sell your books. I look forward to the fourth – somebody who is as much an artist as you will have to write it whether he wants to or not.

Brighton Rock has done well critically, but it's by no means a best-seller – somewhere about 6,000 which is good for me. But I'm feeling horribly sterile – my only idea one of frightening difficulty & hazard.[30] When one has a family to support one hates to try something new which may drop one's sales back to the old level.

Vivien is well & sends her remembrances to you & your wife, & we both look forward to seeing you in the flesh next year.

Yours ever,

Graham Greene

TO JOHN BETJEMAN

14 North Side: Clapham Common: S.W. 4 | Dec. 30 [1938]

Dear Betjeman,

How nice of you to write. I was very worried because the *Spectator* printed vowels instead of towels.[31] O well.

Can I enlist your support to an Association of Perpetual B.A.'s, to sign a manifesto pledging themselves never to take an M.A. & add

29 *The Dark Room.*

30 Presumably, *The Power and the Glory.*

31 Graham's review of Betjeman's *An Oxford University Chest* in the *Spectator* (16 December 1938) contains this phrase: '. . . the hollow donnish voices mildly complain, hands are raised in little Pilate gestures with dainty North Oxford vowels . . .'

thus to the funds the university misuses? The words Perpetual B.A. have a pleasant Barchester ring, I feel, & recall Mr. Crawley, the high-minded & tiresome perpetual curate.

I wish I could see Piper's aquatints.[32] I have met him – but I am always frightened by the nobility of artists.

Yours

   Graham Greene

TO HUGH GREENE

14 North Side, Clapham Common, SW4 | April 7 [1939]

Dear Hugh,

Sorry I couldn't manage Paris. I wanted to badly, but money and notice were both too short. Curiously enough for other reasons I had been having a passionate nostalgia for Paris the last ten days.

In confidence, life at the moment is devilishly involved, psychologically.[33] War offers the only possible solution. Glad you liked *The Lawless Roads*. Considering it was written in six months. I don't think it's bad. [. . .]

A new shade for knickers and nightdresses has been named Brighton Rock by Peter Jones.[34] Is this fame?

   [. . .]

TO DAVID HIGHAM

In The Confidential Agent *important characters are represented merely by initials. Collier's Magazine in the United States, which was serialising the book, complained about the lack of names to the agent Mary Pritchett, who suggested that Higham and Graham take up the matter with Heinemann.*

32 The designer and artist John Piper (1903–92).

33 A reference to the beginning of his ten-year relationship with the stage-designer Dorothy Glover.

34 A large shop in London, now owned by the John Lewis Partnership.

Dear David,

No, I haven't heard from Mary yet. On no account take up the name point with Heinemann's. Let them think of it themselves if they want to. My own feeling is that the initials which take the place of three names are important as not localising the country from which these people come. Ruritanian names to my view stink of grease paint. I have always found too that Americans – I have noticed it in proof readers – resent any departure from the usual practice. How often have I had an adjective queried and some banal cliché suggested in its place. However if Charles or Frere feel anything about it, we can argue it out.

Any chance of getting contract and cash through next week?

Yours,

Graham

TO R. K. NARAYAN

Narayan's young wife Rajam died of typhoid in June 1939.

14 North Side | Clapham Common | SW4 | July 4 [1939]

Dear Narayan,

To send the sympathy of strangers at such a cruel time seems like a mockery. But I've been happily married now a long time, and I can imagine how appalling everything must seem to you now. I don't even know what your faith allows you to hope. I'll let Higham know. We were talking about you only the other day, and of how Murray's admired your work. And I was saying how you had a long book in mind. I'm glad of that. I don't suppose you'll write again for months, but eventually you will, not because you are just a good writer (there are hundreds), but because you are one of the finest. My wife sends her deepest sympathy, feeling too how cold the words sound. If you ever have a snapshot of yourself and your child, do send it us. We still hope that one day we shall see you, here or in

India. If there is no war. Write again, please, as soon as you feel able to.

    Ever yours,

      Graham Greene

Narayan did not remarry but found comfort in spiritualism. He described his experience of Rajam's sickness and death in The English Teacher *(1945), which he characterised as 'autobiographical in content, very little part of it being fiction'.*[35]

TO NANCY PEARN

14 North Side, Clapham Common, SW4 | July 15 [1939]

Dear Nancy,

David will tell you of a contract he is just fixing up for me with Heinemann called *Refugee Ship*. My idea is a non-fiction book, describing one of these rather appalling voyages from Constanza in Rumania on old wooden Greek boats carrying 3 or 400 Jews. They try to smuggle them into Palestine and are generally nabbed by British destroyers. Don't you think there's a very good human interest story for the *Express*? I should have thought it worth say three articles: the port, the voyage, the landing – or the arrest.

    Yours,

      Graham

Shelden (145–55) carefully selects evidence to make the claim that until the war was over Greene ignored the oppression of Jews in Europe. The book about the refugees was the second Greene proposed that would have taken up Jewish concerns (see p. 86). For Greene's own remarks on Jewish stereotypes in his early fiction, see pp. 398–9. It is worth noting that the plight of the Jewish refugees seems to have been on Greene's mind at just this time, as he speaks of the whisky priest as 'a man without a passport who is turned away from every harbour'.[36]

35 RKN, 129.
36 *The Power and the Glory*, 102.

TO VIVIEN GREENE

14 North Side: Clapham Common: SW4 | Aug. 30 [1939]

It was lovely hearing from you, dear heart: I was getting anxious. I miss you so much particularly in the evening which makes me rather moony and uncommunicative over my pint. I saw Goronwy Rees[37] yday, and the editor is quite ready to take a weekly London diary in the event of war. This would help a great deal. I've found the wills which I enclose, but not any bank receipts. News seems a tiny bit better. London very odd. Dim lighting, pillar boxes turned into white zebras in some parts. The common a mass of tents, and nobody about on North Side. A dubious old man living in Clapham who has for fifty years collected Victorian curiosa has written to Henry Ash and it has been forwarded here.[38] Our cobbler has a daughter in the Bank of England. All the old shabby notes which would have been destroyed are being stored in the country in case the printing works is destroyed. *Spectator* may go to Yeovil at weekend. Derek refuses to cut short his holiday in France by a day which is causing much work. Says the Embassy have told him there's no reason to leave but they don't, as Goronwy remarks, tell anybody else that. I like the conscienceless savoir faire.

You are missing nothing here. Only the faint susurrus of the intellectuals dashing for ministry posts. Spender feathered his young nest in Ministry of Information.[39] Had Clack in yday. A mistake. She broke the latchkey in the door (I've got a new one) and messed up a telephone call. I was having my bath when the Clack voice

37 Goronwy Rees (1909–79), a Welsh novelist and assistant editor of the *Spectator*.

38 Something very odd seems to have happened. Henry Ash was one of several pseud-onyms Greene used when writing letters to the editor. However, there was a real Henry Ash, a draughtsman best known for his sketches of cable-laying expeditions in the 1870s and 80s. He was by now eighty-nine and living in Brighton. The letter Greene received was possibly meant for this man – and although Greene would later make much of there being another Graham Greene (see pp. 246–7), in this case he was himself merely the other Henry Ash. (See Judith Adamson, *Graham Greene, the Dangerous Edge: Where Art and Politics Meet* [London: Macmillan, 1990], 184–6. I am grateful to Bill Turner for information about the draughtsman.)

39 Stephen Spender had actually attempted to enlist but was twice deemed medically unfit. He joined the Auxiliary Fire Service in 1941. (ODNB)

called outside, 'Go round at once', and disappeared. I got out and
dried and went, towelclad, to find her. She didn't know who had
called. Wasn't sure of message. It was a man. I said, 'Next time, tell
them to hold on, and fetch me.' I had got my pants on, when she
pounded up. Same man. She had asked him to hold on. Ran down;
to find she had put back the receiver! He never rang again. Might
have been Pat[40] to tell you to go at once. Might have been anything.
I think one gets on better without the Clack. Sully's carpenter is in
now, fitting plywood over the skylight, to prevent glass falling in.
Good bye, my dearest, for a little while.

   With all my love,
   Tyg

TO VIVIEN GREENE

14 North Side: Clapham Common: SW 4 | Sep. 4 [1939]

My dearest, a very hurried letter in return for your lovely long one.
Yes, we had two warnings yday, one just as I'd begun my cinema
article and the other about 2.45 this morning, both false alarms.
Nobody seems to mind much. No scurrying at all. I went into
central London for the second black-out on Saturday night, and
heard Douglas Byng very funny and Nellie Wallace like[wise?] at the
Prince of Wales.[41] Very lovely and impressive with all the sky signs
gone and little blue phosphorescent milk bars and a hurdy-gurdy
invisibly playing – rather like a Paris back-street. Newspaperman
calling, 'Ave a paper tonight', plaintively. Another one very
conversational, 'Reminds me of the trenches. Never knew which
way you was going.' [. . .]

   After the all-clear went last night it was curiously like Christmas
morning: the voices of air raid wardens going home like people

40 Vivien's brother Patrick, an artillery officer who fought in Italy and achieved the
rank of brigadier.
41 Douglas Byng (1893–1988) and Nellie Wallace (1870–1948) were famous music
hall entertainers. Wallace generally sported a threadbare boa and Byng worked in
drag.

returning from Midnight Mass. After the sirens began yday morning a woman passed slowly along leading a dog, no hurry, and all the balloons began to rise round the sky; the pigeons made a mass dive for shelter. I'm very snug: work in the morning, then go out and see people and have my three halves, and wander round.

[. . .]

TO JOHN HAYWARD

The anthologist and critic John Hayward (1905–65), who suffered from muscular dystrophy, is now remembered chiefly as the close friend and adviser of T. S. Eliot, with whom he shared a flat in Chelsea from 1946 to 1957. Graham had first consulted him in 1931 about the Earl of Rochester, whose works Hayward had edited while still an undergraduate.

14 North Side: Clapham Common: SW 4 | Thursday
[14 September 1939]

Dear John,

I've just been ringing up your flat to see whether you were still in London &, if you were, to beg a cup of tea from you. I don't like shop tea, & I can't be bothered to make my own, & at the same time tea I love above all things. I've evacuated all my family & wait here, having finished a novel yesterday,[42] to be called up on this Army Officers' Emergency Reserve, as a second-lieutenant. Horrible to think of the lieutenants one will have to salute.

I was thinking out an idea yday of an organisation of war authors parallel to the war artists. They would be given acting rank & assigned to the various fronts, to do an objective, non-newsy & unpropaganda [?] picture of the war – for publication in England & America – composite books probably. I can't help feeling there's something here: they should be people who are published in America anyway on their name [?]. Of course the idea behind it is to avoid being sent for six weary months of training to

42 *The Power and the Glory.*

Catterick[43] or some other hole. If you know someone in the War Office (not in that beastly den, the Ministry of Information) won't you put it up, organise it & assign me to some picturesque theatre of war?

I suppose you've succeeded in either letting your flat or surrendering the lease. I ask because a nice, intelligent & reliable friend of mine, a girl who designs theatre costumes,[44] asked me to look out for someone who couldn't let his flat & would accept a nominal rent of not more than 30/- a week in return for a careful eye being kept on his things.

I must stop & read an incredibly funny & indecent Hugh Walpole (I am doing *Spectator* fiction to earn some money).[45]

'Standing up they embraced until they were indeed one flesh, one heart, one soul. But it hurts to make love standing, so Joe said: "Let's not bother about lunch."'

Yours,

Graham

Another gem: 'For weeks they had been constantly together, & during the last week had been without a break in one another's arms, spiritually when it had been too public to be so physically.'

TO LAURENCE POLLINGER

By April 1939, Graham was involved in a very serious relationship with Dorothy Glover (1901–71), which continued until the late 1940s. Although Glover's short, stout appearance was hardly prepossessing, he admired her direct and forceful character, which offered a decided contrast to Vivien's. She lived with her mother in Mecklenburgh Square and met him when he came to rent a studio from them.[46] The two remained in London

43 Catterick Camp, now Catterick Garrison, is a large military training facility in North Yorkshire.
44 Dorothy Glover.
45 Review of *The Sea Tower* by Hugh Walpole in the *Spectator* (22 September 1939).
46 See NS 2: 19–20, but note that in a letter of 15 October 1942 (p. 120 below) Greene says that the relationship is actually four years old.

*through the blitz, mainly at another studio at 19 Gower Mews. Graham did
his best to promote Dorothy's career and went on to collaborate with her on
several children's books. In later years Dorothy became a Catholic. Hard
drinking eventually destroyed her health.*

14 North Side, Clapham Common, SW4 | Feb. 8 [1940]

Dear Laurence,

I have advised a friend of mine, Dorothy Glover, to send you a
play she has written. She is a theatrical designer, costume and sets,
so, although this is her first, she has had plenty of experience of the
stage. I read it in the rough and it seemed to me as good as most
plays one sees put on. A farcical-thriller. Anyway perhaps you'll look
out for it.

I've just heard from Gyde that the novel is not being published
till March 11.[47] Isn't this rather a lousy date, as it only gives it ten
days to run before Easter gums up the works? Good Friday is the
22nd. What do you think?

Yours,

Graham

D.G. asked me how many copies you'd need of a play. I said I
thought two – one for managements & one for files. Is that right?

TO MICHAEL RICHEY

In this letter Graham responds to comments on The Power and the Glory
*from Michael Richey (b. 1917), who became one of his closest friends.
Briefly a monk, then an apprentice to the artist Eric Gill, Richey served on
a minesweeper and other ships in the Royal Navy. After the war he became
a prominent navigator and author.*

47 Arnold Gyde was head of the editorial department at Heinemann and the firm's
chief publicist. (St John, *passim*) *The Power and the Glory* was actually released on
4 March 1940.

14 North Side | Clapham Common | S.W.4 | June 5 [1940]

Dear Michael,

I'm afraid I've been a long time answering your letter. Frantically busy about affairs of no earthly importance. I'm glad you like P. and G., and you are probably right about the length. I don't agree with you otherwise. The priest may have kicked up a fuss, but his rightness is neither here nor there. He was the sort who would. Read some lives of the saints and see what a fuss they make. He was a bit of a religious materialist, I meant him to be, though I think you are wrong in saying that he found the toothglass odd. In fact you are objecting to him on the same grounds as people who object to a book because it has no nice characters. The answer is: they are not meant to be nice.

If you ever get leave, do come and see us. You certainly live now in a stranger world than that priest's.

Yours,

Graham

TO MARION GREENE

On 18 October 1940, 14 North Side was bombed. Vivien and the children were in Oxford and Graham was at the studio in Bloomsbury, so the house was unoccupied.

as from 99 Gower St. [c. 19 October 1940]

Dearest Mumma,

Alas! our house went at 1.30 a.m. on Friday. I arrived to collect some objects at 8.30 to find a scene of devastation. There has been no fire & no flood & the structure is still standing, so something may be salvaged when the demolition people have made it safe to enter. Either a landmine at the back or else a whole load of bombs. The secret [?] workshop in the garden next door destroyed, part of the L. C. C. flats & damage all along the row, but the back of our house got the worst blast. Impossible to get beyond the hall for wreckage. I only hope some of my books & some of V's things will be saved. But there was still an unexploded bomb nearby to go off, & the whole place is likely to tumble at much more shock. Rather heartbreaking that so lovely a house that has survived so much should go like that. And I feel over-awed without my books. No hope of salvage starting before Monday. However there were no casualties.

   Much love,
      Graham

Graham's shock at the destruction of a fine old house was not the whole story. He was certainly glad to be rid of a financial worry. Stocked with costly antiques, the house had stood as Vivien's recompense for an unstable childhood. Graham felt more and more engulfed in a middle-class way of life, from which he had sought escape since adolescence. The destruction of the house brought these differences of temperament and expectation into sharper focus.

TO ANTHONY POWELL

From April–September 1940 Graham was in charge of the writers' section of the absurdly bureaucratic Ministry of Information. In this letter he tells the novelist Anthony Powell (1905–2000) how the new Director-General, Frank Pick (1878–1941), formerly Managing Director of London Transport and the man responsible for the development of the Tube Map, had eliminated his position as unnecessary.[48]

The Spectator | 99 Gower Street | London W.C.1 |
Dec. 16 [1940]

My dear Powell,

   How good to hear from you. I have only had second hand news via Malcolm.[49] I've been leading a chequered and rather

48 See NS 2: 38

49 '[Greene] was staying near the ministry in a little mews flat where I spent an occasional evening with him, the invariable supper dish being sausages, then still available. Whatever his circumstances, he had this facility for seeming always to be in lodgings,

disreputable life. After passing the medical board for general service I was given till last July to amass some money for my family:[50] then in April I was suddenly offered a job at the M. of I. – the job A. D. Peters once had. I stayed there six months, having resigned from the Officers Reserve . . . an absurd hilarious time I shouldn't have had the vitality to break. Luckily Pick axed me at the end of September, and I am now literary editing this rag . . . which isn't quite as I pictured war. However London is extraordinarily pleasant these days with all the new open spaces, and the rather Mexican effect of ruined churches.

I have a private ambition to do Free French propaganda in French Guinea and the Ivory Coast from a base in Liberia, but so far I haven't [been?] contacted. All my family are parked in Trinity: my house has been blasted into wreckage by a land mine, and I sleep on a sofa in a Gower St. mews. As I'm under a skylight I go into a basement when the barrage is heavy. A direct hit next door and escaping gas and a midnight flit has been the most exciting evening yet.

I find it impossible to write anything except reviews and middles, but there's nothing to spend money on and I find one can live admirably on about 500 . . . which I suppose is a fortune to a soldier. Would it be possible for you to work off some of your bile in book reviews? I wish to God you would do some for me.

If you ever get up to town, do ring me up and have lunch. Hope you get leave at Christmas.

Yours,

   Graham Greene

and living from hand to mouth. Spiritually, and even physically, he is one of nature's displaced persons. Soon after his house on Clapham Common had been totally demolished in the Blitz, I happened to run into him. There was no one in the house at the time, his family having moved into the country, and he gave an impression of being well content with its disappearance. Now, at last, he seemed to be saying, he was homeless, *de facto* as well as *de jure*.' Malcolm Muggeridge, *The Infernal Grove* (London: William Collins, 1973), 82–3.

50 Graham managed to get £2000 from a film contract with Alexander Korda. To the great disappointment of an Inspector of Taxes who menaced Vivien while Graham was serving in Africa, the payments were split between two tax years.

TO MARY PRITCHETT

The Spectator | 99 Gower Street, | London, W.C.1, |
March 18 [1941]

Dear Mary,

I've been very remiss in writing to you, but as you can guess life is quite crowded. I'm literary editing this paper, acting as dramatic critic, reviewing a good deal, completely failing to write any books, doing some B.B.C. scripts, and at least three nights a week act as an air raid warden from 10 till 2 in the morning, or until the Raiders Passed goes. I'm glad to say I saved practically all my books from the house, though poor Vivien lost most of her Victorian furniture and objects. It's sad because it was a pretty house, but oddly enough it leaves one very carefree.

The whole war is good for someone like me who has always suffered from an anxiety neurosis: I turn down work right and left just for the fun of not caring. The M. of I. asked me to return the other day which gave me an opening for a cheery raspberry . . . If you ever feel inclined to drop a line to Vivien her address is President's Lodging, Trinity College, Oxford. She has the thin end of things. I have a most interesting and agreeable time in London. It all seems most right and proper.

[. . .]

TO MARION GREENE

Wednesday, 16 April 1941, brought one of the worst raids of the war. One bomb fell on the Victoria Club in Malet Street where 350 Canadian soldiers were sleeping.[51] *Graham was often in the streets as bombs were falling.*

51 Ways of Escape, 84–8.

The Spectator | 99 Gower Street | London W.C.1 |
April 18 [1941]

Dearest Mumma,

Just off for a weekend with the family at Blockley. You'll have seen
about Wednesday night. It really was the worst thing yet. On my beat
which only consisted of about three quarters of a mile of streets we had
one huge fire, one smaller fire, one H.E.[52] and, worst of all, a landmine.
The casualties were very heavy, as the landmine which got the
Canadian soldiers' home by the M. of I. blasted houses right through
Gower St. The fires are not quite out yet. I got off with a cut hand
from having to flop down flat on the pavement outside the landmine
place. One thought the night was never going to end. Hardly three
minutes would pass between two and four without a salvo being
dropped. I feel very stiff and bruised . . . I think from carrying a very
heavy young woman down from the top of the R.A.D.A.[53] building in
Gower St. and helping to carry a very fat, very vocal foreign Jew, who
had had his foot crushed, to the M. of I. where they had an emergency
dressing station. One's first corpse in the Canadian place was not
nearly as bad as one expected. It seemed just a bit of the rubble. What
remains as nastiest were the crowds of people who were cut by glass, in
rather squalid bloodstained pyjamas grey with debris waiting about for
help. I was very lucky when the mine went off as I was standing with
two other wardens in Tottenham Court Rd. We got down on our
haunches, no time for more, and a shop window showered on top of us
without cutting any of us. One felt rather pursued. I was having my
hand bound up at my post under the School of Tropical Medicine in
Gower St when a stick came down, and we were all over the floor
again with the windows blown in.

[. . .]

TO MARION GREENE

Graham's sister Elisabeth joined SIS in 1938 at Bletchley and recruited

52 High explosive.
53 Royal Academy of Dramatic Art.

Graham and Malcolm Muggeridge to the service.[54] *After training at Oriel College, Oxford, Graham sailed for his first posting in early December.*

The Spectator | 99 Gower Street | London W.C.1 |
Aug. 20 [1941]

Dearest Mumma,

This is just to tell you that I am going out to West Africa for the Colonial Office. I shan't be going for two or three months as I shall be working in London first. The pay is very good, & the job interesting, & the shadow of a private's pay – or even a lieutenant's – is raised. I shall be able to leave plenty behind for the family. How long I shall be out there I don't know. I hope not more than 6 months, but it might be a year – though I doubt if the war will last that long. I gave in my notice here yday.

[. . .]

TO JOHN BETJEMAN

On the first anniversary of the bombing of his house Graham used old letterhead with the address crossed out and a note in the margin, 'Obit. 18.10.40 1.a.m.' Betjeman, who was then press attaché to the British Representative in Dublin, described himself as 'a bloody little diplomatic sunbeam'. He sent Graham a poem by Patrick Kavanagh and invited him to come over and lecture.[55]

North Oxford Nursing Home, | Banbury Rd. | Oxford. |
Oct. 18 [1941]

Dear John,

It was good hearing from you in this place which is one after your own heart – diamond panes looking out on North Oxford chimney

54 Christopher Hawtree, obituary of Elisabeth Dennys, *Guardian*, 10 February 1999.
55 See Bevis Hillier, 'The Graham Greene Betjeman Knew', *Spectator* (2 October 2004).

pots, fumed oak furniture, and a few roses in a tooth mug, and water pipes which whistle sullenly in the wall. I left the *Spectator* nearly a month ago as I felt that very soon I shall find myself in the Pioneer Corps, the haunt of middle-aged professional men like myself. But the pay they tell me is *hardly enough to make both ends meet*. So I joined the Colonial Office & am supposed to be going out quite soon to West Africa, the pay being good but with a sinister absence of competition.

Then for reasons only known to themselves the C.O. thought it would do me good to get a military background, so I was sent for four weeks to a college here & taught how to salute with a little stick under my arm on the march (a thing I shall never have to do.) They also tried without success to teach me to motorcycle on Shotover – this always ended in disaster. As I seemed to be surviving better than the bicycles they gave it up, & gave me flu instead. This was definitely the military background – the hideous little M.O. with dirty yellow fingers, the no heating, the lavatories on the other side of a cold quad, the struggle for water to drink, the dreadful cold soggy steak & kidney pudding on iron trays . . . I packed a suitcase and fled here, but they'd already added bronchitis to the flu.

How I should love to come to Dublin & see you, but I'm a bad lecturer & I don't think this time . . . I've got to gather my strength & shave now. One of the nurses said I looked like an old man & yesterday on the way to the lavatory I caught sight of myself in a glass huddled in an old yellow overcoat like a humble character in Dostoievsky pursuing the scent of a samovar into somebody else's flat . . .

I'm sorry I couldn't do anything about Kavanagh: my successor is W. J. Turner.[56]

And I'm sorry too about my writing which gets worse every day here.

If W.A.[57] should get delayed – I'll write & tell you, & do fix up something.

Yours,

Graham Greene

---

56 The poet W. J. Turner (1889–1946) took over as the literary editor of the *Spectator*.
57 West Africa.

4

THE HEART OF THE MATTER

TO MARION GREENE

After three months in Lagos, Graham took up his post in Freetown, where he remained until February 1943. In a drab bungalow where rats swung on his bedroom curtains and one servant chased another with an axe, he quickly wrote The Ministry of Fear, *his most successful thriller. His experiences there led also to the writing of* The Heart of the Matter *(1948). In this letter, he complains about difficulties and inconveniences of his posting, yet his attitude towards this place was surprisingly passionate. He believed that what was essential about life was most likely to be apprehended on the move or in conditions of privation and danger. He wrote of 1942: '"Those days" – I am glad to have had them; my love of Africa deepened there, in particular for what is called, the whole world over, the Coast, this world of tin roofs, of vultures clanging down, of laterite paths turning rose in the evening light'.*[1]

> C/O Bank of B. W. A. | Freetown | Sierra Leone |
> April 2 [1942]

Dearest Mumma,

I had a very pleasant surprise today with a letter from you and your present of books. Thank you so very much: the letter was as welcome as the books. My last mail missed me here and is now pursuing me up and down the coast, so I hadn't heard anything for a long time.

---

1 *Ways of Escape*, 89–95; see also 'The Soupsweet Land' in *Collected Essays*, 339–45.

I left Lagos last Saturday (today's Thursday) and flew to Accra. What I saw of it I didn't like – except the superbly beautiful old Danish fort in which the Governor lives – like a stage set of Elsinore in dazzling white with the surf beating below on two sides. I stayed in an American transit camp for the night: a wind blowing up the red dust all the time, bad food and morose or drunk tough Americans belonging to the airline. Then on the Sunday I flew on here coming down in Liberia at a new aerodrome the Americans have made, for lunch – an overcooked steak literally a foot long. The planes are uncomfortable – freight planes in which the passengers sit upright facing each other the whole length on little metal seats like lavatory seats. The heat until you get well up is appalling and then of course the metal turns cold.

I arrived in Freetown with no accommodation in the evening but the Governor[2] – a very kind and intelligent man – put me up a couple of nights until I'd got a couple of boys and a cook, and then I moved into my dingy little Creole villa about two miles out of town in the flats. It's terribly difficult to get anywhere to live alone in these days, so one can't look a gift horse in the mouth. All the same I wish I was not just across the road from a transport camp in process of erection with two steam shovels going all day. And there's no water although there are taps. Freetown has 147 inches a year, but distribution is so bad that there won't be any water in my part till the rains six weeks hence. Drinking water I have to fetch in empty bottles from Freetown and then of course boil it, and bath water is fetched from a water hole. One tries not to think of germs and what the blacks do there and one pours in sanitas . . . I'm hoping that the police are getting me an oil-drum of water out in a few days. Sanitation of course is nonexistent.[3] I shouldn't mind this a bit if I was in the bush, but it's depressing trying to keep clean to entertain and be entertained. This sounds a depressed letter, but I'm not really depressed. Just a bit badgered with housekeeping worries: it's a little difficult at present to find time to work.

2 Sir Hubert Craddock Stevenson (1888–1971) served as governor of Sierra Leone from 1941 to 1947.

3 Other letters at this time indicate that the area around the house was essentially an open latrine.

[. . .]

I'm afraid letters from me will be rather few and far between. I have no assistant or secretary, and God knows how I shall get through the work. I'm turning my minute dining room here into an office as soon as I can get any desk or other furniture but practically everything is unobtainable here. For instance even ink can't be bought for love or money, no soda water – a trial in a country where you have to boil and filter every drop – if you can get a drop. Even in the town taps stop running about 11 in the morning. People keep the two inches of their morning bath to serve again at night – this isn't so good when you've sweated all day, but when the rains come it will be better.

Well this has been a moan. I hadn't meant it to be. In many ways we are better off than at home. Tomorrow's Good Friday . . . Good Friday four years ago I went to a secret illegal Mass in Chiapas. I've had an odd life when I come to think of it. Useless and sometimes miserable, but bizarre and on the whole not boring.

My love to all of you,
     Graham

I've sent on the letter to Lagos and asked them to forward by air mail. It should get to Elisabeth in about a week to ten days. If a bag is going it will get there earlier. I suddenly realized that I hadn't told you that it would probably have to go through the Egyptian censorship[4] so I took the necessary liberty of reading it first. Now that I've told you I shan't have to again. Sorry. C'est la guerre! I'm so glad you've got airgraph letters now.

     Much love.

4 Elisabeth's war years were divided between Cairo and Algiers.

TO MARION GREENE

C/O Bank of B. W. A. | Freetown, | Sierra Leone, |
May 4 [1942]

Dearest Mumma,

[. . .]

I'm reading *North and South* by Mrs Gaskell at the moment. Some
of it is very good – and the acid humour is most pleasant. Only
people in Victorian novels do seem to behave so oddly whenever sex
rears its ugly head! Tremors and horrors and indignations. Would
they think we behaved oddly? perhaps they'd think just disgustingly.
I'm leaving *The Eustace Diamonds* till my railway journey. I ration
myself to one Trollope a month which will take me through
November. Last night I had my first film for a long time. I went on
board one of the naval ships and saw the full length Disney *The
Reluctant Dragon*. It's the one which takes one [on] a tour of the
studios and throws in two or three films. I liked it more than any
Disney for a long time. One sat on deckchairs on deck, and though
the sound was a bit off, it was quite delightful with the lights of
Freetown over the water.

Freetown always looks its best from the water. On shore after the
rain the plague of house flies has come back to my part. And at night
there are far too many objects flying and crawling for my liking.
Wherever one wants to put one's hand suddenly, to turn on a switch
or what not, there always seems to be a gigantic spider. Whenever
one kills something which has flopped on the floor the ants come
out and get to work, stripping the corpse and then heaving and
pushing the skeleton towards the door. Last night I counted a slow
procession of four black hearselike corpses: you couldn't see the ants
underneath. And I never get quite used to seeing a vulture sitting
complacently on my roof as I come home. Their walk is peculiarly
ugly. Putting up their wings like an umbrella they make a quick
tottering reel forward.

However I'm really comfortable now, and very lucky to have a
house all to myself, a good cook, a fairly good steward . . . my small
boy has gone off to join the army. Work at present is uneven. Days of

extreme rush when I long for a secretary to take off the donkey work of typing etc., and then days of almost inertia which I dislike intensely. I've converted my dining room into my office, and eat and live in one large room.

Give my love to Da.[5] I'm glad he's got over his cold. I believe you are having good weather at last or were four weeks ago. Good news today about Madagascar[6] on the wireless, I gather. I haven't been able to get a radio myself.

Much love,
    Graham

TO MARION GREENE

Graham learned by telegraph that The Power and the Glory *had been awarded the Hawthornden Prize.*

C/O Bank of B.W.A. | Freetown. | June 11 [1942]

Dearest Mumma,

I'm afraid it's a long time since I've written, but I've been pretty busy this last month. It's funny how things always seem to go well when I'm away; I've just heard about winning the Hawthornden prize and the film of *A Gun for Sale*. Vivien tells me it's an extremely good film. I wonder whether you would be able to get up to London and have a look at it. But I expect it's off again by this time: maybe it will come to Crowborough. Rather sad that one can't have the presentation and speeches and so on of the Hawthornden, though the prizewinner always looks a little silly. And it's odd that one feels pleased – apart from the hundred pounds which is always useful. There's no real distinction in the prize: a few good books have won it, and a great many very bad ones – like Charles Morgan's.[7] I

---

5 James Greene, Hugh's son, suggests that Graham's letters to his mother were, in effect, letters to both parents.
6 The British assault on Vichy-held Madagascar quelled all resistance by 7 May.
7 Morgan's novel *The Fountain* had taken the award in 1932.

suppose at the bottom of every human mind is the rather degraded love of success – any kind of success. One feels ashamed of one's own pleasure.

I had a very nice week away from this loathly town in the Protectorate, visiting old haunts and seeing a few ghosts of the past. I went up to Kailahun and found the D. C. there was the man who had been headmaster of Bo School with whom I had had a good party when I was here before. Of course the result of being away a week was an awful accumulation of stuff here, which it took me a long time to clear. And travel now is appallingly tiring.

The house is looking reasonably human now and as the rains are beginning there's plenty of water, thank God. But none of my stuff has yet arrived from Lagos. It's been waiting shipment twelve weeks. I feel that it could have been managed if anybody at the other end had taken trouble. Half my clothes are mouldering in a wooden case there, all my china and cutlery, and of course my car.

Some friends of Vivien passed through the other day going out to Elisabeth's part of the world, so I was able to send a letter. I'm extremely well, though I humbugged my knee a bit the other day. Humbug is the local expression. A thief got into my living room and stole a loaf of bread, a table cloth, two bottles of beer, an unopened bottle of sherry, the fountain pen which I've had since 1926, and my sole remaining pair of glasses. (I cabled for more). So I got wire put up over all the windows which gives the impression that one is either living in a prison, a nursery, or a loony bin. The wretched carpenter left a coil of this rusty criss cross wire on the path, the same colour as the stones, and running out in the rain to a taxi I caught my foot in it, twisted my knee and cut it. I could hardly walk for 24 hours, but now it's only a little stiff. The cut of course festered in a small way – you can't scratch yourself here without festering, even if you swab on iodine at once, but I think the pus has all come out now and it should heal in a day or two.

Last week was rather frantically social with dull people in every night for dinner or drinks, but this week, thank God, looks like being a little quieter. I see my cook approaching in the distance proudly escorting two carriers: the lord knows what he's been buying: one has a pail on his head and the other a large box. I suppose I shall know soon. Things are a bit short here as we haven't had any ships in for a good while. Milk (tinned of course) has been unobtainable, and butter too. (I see now it's logs for the stove and not a box). But of course we are really very well off compared with England – though not quite so disgustingly so as Lagos.

There's a chance of sending this letter off by a quick route, so I must close. I hope Da's keeping well. It really looks as if the war may be over next year. Don't you feel so? Much love to you all from

Graham

TO RAYMOND GREENE

C/O Bank of B. W. A. | Freetown, | Sierra Leone |
July 23 [1942]

Dear Raymond,

It was extremely pleasant hearing from you. No, this isn't an ideal spot, but in some ways it's a good deal better than Lagos, and I have a house of a kind to myself and can close the door when I want to and be as morose as I like. The water difficulty of course is solved now by nature. So far I've rather liked the rains except on the occasions when it rains continually for three days and nights.

Life was helped at the beginning by an excellent cook, but he's gone off his head and my steward who is acting as cook has a rather horrifying range of dull dishes not too well done.

I suppose one never enjoys what one is doing at the moment – even writing books, and I rather envy you the sense of a useful job. I'm not in the least convinced that I would not be far more useful in a munitions factory, and certainly one would prefer any factory town to this colonial slum. I shall probably rebel eventually and find myself at home again.

[. . .]

I heard of your commando activity.[8] It must have been fun. I wish

---

8 The specific reference is not clear, but during the war, Raymond worked with SOE (Special Operations Executive), which specialised in sabotage, subversion and

they would take me on as a kind of war historian-observer. With honorary rank and no dull regimental duties. These are the idle dreams of an exile.

I get away from this place up-country when I can and have revisited a few old spots and met ghosts of the past, but it's difficult to get away and when I do I pay for it by several 12 hour days getting through the arrears of dull routine stuff that has stacked up for me.

Well you know the S.P. has quite a function even in the tropics – security.[9] Of which there is never very much when more than three Englishmen are together. The ideal of security I suppose is one man in an igloo surrounded by 500 miles of snow.

Do write again and let me know more about your nurses' constipation. I've been very well so far; the irritating thing about this climate is that you can't scratch yourself without going septic.

The rain is drenching down and I must back to work. My love to Eleanor.

> Yours,
>   Graham

TO HUGH GREENE

In a letter of 28 June 1942, Hugh had told Graham that a 'very nice piece and a good drinking companion' would be taking up a government job in Freetown. He thought she might be a 'comfort' to him. He also said that he saw Dorothy Glover from time to time and that they were planning an illustrated book called 'Sights of London' to be published after the war.

guerrilla warfare. He helped them with high-altitude and cold-climate military plans that, as a doctor, he was expert on given his Everest experience. He spent a lot of time at the SOE Station at Grendon Underwood and at Scapa Flow, from which a number of secret expeditions were launched across the North Sea. (Information from Oliver Greene)

9 Probably the Field Security Police, a branch of military intelligence also known as MI11.

c\o Bank of B.W.A. | Freetown, | Sierra Leone. |
August 1 [1942]

Dear Hugh,

Many thanks for your note. I'll look out for the girl, but I don't
feel inclined really for a playmate. Life is quite complicated enough
as it is, and I'm still in love! A drinking companion would be a boon
if there was anywhere to drink and anything to drink. But there's
only one hotel, and nothing to get but bad bottled export beer of
uncertain kinds, Scotch if you are lucky, gin which is a depressant,
and South African wines that make you feel like hell next morning.

I should certainly warn the poor thing off these parts: they really
are not a catch, unless she likes being swarmed around by subalterns.

Doll wrote me about the bawdy book she's planning with you as
evasively as you. I long to hear more. I wish you'd told me how she
was looking, whether she seemed well, could down her pint and Irish
as readily, etc. Give her my love. In the ordinary course of things I
should have been most grateful for your tasteful and reliable pimping,
but I've become terribly one-idead. This letter is not for circulation!

O, I hear your two teeth have been taken out and put back,
straight. I can't help feeling you will lose some of your charm.

This place will be most amusing to look back on, I daresay, but it's
extraordinary how dull and boring the bizarre can be at the time. I'm
getting grey, more and more bad tempered, and rather a bully.

Elisabeth's engagement was pleasing. The man is very nice and
intelligent. I was afraid that she was emotionally tied up with the
middle-aged married sailor. God knows what size the children will
be, as the man is a good bit taller than me.[10] I envy you Sweden.[11] I
suddenly realise I'd better not send this off till you return. God bless.

Graham

10 After an on-and-off engagement, Elisabeth married an intelligence officer named
Rodney Dennys in 1944. In the early days of the war, he had pulled off a daring
escape from the Nazis in Holland. The couple met at Bletchley and again when they
were both stationed in Cairo. (See Christopher Hawtree, obituary of Elisabeth
Dennys, *Guardian*, 10 February 1999)

11 In August and September 1942 Hugh was in Stockholm trying to find out how the
BBC might counteract the jamming of its transmissions. His eventual recommenda-
tion was that presenters should speak very clearly. (Tracey, 85)

TO ELISABETH GREENE (LATER DENNYS)

c/o Police H.Q. | Freetown, | October 15 [1942]

Dear Elisabeth,

I've just got your letter of Sep. 19. I'm so sorry things have not gone too well. Things can be hell, I know. The peculiar form it's taken with me the last four years has been in loving two people as equally as makes no difference, the awful struggle to have your cake and eat it, the inability to throw over one for the sake of the other. . . . This, of course, is confidential. Yours is different and I imagine just as hellish. I always used to laugh at emotional situations and feel they couldn't any of them beat toothache. One lives and learns.

You say you'd like any suggestions, though as you quite rightly say other people's suggestions are no bloody good. My own feeling is that climate can play the absolute devil with things: the whole atmosphere of a place like this is artificial in the extreme and I imagine it's a bit the same with you. A kind of feverish mental sexuality with much impaired vitalities. People talking the whole time and the doing not so hot. (Here comes a tornado – blast it: I'd much rather have a blitz than a bad thunder-storm). And that's hellishly wearing on the nerves. I don't personally suffer from it because my life is too complicated to want any further complications.

What I'm circuitously getting at is that I'd humbly and probably impracticably suggest that you, as it were, break off officially with the mutual understanding that you've no objection to his making love to you again whether you are engaged or not if he wants to when you are both back in a reasonable climate – put it up to your respective parents that you've decided that it's better to wait and see whether you like each other when circumstances are normal. Then make head office give you over-lapping leaves. Not leaves at the same time, that's too purposeful like making a date to sleep with a new lech on a certain day.

Of course, I don't know what your relations with Rodney are, but remember that if you are just engaged, even in a temperate climate a man can lose about five of his skins . . . I remember ghastly headaches . . . I'm assuming for the sake of argument that you are just engaged. In which case, for God's sake, remember that it's a distinct possibility to fall badly in love *after* sleeping with a man, and that's the kind that goes on. A man improves enormously too under that treatment in the way of nerves, thin-skinnedness, sociability and the like. Only, of course, it mustn't be done as an 'experiment', but because one's feeling cheerful and a little drunk perhaps and in the mood. . . . I'm rambling on and teaching you to suck eggs. I'm sorry.

I had about two months ago a violent quarrel with my local boss and resigned. I was supported on the point at issue and offered a new position for which I was totally unfitted by lack of languages, though it would have been most interesting. I'm not quite sure or not whether I'm now going home under a cloud. I think not as I am not being replaced. This is a quite useless spot. Anyway you'll probably hear of me yet cleaning latrines on Salisbury Plain.

[. . .]

Much love and I hope things improve one way or another.

   Graham

Reading this over I feel it's an awful flow of platitudes already familiar. I'm getting rapidly middle-aged in this climate. Forgive them.

TO MARION GREENE

Long a sufferer from diabetes, Charles Greene died on 7 November 1942: 'The news came in two telegrams delivered in the wrong order – the first told me of his death – the second an hour later of his serious illness'[12]

Freetown, | Nov. 30 [1942]

Dearest Mumma,

I have only heard today about Da's death and I wrote to you yesterday inquiring after him and full of silly minor personal

12 *A Sort of Life*, 20.

troubles. I feel it was rather a selfish act taking on a job abroad at this time, and I ought to have been home. I wish Elisabeth had been. I can't write about how sorry and sad I feel: he was a very good person in a way we don't seem to be able to produce in our generation. I wish he could have seen the end of this wretched war and better times, but I'm glad all happened so quietly and suddenly, so that he had no time to miss Elisabeth being away at the end. And I'm glad too that I belong to a faith that believes we can still do something for him and he can still do something for us. It will be such a long time after that you'll get this letter, and that will hurt. I'm glad the children saw him again in September and Hugh and his family were down not so long before. I can't write more now, but I think I shall be seeing you before very long.

So much love and more sympathy than I can put in words.

Graham

Later.
This may seem Popish superstition to you, or it may please you, that prayers are being said every day for Da in a West African church, & that rice is being distributed here in his name among people who live on rice & find it very hard to get.

TO RAYMOND GREENE

Freetown | Jan. 4 [1943]

My dear Raymond,

[. . .]

Forgive this rambling and not very lucid letter. Yesterday I began the second year on the coast, and I think quinine and the dreary colonials and the even drearier services turn one into a complete nit wit. I expect, however, to be home, for a time at any rate, quite soon now.

The letter about Da's death was a bit of a shock. I agree with you. Having children of one's own makes one appreciate the position much more. I felt terribly sorry I hadn't been down oftener since the war came, and when one did go down his rather noble old Liberalism was always inclined to make one bring out one's cynicism stronger than need have been. About the chattels: it's very difficult to think of things at this distance. I agree entirely with you that we should buy the things. I can think only of the DNB which would be extremely useful to me, and, if I could have a gift, his copy of Hardy's *Dynasts*. The DNB of course I would buy. It's very nice of you to have let me have first choice. May I suggest that Elisabeth ought to choose a chattel or two? She can hardly be expected to buy. And perhaps when you have chosen, you would consult Vivien on my behalf. There might be something she would like to buy with a view to having a house of our own again. I am writing to Mumma about the DNB and *The Dynasts*.

My homecoming shortly does not depend I am glad to say on the major war situation. I agree with you about that, and resolutely refuse to be optimistic, though actually the prospect of peace now would fill me with utter gloom. War has not yet touched enough people of ours to alter the world. Here the complacency, ignorance and well-being is incredible. I should like to make a poster: 'Come to Sierra Leone and Forget the War. No Rationing. No Income Tax. All the Fun of the Fair.' Three day public holiday at Christmas and another three days at the New Year. The consumption of food and drink during those days quite enough to fill a cargo boat. One will be glad to get back to decent austerity again and at least the possibility of air raids. I imagine Churchill's reference to the services of West Africa in the war was ironic.[13] As far as I can see their contribution has been confined to cowardice, complacency, inefficiency, illiteracy and thirst . . . Of course one is referring only to the Europeans. The Africans at least contribute grace. However it is all admirable copy. But how tired one is of little plump men in shorts with hairless legs, and drab women, and the atmosphere of Balham going gay. People say the African is not yet ready for self-government. God knows whether he is or not: the Englishman here certainly isn't.

Yours,

Graham

13 On 29 November 1942, Churchill had referred to Operation Torch, the landing of Allied forces in Vichy-controlled Algeria and Morocco, as a 'majestic enterprise'.

TO LAURENCE POLLINGER

*Graham returned to England at the beginning of March 1943 and was
faced with an array of uncertainties concerning Vivien, Dorothy and his
future as a writer. After a visit to his mother at Crowborough, his first
order of business was to make sense of the stage production of* Brighton
Rock. *Despite the presence of a young Richard Attenborough, whom he
admired greatly, Graham found that Hermione Baddeley (1906–86), now
best remembered as Mrs Cratchit in* Scrooge! (1951), *was eating up the
scenery in the role of Ida. Worse still, the final script had omitted the key
phrase in the novel.*

C/O President's Lodging, | Trinity College, | Oxford. |
March 4 [1943]

Dear Laurence,

Apropos of our telephone conversation this morning. I went to
see *Brighton Rock* at Oxford on Tuesday & was horrified by certain
changes: these seemed to me to ruin the play for the sake of allowing
Hermione Baddeley to fling a heart throb to the back of the gallery.
She is a very bad piece of miscasting: her performance is on the
overacted level of a revue sketch & her grotesqueness is all wrong for
the part – but that is beside the point. These are my quarrels with
the production & unless Linnit[14] will agree to meet our wishes over
(1) & (2) I must insist that my name be removed from all
programmes & posters, & that no reference to me or my book be
made in any publicity put out by the firm.

1. Certain passages have been added to Hermione Baddeley's
   part to enable her to pull out an emotional stop – which she
   does with grotesque inefficiency. Not having the script, &
   my memory of so ineffective a production being a bit dim, I
   find it hard to particularise. To anyone visiting the
   production they are made obvious by a preliminary break in
   Miss Baddeley's voice which sounds rather like a gargle &

14 The producer Bill Linnit.

can obviously be heard at the back of the gallery. The passages generally refer to her desire to be a mother to Rose. One such heart throb occurs in Act. 2 Scene 2: the worst in Act 3 Scene 2. Here lines are spoken which destroy the whole point of the play. Presumably Linnit has never spotted the point, but the dramatist in his original version certainly did.[15] The idea is that Pinkie and Rose belong to a real world in which good & evil exist but that the interfering Ida belongs to a kind, artificial surface world in which there is no such thing as good & evil but only right & wrong. The dramatist brings this out several times in the attitude of Rose to Ida – though I suspect certain lines of importance have been cut. Now new lines have been inserted in Ida's mouth in Act 3 Scene 2, when she tells Pinkie that he belongs to a small crooked perverted world which can't hurt her – *she* belongs to the real world. The result is to give Hermione Baddeley another chance to gargle to the gallery, but makes the poor audience wonder what in hell the play's about then. If they have any sense they won't wonder for more than 50 nights.

2. The removal of the last scene – & the priest's speech about – 'the appalling strangeness of the mercy of God' – makes the play more than ever pointless. Has this been removed in order to shorten the play – a case of *Hamlet* being shorter without the Prince of Denmark? We must have an explanation about this – I made an explicit condition of approving the script that the ending should be unchanged – & I am quite prepared to seek an injunction if I am not satisfied with Linnit's explanation.

[. . .]

Changes were made to the script to meet Greene's criticisms, and even though he was never happy with the production, he made sure that his royalties were paid and that his relatives had complimentary tickets.

15 The script was written by Frank Harvey.

TO VIVIEN GREENE

*The end of the marriage of Graham and Vivien can probably be dated from
the beginning of the war when she evacuated to Crowborough, then Oxford,
and he remained in London with Dorothy Glover. His time in Africa merely
postponed a reckoning. A month after his return, Vivien had apparently confronted him with evidence of infidelity – he was still very much involved with
Dorothy.*

King's Arms (Oxford) | April 8–9 [1943]

My darling, I've read your letter and I've had a party in the bar till
now! I hadn't meant to get involved but they were all friends of
Raymond . . . I love you so much, my darling. Please believe that.
Things have been difficult these last years, but I want so much to
make you happy. That's what I always said I'd do. My darling, *in vino
veritas*. You are the best, the most dear person I've ever known. Life
is sometimes so beastly that one wishes one were dead,[16] & I go to
places like Mexico & Freetown in a half hope that everything will
be finished – but like in that Prior poem 'you are my home'[17] & back
I come and ask you to like me & go on liking me. You mean more to
me than the children, though I may seem nicer to them! Sometimes
I wish I could twist a ring & skip twenty years & be old with you,
with all this ragged business over. I've never wanted to be old, but
with you I could be old & happy. God bless you, dear. God bless you,
dear. I've told a lot of lies in 38 years – or I suppose in 35 years, one
couldn't lie from the cradle – but this is true. I hate life & I hate
myself & I love you. Never forget that. I don't hate life ever, when
I'm with you and you are happy, but if I ever made you unhappy

16 Graham originally wrote and then amended 'I wish I were dead'.
17 The allusion is to Matthew Prior's 'A Better Answer to Cloe Jealous' (1718),
which includes these lines:

> *What I speak, my fair Cloe, and what I write, shows*
> *The diff'rence there is betwixt nature and art:*
> *I court others in verse; but I love thee in prose:*
> *And they have my whimsies, but thou hast my heart.*

really badly & hopelessly or saw life make you that, I'd want to die quickly. There's a cat moving outside the door. If it were you how quickly I'd let you in. I love you dear, good night. Keep this.

TO CHARLES EVANS

at 19 Gower Mews, | Gower St. | London, W.C. [early May 1943]

Dear Charles,

I have just been down to Oxford to see Vivien & have heard for the first time of your son's death.[18] I am so sorry to think that I've bothered you only two days ago with so trivial a thing as a dust jacket. Please forgive that & accept this halting sympathy. While I was in Africa I lost my father – that is a much smaller loss than a son's because one accepts it as inevitable but I think it makes it easier for me to understand a little of what you feel. I always pray that I shall never see the death of one of my children. I'm so very sorry.

Yours in friendship, I hope, & in gratitude most certainly.

Graham.

The god of us verse-men (you know, child) the sun,
How after his journeys he sets up his rest:
If at morning o'er earth 'tis his fancy to run,
At night he reclines on his Thetis's breast.

So when I am wearied with wand'ring all day,
To thee, my delight, in the evening I come:
No matter what beauties I saw in my way;
They were but my visits; but thou art my home.

18 In early 1942, Evans's youngest son David had been shot down in a bombing raid and was posted missing. After five months his death was confirmed. The loss seems to have broken Evans's health, as he died himself on 29 November 1944. (St John, 305)

TO VIVIEN GREENE

Friday [late May? 1943]

Dear heart, I got your second sad letter quickly. I can't tell you how
sorry I am about things – I feel I've fooled you. I think for ten years I
kept you happy, but then things went to pot. I hate your being
unhappy, & I do understand why. I never think you are lucky – I
think you are having a tougher war than anyone I know – except
perhaps people like Charles.[19] You are having a tougher war than
people even whose husbands are killed because death is a kind of
distraction, a jerk that sets one into a new life. I really feel that it
would have been better for you if I'd been torpedoed or plane
crashed because a novel sort of vitality would have been handed
over to you after the first shock. My dear, my dear, my dear, I love
you [so] much – that's true however badly now I show it – even
when it seems untrue, it's true.

   [. . .]

The marriage staggered on for another four years, when Graham's rela-
tionship with Catherine Walston led to a final separation. Vivien refused to
grant a divorce in the belief that sacramental marriage is indissoluble. The
sentiment Graham expresses here, that a wife might be better off with such
a husband dead, reappears as part of Scobie's motive for suicide in The
Heart of the Matter.

TO ELISABETH GREENE

Aug. 18 1943

Dear Elisabeth,

   [. . .]

   I've just had a week's holiday in South Wales with my family –
rather cold, but a lovely place – a few pubs, a ruined castle, woods

19 Evans: see preceding letter.

sloping down to a wide muddy estuary, a few 18th century houses: sands & caves a bus ride away.

Have you heard that I'm now contracted to be a full-blown publisher immediately the war's over: after 18 months training I am to have full charge of Eyre & Spottiswoode, which should be fun – but is anything fun when one gets down to it? *The Ministry of Fear* has sold 15,000 before reprinting which is monetarily satisfactory. I quite enjoy my work now – which is more varied & interesting than what I did at first, but all the same one does long for an end of this boring war.

Your letters to Mumma fill me with claustrophobia. Malcolm is back, for a while anyway. I wish we could do something together.

God knows what a dull letter this is, but one's brain becomes progressively more torpid, & the tightrope one walks gets tighter & tighter.

 Much love,
  Graham

TO MERVYN PEAKE

Greene met the novelist and illustrator Mervyn Peake (1911–68) in Chelsea in the spring of 1943. In June, Chatto and Windus rejected the long, unfinished manuscript of Titus Groan *when Peake refused to make cuts. Greene suggested that Peake should meet with Douglas Jerrold, the managing director of Eyre & Spottiswoode, to discuss the novel and an illustration project. By the end of August he had written the last chapters and sent the whole manuscript to Greene.*

Reform Club [c. October 1943]

Dear Mervyn Peake,

You must forgive me for not having written before, but you know it's a long book!

I'm going to be mercilessly frank – I was very disappointed in a lot of it & frequently wanted to wring your neck because it seemed to me you were spoiling a first-class book by laziness. The part I had seen before I, of course, still liked immensely – though I'm not sure that it's gained by the loss of the prologue. Then it seemed to me one entered a long patch of really bad writing, redundant adjectives, a kind of facetiousness, a terrible prolixity in the dialogue of such characters as the Nurse & Prunesquallor, & sentimentality too in the case of [Keda] & to some extent in Titus's sister. In fact – frankly again – I began to despair of the book altogether, until suddenly in the last third you pulled yourself together & ended splendidly. But even here you were so damned lazy that you called Barquentine by his predecessor's name for whole chapters.

I'm hitting hard because I feel it's the only way. There is obviously good stuff here but in my opinion you've thrown it away by not working hard enough at the book – there are trite unrealised novelettish phrases side by side with really first class writing. As it stands I consider it unpublishable – about 10,000 words of adjectives & prolix dialogue could come out without any alteration to the story at all. I want to publish it, but I shall be quite sympathetic if you say 'To Hell with you: you are no better than Chatto' & prefer to take it elsewhere. But at least I can claim to have read it carefully, & I do beseech you to look at the M.S. again. I began by putting in pencil which can easily be rubbed out brackets round words & phrases which seemed to me redundant, but I gave up after a time.

Write & let me know how you feel about all this. If you want to call me out, call me out – but I suggest we have our duel over whisky glasses in a bar.

    Yours,
        Graham Greene

Peake was shocked, but this letter marked a turning point in his career as he finally accepted the importance of 'the blue pencil approach'. Delayed by revisions and the wartime shortage of paper, Titus Groan *finally appeared on 22 March 1946.*[20]

20 See G. Peter Winnington, *Vast Alchemies: The Life and Work of Mervyn Peake* (London: Peter Owen, 2000), 166–9.

TO WILLIAM H. WEBBER

Editorial Unit: | 43 Grosvenor Street, | London, W.1. |
22nd July, 1944

To: Mr. Webber.
From: Mr. Graham Greene.

It will perhaps interest you to hear the reactions of a Londoner to your fantastically inefficient and childish ideas of organising a fire-guard, though it will probably seem odd to you that anyone should take fire-guard duties seriously. But you should remember that in London we have had some experience of fires.

Understanding that one had to report not later than half an hour before black-out, I arrived at 25 Gilbert Street last night about 10.15. I was told to go to 47 Mount Street. I went to 47 Mount Street and found the house locked. Half an hour later I tried again and found a guard there. He had an office chair to sit on – nothing else, not even a blanket. I returned to Gilbert Street to raise Cain and found I had been sent to Mount Street by mistake: I went back to Mount Street for the final time and collected my things. By this time I was getting a little irritable. I was then told that my room as fire-guard was No. 2552. The passages were in darkness; there was no black-out in the rooms and no-one knew where 2552 was. After a long search with the help of a watchman, I found it at the top of the building, at the head of a twisting iron emergency ladder. No fire-guard had apparently ever in fact slept in this absurd death-trap and I set up my bed on the floor below in room 2541. To this room on the third or is it the fourth floor? – one had to carry one's own bed, blankets, mattress, pillow – a dubious example of courtesy and consideration to fire-guards.

There were no instructions as to where one found the tools of one's trade – stirrup pump, etc., no directions where water was available, no issue of torches in case the electric-light failed. Incidentally there seemed to be no other fire-guard on duty.

However, I must admit that the Gilbert Street fireguard is a little better off than the wretched guard in Mount Street whose treatment is really scandalous.

If at any time you care to ring me up at 49 Grosvenor Street, I will be delighted to tell you what you can do with your fire-guard duties.

Despite this outburst, Greene continued to work as a fire guard.[21]

TO R. K. NARAYAN

Eyre & Spottiswoode (Publishers) Ltd., 15 Bedford Street W.C.2
| [31 October? 1944]

Dear Narayan,

I am delighted to welcome you as an author to Eyre & Spottiswoode, and I very much enjoyed reading your new book. I think Pollinger has already written to you saying that I want to change the title to 'The English Teacher'. The present title sounds in English ears rather sentimental and gives a wrong idea of the book.

We are taking over the cheap rights of 'Swami and Friends' and 'The Bachelor of Arts' and I hope that when the paper situation is eased after the war we shall be able to put these back into print.

It seems a very long time since I heard from you and I hope that you can spare the time one day to let me know how you are. I still hope when all this foolishness is over to see you one day in England.

Yours ever
Graham Greene

TO EVELYN WAUGH

15 Bedford Street | W.C.1 [January 1945]

Dear Evelyn,

Just a line which please don't bother to answer – to say how immensely I enjoyed *Brideshead*. I liked it even more than *Work in*

Progress which was my favourite hitherto, & I find it grows in
memory.

  Yours,
    Graham

Graham later wrote: '. . . I, for one, had been inclined to dismiss
Brideshead Revisited. *When he had written to me [27 March 1950] that
the only excuse for it was Nissen huts and spam and the blackout I had
accepted that criticism – until the other day when I reread all his books, and
to my astonishment joined the ranks of those who find* Brideshead *his best,
even though it is his most romantic.'*[22]

TO VIVIEN GREENE

Eyre & Spottiswoode | 14, 15, 16 Bedford Street| Strand,
London, W.C.2 | Tuesday [20 March 1945]

[. . .]

Had a grim evening with the Peakes. I'll tell you about that and
their persecution by a dotty old widow of an oldtime painter. I
should hate to live in Chelsea. So dirty and the real fume of creepy
evil. On Sunday I was lying late in bed and there was a huge crash,
followed by a terrific rumble and the sound of glass going. The
loudest I've heard. From bed I could see a pillar of smoke go up
above the roofs. Actually it was quite a long way away and a very
lucky rocket. Just inside Hyde Park at Marble Arch where the tub
thumpers would have been later in the day. I went and looked. The
blast had missed the Arch and swept though the poor old Regal
which was on the point of reopening after being flybombed and
knocked out the windows in the Cumberland. American soldiers fat
with their huge meat ration stood around grinning and taking
photos (which we are not allowed to do). I wandered around making
anti-American cracks!

  [. . .]
    Graham

22 *Ways of Escape,* 200.

TO GEORGE ORWELL

Graham devoted considerable effort to The Century Library, his firm's modern reprint series. Here he comments on George Orwell's suggestions for the series.

Eyre & Spottiswoode (Publishers) Limited | 27th August 1945

Dear Orwell,

Forgive the delay in replying to your letter, but I have been away for a long weekend.

I am glad you have managed to get hold of the Merrick books and as soon as you let me know which you think we should include in the Century Library I will get on to the publishers. There will be no need whatever to keep the Introduction which was supplied in the collected edition.[23]

I am delighted to have suggestions from you for other books as I have very little time for seeking around myself. I will have a look at Barry Pain.[24] I read two W. L. Georges recently and they were pretty poor stuff, but I will find a copy of *Caliban*.[25] I should have thought that Guy Boothby[26] was dropping a little too low – much lower than Richard Marsh who, I do think, can be very good indeed. I am not sure when *The Beetle* was published but I think it was before the century.[27] However, there are several Marshes published later and I certainly agree we ought to have one.

Hornung's books, other than *Raffles* have generally struck me as too homosexually sentimental. I tried the other day *The Camera*

23 Orwell wrote a new introduction to Leonard Merrick's *The Position of Peggy Harper* (1911), but the projected reprint did not appear. See 'Introduction to "The Position of Peggy Harper"', in *The Collected Essays, Journalism, and Letters of George Orwell*, ed. S. Orwell and I. Angus, 4: *In Front of Your Nose, 1945–1950* (1968), 52–6.

24 Barry Pain (1864–1928) was a parodist and humorist well known for sketches of working-class life. His most successful novel was *Eliza* (1900).

25 Walter Lionel George (1882–1926), biographer and novelist; his *Caliban* was published in 1920.

26 Guy Boothby (1867–1905), Australian playwright and novelist, best known for *Dr. Nikola's Vendetta* (1895) and its sequels.

27 Richard Marsh (Heldmann) (1857-1915) was a prolific mystery writer whose best-known work *The Beetle* was published in 1897.

Fiend and *Witching Hill*, both of which I had liked as a boy, but they ring no bells at all now.[28]

Do give me a ring when you get back from your holiday and let us have lunch together.

Yours,

Graham Greene

TO JOHN BETJEMAN

As a publisher, Greene had to promote his firm's books with reviewers, including Betjeman, who was then reviewing for the left-wing Daily Herald.

Eyre & Spottiswoode (Publishers) | 22nd August, 1946.

Dear John,

I am not going to pretend that you will like, from a literary point of view, this book I am sending you, *The River Road* by Mrs. Parkinson Keyes, but I think it may amuse you as a curious example of popular favour. For about ten years now, Mrs. Parkinson Keyes' books have been selling in enormous quantities. In fact we cannot print enough to meet the demand. I do not think any of us feels able to explain this odd popularity. She does not tell an exciting story, the sexual element is there but is not really very pronounced and she gives in vast detail the every-day life of America. From this book, for example, one could almost learn how to run a sugar plantation and yet, as I say, she sells in a way that even Priestley would envy. I would not, in the ordinary course of events, send you this book but it occurred to me that during the 'Silly Season' you might be amused to do something on the 'Popular Novel'!

Yours ever,

Graham

28 The brother-in-law of Arthur Conan Doyle, Ernest William Hornung (1866–1921) wrote a popular series at the turn of the century recounting the feats in burglary and cricket of A. J. Raffles. Two collections of the stories were reprinted in The Century Library. His other novels including *The Camera Fiend* (1911) and *Witching Hill* (1913) had no comparable appeal. Greene's play *The Return of A. J. Raffles* was first performed at the end of 1975.

TO JOHN BOULTING

John Boulting (1913–85) and his twin brother Roy (1913–2001) founded Charter Film Productions in 1937. Working from a script by Greene and Terence Rattigan (1911–77), John Boulting directed Richard Attenborough in Brighton Rock *(1947).*

18th September, 1946

Dear John,

I have finished reading through Terence Rattigan's outline treatment of *Brighton Rock*, and I agree with you that it provides a good skeleton to work on. There is no point in criticising small details of dialogue or scene at this stage, and I think my only major criticisms are as follows: –

(1) I think the boy Pinkie has got to be established as the solitary central figure of the film, and we must to some extent reduce the importance of Ida so as to throw him in solitary relief.

(2) This arises partly out of (1) and partly out of what you may consider a personal fad. I never feel that films that start on long shots are satisfactory. I feel the American practice of nearly always starting on close-up is much more imaginative. How often one has seen an English film which begins with a long shot of a holiday resort: to my mind the opening shot suggested here would stamp the film unmistakably as pre-war British. My own rough idea of the opening of the film is to present by a succession of close-ups the atmosphere of Brighton waking up for Whit Monday – curtains being raised or shutters drawn back in the shops: the day's newspaper poster featuring Kolley Kibber being squeezed under the wire framework of a poster board: the fun cars on the pier being polished: all the shots close-up or semi close-up and culminating in a close-up of the boy spread-eagled in his clothes on the brass bedstead: entrance of Dallow: a newspaper spread in front of the boy's eyes by Dallow with the headlines about Kolley Kibber: the boy sitting up in bed: cut stop. I express this very roughly and loosely but perhaps you will see the kind of tempo I feel the film should begin on. In this way the boy is established

before Hale who is after all a minor character disposed of very quickly.

(3) I am very pleased at the way in which Rattigan has tried to keep the central theme of the book: that is to say, the difference between Ida who lives in a natural world where morality is based on Right and Wrong, and the boy and Rose who move in a supernatural world concerned with good and evil, but I feel this is sometimes a little over-emphasised (a small example is the play on the name of the horse Satan Colt), and in a more important place under-emphasised – that is to say I think somehow we ought to insert in the film after Pinkie's death the notion expressed in the book by the anonymous priest in the confessional of 'the appalling strangeness of the mercy of God'.

(4) I like Rattigan's idea of the murder in the Fun Fair train, but it does make the coroner's verdict rather inexplicable.

(5) I like his idea of making Corkery into a bookmaker. This certainly tightens up the story.

(6) A last and really not very major point is that one has lost any point to the title. The title of the book had two significances: first, the murder of Hale took place in one of the small booths underneath the pier where Brighton Rock is sold, and secondly, a point we can easily introduce into the later treatment, the passage where the boy speaks of himself as knowing nothing but Brighton and the comparison with Brighton Rock which, wherever you bite it, still leaves the name of the place showing.

[. . .]

TO CATHERINE WALSTON

Catherine Walston (née Crompton) was the American wife of the wealthy Labour politician Harry Walston (later Lord Walston). Introduced to him by John Rothenstein in early 1946, she asked Graham to serve as her godfather, since his books had influenced her decision to become a Catholic. Within a few months they had embarked on a serious affair that continued, with interruptions, for more than a decade. It is commonly said that she is the 'original' of the saintly and promiscuous Sarah in The End of the Affair.

This is largely true, but not entirely so. Greene chose to set the novel in the war years and so, to some degree, was drawing on his relationship with Dorothy Glover, conducted at times under the bombardment. Sarah is much more passive than either Glover or Walston. In any event, the difference between the novel and the lives that inspired it is considerable.

Eyre & Spottiswoode [25 September 1946]

Dear Mrs. Walston,

This is a shockingly belated note of congratulation & best wishes. I gave my secretary a telegram to send, but in the rush of work (I had been away on the Continent for a fortnight) she never sent it! I feel I am a most neglectful god-father! I haven't even sent you a silver mug or a spoon to bite.

I heard all about the breakfast from Vivien. I wish I'd been there. Again all my wishes for the future.

Yours,
    Graham Greene

TO CATHERINE WALSTON

Eyre & Spottiswoode [c. October 1946]

Dear Catherine,

I wrote off the other day – to a wrong address apparently, in Ireland – explaining my apparent chilling silence on the day of your reception, & now my sense of guilt is increased by your letter! However what would a novelist do without a sense of guilt?

I think the whole business of your becoming a Catholic was extraordinarily courageous – I became one before I had any ties.

How lovely the West of Ireland sounds. Do come & tell us about it in Oxford when you get back.

Yours,
    Graham Greene

TO EVELYN WAUGH

Eyre & Spottiswoode | 14, 15, 16 Bedford Street | Strand,
London, W.C.2 [1947]

Dear Evelyn,

I was delighted & flattered by your letter. The sweetest form of praise comes from those one admires.

Who on earth told you I was going to Kenya? It was probably a half-hearted melancholy joke. I shall stay & be atomised [?] quietly with all home comforts. I should like to compromise & go to Ireland because I like the Irish & approve so strongly of their recent neutrality, but Vivien has an anti-Irish phobia, so I can never do that. We *are* looking for a Regency house – or Georgian, with a walled garden & a paddock to keep a pony in, & costing not more than £5000 – but that seems hardly likely to come our way.

Do let us see you before you go to Ireland.

Yours ever,

Graham

TO CATHERINE WALSTON (POSTCARD)

[Amsterdam | 3 March 1947]

I love onion sandwiches.

G.

Bendrix writes in The End of the Affair *(44): 'Is it possible to fall in love over a dish of onions? It seems improbable and yet I could swear it was just then that I fell in love. It wasn't, of course, simply the onions – it was that sudden sense of an individual woman, of a frankness that was so often later to make me happy and miserable. I put my hand under the cloth and laid it on her knee, and her hand came down and held mine in place.'*

TO CATHERINE WALSTON

Monday [5 May 1947]

You won't be able to read this so I can put what I like!

I missed you so much on Sunday. Mass wasn't the same at all. We went to 12 o'clock at St. Patrick's, Soho, & had a drink afterwards at the Salisbury in St. Martin's Lane. I just missed you all the time & felt depressed & restless. A bit of a row blew up before I left – she said I had changed so much in Ireland,[29] but she still believes that it's simply that I've come under influence of a pious convert! Tried to ring you from Charing Cross.

Got to sleep by reading about 1 still depressed, but woke up blissfully happy. You had been with me very vividly saying, 'I like your sexy smell' – & of course I had a sexy smell! It had been one of those nights!

Then there was a line from you (how beautiful your handwriting is), & then I got you on the telephone. Result I feel cheerful & I've written 1000 words! And you love me – you do you know. And I see you on Thursday.

[. . .]

TO RAYMOND GREENE

16th May, 1947

Dear Raymond,

Many thanks for your most useful letter. I begin to see how my character[30] is going to commit suicide now. I should imagine that a man posing as having angina would have every reason to suffer from insomnia.

I should imagine, too, that as you have to bury somebody within a

---

29 Graham had spent most of April with Walston in a cottage on Achill island in the west of Ireland.

30 Scobie in *The Heart of the Matter*.

few hours in Sierra Leone (there is always an awful scramble to get a coffin in time) they would not bother about a post mortem on somebody known to be suffering from angina.

I expect to be down at Oxford by Whitsun and I hope we shall meet some time after that.

Yours,
   Graham

TO CATHERINE WALSTON

15 Beaumont Street | Oxford [29 May 1947]

O hell! darling. Achill looks like being the only good thing in 1947. One feels like investigating one's policies. Perhaps the ban on killing oneself is only during the first three years of a policy. Something whispers the idea to me anyway. At the moment I'm feeling rather like a cornered rat (rat is probably the right word). Something else happened this morning. I'll tell you about it when I see you. One would laugh if it was a book. I ought to write funny books. Life is really too horribly funny, but unless one's an outsider looking on, it's all such a bore.

Now about Thriplow.[31] Vivien thoroughly fed up with the whole idea, & finally calmed & smoothed by having *part* of her own way – that is to say I can't come till Friday & then have to be back Tuesday night. Any good? and how shall I get to you? Can you pick me up at Cambridge – or possibly Bletchley which is where one is delayed for hours? Or would you be in town & I pick *you* up? In return for these four days I have clamped the handcuffs on my wrists & said that in future I shall be spending all my weekends at Oxford (except for emergencies). 'Am I happy?' The answer is definitely negative.

I loved seeing you – on Tuesday especially, but what the hell is the use? I rather hoped that I wouldn't love seeing you.

31 The Walstons' home was at Thriplow, six miles south of Cambridge.

I can't live permanently in handcuffs, so I suppose either the handcuffs will go again, or I shall.[32]

Love,

    Graham

TO CATHERINE WALSTON

Sir Alexander Korda produced The Fallen Idol (1948), *based on Graham's short story 'The Basement Room', and* The Third Man (1949), *and he introduced Graham to Carol Reed (1906–76), who directed both films. As a reviewer, Graham had praised Reed's work lavishly, and despite annoyance over his handling of* Our Man in Havana (1960), *he always believed that Reed's skills were nearly unrivalled.*

15 Beaumont Street | Oxford | Tuesday 7.45 [10 June 1947]

I've been in town all day seeing Korda & Carol Reed ('Odd Man Out'): they are buying a short story of mine called 'The Basement Room' & want me to work on it.[33] Once I suppose I'd have been excited & pleased by all this (it means about £3000), but I feel dreary. Thank you for the keys, darling, & for the letter. I think a lot of it is self-deception. (I think perhaps your love for me is too. I don't know.) If I'm going to tell the whole truth to Vivien, what's the good of keeping us back? Within 12 months a new line of deception would have developed. The whole subject must be a bore for you, & I think we'd better drop it – unless I take action when I'll report what the end of the affair is for your interest. Well, my darling, you may as well have these letters. I think they are quite

32 '[Louise] had joined [Scobie] the first year of the phoney war and now she couldn't get away: the danger of submarines had made her as much a fixture as the handcuffs on the nail.' (*The Heart of the Matter*, 7)

33 Reed's most recent film was *Odd Man Out* (1947) about the last twenty-four hours of a wounded IRA man. The short story was made into *The Fallen Idol*, in which, in a memorable scene, Baines asks his wife for his freedom. The film also presents a symbolic emasculation when Mrs Baines destroys MacGregor, the little boy Philippe's pet snake.

sensible. I expect this is the end. If it is you've given me the best morphia I've ever had. Thank you.

Thank God, anyway that there's somebody I can't hurt.

With love,
Graham

TO CATHERINE WALSTON

Eyre & Spottiswoode | Friday morning [27 June 1947]

You are in the air, Cafrin, & I'm – very much – on the earth. This is just a note to pursue you as quickly as possible to Achill & to remind you of three things – that I'm still terribly in love with you, that I miss you (your voice saying 'good morning, Graham' at tea time), & that I want you. I want to be filling the turf buckets for you & sitting next door working, hearing the clank of washing-up, & your whistle, & I want to help you make lunch. I am thirsty for orange juice at 3 in the morning. I want to see you in your pyjama top nursing the sod of the fire.

Now I pin a lot of hope on India. It might be a way of being with you for 3 months, & by God I'd get into your skin before that time was over.

I kiss you, my dear, here, here – & there.
Graham

Have I written a love letter?

TO CATHERINE WALSTON

15 Beaumont Street, | Oxford | Sunday [29 June 1947]

Cafryn, dear, I've missed you like hell this week-end – back at the obsession level. Dreamed last night that you telephoned as usual & woke happy. Here my relations with Vivien seem to be slumping back to the old level. An individual can't of course be heroic all the time: last time she was heroic, now the heroism is worn out. I dragged with her on Saturday to a meeting of the Georgian Group at Badminton, the Duke of Beaufort's house – four hours hot railway travel & a picnic lunch among flies – one needs to be in love to enjoy that kind of thing. I am beginning positively to hate beautiful houses & beautiful furniture. And a private house open to public inspection seems more dead than a museum. Suddenly on the way back I felt I'd *got* to get a few days happiness, & quite literally the only way I get any happiness now is either with you or with work. And work is for the time being over. So tomorrow unless wiser counsels prevail I shall set about pursuing you to Ireland. I think it can be arranged, though I can't drop the film script while I'm there. Cafryn, dear, I want to kiss you, touch you, make love to you – & simply sit in a car & be driven by you. Tomorrow (unless I'm wise & only the very young can be wise) I shall telegraph proposing a date.

I nearly slept at Mass today. How dead it was – not dead in the amusing phosphorescent way of last Sunday, aware of your shoulder half an inch from mine, but just limp & meaningless & boring. I'm not even a Catholic properly away from you.

Love,

Graham

TO CATHERINE WALSTON

Monday 25th [August 1947]

Now you'll be able to read what I write.[34] So I can't say nearly as much. When I got to the office the first thing I saw was your letter. O, I am falling in love again. You are right – nothing is ever dull when we do it. If we get to India it will be odd – the exciting thing in exciting company. I have a feeling that even being in a massacre in the Punjab (I enclose a good account of one) won't really be as exciting as sitting on a cliff watching for salmon. My dear, before you

34 This typed letter was sent with another, handwritten, from the day before.

cropped up, I used to have odd dreams of peace – that dream of the moon I gave to Scobie for instance,[35] but now I dream of you instead, especially when I'm at Oxford. I also dreamed this last time that Vivien died. She was dying and I was walking up and down trying to pray. I found I simply couldn't pray for her life, so I simply prayed that she wouldn't have any pain. Then I woke up and thought that I was in bed with someone else. All very odd and confusing.

[. . .]

TO CATHERINE WALSTON

Addressed to Catherine in Wilton, New Hampshire, this letter indicates another layer of trouble in Graham's dealings with women. He had failed to break off with Dorothy Glover ('my girl') and was hoping that a long sea voyage might help her accept the change in their relationship.

15 Beaumont Street, | Oxford | Friday, Sep. 5 [1947]

Cafryn dear, at last the arrangements for my women are coming off & it will only remain with your assistance to make arrangements for myself! Vivien *is* coming to the States as the guest of my agent, & though I should have liked to have weekended (my grammar's gone wrong) at Westbury, I shall feel much happier in mind in Ireland, especially if I can arrange for her to stay till mid-November with someone. I shall try.

Now for My Girl. Today I wangled her a passage on an Elder Dempster cargo ship down the West African coast & back, mid-September to mid-December – so she'll be happy. I must say when I saw the list of stops my heart missed a beat. Las Palmas, Dakar, Bathurst, Freetown, Cotonou, Lagos – it's like hearing Maynooth, Athlone, Galway, Westport, Newport, The Sound, Dooagh. I think this will be very good for her – getting away from me & new places & being made much of – as any white woman is there. Elder Dempster

---

35 'Once in sleep [peace] had appeared to him as the great glowing shoulder of the moon heaving across his window like an iceberg, Arctic and destructive in the moments before the world was struck . . .' (*The Heart of the Matter*, 50)

too are treating her as a V.I.P.! She's been very sweet this last week & much more ready to accept the fact that one can love two people!

[. . .]

TO CATHERINE WALSTON

Tuesday, Sep. 30. [1947] | 11 p.m.

Dear Catherine,

I believe I've got a book coming. I feel so excited that I spell out your name in full carefully sticking my tongue between my teeth to pronounce it right. The act of creation's awfully odd & inexplicable like falling in love. A lock of hair touches one's eyes in a plane with East Anglia under snow,[36] & one is in love. . . . Tonight I had a solitary, good dinner where I usually go with My Girl & afterwards felt vaguely restless (not sexually, just restless). So I walked to the Café Royal & sat & read *The Aran Islands*[37] & drank beer till about 10 & then I still felt restless, so I walked all up Piccadilly & back, went back in a gent's in Brick Street, & suddenly in the gent's, I saw the three characters, the beginning, the middle & the end, & in some ways all the ideas I had – the first sentence of the thriller about the dead Harry who wasn't dead, the risen-from-the dead story, & the one the other day in the train – all seem to come together.[38] I hope to God it lasts – they don't always. I want to begin the next book with you in Ireland – if possible at Achill, but on Aran or Innishboffin or the Galway hotel or anywhere.

Now I shall go to bed with lots of aspirin, but I shan't sleep.

Love,

Graham

36 Early in their relationship, Catherine had organised on short notice a plane ride for Graham from her home in Cambridgeshire to Kidlington, near Oxford.

37 J. M. Synge's travel book first published in 1907. Graham regarded his time with Catherine in Ireland as edenic.

38 The letter is written in pencil, and this sentence is especially difficult to read. Among several points of uncertainty is the word 'character' which could also be rendered as 'chunks' (see NS 2: 242). The dash between 'train' and 'all' has been added and may alter meaning.

P.S. I'm better than Mauriac [?] you know! Today I read an article which said 'unlike such writers as James Joyce & Graham Greene' – damn you, I'm not played out yet. Let's fall in love.

TO JOHN BOULTING

2nd December, 1947

Dear John,

I have been meaning for some time to write and tell you how delighted I was with the production of *Brighton Rock*. I think that Attenborough's performance was outstanding in the part of Pinkie, the art direction was the equal of any French film in its realism, and your direction seemed to me most impressive. I think this is the first time I have seen one of my own books on the screen with any real pleasure.

Yours ever,
Graham

TO ELIZABETH BOWEN

This and the following letter are Greene's contribution to a formal discussion on the role of the writer with Elizabeth Bowen and V. S. Pritchett, who had first proposed the exchange in the spring of 1946. The three read their letters on the BBC Third Programme on 7 October 1948. A short version of the exchange was published in the Partisan Review *(November 1948) and a longer form in the pamphlet* Why Do I Write? *(London: Perceval Marshall, 1948). The letters generally reflect unease with the whole idea of the writer's social function being paramount; as Pritchett remarked in his preface, 'we had had enough of the formal declarations, statements and manifestos that stereotyped discussion in the thirties and that strapped the writer to a bed too short – or vastly too large – for him. We did not want the easy finality of an essay or the open yawns of the hurried article. We wanted an enquiry which would not exhaust the subject; the value of it for ourselves would be self-discovery not decision – though one principle slips out and*

remains, intransigent: the assertion of our liberty . . .' Greene re-used parts
of his letters when writing his lecture 'The Virtue of Disloyalty' (1969),
published in Reflections *(266–70).*

London [1948]

When your letter came, I had just been reading Mrs. Gaskell's *Life of*
Charlotte Brontë, and this sentence from one of Charlotte Brontë's
letters recurred to my mind. It certainly represents my view, and I
think it represents yours as well: 'You will see that Villette touches
on no matter of public interest. I cannot write books handling the
topics of the day; it is of no use trying it. Nor can I write a book for
its moral. Nor can I take up a philanthropic scheme, though I
honour philanthropy . . .'

Pritchett, too, I think, would agree with that, though perhaps
it was easier for Charlotte Brontë to believe that she had excluded
public interest than it is for us. Public interest in her day was
surely more separate from the private life: a debate in Parliament,
a leading article in the *Thunderer*. It did not so colour the
common life: with us, however consciously unconcerned we are, it
obtrudes through the cracks of our stories, terribly persistent like
grass through cement. Processions can't help passing across the
ends of our imaginary streets; our characters must earn a living: if
they don't, what is called a social significance seems to attach
itself to their not-earning. Correcting proofs the other day, I had
to read some old stories of mine dating back to the early thirties.
Already they seemed to have a period air. It was not what I had
intended.

'The relation of the artist to society': it's a terribly vague subject,
and I feel the same embarrassment and resentment as you do when I
encounter it. We all have to be citizens in our spare time, standing
in queues, filling up income tax forms, supporting our families: why
can't we leave it at that? I think we need a devil's advocate in this
discussion to explain the whole thing to us. I picture him as a
member of the PEN Club, perhaps a little out of breath from his
conference in Stockholm where he has been discussing this very
subject (in pre-war times he would have returned from the

Adriatic – conferences of this kind were never held where society was exactly *thick*). Before sitting down to add his signature to an appeal in *The Times* (in the thirties it would have proudly appeared with Mr. Forster's, Mr. Bertrand Russell's and perhaps Miss Maude Royden's),[39] he would find an opportunity to tell us what society is and what the artist.

I'm rather glad, all the same, we haven't got him with us. His letters confirmed the prejudice I felt against the artist (there the word is again) indulging in public affairs. His letters – and those of his co-signatories – always seemed to me either ill-informed, naïve or untimely. There were so many petitions in favour of the victims of arbitrary power which helped to knot the noose round the poor creatures' necks. So long as he had eased his conscience publicly in print, and in good company, he was not concerned with the consequences of his letter. No, I'm glad we've left him out. He will, of course, review us . . .

We had better, however, agree on our terms, and as you have suggested no alternative to Pritchett's definition of society – 'people bound together for an end, who are making a future' – let us accept that. Though I'm not quite happy about it. We are each, however anarchistically and individually, making a future, or else the future, as I prefer to think, is making us – the death we are each going to die controlling our activities now, like a sheepdog, so that we may with least trouble be got through that gate. As for 'people bound together for an end,' the phrase does, of course, accurately describe those unfortunate prisoners of the French revolution of whom Swinburne wrote in *Les Noyades*: they were flung, you remember, naked in pairs into the Loire, but I don't think Pritchett had that incident consciously in mind.

The artist is even more difficult to define: in most cases only time defines him, and I think for the purposes of this argument we should write only of the novelist, perhaps only of the novelist like ourselves, for obviously Wells will be out of place in any argument based on, say, Virginia Woolf. The word artist is too inclusive: it is impossible to make generalizations which will be true for Van Gogh, Burke,

39 Maude Royden (1876–1956) was a suffragist, social hygienist and preacher.

Henry James, Yeats and Beethoven. If a man sets up to be a teacher, he has duties and responsibilities to those he teaches, whether he is a novelist, a political writer or a philosopher, and I would like to exclude the teacher from the discussion. In the long run we are forced back to the egotistical 'I': we can't shelter behind the great dead. What in *my* opinion, can society demand of *me*? What have I got to render to Caesar?

First I would say there are certain human duties I owe in common with the greengrocer or the clerk – that of supporting my family if I have a family, of not robbing the poor, the blind, the widow or the orphan, of dying if the authorities demand it (it is the only way to remain independent: the conscientious objector is forced to become a teacher in order to justify himself). These are our primitive duties as human beings. In spite of the fashionable example of Gauguin, I would say that if we do less than these, we are so much the less human beings and therefore so much the less likely to be artists. But are there any special duties I owe to my fellow victims bound for the Loire? I would like to imagine there are none, but I fear there are at least two duties the novelist owes – to tell the truth as he sees it and to accept no special privileges from the state.

I don't mean anything flamboyant by the phrase 'telling the truth': I don't mean exposing anything. By truth I mean accuracy – it is largely a matter of style. It is my duty to society not to write: 'I stood above a bottomless gulf' or 'going downstairs, I got into a taxi,' because these statements are untrue. My characters must not go white in the face or tremble like leaves, not because these phrases are clichés but because they are untrue. This is not only a matter of the artistic conscience but of the social conscience too. We already see the effect of the popular novel on popular thought. Every time a phrase like one of these passes into the mind uncriticised, it muddies the stream of thought.

The other duty, to accept no privileges, is equally important. The kindness of the State, the State's interest in art, is far more dangerous than its indifference. We have seen how in time of war there is always some well-meaning patron who will suggest that artists should be in a reserved class. But how, at the end of six years of popular agony, would the artist be regarded if he had been reserved, kept safe and fattened at the public expense, too good to die like other men? And what would have been expected of him in return? In Russia the artist *has* belonged to a privileged class: he has been given a better flat, more money, more food, even a certain freedom of movement: but the State has asked in return that he should cease to be an artist. The danger does not exist only in totalitarian countries. The bourgeois state, too, has its gifts to offer to the artist – or those it regards as artists, but in these cases the artist has paid like the politician in advance. One thinks of the literary knights, and then one turns to the plain tombstones with their bare hic jacets[40] of Mr. Hardy, Mr. James, and Mr. Yeats. Yes, the more I think of it, that is a duty the artist unmistakably owes to society – to accept no favours. Perhaps a pension if his family are in danger of starvation (in those circumstances the moralists admit that we may commit theft).

Perhaps the greatest pressure on the writer comes from the society within society: his political or religious group, even it may be his university or his employers. It does seem to me that one privilege he can claim, in common perhaps with his fellow human beings, but possibly with greater safety, is that of disloyalty. I met a farmer at lunch the other day who was employing two lunatics; what fine workers they were, he said; and how loyal. But of course they were loyal; they were like the conditioned beings of the brave new world. Disloyalty is our privilege. But it is a privilege you will never get society to recognize. All the more necessary that we who can be disloyal with impunity should keep that ideal alive.

If I may be personal, I belong to a group, the Catholic Church, which would present me with grave problems as a writer if I were not saved by my disloyalty. If my conscience were as acute as M. Mauriac's showed itself to be in his essay 'God and Mammon', I could not write a line.[41] There are leaders of the Church who regard literature as a means to one end, edification. That end may be of the highest value, of far higher value than literature, but it belongs to a different world. Literature has nothing to do with edification. I am

40 Hic jacet: here lies . . .

41 The French novelist François Mauriac (1885–1970) had argued that the dilemma for Christian writers was to show readers the evil in human nature without tempting them.

not arguing that literature is amoral, but that it presents a personal moral, and the personal morality of an individual is seldom identical with the morality of the group to which he belongs. You remember the black and white squares of Bishop Blougram's chess board.[42] As a novelist, I must be allowed to write from the point of view of the black square as well as of the white: doubt and even denial must be given their chance of self-expression, or how is one freer than the Leningrad group?[43]

Catholic novelists (I would rather say novelists who are Catholics) should take Newman as their patron. No one understood their problem better or defended them more skilfully from the attacks of piety (that morbid growth of religion). Let me copy out the passage. It really has more than one bearing on our discussion. He is defending the teaching of literature in a Catholic university:

'I say, from the nature of the case, if Literature is to be made a study of human nature, you cannot have a Christian Literature. It is a contradiction in terms to attempt a sinless Literature of sinful man. You may gather together something very great and high, something higher than any Literature ever was; and when you have done so, you will find that it is not Literature at all.'

And to those who, accepting that view, argued that we could do without Literature, Newman went on:

'Proscribe (I do not merely say particular authors, particular works, particular passages) but Secular Literature as such; cut out from your class books all broad manifestations of the natural man; and those manifestations are waiting for your pupil's benefit at the very doors of your lecture room in living and breathing substance . . .

42 Graham often quoted or alluded to Robert Browning's 'Bishop Blougram's Apology':

> All we have gained then by our unbelief
> Is a life of doubt diversified by faith,
> For one of faith diversified by doubt:
> We called the chess-board white — we call it black.

43 In 1946, Andrey Zhdanov, the Leningrad Party chief, denounced the poet Anna Akhmatova and the satirist Mikhail Zoshchenko in a speech to the Leningrad Union of Writers. The two were immediately expelled from the Union and so could no longer publish.

Today a pupil, tomorrow a member of the great world: today confined to the Lives of the Saints, tomorrow thrown upon Babel . . . You have refused him the masters of human thought, who would in some sense have educated him because of their incidental corruption . . .'[44]

Graham Greene

TO V. S. PRITCHETT

Pritchett observed that since the days of patronage were over and taxation policy had ended the 'private income', the state ought to provide endowments and scholarships for writers. He also argued for a tax on the classics and a reorganisation of libraries to compensate authors for the use of single books by many readers. Greene rejected all but the last of these proposals since they would undermine the writer's independence from the state.

London [1948]

The last time I received a letter in this series I was reading the *Life of Charlotte Brontë*: this time the poems of Thomas Hood, and the change of mood may account for my uneasy suspicion that in my last letter I simplified far too much. Perhaps that magnificent poem, 'The Song of the Shirt', has unduly influenced me, for I am not quite so sure now that the writer has no responsibility to society or the State (which is organized society) different in kind from that of his fellow citizens.[45]

44 The quotations are taken from Newman's Discourse IX: 'Duties of the Church towards Knowledge', sections 7 and 8.

45 Hood's poem opens:

> With fingers weary and worn,
> With eyelids heavy and red,
> A woman sat in unwomanly rags,
> Plying her needle and thread –
> Stitch! stitch! stitch!
> In poverty, hunger, and dirt,
> And still with a voice of dolorous pitch
> She sang the 'Song of the Shirt!'

You remember Thomas Paine's great apothegm, 'We must take care to guard even our enemies against injustice,'[46] and it is there – in the establishment of justice – that the writer has greater opportunities and therefore greater obligations than, say, the chemist or the estate agent. For one thing he is, if he has attained a measure of success, more his own master than others are: he is his own employer: he can afford to offend; for one of the major objects of his craft (I speak, of course, of the novelist) is the awakening of sympathy. Now the State is invariably ready to confuse, like a schoolmaster, justice with retribution, and isn't it possibly the story-teller's task to act as the devil's advocate, to elicit sympathy and a measure of understanding for those who lie outside the boundaries of State sympathy? But remember that it is not necessarily the poor or the physically defenceless who lie there. The publicans and sinners belong to all classes and all economic levels. It has always been in the interests of the State to poison the psychological wells, to restrict human sympathy, to encourage cat-calls – Galilean, Papist, Crophead, Fascist, Bolshevik. In the days of the totalitarian monarchy, when a sovereign slept uneasily with the memories of Wyatt, Norfolk, Essex,[47] in his dreams, it was an act of justice to trace the true source of action in *Macbeth*, the murderer of his king, and Shakespeare's play has for all time altered our conception of the usurper. If at times we are able to feel sympathy for Hitler, isn't it because we have seen the woods of Dunsinane converging on the underground chambers of the Chancellory?

Here in parenthesis I would emphasize once again the importance and the virtue of disloyalty. If only writers could maintain that one virtue – so much more important to them than purity – unspotted from the world. Honours, State patronage, success, the praise of their fellows all tend to sap their disloyalty. If they don't become loyal to a Church or a country, they are too apt to become loyal to some

46 Presumably, Greene is thinking of Paine's remark in *Dissertation on First Principles of Government* (1795), 'He that would make his own liberty secure, must guard even his enemy from oppression; for if he violates this duty, he establishes a precedent that will reach himself.'

47 Sir Thomas Wyatt the Younger (*c.* 1521–1554), Thomas Howard, 4th Duke of Norfolk (1538–1572) and Robert Devereux, 2nd Earl of Essex (1565–1601) were all executed for treason.

invented ideology of their own, until they are praised for consistency, for a unified view. Even despair can become a form of loyalty. How few die treacherous or blaspheming in old age, and have any at all been lucky enough to die by the rope or a firing squad? I can think of none, for the world knows only too well that given time the writer will be corrupted into loyalty. Ezra Pound therefore goes to an asylum . . . (the honorable haven of the uncorruptible – Smart, Cowper, Clare and Lee).[48] Loyalty confines us to accepted opinions: loyalty forbids us to comprehend sympathetically our dissident fellows; but disloyalty encourages us to roam experimentally through any human mind: it gives to the novelist the extra dimension of sympathy.

I hope I have made it clear that I am not advocating a conscious advocacy of the dispossessed, in fact I am not advocating propaganda at all, as it was written by Dickens, Charles Reade or Thomas Hood. The very act of recreation for the novelist entails sympathy: the characters for whom he fails in sympathy have never been truly recreated. Propaganda is only concerned to elicit sympathy for the innocent, or those whom the propagandist likes to regard as innocent, and this he does at the expense of the guilty: he too poisons the wells. But the novelist's task is to draw his own likeness to any human being, the guilty as much as the innocent. Isn't our attitude to all our characters more or less – There, and may God forgive me, goes myself?

If we can awaken sympathetic comprehension in our readers, not only for our most evil characters (that is easy: there is a cord there fastened to all hearts that we can twitch at will), but of our smug, complacent, successful characters, we have surely succeeded in making the work of the State a degree more difficult – and that is a genuine duty we owe society, to be a piece of grit in the State machinery. However acceptable the Soviet State may at the moment find the great classic writers, Dostoevski, Tolstoy, Chehov, Turgenev, Gogol, they have surely made the regimentation of the Russian spirit

48 Ezra Pound (1885–1972), under indictment for treason arising from his wartime broadcasts, was incarcerated at St Elizabeth's Hospital for the Insane, in Washington, DC. Christopher Smart (1722–71), William Cowper (1731-1800), John Clare (1793–1864) and Nathaniel Lee (1653–1692) were all confined for madness.

an imperceptible degree more difficult or more incomplete. You cannot talk of the Karamazovs in terms of a class, and if you speak with hatred of the kulak doesn't the rich humorous memory of the hero of *Dead Souls* come back to kill your hatred? Sooner or later the strenuous note of social responsibility, of Marxism, of the greatest material good of the greatest number must die in the ear, and then perhaps certain memories will come back, of long purposeless discussions in the moonlight about life and art, the click of a billiard ball, the sunny afternoons of that month in the country, the blows of an axe that has only just begun to fell the cherry trees.

I am sorry to return over and over again to this question of loyalty or disloyalty, but isn't disloyalty as much the writer's virtue as loyalty is the soldier's? For the writer, just as much as the Christian Church, is the defender of the individual. The soldier, the loyal man, stands for the mass interment, the common anonymous grave, but the writer stands for the uneconomic, probably unhealthy, overcrowded little graveyard, with the stone crosses preserving innumerable names.

There is a price to be paid, of course. We shall never, I suppose, know how many Russian writers have taken the same stand as Ivan Karamazov (one has only to substitute the words the State for the word God) and studied a long silence:

'This harmony has been assessed too dearly; the price for entry is already too high for our pockets. I prefer to hand back my entrance-ticket; and as an honest man I am bound to return it as soon as possible. So that is what I am doing. It is not that I reject God, Alyosha; I merely most respectfully hand Him back the ticket.'

One mustn't, of course, forget, writing as I have just done, that at the moment the chief danger to us of Russia is the danger the publican represented to Pharisees. We spend so much time as writers thanking God that we are not as the Soviet League of Writers, rejoicing in our freedom, that we don't see in how many directions we have already bartered it, in the interests of a group, whether political or religious.

I realize that I haven't taken up any of your practical and useful points on the question of the State's responsibility to the writer. But I remain intransigent. It seems to me unquestionable that if once writers are treated as a privileged class from the point of view of taxation they will lose their independence. What the State gives it can take away, and it is so terribly easy for a gift enjoyed for a few years to become a necessity. Once give us protection and we shall soon forget how we kept the wolf away in those past winters. And another danger is that privilege separates, and we can't afford to live away from the source of our writing in however comfortable an exile. I am one of those who find it extraordinarily difficult to write away from England (I had to do so at one time during the war), and I dread the thought of being exiled at home. It is possible, though I don't think it probable, that taxation might kill the novel, but it won't kill the creative passion. It may be that we are passing out of the literary period during which the novel has been the dominant form of expression, but there will still be literature. I cannot see why the poet should be affected by high taxation . . .

When you write of means other than State support for the novelist, I find myself more in agreement with you. Some kind of royalty collectable on library lendings is long overdue, but all the same don't let us make the mistake of treating the librarian as an enemy. He is our greatest friend. We have already emerged from the artificial book boom (that strange period when people bought novels) and are nearly back to normal times. In normal times it has been the library (I am not referring now to the public library) which has given the young novelist at least a basic salary. We must be careful not to kill the goose.

As for your proposed tax on the classics, I feel even more doubt, for who is to administer this fund if not the State? A committee of authors? But who is to choose the authors? In any one generation how many authors could you name whom you would trust to show discrimination or even common integrity? And as a matter of publishing fact, don't the classics already subsidize the living writers? A publisher's profits finance his work in progress. The best seller – or the classic – helps to finance the young author, the experimental book, the work of scholarship which cannot expect to show a return. There are certain publishers (we could agree on names) who never by any chance publish a book of literary merit, but these are not the publishers who are making money out of the classics. (I except a few mushroom firms who belong to the boom period and are dying with it.)

You may well ask, have you no plan, have you not one constructive suggestion to make? and my answer is quite frankly, None. I don't want a plan for literature. I don't want a working party, however high-minded or benevolent, to study the standard of life among novelists and decide a minimum wage. Even if by a miracle the State could be excluded from such a plan, I still don't want it. A plan can be taken over later by other authorities. Nor can a craft be trusted to legislate wisely for itself. Think of the Board of Film Censors which was set up by the industry itself, and consider how it has hampered the free development of films in a way that would have been impossible to the Lord Chamberlain's office.

No, our life is too organized already. Let us leave literature alone. We needn't worry too much. Man will always find a means to gratify a passion. He will write, as he will commit adultery, in spite of taxation.

Graham Greene

TO VIVIEN GREENE

Eyre & Spottiswoode | 14, 15, 16 Bedford Street | Strand,
London, W.C.2 | June 3 [1948]

Dear Vivien,

Thank you very much for your note about the book.[49] It was sweet of you to send it.

I have to fly over to New York in connexion with the *Heart of the Matter* affair on Sunday & I am flying back the following Saturday. Then a few days after my return I have to go with Carol Reed to Vienna to help arrange for the film of 'The Third Man' – the story I wrote for Korda in Italy.

If possible I think we should discuss matters before I leave for Vienna, though I don't expect to be away more than ten days. What

49 *The Heart of the Matter* was published 27 May 1948, with a dedication to Vivien and the children.

I suggest is that you read this letter while I am in New York & if you would like to discuss it, I would either meet you in London or Oxford, whichever you prefer.

I hope before I leave for Vienna to have taken a flat by myself in London, so that the present set-up in Gordon Square will be materially altered, though I am trying, if it's humanly possible, to save some relationship there.

You know I am fond of you. Quite apart from that I am aware of the responsibilities I owe you & the children. But, mainly through my fault, we have lived for years too far from reality, & the fact that has to be faced, dear, is that by my nature, my selfishness, even in some degree by my profession, I should always, & with anyone, have been a bad husband. I think, you see, my restlessness, moods, melancholia, even my outside relationships, are symptoms of a disease & not the disease itself, & the disease, which has been going on ever since my childhood & was only temporarily alleviated by psycho-analysis, lies in a character profoundly antagonistic to ordinary domestic life. Unfortunately the disease is also one's material. Cure the disease & I doubt whether a writer would remain. I daresay that would be all to the good.[50]

For nearly nine years, as you know, I have had a second domestic life in London, but the fact that that has been without the ties & responsibilities of a husband has not made it any more of a success. I have failed there just as completely as at Oxford, so that especially during the last four years, though the strain began much earlier, I have caused her a great deal of misery.

So you see I really feel the hopelessness of sharing a life with anyone without causing them unhappiness & disillusion – if they have any illusions. If you feel that a life is possible for us in which, though Oxford is my headquarters, there are no conditions, no guarantees or time tables laid down for either of us (you will have more liberty yourself soon), then let us try it. But, my dear, if as you reasonably may, you feel this arrangement (or lack of an arrangement) would only make for more misery, then I think we had better have an open separation which will be less of a problem &

50 Greene's bipolar illness had not yet been diagnosed.

nerve-strain for both of us than the disguised separation is now. The financial arrangements would be agreed between us, & I would see the children sometimes during their holidays: that could be discussed later. This could be a legal separation or not as you chose, but on my side I see no reason why we should not correspond directly on any problems that might arise, & I would always be only too anxious to meet you at any time.

    With affection,
        Graham

TO EVELYN WAUGH

Scobie's suicide in The Heart of the Matter *startled Catholic readers, many of whom held to the orthodox view that despair is an unforgivable sin. In two reviews of the book, Waugh had suggested, hesitantly, that Greene thought Scobie a saint, but also wondered whether Scobie's offering of suicide was 'either a very loose poetical expression or a mad blasphemy'.*[51] *Responding to Waugh, Canon Joseph Cartmell had dismissed Scobie as 'a very bad moral coward'. He said that the only good that came of Scobie's death 'was a negative one, the removal of himself as a source of sin'.*[52]

                    In Flight: American Airlines [July 1948]

Dear Evelyn,

    You've made me very conceited. Thank you very very much. There's no other living writer whom I would rather receive praise (& criticism) from. A small point – I did not regard Scobie as a saint, & his offering his damnation up was intended to show how muddled a mind full of good will could become when once 'off the rails.'

    I'm on the way to N.Y. to draw up a contract! Thank you so much for your advice. I fly back in 6 days & on to Vienna. Can I visit you some time in July? My time is going to be freer. I'll write & propose myself.

51 *The Tablet* (5 June 1948) and *The Commonweal* (6 July 1948). Cartmell's remarks appear in *The Tablet* (5 June 1948).
52 See Amory, 280, and NS 2: 294–300.

I thought the Canon rather complacent. Can't one write books about moral cowards?

Yours gratefully,
Graham

TO CATHERINE WALSTON

Sunday [22 August 1948]. In plane.

Cafryn dear, you'll have got my note posted by Carol. I feel bad at interrupting your retreat,[53] but not knowing how these things are run, I thought you might have telephoned & found it odd that I wasn't at home.

I had rather a beastly 24 hours wondering whether all was up with us. Not by death which I wouldn't mind but by sickness. An hour before going off to catch the plane I had a beastly hemorrhage, got in a doctor who said I mustn't fly but must go into hospital for examination. Carol unwillingly went off & I lay drearily in The Medical Arts Centre Hospital,[54] wondering. One has seldom felt so lonely, but that came to an end with a blessed Nembutal.

Yesterday they first X rayed me, then put me to sleep with an injection (an extra heavy dose because I kicked so) to examine me more intimately. The result was 'satisfactory' – no alcohol for 10 days & rather less permanently, a certain amount of treatment. All yesterday I was dopy, waking only at intervals, & all yesterday I dreamed of you – I do so so seldom – & all 'nice' dreams. So often I have angry or suspicious ones. I would wake up & fall asleep & at once back you were – very dear & sweet. It was really worth being doped.

[. . .]

53 Walston was staying at a convent in Surrey.
54 In New York.

TO ANTHONY POWELL

After a row at the Authors' Club in mid-September 1948 over delays in publication of Powell's John Aubrey and His Friends, *which Greene described as 'a bloody boring book,' he agreed to release Powell from his contract to Eyre & Spottiswoode.*[55] *The Board of Directors rejected this arrangement. Douglas Jerrold wrote to Powell on 29 October: 'Graham has no more power to release you from your contract with this firm than I have to sell the company's furniture and premises.' The episode led to Greene's quitting the firm.*

5 St. James's Street, | London, S.W.1. | 14th December 1948

Dear Tony,

I am afraid I had just left for Italy when your letter came and so I can only answer it now.

I expect you have heard by this time that I have resigned from the board of Eyre and Spottiswoode. Your case really brought matters to a head but [the] boil had been growing for many months. It is quite true that I offered to release you from your novel contract and, between ourselves, I was not prepared to remain on the board of a company which kept any author to the letter of a contract. I did, however, very much hope after our meeting in the Authors' Club that the whole thing might blow over and I had understood from David Higham that it was unlikely you would press the withdrawal of your novels.

Amongst the mass of letters waiting for me there is a letter from the Spanish Embassy and I suppose it is from your friend Carcer.[56] I will be writing to him.

Now that we are again in the position simply of friends and not of author and publisher, do look in for a drink!

Yours,

Graham

55 NS 2: 200–01.

56 A second secretary at the Spanish Embassy who was writing an article on Greene.

TO CATHERINE WALSTON

[Paris] | Saturday [22 January 1949][57]

Cafryn dear, I count the days in the quarter hours between engagements.

It's all too fantastic. My books in every shop – a whole display in the Rue de Rivoli. Three different people writing books on me for three different publishers. The Professor of English at the Sorbonne has asked me to lecture & says that he can fill the hall twice over. Charles Morgan vanquished. Three of his post-graduate pupils writing theses on me, one on 'L'Univers de G.G.', one on 'Le Malheur dans les Oeuvres de G.G.' & one on 'The Technique of the novels of G.G.' Priests flock reverently around. I'd really be rather enjoying it if I believed it, but I don't, quite . . . commonsense tells me it's all a joke that will soon pass. But I wish you could see the joke too. I'd love to preen my feathers in front of you.

I was so glad to get your letter. Though now of course I take the opposite view to Scobie – that nobody can ruin another person.[58] Harry has been happy, really happy, & that's your achievement. We others haven't made such a staggering success of adult marriage.

[. . .]

TO MIECZYSLAW GRYDZEWSKI

Mieczyslaw Grydzewski (1894–1970), editor of the Polish-language journal Wiadamosci, *asked Greene to discuss his views of Joseph Conrad.*

5 St. James's Street | London, S.W.1 | 5th April 1949

Dear Mr. Grydzewski,

I have always since the age of sixteen been a very great admirer of

57 See NS 2: 303.

58 Greene had told Waugh that the book showed not that Scobie was a saint but what happens when a person with good will gets off the rails (see p. 160). This letter suggests that at some point Greene shared Scobie's basic views. Waugh may have been uncomfortably close to the mark.

the works of Joseph Conrad, in particular *The Secret Agent* and *The Heart of Darkness*. It is, therefore, very easy for me to reply to your first question, that I believe he has a permanent place in English letters which at least compares with that of Dostoievsky in Russian, and that the reaction against his work which was experienced in the thirties is very temporary. Certainly, I would place him far and away above Virginia Woolf, who, perhaps, was responsible for that reaction.

As far as the other question is concerned, it is of course possible to detect in Conrad's work a certain rhetoric which is not in the main lines of English prose style. I think it is possible to say that his books sometimes read as though they were extremely brilliant and understanding translations from the French, but this does not destroy in any way the value of his contribution to English letters.

Yours faithfully,
Graham Greene

TO FRANÇOIS MAURIAC

Hotel Pont-Royal [Paris] | May 19 [1949]

Cher maître et ami,

I wanted to see you after the Conférence,[59] but you were busy signing books, & I had to leave the reception afterwards before you had arrived. May I say once again how much pleasure & pride I receive from knowing you, & how I regret the barrier between our languages? Your remarks in the *Figaro* were very generous.[60] Please believe that though I am no longer your English publisher, I am your admirer, your disciple & your friend.

Very sincerely yours,
Graham Greene

---

59 Both Greene and Mauriac were participants in the *Grand Conférence Catholique*.
60 Greene is referring to a tribute paid to him by Mauriac in *Le Figaro* (30 October 1948) and often reprinted. He remarks on Greene's exploration of the realms of sin and grace and how grace utilises sin in *The Power and the Glory*.

THE END OF THE AFFAIR

TO CATHERINE WALSTON

5 St. James's Street | London [8 July 1949]

My dear, after all this time have we got to say goodbye. Harry says I am not to speak to you. Is this final?

You always said you would stick to me. I don't know what to do. For God's sake send me a line.

TO CATHERINE WALSTON

5 St. James's Street | London S.W.1 | Sunday [10 July 1949] | off to Mass.

Dear,

I loved getting your letter. I still feel in a curious way knocked out by Thursday & the awful Friday when I believed an iron curtain had dropped & you had chosen the other side of it. I shan't ring up today. Twinkle's[1] letter, that like everybody else, I was 'time-demanding' is, I think, true – nor do I want to hear Harry's voice at the other end. My dear dear dear, I mustn't be time-demanding. When you feel like a word ring me up, & see me or not as you like on Tuesday or as circumstances demand.

1 Beatrice Ball, the Walston's nanny.

At 10 tomorrow morning I'm off to Shepperton to see the film. This afternoon I go to see Korda who wants me to produce an idea for Carol Reed & Laurence Olivier. A French company want to do a play of *The Power & the Glory*. I have provisionally accepted a free luxury holiday in Biarritz from July 29 to August 5 in the company of Cocteau, Charlie Chaplin, Marlene Dietrich & Orson Welles! (This is part of my effort not to be time-demanding).

[. . .]

TO CATHERINE WALSTON

Greene and Basil Dean collaborated on a dramatisation of The Heart of the Matter, *with Dean mainly responsible for the structure and Greene for the dialogue. In December 1949, they visited Sierra Leone to take photographs that would be helpful for sets and atmosphere. When the play was produced by Rogers and Hammerstein, it flopped.[2]*

Air France Transit Camp | Dakar | Thursday [8 December 1949]

Cafryn dear, we got here, after a rather awful journey starting from the Invalides at 6, at about 1 in the morning, & the plane for Freetown today has been cancelled!

What a time it was on Tuesday. I had to be revaccinated & get a bogus medical certificate to say that we were both unfit to be inoculated. That allowed Air France to put us on the plane, but we may be still quarantined by the strict English when we get to Freetown. It was a day of frantic telephonings, taxiings & visits to police stations – Marie[3] was an angel & did most, though the British Embassy & a mysterious employee of Cecil King called Mme Vanon also pulled wires.[4] Now we are confined to this rather beastly camp (we have no visas) unless a friend of a friend of Marie's helps us.

2 See Basil Dean, *Mind's Eye: An Autobiography 1927–1972* (London: Hutchinson, 1973), 305–7.

3 Marie Schebeko (later Biche), Greene's French agent. See p. 177.

4 Cecil King (1901–87) was the newspaper magnate who organised the Mirror Group of newspapers. His mysterious employee has not been identified.

Dean was rather depressed by this place, but suddenly getting under a mosquito net in the damp stuffiness, I felt at home – a familiar austere narrow home of four muslin walls. And this morning the light was beautiful & the black women passed by the window in robes of the loveliest colours, slouching by, chewing their sticks. I can never get this put right out of my system.

Interrupted by an unimportant first-drink-of-the-day with the steward of the plane at 7 in the morning. This encouraged me to get on the phone to Marie's f. of an f. & she's fetching us in her car at 2. I'm too happy to be in West Africa simply to mind what happens (Dean is still asleep). Next to you I love this hot wind & the black decorative women & the rather raffish kindly men in shorts & the mosquito net & the camp bed & the washed out madame behind the bar & this grey bright light. If I couldn't be with you, I'd like to be here. I believe I could even work in West Africa – I did once. But I hope tomorrow we get to Freetown, & one will see & smell the place again, & look up Ali who is in the police band now.

This is all very sentimental, but you & West Africa both make me sentimental. The French language here seems oddly natural like a native dialect. And at the airport at 1 in the morning people were so charming – the Santé man who rocked with laughter at our yellow fever letters but passed us through. 'Tell me what happens,' he said. 'Eight days quarantine. My English colleague very strict. You are the first British I have seen without proper certificates. O, what fun you are going to have. 8 days quarantine. We French we know how to dance' & he began to dance on the floor, 'we dance this way, that way, we dance . . .'

'The polka,' I said.

'Yes, the polka, but my English colleague he doesn't know how to dance.'

And the elderly customs man – I had tried ½ an hour before to get my bag cleared out of turn, because I should have done police & Santé first – greeted me again with a huge beam, 'Ah, it is the poor M. Graham,' & chalked them up with a grin.

(Oh, I haven't told you that when Dean & I were filling up the police forms at Les Invalides, an official brought me an extra form & asked me to sign the back of it because his wife was a Catholic &

liked my books! Dean was rather impressed!)

This must be the longest letter you've ever had from me with the least love stuff, & yet really the love stuff is in every word – I have loved no part of the world like this & I have loved no woman as I love you. You're my human Africa. I love your smell as I love these smells. I love your dark bush as I love the bush here, you change with the light as this place does so that one all the time is loving something different & yet the same. I want to spill myself out into you as I want to die here. And I am happy talking nonsense about you as I am about Africa.

On Tuesday night Marie & I talked about you. She loves you after this visit. After the first visit she said she was worried that you seemed hard but now she said from the first in the Ritz room, when you were relaxed & content, she saw the point, aesthetically & psychologically, & she liked you more & more each time of this visit. Please let's go again before the awful disappearance.

[. . .]

TO CATHERINE WALSTON

[Paris] | Sunday. 11:30 a.m [18 December 1949]

Dear, forgive this letter in advance, a humiliating wail of self-pity that I am ashamed of. But I'm missing you terribly here – the fortnight doesn't seem to have helped & I just feel at the end of my tether, or near it. After Mass I was stupid enough to walk across the river, & I found myself crying in the Tuileries Gardens. I don't know what to do. It was all right yesterday when I spoke to you, but one can't telephone all the time. Then I held you at bay till 3 in the morning drinking with Marie, but one can't go on doing that, though I am going out again with her tonight. You captured Rome & Dublin, & now at the second assault you've captured Paris. I talked to Marie last night about the house & she's going to set about finding one, but what's the good? My dear my dear. I used to like being alone, but now it's a horror. One thinks of times when we were happy & one tries to shut off thought. It's horrible that one can't be

happy thinking of happy times like one can in an ordinary
relationship.

I don't know what to do about next year. One wishes over & over
again that one of these planes will crash & they never do. I so long
for your company – I don't, at this moment, want to make love. I
want to sit on the floor with my head resting between your legs like
at the Ritz & be at peace. The telephone pulls at my elbow but
what's the good? My dear, I never knew love was like this, a pain
that only stops when I'm with people, drinking. Thank God, from
tomorrow there are lots of engagements.

For God's sake, dear, don't hold this letter against me, & be sweet
on Thursday. You can always cure this pain by coming in at a door.
You don't know how I need you.

Pray for me.

Graham

TO CATHERINE WALSTON

5 St. James Street | London S.W. 1 | Monday [30 January 1950]

Dear heart,

I'm so sorry that all the trouble has started again. Please
remember that I love you entirely, with my brain, my heart & my
body, & that I'm always there when you want me.

I don't like or approve of Harry's judgements. When a man
marries, he is like a Prime Minister – he has to accept responsibility
for the acts of a colleague. My marriage failed (only God can sift all
the causes), but the *responsibility* for failure is mine. One can't lay the
blame on one's wife. Your marriage, intrinsically, had failed before I
knew you, & the man must accept responsibility – which doesn't
mean guilt. It had failed because marriage isn't maintaining a friend,
a housekeeper or even a mother. The Catholic service says 'with my
body I thee worship', & if that fails the heart has gone out of it.

My dear, any time you say I would lay out a plan of action for
living together. I'm certain I could make you happy, & the church
would not be excluded. You would be unhappy for a time – that's all,

but the division would be over. Harry could not divorce you without your consent & *therefore* he could not shut down the doors between you & the children. You could insist on sharing them in any separation, just as if I chose I could insist on mine. He is not legally in a position to lay down terms or a way of life for you.

Dear, this letter may make you angry. Don't be. I must, at times, present a practical plan. It's the dearest wish I have – the only wish – to have you with me & to make you happy with me. I believe I could do it, after the bad period was over. I love you now so infinitely more than even a year ago. I have great trust, admiration & gratitude (because of the amount of happiness you have given me & patience you have shown during my bad period). I want you to come away with me for six months & test me. That was what Vivien suggested to me – I think in the long term she is proving more generous[5] & more loving than Harry. I'm sorry (& this will anger you) I don't believe in Harry's love for you or anybody, but his small unit of power.

Dear heart, the cabins [?] are there. Come with me on the 15th & stay with Binny[6] until you are rested & can sort things out. I'll stay with you & look after you for weeks, months, years, a lifetime. (Strike out the phrase not required!) I want to grow old with you & die with you.

Your lover, who loves you for ever. God bless you & pray for me.

TO CATHERINE WALSTON

5 St. James's Street | London S.W.1 | Monday 2 p.m.
[30 January 1950]

My dear, if things are getting bad, & the curtain is liable to fall, you must forgive me for presenting my case. I wouldn't love you so much if I wouldn't fight to the last ditch.

My previous letter was one to be burned. This one put in the

black box because it really is the sketch for a plan of action – &
though you may not need it now, you may need to consider it one
day.

How I want to be with you when you are in trouble, & put my
arms round you, with your face turned to my face, & hear you
sleeping.

Dear dear dear

Graham.

Order of Battle in the unlikely event of your choosing me.

1. During the 'unhappy period' we would consider basing
   ourselves on Achill and Anacapri,[7] or we would take a
   long trip into strange territory with the help of the
   Express – South Seas, India, Palestine, what you will.
2. We would immediately begin steps to see whether I could
   get my marriage annulled on *two* possible grounds.
3. In the meanwhile proper arrangements would be made for
   you to have access to your children.
4. While the annulment proceedings went on, it might be
   worth while considering changing your name by deed poll
   to mine, for two reasons
   1) I think it would make the whole business go down all
      right with your family.
   2) It would enable us to economise when we travelled in
      only taking one room!
5. I would hand over to you half my controlling shares in
   the new company which would in effect give you 1/3 of
   all film and theatrical earnings in perpetuity. (After all a
   husband can be expected to make financial provision).
6. Our finances – apart from my arrangement with Vivien &
   the children – would be in common, & we would make a
   mess in common or a success in common.
7. Wherever we settled for any length of time, we would
   have two rooms *available*, so that at any time without
   ceasing to live together & love each other, you could go

7 In 1948, Graham acquired the Villa Rosaio, a small house in Anacapri, where he did
much of his writing in the years that followed.

to Communion (we would break down again & again, but that's neither here nor there).

8. I love your children, & you would spend any time you wanted with them.

9. My love for you will go on till death, & I would guarantee never to break up our relationship except by your wish. No 'tipsy frolic' would make me walk out. It might make me sore as hell for 24 hours, but so far I don't think I've managed to be sore that time!

10. I would tell the truth to you always. Your part of our life should be yours. I trust you as I trust no other living person. I am yours entirely. I love you & will always love you. As I said in Paris you are the saint of lovers to whom I pray. God bless you & treat this seriously.

TO MARCEL MORÉ

A greatly condensed version of this letter to a French scholar was published in Dieu Vivant *(17 November 1950) as a sequel to two other pieces on Greene. It constitutes Greene's most detailed statement on the Catholic dimensions of* The Heart of the Matter.

5 St. James's Street | London S. W. 1 | 12th July 1950

Dear Mons. Moré,

Very many thanks for your letter and for the copy of *Dieu Vivant* with the two articles. I did not realise that I was quite so dogmatic at the Table Talk, but it is nice to be made to appear to speak French so fluently and well! Your article on 'Les Deux Holocaustes de Scobie'[8] interested me very much and it seemed to me to be a very close and acute study of the character, enlightening me a little. A few points I would like to point out –

1. *On page 91.* If I said at lunch that the point of the child's

death had no other purpose than to show Scobie making a gesture natural to any man under the circumstances I was talking loosely. You know how it is with authors – in conversation we feel embarrassed at talking about our own books and are apt to try and cut the conversations short by an abrupt half-truth. Obviously one did have in mind that when he offered up his peace for the child it was a genuine prayer and had the results that followed. I always believe that such results, though obviously a God would not fulfil them to the limit of robbing him of peace for ever, are answered up to a point as a kind of test of a man's sincerity and to see whether in fact the offer was one merely based on emotion.

2. I knew very well what I was about when I used the Portuguese captain's daughter as a comparison with Scobie's dead child, but I had not thought of the explanation which you give on *page 94* of his first act of faith. It seems to me an admirable point and I wish it had been consciously in my mind as it certainly explains an otherwise rather abrupt revelation of character.[9] Curiously enough the book I am writing now deals also with a holocaust and I have been very discontented with the psychology of the moment of holocaust. In this case it is a prayer of a non-Catholic and a non-Christian, and I have not satisfactorily explained how it came about. Your remarks on *page 94* have given me the clue to the whole situation and will make, I hope, all the difference to the book and I am very grateful to you for that fact.

3. I have not read the passage from Père Surin[10] which you

---

9 Moré argued that when Scobie opens the letter the reader learns that the two daughters, one still on earth, the other in heaven, are praying for their fathers.

10 Jean-Joseph Surin was a seventeenth-century Jesuit and spiritual writer, whose life offers a bizarre parallel with Scobie's. He performed an exorcism on three Ursuline nuns, but was so horrified at the sacrileges intended for them that he prayed he himself would be possessed instead. His prayer was granted, and for twenty years he was plunged into despair over his own damnation. According to the *Catholic Encyclopedia*, 'He was healed eight years before his death and was thenceforth absorbed in the abundance of Divine communications.' The quotation in the article refers to Surin's experience of the violent conflict between demons and the spirit of God.

quote on *page 99* and I am grateful, too, for your drawing my
attention to it. It seems to me to be a remarkable description
of a state of mind which comes home to many of us: a kind
of religious schizophrenia.

4. *Page 101.* Scobie's last prayer has lost the point that I
intended in the French because of the inability to translate
into French 'Oh God, I love. . . .' without adding the subject
of the love. My own intention was to make it completely
vague as to whether he was expressing his love for the two
women or his love for God. My own feeling about this
character is that he was uncertain himself and that was why
the thing broke off. The point I would like to make which is
probably heretical is that at the moment of death even an
expression of sexual love comes within the borders of
charity. After all when a man knows that he is dying in a
few moments sexual love itself becomes completely
altruistic – pride can no longer enter into it, nor can the
hope of receiving or giving pleasure, it is love pure and
simple, and therefore there must be some confusion in the
mind as to the object of love. This was what I intended but
in the translation, owing to the exigencies of the French
language, we are definitely told that Scobie makes an act of
love towards God which of course rules out the ambiguity of
his future.

5. *Page 102.* I was very interested to see the parallels you found
between certain passages in the book and the Letters of Ste.
Thérèse as I had not read the Letters at the time that I was
writing the book.

6. *Page 105.* I am fascinated and interested by the quotation
you give from Marie Des Vallées.[11] It is always pleasant to
find one's own thought confirmed in the work of people who
know more about faith than I do. There is a parallel passage,
I think you will find, to this in 'La Puissance et La Gloire' on

11 Marie Des Vallées was the adviser and friend of the seventeenth-century Saint Jean
Eudes, founder of the lamentably named Eudist Fathers. The quotation begins:
'L'Amour divin est plus terrible que la Justice elle-même.'

page 314 where the terror inspired by the love of God is expressed.

Again very many thanks for so interesting and acute an essay.
Yours sincerely,
Graham Greene

TO EVELYN WAUGH

Greene discusses the plan that he should write a screenplay of Brideshead Revisited *for the American producer David O. Selznick.*

5 St. James's Street | London S. W. 1 | July 17 [1950]

Dear Evelyn,

I completely missed the announcement in *The Times* of the new son[12] and only heard about it at secondhand on Sunday. Very many congratulations.

Thank you so much for your card. I have in theory agreed to do the script of *Brideshead*, but it is with great trepidation. For one thing I am very anxious that it should not in any way damage our relationship, and as you know a script writer does not have complete control over a film! I would rather it had been any other man almost than Selznick behind this, because he is an extraordinarily stupid and conventionally-minded man. I told Stone[13] that I would not agree to work in California and I urged him to get a French director for the film, by suggesting the man who made Gide's *Symphonie Pastorale*.[14] This director, whose name I have forgotten, is a believing Protestant and the Protestants in France have somewhat a similar position as a minority religion to the Catholics in this country. He struck me when I met him as an extremely perceptive man. I don't suppose however that Selznick will pay any attention to

12 Septimus Waugh.
13 Louis T. Stone, executive assistant to Selznick.
14 *La Symphonie Pastorale* (1946) was directed by Jean Delannoy (b. 1908). In 1956 he directed Anthony Quinn and Gina Lollobrigida in *The Hunchback of Notre Dame*.

this suggestion. The trouble is that in order to get a good script one must work almost daily with a sympathetic director, and I can't think of anyone in England who would have the faintest idea of what *Brideshead* is about. Anyway we might have a certain amount of fun if you would collaborate with me and I think it would be essential if one had to go to California to discuss this script with Selznick that we went together. One man is more easily talked round than two.

I expect I will see you at the D'Arcy[15] dinner for which I am sending my cheque today.[x]

Yours,

Graham

[x]Do sit me far away from Jeannie[16] & near somebody I like!

The plan was abandoned, apparently because Waugh, who had initially been enthusiastic, felt that if he relinquished control of the script the studios would produce a horror.

TO REV. WILFRED HARRINGTON

The Roman Catholic chaplain at Whittington Hospital in London wrote to Greene about The Third Man *saying that there is no evidence that diluted penicillin is dangerous. He also queried the role of an army orderly in the plot. He asked, 'Is the story – as it seems to me – just a leg-pull?'*

15 Rev. Martin D'Arcy, S.J. (1881–1976) was a prominent priest and author responsible for the conversion to Catholicism of numerous writers and poets including Waugh.

16 Presumably Jeanne Stonor (Lady Camoys). Graham was very fond of her husband Sherman (Baron Camoys), and often visited their estate near Oxford, which had a long recusant history. Something of a trophy hunter, Jeanne often flirted with Graham and maintained that she had had an affair with him – a claim he denied. He later became a friend to their daughter the Hon Julia Camoys Stonor, who has written a memoir of her mother, *Sherman's Wife* (London: Desert Hearts, 2006). See p. 395.

28th July 1950

Dear Father Harrington,

Yes, I am the author of *The Third Man*. The penicillin story is not a leg-pull as it was a definite racket of which a description was given me by the Chief of Police in Vienna. The same kind of racket took place I believe in Berlin. The point of danger in using diluted penicillin is the fact that even if you injected somebody with plain water the chances would be that you would cause death, or so I am told by doctors. There is the other point that in cases of meningitis very quick treatment with penicillin is needed, and in the case of the children in Vienna the diluted penicillin was not strong enough to work and it was too late for any other remedy, but in the cases of children losing their minds I am told that this might have been caused by the polluted water. The reason why a medical orderly was shown as taking part in this racket was that at the period of the film penicillin was only allowed to Military hospitals. There was therefore a big temptation to steal on the part of orderlies for the private and civilian market. I feel sure that there are several medical inaccuracies in the story but the general idea is based on fact.

Yours sincerely,

Graham Greene

TO MARIE SCHEBEKO (LATER BICHE)

After the death of Denyse Clairouin, her associate Marie Schebeko, who later married Jean Biche, became Greene's agent in Paris. With absolute command of many languages and expertise in all matters pertaining to publishing, she was a formidable figure. She became one of Greene's closest friends and devoted an enormous effort to his business and to his personal concerns.

5 St James's Street | London S.W.1 | 27th October 1950

Dear Marie,

I got back two days ago from Stockholm where I spent the last week of the holiday. Strictly between you and me it was to nurse my constituency! I am one of the three candidates this year for the Nobel Prize, but the other two are much more the favourites in the running. Don't tell Laffont or it will get into the press. As it was Stockholm papers made cracks about my having arrived two months too early.[17]

As a result of a letter from my younger brother who has gone to Malay to conduct political warfare I have decided to spend a couple of months with him. He assures me he can lay on anything from a jungle patrol to a Chinese dance girl!

[. . .]

TO EVELYN WAUGH

5 St. James's Street | London S.W. 1 | Oct. 26 [1950]

Dear Evelyn,

I only got back yesterday afternoon from three nice weeks in Italy & one rather wearing week in Stockholm & found your sumptuous present.[18] Thank you again & again. I've read the book with enormous interest in *The Month* but from all accounts the untruncated version is better still. I shall now have to buy a reading copy though because one can't mark a limited edition & I never feel as though I own a book until I've done | for approval & wwwww for disapproval. I've never got to the Victorian point of ? & !!

In Italy we saw Harold.[19] How nice & dear he is, & how I didn't realise it at Oxford.

I'm planning to go to Malaya in December & January. I wish you'd come too. There are a lot of very proud Portuguese Eurasian Catholics in Malacca.

Affectionately,

Graham

17 Two prizes were given. One held over from 1949 went to William Faulkner, the other, for 1950, to Bertrand Russell. Over four decades the Nobel Committee, influenced by the anti-Catholic Artur Lundkvist, failed to honour Graham Greene.

18 Waugh's novel *Helena*.

19 The aesthete Harold Acton (1904–94) whose home was at Villa La Pietra near Florence. Graham's contemporary at Oxford, he had written a crushing review of *Babbling April*, which Graham eventually accepted as accurate.

TO SIR OSBERT SITWELL

Left Hand, Right Hand (5 vols, 1945–50), the autobiography of Sir Osbert Sitwell (1892–1969), describes an eccentric father, a genially domineering butler, a feckless mother, and three siblings of genius, through decades of bizarre entanglements. Though now neglected, the series was regarded at the time as a masterpiece of English prose. Graham's comments on books written by his acquaintances were usually drawn from the well of faint praise. Not in this case.

5 St. James's Street | London S.W. 1 | Friday, Oct. 27 [1950]

Dear Osbert Sitwell,

I've returned home to find – as I confess I'd hoped – the last volume of your autobiography. How one wishes one did not say last. Thank you so much for completing a set which I value more, I think, than any other book of my time – Proust is before my time! I am not going to read it yet, for in three weeks I depart to Malaya for awhile & I feel I should need your sense of style & values deeply there.

With so many regrets that the book is finished.

Yours,
Graham Greene

TO EVELYN WAUGH

5 St. James's Street | London S.W. 1 | [before 16 November 1950]

Dear Evelyn,

I must write you a hasty line to say how much I like *Helena*. The truncated version in *The Month* didn't do it justice. It's a magnificent book. I think particularly fine & moving was Helena's invocation to the three wise men. How it applies to people of our kind – 'of all who stand in danger by reason of their talents.'

With great admiration & affection.

Graham

TO CATHERINE WALSTON

*After Communist rebels in Malaya killed three planters in June 1948, the
British declared a state of emergency and found themselves engaged in a
jungle war, involving constant attacks by guerrillas on civilians. Hugh
Greene went to the country to organise psychological warfare and invited
Graham to come out as well. One of the highlights of his trip was a patrol
with the Gurkhas. The visit to Malaya led to a major article in* Life *(30 July
1951), later incorporated into* Ways of Escape.

[Kuala Lumpur | 22 December 1950]

[. . .]

Now for the Gurkhas. After a wild night which included shooting
billiard balls at an opponent's finger (3 hits a win!) ending with
dinner at 1.15 a.m. Cheers,[20] 21 Gurkhas & myself set out. I'd never
realized the heaviness of a pack before. They gave me a revolver
instead of a rifle or I could never have stuck it. Our job was to make
our way – on a compass bearing not a track, hacking our own trail –
through a patch of jungle between two roads. 150 bandits were
supposed to be in the area, & they had had an air strike at them.
The going was awful. Heavy rubber soled anti-leech boots slipped all
the time on the wet clay slopes. Elevations were sometimes this
much / & the first day ended with 500 feet of climbing, hauling on
to trees [?] which generally left thorns in one's hands. At the end of
the first day, as the crow flies, we had done 3 miles. I felt absolutely
whacked. We started camping at 4 & the Gurkhas had to make a
clearing with their kukris[21] for the wireless set & also hack down
trees for shelter. My batman had forgotten my spare trousers, so I had
to sleep in trousers already dripping with sweat & rain. They built
for Cheers & myself a kind of double bed with four posts, logs laid
across a mattress of poles, leaves & a mackintosh covering & a
mackintosh shelter which kept out the torrential rain in the night
perfectly. But we both suffered badly from cramp & got very little
sleep.

20 Major Joey MacGregor-Cheers, one of Greene's companions in Malaya.
21 A curved knife or short sword used by the Gurkhas.

Second Day. The wireless failed to work & we were having an air drop by parachute of rations at 10. a.m. So after our early tea the Gurkhas had to make a clearing by simply knocking down a few 100 foot trees with their kukris. Then we sent up smoke bombs to mark our position & half an hour late the air drop was made: the parachutes dropping within 30 feet of a clearing no larger than a tennis court. Then we set out again – still going bang straight by compass, hill or no hill, path or no path. Our second camp was on the side of a hill & I felt much better – the day had produced a couple of abandoned bandit camps. And there was a running stream in which we could bathe: found a leech had been at work on my right bottom. Too tired to eat any supper & felt rather sick.

3rd Day. This was awful. I felt completely uninterested in bandits – the only effort was to keep up & not delay the patrol. Felt very sick & destroyed the silence of our halting places by retching. We had to climb up & down a 1500 foot hill – again this sort of angle of wet slippery clay ╱ . Of course when we came out of the jungle again all the excitement had been near the place where we entered the jungle – a concentration of 100 Communists having been engaged, wearing the Gurkha hats & identity marks, by 7 police.

[. . .]

TO MARIE SCHEBEKO (LATER BICHE)

as from Majestic Hotel, | Kuala Lumpur, | Dec. 25 [1950]

Dear Marie,

Forgive this very tardy wish for a happy Christmas. Life has been a bit tiring here what with Gurkhas dragging me round the jungle in full kit & planters dragging me from bar to bar. I haven't seen a bandit yet, but one of my new friends here has already been killed. There's a daily casualty list of civilians & police. Apart from this the country isn't wildly interesting. Difficult to work though & all I've done is some drastic revising of the novel[22] – it's still not right, & I

22 *The End of the Affair*.

know what's wrong, but the book's finished & I can't bring myself to write new scenes.

I'm in Malacca at the moment with my brother. The only attractive (to me) part of the country because the only old part. Nature doesn't really interest me – except in so far as it may contain an ambush – that is, something human.

[. . .]

TO CATHERINE WALSTON

The Residency, | Malacca. | Dec. 25 [1950]. | 8 a.m.

[. . .]

I filled up the time with Hugh to Midnight Mass at the City Park drinking whisky & watching the taxi girls dance around. I had forgotten till it was too late that Christmas Eve was Sunday & I didn't go to Mass, but it was such complete inadvertence that I went to communion just the same. We went to an 18th century church in walking distance of the City Park which specialises in the Portuguese Eurasians. Such a crowd. It took half an hour to get through the communicants. Then we drove home in bright moonlight in two trishaws.

One sad thing. Did I tell you how I met on my last visit here a young Englishman who was crackers about Macao, dreamed of going back & living there (the earthly paradise), could talk of little else? We met in the City Park dance place & he had a Chinese girl with him who he fondly believed was a virgin – 'see her home every night: can't touch her.' He had extraordinary clear wild blue eyes & loved the Chinese. When I came with Hugh to the dance hall I saw his girl – she was taxiing, & I was afraid of seeing him because I couldn't remember his name for introductions. I described him to our companion. He said, 'Oh, that was Jolly.' Jolly I knew as the name of a young man who was shot a week ago. I had noticed his tiny absurd car & had said to Noel Ross,[23] 'That would be good for an ambush,' but they put five bullets in him very accurately in spite

---

23 The colonial adviser. He had once been a Dominican novice.

of the tiny car. It was oddly sad being afraid of meeting him & seeing his 'virginal' Chinese girl taxiing & then finding he wasn't here or back in Macao or anywhere at all.

Another queer encounter just before I came away. A man came up to me in the Cold Storage shop where I was buying drinks – a tall foxy faced rather heavy man, who introduced himself as Wheeler. Wheeler was at school with me & belonged to the bad period. We were in the junior school together & then in the same house. (He told me, though I'd forgotten it, that I used to do his Latin prep for him). The real misery of that time began when he was suborned onto the side of my great enemy, Carter (who he told me the other day was dead). I put Carter into *The Lawless Roads* – 'spreading terror from a distance.' What a lot began with Wheeler & Carter – suspicion, mental pain, loneliness, this damned desire to be successful that comes from a sense of inferiority, & here he was back again, after thirty-five years, in a shop in Kuala Lumpur, rather flash, an ardent polo player. And instead of saying 'What hell you made my life 30 years ago,' one arranged to meet for drinks!

[. . .]

In his work Graham depicts in various guises the figure of Lionel Carter (b. 1904), a boy who attacked him physically and subjected him to ingenious mental cruelties. Carter offered him friendship, then withdrew it and taunted him as a traitor in the dormitory. In The Lawless Roads he is called Collifax, 'who practised torments with dividers' (14). The most detailed account of these episodes is found in A Sort of Life (59–62), where Augustus Henry Wheeler (b. 1904) is given the name Watson. As David Pearce, a retired housemaster at the school and an authority on Old Berkhamstedians, notes, Wheeler's father, a military officer from Eastbourne, was dead by 1916 and his mother sent him to a distant private school, a recipe for bullying. Sherry (1: 75), relying on information from Carter's widow, says that Carter died in 1971. Pearce remarks: 'The Wheeler mention of an earlier death sounds like the blarney of an alcoholic OB. "Dead, my dear boy, dead."'

TO FRANCIS GREENE

Hotel Majestic | Kuala Lumpur | Jan. 7 [1951]

Dear Francis,

I got back from Kalantan & the China Sea (where I bathed twice in big breakers) to find a small parcel which I think was in your handwriting – it contained a very pretty plaque of St. Christopher. Was this from you? Thank you very much indeed if it was – otherwise you must pass on the thanks to the real giver.

There's really no news, & I've had no real adventures since I went with the Gurkhas. The nearest I've come to an ambush was when a convoy that had taken me somewhere last week was ambushed on the way back (when I wasn't with them). It was a very small ambush – one soldier had a finger shot off. That's all.

Will you let me know when you go back to Ampleforth? I shall be back about mid-February – I go to look at the war in Indo-China on the 25th.

Lots of love,
Daddy.

P.S. I'll send you soon a photograph of myself all dressed up like a Gurkha officer!

TO EMMET HUGHES

After a brief visit to Vietnam in January 1951, Greene received a request from Hughes (1920–82), then articles editor at Life, *to write on the country. However, the magazine rejected an important piece that subsequently appeared in* Paris Match *(2 July 1952; reprinted in* Reflections, *129–47). During his first visit, Greene had met the ferociously anti-communist Colonel Leroy, who controlled the area of Ben Tre near Saigon, and the Bishop of Phat Diem, Le Huu Tu, who ruled his diocese like a medieval prince-bishop and maintained a small army. After an initially warm reception, the French Commander-in-Chief General de Lattre concluded that Greene was a spy.*[24]

5 St. James Street | London S. W. 1 | 15th February 1951

Dear Emmet Hughes,

I shall try and get down to a Malaya article this week-end and send it to you as soon as possible. I received your telegram about Indo-China, but although I think this is a fascinating and interesting country I was only there for ten days and I don't feel I could write any general article on it. I concentrated mainly on seeing some of the queer little private armies that are operating there now for the moment in support of the French. For instance, I visited a young ex-Catholic Leroy in the south who is keeping the islands round his own estates clear with an army of 2,000 Annamite catholics;[25] I spent a night with the Annamite Bishop of Phat-diem who is Commander-in-Chief of a small army of 2,000 to protect his diocese. This was both interesting and moving as here there was some genuine antagonism to Communism. I also visited the Caodaists, a new Annamite religious body who have a highly disciplined army of 25,000 men, who worship by means of spiritualism, Buddha, Christ, and Confucius, and have three lesser Saints, Dr. Sun Yat Sen, Victor Hugo and an ancient Chinese philosopher! The whole place was very reminiscent of the middle ages with the barons juggling for position according to the skill of their armies and the border towers, similar in structure to our own Welsh border fortresses, going up every kilometre along the roads.

This might make one particular article, but if at any time you felt it worth while and if the fighting intensified again, as it certainly will before long, I should be very ready to go out there again and to study the country properly. The months I would most favour are March–April or August, but of course [the] Viet Nimh may not

---

24 *Ways of Escape*, 126.
25 Greene admired Jean Leroy for his skill as a soldier and his refusal to be corrupted. See Greene's introduction to Leroy's memoir *Life of Colonel Leroy* (1977), reprinted in *Reflections*, 298. Annam is an area in central Vietnam.

decide that those are suitable months for attack! The French received me extremely cordially and I had cars and 'planes whenever I wanted them, and General de Lattre I am quite certain would give me every facility if I returned.

As for Malaya, I never want to see the place again!

Yours ever,

   Graham Greene

TO EVELYN WAUGH

On 17 March 1951, Waugh wrote to thank Greene for sending The Lost Childhood and Other Essays, *especially praising those on Henry James, but he added that the praise of Lawrence 'sickens me'. He suggested that Greene sometimes confused the terms 'artist' and 'genius'.*

5 St. James's Street | London S.W.1 | 19th March 1951

Dear Evelyn,

How nice it is to know you are back in England. Rumours of it reached me a day or so ago from Dame Robert Speaight.[26] I don't suppose you knew that she knew! I long to see you again and to hear about the Palestine trip – my trip in Malaya was rather dreary and wet, but I loved Indo-China and finding a new Eastern religion in which Victor Hugo is venerated as a saint.

I feel sure we would not agree about many people, but don't you like Rider Haggard? I am puzzled by your reference to my praise of Lawrence as I don't like the man much. Surely it must have been a very incidental reference and I imagine I was using genius in a particular way. It seems to me genius is not a term of praise but a psychologically descriptive one. It always seemed to me that Lawrence was ruined as an artist by his genius.[27]

26 A facetious reference to Robert Speaight (1904–76), actor, author, and Catholic convert.

27 The disputed reference is probably that in 'Henry James: The Private Universe': 'The sense of evil never obsessed him, as it obsessed Dostoyevsky; he never ceased to be primarily an artist, unlike those driven geniuses, Lawrence and Tolstoy . . .'

I wish that I could be at Downside with you[28] even though I hate the headmaster so much, but I am going to be in France at that time. Do let me know when you have any plan to be in London. I shall be back here sometime in April.

Naturally I rather liked Moré's article in *Dieu Vivant*, but I thought like everything about him it was a little bit exaggerated. I don't really like these Léon Bloy[29] converts.

Yours affectionately,

Graham

TO HUGH GREENE

26th June 1951

Dear Hugh,

[. . .]

Paris Match is pressing me for [a] definite date for Indo-China and I have told them that I am prepared to go after July 20 but I am still waiting to hear from Trevor Wilson in Hanoi. He is taking a holiday sometime and I definitely don't want to go when he is away as he gives me free accommodation in Hanoi as well as being an immense source of information.[30] I seem to have missed the bus in the last few weeks when Ho Chi Minh put on a big offensive to cover the infiltration of guerillas in an attempt to steal the rice crop. My nice Bishop was completely surrounded in his diocese and had to be rescued by parachute troops. It would have been fun to have been

28 Waugh was going to what he called 'that centre of Sadism', Downside Abbey near Bath, for Holy Week.

29 The novelist, poet and essayist Léon Bloy (1846–1917) exercised enormous influence over French Catholicism, promoting the spiritual value of poverty and suffering. Greene cannot have thought too badly of Bloy as he quotes him in the epigraph to *The End of the Affair*: 'Man has places in his heart which do not yet exist, and into them enters suffering in order that they may have existence.'

30 Trevor Wilson was the British Consul in Hanoi and a fellow Catholic whom Greene had met at the SIS headquarters at St Albans during the war. Wilson introduced him to Vietnam, from which he was himself expelled in December 1951 for anti-French activities. In 1968, he rescued Francis Greene from a likely death in Laos (see pp. 294–5).

with him and seen him in a crisis. I will let you know directly I am
certain when I am going to be there and it will be enormous fun if
you can make the excuse of a tri-partite conference to come too.
The weather will be foul but I suppose one can put up with that.

   Love

      Graham

TO CATHERINE WALSTON

5 St. James's Street | London S.W.1 | [10 August 1951]

My dear,

   In this nervous condition, speaking on the telephone, it seems
impossible to convey a meaning without over-emphasis or
abruptness.

   What I want to say is this. A human relationship, like ours has
been, is inextricably physical & mental. I have no *real* belief that the
physical side is seriously wrong in the particular circumstances, but
you will remember that for the last two years I've urged you to go to
confession & communion between our meetings. I can see a great
benefit in that. Communion might help to reduce the occasions
happily. All *that* I would support to the hilt.

   I don't however believe that as long as there's strong desire it's
possible to tease oneself while we are together without nerves, anger,
impatience – all the things that ruin a relationship finally. You know
the peace & quiet we had last time in Anacapri. That was only
because the relationship was complete. Do you really think we could
go back there now, & live in separate houses for safety, without even
the friendly silly cheerful drinking together, working together
atmosphere disappearing.

   You say the last 4½ years have been a fairy tale. Thomas[31] has
probably said that, but he hasn't lived them. It was at least a fairy

---

31 Thomas Gilby, a Dominican priest and a friend of both Greene and Walston. It has
been argued on fragmentary evidence that he had an affair with Walston. (See NS 3:
391–400).

tale which might have lasted another five before one side of the
relation died slowly & naturally out. The fairy tale you are
substituting is one in which one will be afraid to come into the same
bedroom, afraid to kiss, afraid to touch you, when we shall be so self-
conscious that the body will be always in one's mind because never
at peace. I don't know what kind of 'intellectual companionship' we
shall get out of that.

[. . .]

I'm afraid I'm wholly on Browning's side, 'Better sin the whole sin
sure that God observes.'[32]

I think the only way to stay together for life is to go back & back
to Confession & Communion after every time or period, but I *don't*
believe – even Thomas doesn't believe in the possibility, I think – of
suddenly switching a relation onto the unphysical level. We should
try, I agree, when we go away together not to think & emphasise in
our own minds beforehand what it entails, there are other motives
in being together, but a teasing affair of – let's hold out another day,
another two days etc, would only *prevent* the physical love from
taking the right proportions.

And whatever the Church may say it gives a lot of scope to the
individual conscience, & it goes dead *against* my conscience to
believe that it hasn't been far better for you & me to have been
faithful to one person for four & a half years than to have lived as we
were apt to live before.

Dear heart, if all you mean is this: that in future we should get
back to confession & communion as frequently as we can, that we
should want to want God's will (which we don't & can't know),
then I am with you all the way. I don't question the value of an
eventual intention, but if we are simply to cut off the whole physical
side of loving each other, I can't share the immediate intention &
can't go further than praying 'to want to want'. And as I can't share

32 From Browning's poem 'Before':

> *Better sin the whole sin, sure that God observes,*
> *Then go live his life out! Life will try his nerves,*
> *When the sky which noticed all, makes no disclosure,*
> *And the earth keeps up her terrible composure.*

that *immediate* intention, it would be better – if that's in your mind –
to cut right away.

I hope & pray you don't because life would be a real desert
without you, & God knows what shabby substitutes one would
desperately try to find. But try & answer clearly, dear love.

I love you & I want you & I can't separate the two.

    God bless you,

      Graham

TO EVELYN WAUGH

5 St. James's Street | London S.W.1 | August 20 [1951]

Dear Evelyn,

I'm typing because I know how impossible it is for you to read my
writing. Your letter came as an absolute Godsend. Several times in
the last day or two I've nearly wired you. Things have been battering
one about like nobody's business. Will you mind a semi-corpse who
will try to work and will succeed in drinking? About dates I expect
to go with Thomas Gilby to Austria tomorrow or the next day until
the end of the month. Could you after that put up with me for ten
days? Say frankly if that's too long. What I'd do would be to come
down in the afternoon of Sep. 3 and leave on Sep. 14. Catherine
might be able to come down for Sep. 11, 12, and 13. If you'd rather I
came later than Sep. 3 tell me.

I had an awful time the other day with Cyril Connolly[33] who said
he'd been commissioned to do a profile of you for *Time*. He kept on
saying what a friend he was of yours till I asked God to save me from
such friends.

I like your Knox story. Could we meet? I hardly know him.[34]

33 Cyril Connolly (1903–74), author of *Enemies of Promise* (1938) and editor of
Horizon, was a friend of Waugh and often the butt of his jokes. It is possible that the
character of Waterbury, a literary journalist who appears in the last pages of *The End
of the Affair*, is modelled on him.

34 Monsignor Ronald Knox (1888–1952) had been chaplain at Oxford and was
known for an anarchic wit. He was a translator, detective writer and Catholic apolo-
gist. Waugh esteemed him and wrote his official biography. Greene found him precious
and boring.

I wish I could tell you how glad I was of your letter.

    Affectionately,

      Graham

P.S. Shall I bring a dinner jacket?

TO EVELYN WAUGH

5 St. James's Street | London S.W. 1 | [22 August 1951]

Dear Evelyn,

Your account doesn't in the least deter me. I like boiled or scrambled eggs and I can do without hot water indefinitely. I can't drive as I haven't a licence, but Catherine can and if she manages to come we could drive and see Knox. I will bring a supply of postage stamps, but as a matter of fact I like walking. Nor do I even mind a dinner jacket. The Swiss Family Robinson life is exactly what Catherine and I used to live when the world allowed us to. So that won't put her off. We are both drinkers rather than eaters.

I'm off tomorrow to Salzburg with Thomas Gilby until about the end of the month. I don't know my address, but Mrs Young at No. 6 will by the time you get this. I'll wire you on my return about trains. I'll get a taxi in Dursley. I look forward so much to this visit. Perhaps I'll be able to work again.

    Affectionately,

      Graham

TO EVELYN WAUGH

5 St. James's Street | London S. W. 1 | Sep. 29 [1951]

Dear Evelyn,

Maybe we've been wrong about Perry Mason. I've just been reading an early one – perhaps the first. *The Case of the Velvet Claws.* He kisses Della right on the lips & when his client notices the lipstick, he says 'Let it stay.' His client's a girl & at one time he pushes her roughly onto a bed. He also makes her faint by third degree & slaps her with a wet towel to bring her round.[35]

Or maybe that was the turning point. Though in the next case he drinks some red wine with a little French bread.

The Korda trip has begun & then I go to Indo-China to do an article for *Life*. Hanoi about Oct. 21.

Love,

Graham

TO ELISABETH DENNYS (NÉE GREENE)

M. Y. Elsewhere[36] | Oct. 11 [1951]. nearly Athens.

Dear Elisabeth,

I was so disappointed not to get to Istanbul & do tell Rodney how sorry I am for all the trouble I must have given him with my cables. We got as far as Skiathos, an island in the Sporades, & there north-east gales stopped us for three days – there was no sign of a change (one Greek ship was lost off Lemnos), so we had to break south again. I'd have so loved seeing you all – & the ship's company might have amused you – Korda, Laurence Olivier, Vivien Leigh & Margot Fonteyn. I've lost my heart to the last, though she's only sporadically pretty, but she likes cheap cafés & retsina wine & is a companion spirit. 'Larry' I like very much, & Vivien – who was terribly actressy for the first three days – is now great fun. We play endless canasta & eat enormous meals & drink a lot.

[. . .]

---

35 Greene remained convinced of the eroticism of these stories. In *The Honorary Consul* (1973), 27, he writes: 'Perry Mason's secretary Della was the first woman to arouse Plarr's sexual appetite.'

36 Korda's yacht. 'For the first time – and I think the last – I drew a principal character from the life. Dreuther, the business tycoon in *Loser Takes All*, is undeniably Alexander Korda, and the story remains important to me because it is soaked in memories of Alex . . .' (*Ways of Escape*, 167) Bertram, the central character, and his wife Cary wait in Monte Carlo for the arrival of Dreuther in *The Seagull*, a boat modelled on *The Elsewhere*.

TO FRANCIS GREENE

c/o British Consulate, | Hanoi, | Indo-China, | Nov. 16 [1951]

Dear Francis,

I wonder how you are & how things are going. I'd love to get a letter in this hot & rather dull town.

I haven't had a very interesting time so far. The most amusing has been 24 hours with a bombing squadron. I went on two missions. The first was to bomb & machine gun round a town which the Communists had captured. My aircraft went alone. Tiny little cockpit, just room for the pilot (who was also gunner & bomber), the navigator & me – an hour's flight each way & then three quarters of an hour over the objective. We did 14 dives. It was most uncomfortable, coming rapidly & steeply down from 9000 to 3000 feet. You were pressed forward in your seat & then as you zoomed up again your stomach was pressed in. I began to get used to it after about four dives.

Coming back we went down to about 200 feet & shot up a sampan on the Red River.

Next day I went in a formation of three aircraft & we tried to cut a road – I don't think we managed it. This was quite comfortable horizontal bombing at 5000 feet. The leader made two circuits, dropping our trial bomb each time. Then we closed up nearly wing to wing, & sent down three sticks of bombs. It was interesting to watch them drift diagonally below one.

My next trip I want to see the naval boats at work among the islands.

It's very very hot & difficult to write letters, so would you let Mummy see this one if you think she'd be interested in bombing!

Lots of love,

Daddy.

Greene returned to these scenes in The Quiet American *(142), adding details he spared his son: 'Down we went again, away from the gnarled and fissured forest towards the river, flattening out over the neglected ricefields, aimed like a bullet at one small sampan on the yellow stream. The cannon gave a single burst of tracer, and the sampan blew apart in a shower of sparks; we didn't even wait to see our victims struggling to survive, but climbed and made for home. I thought again as I had thought when I saw the dead child at Phat Diem, "I hate war." There had been something so shocking in our sudden fortuitous choice of a prey – we had just happened to be passing, one burst only was required, there was no one to return our fire, we were gone again, adding our little quota to the world's dead.'*[37]

TO CATHERINE WALSTON

[near Macau] | Christmas Day [1951], 10.10 a.m.
[. . .]

There is so much to tell you. I thought I was going to disappear for four weeks with a Foreign Legion officer, but it didn't come off. However I got where no newspaper man was allowed, into surrounded Phat-Diem – the rebels all round within 600 yards, flames, far too many corpses for my taste, & constant mortar fire. One slept in one's clothes in a half wrecked mess with a revolver on the pillow. The bodies, especially those of a poor woman & her small boy who had got in the way of war, drove me to confession. So I went to the Cathedral where the whole town had taken refuge & found my friend, the Belgian priest, quietly reading his breviary at the top of the bell tower. But the French quite absurdly believed him to be a Viet Minh spy, so my friendship with him made me suspect again, & they edged me out. Also I'd gate crashed into a small operation with the parachutists, (on land!) & they weren't happy about that.

[. . .]

Greene wrote in The Quiet American *(45): 'Twenty yards beyond the farm buildings, in a narrow ditch, we came on what we sought: a woman and a small boy. They were very clearly dead: a small neat clot of blood on the woman's forehead, and the child might have been sleeping. He was about six years old and he lay like an embryo in the womb with his little bony knees drawn up. "Mal chance," the lieutenant said.'*

37 See also 'A Memory of Indochina', *Listener* (15 September 1955), reprinted in *Reflections* 187–8.

TO FRANCIS GREENE

5 St. James's Street | London S.W. 1 | Wed. [n.d.]

Dear Francis,

I wish I had seen more of you the other day – I was too busy with 'affairs of no earthly importance' & now it looks as if I shall see nothing of you this holidays. Remember to send me your blue card for next term, & let's see also – if you feel like it – whether we can plan a small trip together somewhere queer or interesting on the Continent in the summer holidays. I mean two males together! Have you any views?

In any case a lot of love,

G.

TO DENIS CANNAN

The playwright Denis Cannan (b. 1919) collaborated with Pierre Bost (1901–75) on the dramatic version of The Power and the Glory. *Greene revised the script before it was staged at the Phoenix in London in 1956 with Paul Scofield (b. 1922) in the lead, directed by Peter Brook (b. 1925).*

24th April 1952

Dear Denis,

I have now got as far as the last scene in your new draft and have made very few corrections indeed. About the last scene, however, I feel extremely doubtful. The trouble is that this scene should really contain the whole dialectic of the play and should be some kind of a debate between the Lieutenant and the Priest with the two points of view clearly but not bluntly expressed. In the book one used the device of the two men first being held up by rain before going back to the city, and afterwards of the night's lodging on the way to the city. This was a reasonable setting for what is really a dialogue between two mystics. What I feel about your draft is that the dialectic has become a little too plain [?] and explanatory, and therefore not very dramatic, while at the same time most of the space is given to dramatic incident. The drama of this last scene surely from the moment of the Lieutenant's arrival must be only the drama of dialectic. I would very much like if it is possible for us to meet and discuss this in detail with the book as well as the play in front of us.

You may have been puzzled by some of my small changes in the dialogue in the scenes I gave back to you. In several cases I went back to the dialogue of the book because I felt that in order to make the meaning clear to the audience you had sometimes lost the dramatic mystical flash. A religious idea is often a paradoxical one and I don't feel that one wants to smooth out the paradox too much. I remember an awful Jesuit once giving a long sermon in Farm Street to explain away the statement about there being more rejoicing in heaven over two sinners being penitent than over ninety-nine just men. By the time the priest had finished he had reduced the paradox to a very reasonable statement by the headmaster of a public school. I don't of course mean that in any place you went as far as this!

    Yours,

      Graham

TO LADY DIANA COOPER

In July 1952 the politician, diplomat and author Duff Cooper (1890–1954) was created 1st Viscount Norwich. His wife was the memoirist and socialite Lady Diana Cooper (née Manners) (1892–1986). She did not use the title Viscountess Norwich since she thought it rhymed with porridge. After his retirement as Ambassador to France in 1947, they lived in Chantilly (ODNB). Graham and Lady Diana Cooper were both close friends of Evelyn Waugh.

        5 St. James's Street | London S.W. 1 | June 6 [1952]

My dear Diana,

    First a thousand congratulations to both of you. Seldom does one feel so wholeheartedly pleased. So many of my generation have been

Duff fans ever since his magnificent Munich resignation.[38] What a
lot of plaudits there will be too from the dead as well as from the
living.

I got back from Italy yesterday & found your card. Well, it is true
in a way, but really the villa is in Anacapri &, for foreign
consumption, it is owned by the Societa Anacapri! I would have
liked to let it – except to you & Duff to whom I'd love to lend it any
time. It's very quiet & simple with one maid who cooks rather
inadequately, shops & launders – perhaps adequately. There are 2
little houses in a small but pretty garden under the slope of Monte
Solario. One house has one double bedded room, one single bedded
room & bathroom. The other has one double bedded room, one
single, living room, dining room, bathroom & kitchen. It will be
empty from now until nearly the end of July.

Catherine will want me to send her love. We hope to be in Paris
for a couple of days at the end of July with her sister, to coincide
with Harold Acton whom we all love dearly. Can we come & see
you if you are at Chantilly?

Devotedly,
    Graham

TO HERBERT GREENE

5 St. James's Street | London S.W. 1 | 17th June 1952

Dear Herbert,

I am sending a lot of pants and vests etc. which I weeded out in
going through my drawers. I don't suppose any of it fits you but I am
sending it on the chance. The queer stains on some are due to a
broken bottle of Chinese wine!

Love
    Graham

38 Duff Cooper had resigned as First Lord of the Admiralty to protest against the
Munich Agreement with Hitler, 3 October 1938 (ODNB).

TO MARY PRITCHETT

At the suggestion of Robert McClintock, an American diplomat in
Brussels, Graham attempted to execute a piece of mischief against the
American government. He revealed in a Time *magazine cover-story (29*
October 1951) that he had been a member of the Communist Party for six
weeks while a student at Oxford. This put him, as a religious and literary
celebrity, on the wrong side of the McCarran Act, which attempted to
keep Communists and other subversives out of the United States. In early
1952 he was denied the usual twelve-month visa and given instead a three-
month one. In the United States he spoke to various newspapers about the
danger of McCarthyism. By September he was planning a return visit and
new provocations.[39]

12th September 1952

Dear Mary,

Partly for the fun of baiting your authorities and partly because
I think it would be useful from the point of view of the play, I
wish to apply for a six-month's visa for the U.S.A. with the
ostensible object of visiting you sometime between January and
April 1953. The authorities demand evidence that necessary funds
for my maintenance are available while I am in the United States.
This should take the form of a bank letter. Is it possible for you to
procure a bank letter which would guarantee that I was supported
whilst there? Naturally I can when the time approaches obtain
the necessary travellers' cheques from the Bank of England,
but I want if possible to put the American authorities in the
position of either granting me or refusing me a visa before the
Elections in November so that I can stir up a little trouble if
necessary! I cannot ask the Bank of England for the funds until
the actual date of my journey is known and therefore I think your
bank letter would be necessary to apply now. I do think from the
point of view of the future it is necessary to clarify the situation
with the U.S. authorities, and I hope you will help me. If it is

39 See NS 2: 437–46.

possible for you to arrange some bank letter by return of post I should be grateful.

> Affectionately,
>
> Graham

Shortly after this letter he wrote a public protest against the treatment of Charlie Chaplin, who had lived for forty years in the United States. The Attorney General ordered that Chaplin be detained when he tried to re-enter the United States because of speeches he had given in support of Russia when it was invaded by Germany. Doubtless as a result of the publicity, Graham was himself granted a visa for only eight weeks.[40]

TO EVELYN WAUGH

Villa Rosaio, | Anacapri, | October 2 [1952]

Dear Evelyn,

I've just finished Men At Arms, which I took with me to read in the relative peace of this place. I do congratulate you. You're completely crazy when you think it not up to the mark – I think it may well be the beginning of your best book. Apthorpe outplays Crouchback in this part, but C. is such a good starter that one looks forward impatiently to the horses coming round again. As for style you've never, except in isolated passages written better, or, I believe, as well. This all sounds pompous & dogmatic, when all I want to say is thank you for a book I admire & love – & I'm no indiscriminate fan. There are two books of yours I don't like!

It rains most of the time & Catherine is ill with bronchitis & I am 48 today – & I don't like any of these inescapable facts. But I love Men at Arms.

> Affectionately,
>
> Graham

40 See *Yours etc.*, 24–7, and NS 2: 445.

TO FRANÇOIS MAURIAC (TELEGRAM)

7 November 1952

A thousand congratulations. The Nobel jury have honoured themselves.[41]

Graham Greene

TO SIR ALEXANDER KORDA

The director George More O'Ferrall (1907–82) faced difficulty bringing the film of The Heart of the Matter *to a close since a suicide by Scobie, played by Trevor Howard (1913–88), would not pass the censors. The script they came up with had Scobie in a parked car ready to shoot himself, when he sees a boy being beaten; he intervenes, only to be shot. His last words are, 'Going on trek. Tell Missus, God made it all right for her.' Graham felt this missed the point of the book.*[42]

17th December 1952

Dear Alex,

I had a very friendly and nice drink the other evening with Trevor Howard and George More O'Ferrall. The subject of the end of the film cropped up again and O'Ferrall was very ready that I should speak to you about it, although he doesn't quite agree with my ideas. So I am making a last appeal to you!

The success of the book was partly based on the controversial aspect of the suicide and the priest's reaction to it. Not only did his attitude come as a surprise to people but it also provided the book with something in the nature of a happy ending. In the last script I was shown the words of the priest were transposed so that they came in before the suicide and therefore had no particular force or

41 In the presentation speech, Mauriac was praised 'for the deep spiritual insight and the artistic intensity with which you have in your novels penetrated the drama of human life'.

42 See Falk, 102–3, and Adamson, 81.

validity. It was merely excusing a man for a deed he had not yet committed.

I know there is censorship trouble with the suicide, but I suggested to Dalrymple[43] and to George More O'Ferrall at our last meeting before O'Ferrall went to West Africa the following means for evading the censorship difficulty and also getting over the full force of the book's subject.

In an earlier scene of the script the doctor had referred to suicide and to the matter of angina pectoris which is undetectable in a postmortem. At the end Scobie can bear things no longer and decides to shoot himself. At the same time he wants to cover up the real motives of his suicide so as to give as little pain as possible. Having loaded his revolver therefore he sits down and writes a letter to his wife saying that the pain he has been secretly suffering proves to be angina and that he cannot face it any longer and asks her forgiveness for his cowardice. At this point he is called out on police duty to deal with Yusef and leaves his revolver behind. As in the present script he is shot, deliberately courting a bullet. Practically the only increase in length is that now his wife or Wilson finds the letter so that she knows he died with the full intention of suicide in his mind. We then have the priest's commentary and rebuke of Mrs. Scobie as at the end of the book. Not only does the film become more controversial and more interesting, but the ending is far less melancholy than if we simply leave it at the death. O'Ferrall objects that this would mean probably at least one more day's shooting if not two, but I would urge you to consider the wisdom of shooting it in this way even if on later consideration you cut it to the form it now takes.

Affectionately,
Graham

No change was made. Howard's performance is generally regarded as brilliant, but the film inevitably suffers by comparison with the book.

43 Ian Dalrymple (1903–89), a producer and scriptwriter.

TO DAVID JONES

The Welsh poet and painter David Jones (1895–1974) is best known for his long poem The Anathemata *(1952), which depicts British history and mythology in terms of the Eucharist. He is regarded by some as a major, if neglected, figure.*

                    5 St. James's Street, | London S.W.1 | 23rd February 1953

Dear David,

Being a little drunk, as perhaps one should always be when reading a really new poem, please accept my homage for *Anathemata*. For weeks now it has been lying on a chair while I waited for the courage to read it. As one grows older one grows more and more disinclined to read a really new thing. One is afraid one won't understand, which hurts one's pride, (and there are great passages in your poem which I don't understand), and one is afraid of being unduly disturbed. But please will you accept from me lying on a sofa, suffering from a bad cold, a sense of excitement which makes one mark passage after passage on page after page. I have read the ending with immense excitement, but I haven't yet got to it. This is a silly letter, but anyway I shall be right out of the country before you receive it.

   Yours,
   Graham

TO R. K. NARAYAN

                    C.6 Albany, | London, W.1. | 19th November 1953

My dear Narayan,

I've been so glad to see first-class reviews of your novels recently in *The New Yorker* and other American papers. It's taken a long time for your genius to come through to the public, but at last it really seems to be making itself felt.

I am going out again East this winter to Indo-China and it occurs to me that it might be possible for me to stop off at Calcutta on the way home and come down to Madras if there was a chance of seeing you. You know how much I should love to do that and how much I should love to see 'Malgudi', but I trust you as an old friend to tell me if it would be in any way difficult or awkward. Alas! politics thrust their way into every human relationship. Please let me trust you to tell me of any difficulty, just as you could trust me if you were living in London and rang up for a drink to say that I couldn't manage it as I had somebody there with whom I wished to be alone!

[. . .]

TO LADY DIANA COOPER

Duff Cooper died of a haemorrhage 1 January 1954.

Hotel Majestic, | Saigon, | Jan. 2 [1954]

Dear Diana,

Please forgive an incoherent note. I have just read of Duff's death. Why does one think selfishly of the loss to his friends & only after a second of time of his loss to you – the real loser? Perhaps because one knows you have him always, & we only had him for a few years. Do please *not* answer this silly inadequate note. When I get to Hanoi tomorrow, I'll arrange for a Mass – you won't mind, will you? It's the expression – the only one we have – of the sense that life isn't over.

Affectionately,
Graham Greene

TO EVELYN WAUGH

In a letter to the Cardinal Archbishop of Westminster, Cardinal Giuseppe Pizzardo (1877–1970), Secretary of the Holy Office, advised that The Power and the Glory *had been 'denounced to this Sacred Congregation'. He noted indulgently that Greene was a convert, but observed that in the novel man's wretchedness carries the day and that the work is injurious to the*

priesthood. 'The novel moreover portrays a state of affairs so paradoxical, so
extraordinary and so erroneous as to disconcert unenlightened persons, who
form the majority of the readers.' Greene was instructed not to permit fur-
ther editions or translations. In a letter of 2 May 1954, Waugh declared
himself ready to join a demonstration on Greene's behalf but assumed he
would not want anything of the kind.

C.6 Albany, | London, W. 1. | May 3 [1954]

Dear Evelyn,

I was very touched by your generous letter & so complete an offer
of help. I think however that for the time being – for the sake of the
Church even, whom the Inquisitor may well injure in the eyes of
non-Catholics – slowness & caution are required, two qualities I
detest. Of course I doubt if the situation would ever have got this far
without our Cardinal Kipps.[44]

My answers go off this week, & if the Inquisitor proceeds to
publication, then I will be very grateful for your support.

I can't tell you how glad I was to get your letter. What a good
friend you are!

Affectionately,
Graham

TO MONSIGNOR GIOVANNI BATTISTA MONTINI
(LATER POPE PAUL VI)

With the advice of his friend Archbishop David Mathew (1902–75), a
papal diplomat, Greene composed a 'casuistical' response and sent a copy to
the cultured Montini (1897–1978), a future pope, who as Pro-Secretary of
State was the most influential of Pope Pius XII's advisers.[45]

44 A facetious reference to Cardinal Bernard Griffin, Archbishop of Westminster, who
in his Pastoral Letter for Advent 1953 had condemned *The Power and the Glory* and
other works by Catholic writers for offending against the sixth commandment. (See
David Leon Higdon, 'A Textual History of Graham Greene's *The Power and the Glory*',
Studies in Bibliography 33 [1980], 234.)
45 See *Ways of Escape*, 67.

[6 May 1954]

Your Excellency will be aware of my profound and filial devotion to the person of the Sovereign Pontiff. I am therefore the more deeply disturbed by the difficulty which has arisen in regard to the judgment of the Holy Office in respect of my book, *The Power and the Glory*. I feel it is only right that I should send to Your Excellency a copy of a letter I have today addressed to His Eminence, Cardinal Pizzardo.

It is not that I ask Your Excellency for any comment on this matter which is so intimately painful to myself. I feel however that I should keep you informed on this question.

I remain with respect

Your Excellency's devoted servant in Christ,

Graham Greene

Montini had already been involved – on 1 October 1953 he had written to Cardinal Pizzardo defending the book.[46]

TO CARDINAL PIZZARDO

[c. 6 May 1954]

It is not without hesitation that I presume to address Your Eminence: but, in the present delicate situation, I have grounds, it seems to me, to present you with an account of the facts.

On 9 April, during an audience which His Eminence Cardinal Griffin, Archbishop of Westminster, granted me, he handed me the copy of a letter which Your Eminence had written to him on 16 November. The delay in the communication of this document is due to my absence from London: I was in Indochina, where I was doing

---

46 See Peter Godman, 'Graham Greene's Vatican Dossier', *The Atlantic Monthly* (July–August 2001), 84–9. While a draft of Greene's letter to Pizzardo is in the Boston College archive, it underwent revisions before being sent to Rome. I have not been able to obtain a copy of that version so rely on Godman's published transcription.

my utmost to make world opinion, for which my articles are intended, understand the difficulties faced by the heroic Catholics of Indochina confronted with the Communist menace.

I wish to emphasize that, throughout my life as a Catholic, I have never ceased to feel deep sentiments of personal attachment to the Vicar of Christ, fostered in particular by admiration for the wisdom with which the Holy Father has constantly guided God's Church. I have always been vividly impressed by the high spirituality which characterizes the Government of Pius XII. Your Eminence knows that I had the honour of a private audience during the holy year 1950. I shall retain my impression of it until my last breath. Your Eminence will therefore understand how distraught I am to learn that my book *The Power and the Glory* has been the object of criticism from the Holy Office. The aim of the book was to oppose the power of the sacraments and the indestructibility of the Church on the one hand with, on the other, the merely temporal power of an essentially Communist state.

May I remind Your Eminence that this book was written in 1938–39 before the menace which I myself witnessed in Mexico spread to Western Europe? I beg Your Eminence, in conclusion, to consider the fact that the book was published 14 years ago and, consequently, the rights have passed from my hands into those of publishers in different countries. In addition, the translations to which Your Eminence's letter refers appeared for the most part several years ago and no new translation is envisaged.

I am sending His Eminence the Cardinal Archbishop of Westminster the names of the publishers concerned. They alone have the right to reprint.

I wish to assure Your Eminence of my profound respect for any communication emanating from the Sacred Congregation of the Index . . .

Your most humble and devoted servant
   Graham Greene

The Vatican quietly allowed the matter to drop.

Berkhamsted School, 1914. Graham sits at the centre of the front row. His father Charles Greene, who was headmaster, sits directly behind him.

Lady Ottoline Morrell was an early supporter of Graham Greene's work. In this photograph from 1930 she stands on the left. Beside her are Vivien Greene, holding a dog, Graham, and the critic and journalist Basil de Sélincourt.

'. . . think of us as moral lepers.' (p. 236) Edith Sitwell shrewdly spotted Graham Greene as a rising talent in the mid-1920s and remained a close friend for forty years.

Lighting up a stinker at 'Stinkers', Evelyn Waugh stands in front of his house, Piers Court in Stinchcombe, Gloucestershire.

Graham Greene as publisher with Eyre & Spottiswoode in 1947. Seated is the managing director Douglas Jerrold. Greene soon resigned after a row with the novelist Anthony Powell.

Graham uncorked. Note the miniature bottles in the background.
A similar collection figures in *Our Man in Havana*.

The Swedish actress Anita Björk, with whom Graham had a love affair in the late 1950s. Here she sits beside Gregory Peck in a still from *Night People* (1954).

Graham Greene and Jocelyn Rickards (front right) had a brief affair in c. 1953. Here they are with John Hayward and an unidentified friend at Battersea Funfair

Graham on a picnic in Switzerland with his grandsons Andrew and Jonathan Bourget.

'It makes one feel there's some point in writing books after all.' (p. 223) Graham helped his daughter Caroline to buy a ranch in Alberta, Canada. Here she stands with her horse Silence, the model for Seraphina in *Our Man in Havana*.

'I can stir up a little trouble if necessary!' (p. 198) Graham trying to slip over the American border from Canada, c. 1955.

'... a *horrible* photo of me and the Pope.' (p. 278) Graham Greene at the Vatican with Pope Paul VI in 1966.

'... he always carried a revolver in his pocket!' (p. 338) A poet and a member of General Omar Torrijos's security guard, Chuchu took Graham to see whatever he wanted in Panama, including the canal and a haunted house.

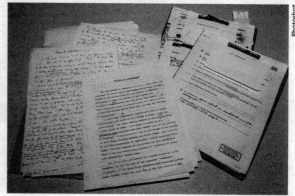

FBI file on Graham Greene offered for sale at Sotheby's. Oddly enough, the file contained almost nothing he had not made public himself.

'I have absolute trust in you ...' (p. 366) Graham and his niece Louise Dennys. She edited his last works and was his Canadian publisher.

'I doubt if the C.I.A. will enjoy having me around!' (p. 336) Graham's travels in Central America were guided by *Time* correspondent Bernard Diederich. Here they are sipping rum punch on the Panamanian island of Contadora.

'You have reached the point when all the little people become jealous.' (p. 317) Greene thought Dame Muriel Spark one of the few brilliant novelists of his time.

Hunting for bargains. Greene believed that if he had not been a novelist he might have been a bookseller.

The burial of Graham Greene in Corseaux, Switzerland, in 1991. In the background are, from left, his estranged wife Vivien Greene, daughter Caroline Bourget and companion Yvonne Cloetta.

TO R. K. NARAYAN

C.6 Albany, | London, W.1. | 19th July 1954

My dear Narayan,

I am about half-way through making small corrections in your book and hope to finish this week. The only title I thought of so far is 'Waiting For The Mahatma' but I don't think this will be a very popular title.[47]

I was fascinated by the portrait you have drawn of Gandhi and that period in India's history, the love story of Sriram and Bharati is charming, and the whole book will do you credit I am sure. I confess myself a little disappointed to find politics entering Malgudi if only because politics either date or become history, and I have always felt a kind of eternal quality in Malgudi.

Yours affectionately,
Graham

TO EVELYN WAUGH

C.6 Albany, | London, W. 1. | 17th August 1954

Dear Evelyn,

I always type my letters to you since the sad day when you couldn't read my signature! I do wish I had been able to come to the fête which from the accounts in the various papers I have read seems to have been great fun for the populace if not for you. Have I ever seen Rossetti's only nude or is it a new acquisition?

I am off tomorrow on the spur of the moment to Haiti to have ten days holiday there with Peter Brook and Natasha. Do you know them? I like them both, especially Natasha, very very much.

No, I don't think you should share my indignation about Colette's

---

47 Published under this title by Methuen in 1955.

funeral[48] as the indignation was really whipped up by an extremely good lunch, a lot of alcohol and some French friends who are dear to me. I wasn't really protesting against the lack of an official mass but only against the way in which the announcement was made, and surely if the relatives want it it's possible to have a few prayers said at a grave-side without involving the church officially. I have a strong impression that something of this kind was done for Conrad who had also lived the greater part of his life outside the Church but on consulting Aubry's *Life* there is no mention of death. Anyway I don't think that my letter has done any harm as it has made the Archbishop write a letter in reply explaining exactly the reasons which will now be understood by non-Catholics.

Yours ever,
Graham

TO CATHERINE WALSTON

Will you keep this letter in case I need it to refresh my mind?

El Rancho Hotel | Port-Au-Prince, Haiti |
Sunday, Aug. 30 [1954]

Dearest Cafryn,

I wonder if this will follow you to Ireland? Last night we were at a Voodoo ceremony until 3 in the morning. One reads about such things[49] but to see them is incredible & terrifying. The first two hours were spent in a kind of parody of Catholic rites – a choir of white-clothed girls jigging & singing & responding, holy banners – one marked St. Jacques, the portrait of a saint, the kissing of crosses & vestments, endless prayers from the Houngan or priest recited in a

48 The French novelist Colette (Sidonie-Gabrielle Colette) died on 3 August 1954. The Cardinal-Archbishop of Paris refused to allow a Catholic funeral because she was divorced. She was given a state funeral attended by thousands, including Graham Greene, who also wrote a public letter of protest, which Waugh thought 'fatuous and impertinent'. See Amory, 429, and *Yours etc.*, 40–2.
49 Graham had begun reading about Haiti at least twenty-five years earlier. See p. 34.

Catholic way, the 'fairy' motions of a server, a kind of Asperges with a jug of water – the horrible really began when the Agape began – a procession carrying fuel & food & dishes & a live hen. The man carrying the hen swung it like a censer, & then would dash to this & that member of the congregation & plaster his face & body with the live bird (you can imagine how I felt about that!). More interminable prayers & then the bird's feet were cracked off like cheese biscuits & the attendant put the live bird's head in his mouth & bit it off – the body of course went on flapping while he squeezed the blood out of the trunk (a small black boy a little older than James watched it all solemnly).

The next startling thing was the initiations after the feast – the initiate wrapped in a sheet like a mummy was carried in on a man's back to the cooking pit flames (extraordinary shadows), & one hand & one foot were drawn out of the cerements & held for as much as a quarter of a minute in the flames while the drummers drummed & the women shrieked their sacred songs. Last of all & quite suddenly (the intervals were filled with a kind of bacchanalian dancing) came 'possession'. They believe that the various gods of war & love etc. start winging their way from Africa when the ceremony starts. They had taken about five hours to cross the Atlantic – & on this occasion it was the God of War. A man started staggering & falling & twisting. People held him up, twisted a scarlet cloth round his middle & put a rum bottle & a panga[50] in his hand. Then he began to whirl around the room, falling & tripping & brandishing the axe; we had to leap up on benches to get out of the way. Sometimes he pressed the blunt end of the panga in someone's stomach, & that man or woman knelt on the ground before him & kissed it, while he sprayed them with rum out of his mouth. Two of those got possessed too, but were quieted by the priest. I was glad when the man gave a shriek & collapsed, & the God had started back to Africa & the party was over.[51]

I like Truman Capote very much. A most queer figure not only in

---

50 A heavy, broad-bladed knife like a machete.

51 Greene drew on these images in 'The Nightmare Republic' (*Sunday Telegraph*, 22 September 1963; *Reflections*, 221–8) and in *The Comedians* (179–83).

the technical sense. He is telling my fortune & it gives one the creeps because one half believes – there's an odd psychic quality about him. The fortune depresses me for obvious reasons even though it might be called a happy one. I'll put it on record.

Between September 1956 & February 1957 I marry a girl 20 years younger who is either Canadian, American, New Zealand or Australian. I am very much in love & she is 5 months gone with a daughter who proves herself a genius by the time she is 18. I see little of my other children. My whole life changes. We have a house abroad by the sea where we are very happy & about the same time I finish (or start) my best book. When I am in the seventies (I remain sexually active till the end!) we spend the summer in the mountains & the winters in the desert. We are very happy, but before we marry I go (in about 2 years time) through a great crisis with myself. Well, there it is – watch out. I'm oddly depressed by it. I want to be with you till death.

[. . .]

TO NATASHA AND PETER BROOK

6th September 1954

Dear Natasha, and Peter,

Oh what a time! When I arrived at Puerto Rico I was formally asked by the Immigration Officer whether I had ever been a member of the Communist Party, and so of course I said 'Yes, for about four weeks at the age of 19.' That put him back quite a bit, and I had to wait reading my P. G. Wodehouse for about two hours until his boss could deal with the situation. I was then told that they couldn't let me proceed and that I would have to be returned to Haiti. I remained extremely equable as I had no engagement in London and thoroughly enjoyed myself. I told them they would get a bit of publicity, but I don't think they believed it.

After a bit of to-ing and fro-ing they decided that I could spend the night at a hotel and not in the Airport if I gave my word of honour not to leave. Earlier before the boss took control I had remarked that perhaps they would let me go as far as the bar for the night and sleep with the drink and was told 'For you this is a dry Airport.' I was then put in charge of two plain clothes Cuban officers and driven to a hotel. I gave them drinks in the bar at the expense of the Government or of P. A. A.[52] I don't know which, and this softened them up a bit and one of them said he would drive me around town if I liked. So back we got into the car and we went around town until two in the morning by which time one of the plain-clothes men was distinctly the worse for drink. The next morning they took me to the airport and a squabble ensued between the Immigration authorities and the airline as of course I hadn't got a Haitian Visa any longer. So I slipped quietly away and sent a cable to Reuters with the results that I expect you know. At last they put me on a plane and at Port-au-Prince I had another quarrel with a disagreeable American manager of Delta, who refused to allow me to go on in the plane for Havana. He told me that he had fixed things with the Haitian authorities that I was to stay two or three days and then he would [be] 'sending me' to Jamaica. I refused to be treated as a parcel and said that I would not go to Jamaica and after a long wrangle I got back into the plane and went on to Havana.[53]

Havana has been a fascinating city, quite the most vicious I have ever been in. I had hardly left my hotel door before I was offered cocaine, marijuana and various varieties of two girls and a boy, two boys and a girl, etc. I smoked my first marijuana cigarette and went to what I am sure exists nowhere else in the world, a public blue film exhibition with advertisements outside, seats in the stalls at $1.20 and a pornographic bookshop in the foyer. I was stuck there for two days before I could get a passage so I sampled most of the delights!

[. . .]

52 Pan American Airways.

53 For more about this episode, see *Ways of Escape*, 162–7, and *Reflections*, 303–5.

TO NATASHA BROOK

C.6 Albany | London, W.1 | 2nd December 1954

Dearest Natasha,

[. . .]

I loved Haiti and we did quite a number of things which we should have done and didn't, i.e. we went up to Le Perchoir,[54] though not for a meal, and to another village right at the top of the mountains with a view towards the D.R.[55] To the D.R. I did not go, nor did I want to. I think I told you on a postcard that we obeyed the Commander in the Marine Gardens this time and it was simply wonderful, being towed on rubber tyres[56] across the reefs and the fishes coming to take food out of one's hands. We also went and bathed on that beach which you and I spotted on the drive back from Cap Haitien and where we planned to go for a Sunday Lunch. We needn't have been dissuaded – there was plenty of shade! We borrowed masks and swam there too but got a severe surprise when a large octopus suddenly opened up with all its tentacles and flashed underneath us. In Havana we found much better blue films than I had and we tried something which was called cocaine but which I suspect was boracic powder. Anyway it had no effect except giving me a hangover next day.

I have decided not to go to the Far East this winter as to escape bankruptcy I must really finish a book. So I am going to Brighton instead. Perhaps you will visit me there. Do you ice skate? I don't. Anyway I still plan the Far East for the year after so we may yet find ourselves all together in Hong Kong or Macao.

Give my love to Peter and lots of it [to] yourself.

Graham

54 An evident typing error resulting from the use of a dictaphone. The original says 'Percheron', but Bernard Diederich advises that this must be Le Perchoir, a restaurant in Boutillier with a tremendous view of Port-au-Prince.
55 In the original 'Diard'. Diederich believes that this should be D. R., since from the top of the mountains there is a view of the Dominican Republic in the distance.
56 Graham must be referring to inner tubes as tyres would sink.

TO MARIA NEWALL

In 1953, Graham visited Kenya to report on the Mau Mau rebellion,
which, among other things, set long-trusted servants against their masters:
'Jeeves had sworn, however unwillingly, to kill Bertie Wooster . . .'[57]
Although Graham was always sympathetic to rebels, he was struck by the
cruelty of the Mau Mau and by the courage of some white settlers, especially
Maria Newall, a former decorator who had gone from England to Kenya in
1949 and operated, without the help of other Europeans, a farm in Nakuru
on the edge of a forest where the Mau Mau were active. In a development
typical of the conflict, she discovered that her very pious servant Stephen had
both taken the oath of the Mau Mau and served as a police informer. She
decided to keep him as there was little chance of her being able to trust
anyone more. Nonetheless, she warned him that if he broke the curfew she
would shoot him. Greene referred to her affectionately as 'Pistol Mary'.

C.6 Albany, | London, W.1. | 31st January 1955

Dear Maria,

I think you ought to know that your letter of the 23rd was neatly
slit open at the side of the envelope. Are your infuriated settlers
beginning to censor the mail or your Africans doing it? It seems
unlikely that it should have been cut open in England.

Forgive this typed letter but I am off to Indo-China next week
and am clearing up things in a great hurry. I hadn't meant to go East
this winter, but when *The Sunday Times* asked me to I couldn't resist
the temptation.

I so agree with everything you say. It is inconceivable that
anybody could wish to hang 5,000 people which was what it would
have amounted to. I do think that it should be publicised that there
were 82 cases of murder pending when an amnesty was given to the
Security Forces, but I won't say a thing about this unless you give me
permission. I would like to draw the attention of an M.P. to it. I
suppose though it is best to let bygones be bygones on both sides.

I hate the idea of your new boy Stephen, and the whole business

57 *Ways of Escape*, 145.

of your living up beside your farm instead of in your nice house, though I suppose there is no real difference in the danger.

I shall be back in England at the end of March and do go on occasionally writing and telling me how you are.

I had a slight hope that Operation Hammer[58] plus the offer of an amnesty might bring the thing temporarily to a close, but as far as one can judge from this end nothing much seems to have resulted.

It is silly to say do look after yourself, but one says it just the same.

Love,

Graham

Although no novel emerged from his time in Kenya, Greene did produce the short story 'Church Militant' (1956), set in Kikuyuland.

TO VIVIEN GREENE

Lucy Caroline eventually went to Canada to work on a ranch and married Jean Bourget. After the break-up of the marriage, she moved with her two sons to Switzerland, where she still lives.

19th May 1955

Dear Vivien,

I have come to the conclusion that the best plan as Lucy seems to be really firmly bent on British Columbia, is for me to arrange a reconnaissance visit this summer which I think I may be able to swing on the expenses of Graham Greene Productions if I can find a sufficient excuse. We would go together for a few weeks and visit some of the ranches out there and see if one can find a suitable one for her to do 6 months as a student. It doesn't seem really feasible to send her out into the blue to find one entirely on her own and I think this is a good solution. Then she would return home and I hope we would have fixed something for her departure in the spring for a trial period.

58 In January 1954, the King's African Rifles began Operation Hammer, which led in time to the capture of 5500 rebels and the deaths of twenty-four band leaders.

I am writing to the Agent General of British Columbia and the Agent General of Alberta to ask for their help in introduction to ranches but I have not let out the real motive as I want the journey on the surface to be connected with one's business.

Love
Graham

TO EVELYN WAUGH

C.6 Albany, | London, W. 1. | July 2 [1955]

Dear Evelyn,

I got back yesterday to find your novel.[59] I am so grateful & proud of my inscribed set, & I am always reluctant to begin a new book of yours & not have it any longer sitting there in mint condition waiting to give pleasure – like a love affair when one was young which hadn't yet begun.

While I was away I had to have a liver cure – injections of grape[60] (why not of Chambertin 29) & no spirits. Still a fortnight to go. But I finished – unsatisfactorily – a novel I've been doodling at for three years & a play.

Affectionately,
Graham

TO GILLIAN SUTRO (POSTCARD)

Gillian Sutro was a fashion journalist and the wife of the scriptwriter and producer John Sutro, who had been Graham's contemporary at Oxford.

---

59 *Officers and Gentlemen.*
60 Pioneered by the South African naturopath Johanna Brandt in the 1920s, the grape cure is supposed to remedy advanced cancers, loosen arthritic joints, detoxify the liver and promote weight loss. A small industry is based on it.

[Calgary, Alberta | 16 August 1955]

'I a stranger & afraid
In a world I never made.'
What am I doing here? I have an instinct to run screaming.
Love,
　G.

*The lines are from 'The laws of God, the laws of man' in A. E. Housman's
Last Poems (1922). Graham's sense of the strangeness of Calgary bore
fruit in 'Dear Dr. Falkenheim' (1963), a short story in which Father
Christmas gets caught in the blades of a helicopter.*

TO MURIEL SPARK

*A recent convert to Catholicism, Muriel Spark (1918–2006), later Dame
Muriel Spark, was seeking a publisher for her first novel* The Comforters,
which was eventually taken by Macmillan and published in 1957.

C.6 Albany, | London, W.1. | 2nd December 1955

Dear Mrs. Spark,

I am delighted to hear that you are better and I do hope that
Macmillan's will publish your book. Perhaps they are not quite the
publisher for anything weird and if you have trouble there don't
hesitate to ask advice on another publisher. At the end of a misspent
life one has quite a lot of experience.

I will certainly speak to anybody I can about the possibilities of a
part-time job, but I am going to be out of London until the end of
next week and again for Christmas. Perhaps early in the New Year
you would come and have a drink and I could find out exactly what
you had in mind, apart from reading. Don't hesitate to use my name
in approaching, say, Tom Burns of Burns Oates, or Jonathan Cape or
A. S. Frere of Heinemann's, in the meantime. Hamish Hamilton,
too, might be worth trying and again say that I suggested it.

Yours sincerely,
Graham Greene

Speaking at Greene's memorial service, Spark recalled how, when she was
young, ill and poor, he sent her £20 each month. With the cheque he would
often send a few bottles of red wine, 'which took the edge off cold charity'.[61]

TO CATHERINE WALSTON

C.6 Albany, | London, W.1. | In bed. | Wed. 3 p. m. [
7 March 1956]

Dearest Catherine,

I feel we are at a critical stage again: it seems to happen every
year, but perhaps each one becomes more serious & although we
haven't quarrelled, this one may be more serious than Rome. I feel
guilty because at least twice I've prevented & fought against the idea
of finishing, even though that may be better for you. The trouble it
seems to me is that we both want to simplify our lives (even your
feeling for walking in Ireland or Switzerland may be part of it) & yet
if you simplify you can only do it by excluding me (after all I'm a
kind of barnacle on your boat), & if I should simplify it would be by
excluding you (living abroad etc).

I've had three aquavits & some beer, so you must forgive a
muddled letter.

We have therefore to think a) whether we want to simplify
enough to separate – except as friends who meet occasionally
and b) whether it's possible to simplify & not lose each other and
c) of course whether we want to stay together because if we don't
there's no point in worrying about a) & b).

I do want you to feel that this letter has nothing – or only a
remote connexion – with one's view through the window last
night.[62] It has far more connexion with Rome, Jamaica 195–
whatever it was, & a division perhaps in my own mind that we
would have talked about sooner or later.

61 Spark, 205.
62 Without indicating the source or date, Cash (228) refers to an episode when
Greene looking though a window spotted Catherine kissing Evelyn Shuckburgh, who
was then an assistent under-secretary of state in the Foreign Office.

Call it a neurosis if you like, but I have the desire to be of use to someone, & in the last nine months particularly I have felt of little use & possibly of real harm to you. You have no responsibility to me, & I have none to you – so that one needs to feel one is not being a clog & a bore & all the rest. The simple thing that we probably both desire is to need & to be needed. I've fought too hard to make you stay – which was purely selfish. You might have been happier now if you'd had your wish in Rome.

I don't think you want or I want holidays at the Ritz, The Grand, luxury holidays here or there, but we began simply in Achill & now think in terms of Hong Kong or Tahiti. Soon we'll have to think in terms of a rocket to the moon. You are so right to go walking in Ireland, or both of us to go walking in Switzerland. We don't want luxury holidays – we want to simplify, but can we? You have against you family, social life, politics; I have against me social life & business. It's easier for me to say, O hell, I'm going to go away & cut it all out than it is for you. Partly because I've already cut out, in 1948, most of the first difficulty – with Lucy in Canada & Francis nearly grown up, & my mother not having long to live, I can soon cut out the rest. But of course it's not only a problem of elimination – in a way it's the opposite, of being of use to someone other than oneself. You (mistakenly) probably consider yourself of no use to me – I'm not talking of sex which will be dead in a few years anyway for me: I (probably mistakenly) feel I am no use to you. We both (perhaps mistakenly too) may feel we can be of use to other people – a draw not only to pride but to any charity that one has left.

Anyway these are the problems – very muddled after three aquavit & another to come soon (it's a new experience getting drunk in bed). Let's think over them in quiet – you in Ireland & me on the Continent & say nothing until we are both back. Then we can 'try' to decide what to do.

Very much love

Graham

TO JOHN GORDON (DRAFT)

Writing for the Sunday Times, *Greene named as one of the three books of the year for* 1955 *Vladimir Nabokov's* Lolita, *and so brought down on himself the thunder of John Gordon* (1890–1974), *the editor-in-chief of the* Sunday Express. *Greene's method of dealing with John Gordon was to set up a mock society in his honour, with himself as President and John Sutro as Chairman. This letter was drafted by Greene; John Sutro was to 'pep it up' and send it on.*

[8th May 1956]

Dear Mr. Gordon,

The President and Chairman of the John Gordon Society are delighted that you will consent to meet the members. They quite understand that you would prefer not to speak on 'The Necessity of Censorship', and are ready to accept your suggestion as the subject of the lecture of 'Pornography.' They regret however that it is not possible to make this occasion a debate as at the first general meeting of the Society it was decided to found a series of lectures under the title of The John Gordon Lectures for which this should be the first. However the Chairman has no doubt that Mr. Greene will be ready to speak in any discussion that follows. However it is unlikely that Mr. Greene would undertake to defend pornography, and the discussion would be more likely to proceed on the lines of what exactly pornography was, about which there is obviously some disagreement between you and the President.

You will understand that the John Gordon Society is a private Society and it is impossible to provide a list of members to someone who is not himself a member. Any of your friends are at liberty to apply for membership, the subscription is only 10/- a year, and their names will be submitted to the Committee at its next Meeting. We propose with your consent to invite members of the Press to attend the Lecture, and of course we would be delighted if you would bring with you one or two personal friends. As each member will be allowed to bring a guest, and space is limited we are afraid we cannot find space for more than two or three of your friends.

Would you perhaps let us have suggestions for the date and time of the Meeting? We would prefer an evening after-dinner Meeting and it is impossible for the officers of the Society to be all present before July.

Yours sincerely,
[John Sutro]

Gordon comes across in all this as a booby, the harrumphing advocate of censorship, but he was in fact one of the grand characters of British journalism. As a junior reporter, he took carrier pigeons to football games to ensure that the results were reported quickly to his office. From 1928 to 1952, he was the editor of the Sunday Express, *where he introduced the first crossword puzzles and features on 'What the Stars Foretell' in a modern British newspaper. He and his astrologer had been prosecuted as rogues, vagabonds and fortune tellers, but escaped conviction when it was shown that their situation was not quite covered by the Vagrancy Act (ODNB). He certainly had enough of a sense of humour to play along with Greene and Sutro.*

TO MICHAEL MEYER

Michael Meyer (1921–2000) was one of Graham's closest friends. A prolific author, he is best known as the translator and biographer of Ibsen and Strindberg. Graham looms large in his Not Prince Hamlet: Literary and Theatrical Memoirs *(1989).*

C.6 Albany, | London W. 1. | 3rd August 1956

My dear Michael,

So many thanks for your subscription to The John Gordon Society. You missed a very amusing and turbulent meeting last week. As a result of John Gordon's invitation to violence in his columns we had the Horseshoe packed to overflowing with people standing all down the stairs and only about a quarter of those present in the hall were members of the Society and their guests. However John Gordon had miscalculated and found that his public were against him. If it hadn't been for Randolph Churchill overdoing his attacks on Gordon all the sympathy would have been against Gordon. Anyway it was all great fun and didn't in fact reach the point of razor blades or fists.

I am surprised to hear that you are still a grass widower!

Affectionately,

Graham

TO JOHN SUTRO

C.6 Albany, | London, W. 1 [Aug? 1956?]

Dear John,

What on earth makes you think that I'd do anything free for the United Nations when I refuse 100,000 dollars to do one of my own much worthier stories![63] I am replying to Adlai Stevenson's phony cable: 'Regret unable help as I consider United Nations combined with American materialism chief threat to world peace.'

Love to you both,

Graham

Who is Lillian?[64] What are you up to now?

TO CATHERINE WALSTON

From 1955, Graham was engaged in a serious relationship with the Swedish actress Anita Björk (b.1923), whose husband the novelist and poet Stig Dagerman (1923–1954) had been thought the great hope of Swedish literature before his suicide in 1954.

---

63 Adlai Stevenson (1900–65), twice the Democratic nominee for president, seems to have wanted Greene to write a filmscript about the UN.

64 The Sutros were friends of the actress Lillian Gish.

C.6 Albany, | London, W.1. [early December 1956]

Dear dear Catherine,

I've just got your note about Jamaica – one of the dearest you've ever written to me, and now I've got to write to you. I've been postponing too long, hoping that things would somehow settle. I love you so much & no one has ever been or can ever be what you've been to me. Nine years are more packed with memory than the rest of life.

This is what has happened. Last November on the way to Poland I fell a little in love with a girl (of 33) & she with me. She was the widow of a young author I admired very much who committed suicide. I didn't mean to or want to – I certainly wasn't looking for it. Then she came to London for 24 hours – nothing had happened in Stockholm except the agreement that nothing should happen, but we slept together once in London & I agreed to see her after Christmas. That's why I went to Stockholm – I hoped to work it out of my system & I thought I had, but I suppose then the gossip started, the result of her belonging to the theatre in her own country. I think all would have been all right, but the same day in September or whenever it was that you told me Harry didn't want you to go to Paris as we'd planned, she rang up, she'd got a holiday & wanted to be with me. So I went to Portugal instead of Paris.

Darling, don't think I didn't want to go to Jamaica – I did & for as long as possible & my meanness on the last night was because it was over.

[. . .]

TO MARION GREENE

Greene-Park Ranch | Christmas Day [1956?]

Dearest Mumma,

There's so much to tell you that it must wait till I come back. Lucy, [illeg.] in blue jeans, met my train & drove me to the ranch. It's a most lovely spot – hills & valley & the Rockies at the end of the vista. If it wasn't for the snow one could walk for hours up hill & down dale without leaving the ranch. No other house in view anywhere. Lucy has turned a little cabin only 23 feet long into a charming bedroom & sitting room, with very nice furniture gathered piece by piece in Calgary, good pictures, a big bookcase made by herself with moveable shelves – very civilized & sophisticated, but the coyotes howl outside & the horses press against the walls at night for warmth – 'I'll huff & I'll puff & I'll blow your house down.'

The weather two days after I arrived turned lovely. 38° & sun & the snow vanishing. We drove 13 miles to Midnight Mass yesterday & tonight drive an hour & a half for Christmas dinner with her friends the Jennings's.

Lucy seems very well & blissfully happy. Adores her new horse Silence.[65] I like the partners, Geoff & Pearl,[66] a nice simple couple very fond of each other. It's a strange feeling looking round at the country, hill & valley & stream, & knowing that Lucy is the owner. It makes one feel there's some point in writing books after all.

[. . .]

Caroline Bourget notes: 'In the letter Graham writes with poetic licence. The horses were in the barn or corral at night. Coyotes did come down and howl in Winter. The Ranch was in a lovely setting with an historic spring where Indians camped in the past. Now, I'm afraid houses have been built all round and there is a paved road through instead of a gravel track.'[67]

---

65 Parts of *Our Man in Havana* were written at the ranch. Milly Wormold's horse Seraphina is certainly modelled on Silence, and the novel contains various private jokes between Graham and Caroline (as an adult, she has preferred to use her middle name); nonetheless, this letter and others confirm that Graham was proud of his daughter's venture in ranching.

66 As partners in the ranch, Caroline provided the land, and Geoff and Pearl Parker provided the livestock and equipment.

67 E-mail to RG, 7 February 2006.

TO EVELYN WAUGH

IF YOU CAN'T READ THIS RETURN TO Mrs YOUNG FOR
TYPED COPY!

C.6 Albany, | London, W.1. | Aug. 7 [1957]

Dear Evelyn,

I only got back on the night of the 5th from Martinique (a
strange island populated by French royalists) & found *Pinfold*.
Yesterday I read it – with enormous pleasure & some horror. It's a
wonderful book – I'm not sure that I don't like it the best of all you
have written.[68]

I am off to Russia with my son on the 14th – a last holiday before
he's called up. Assuming that I don't stay on as Burgess's new
assistant & advisor on Westminster diplomatic activity,[69] do let's see
each other.

Affectionately,
Graham.

---

68 Later, Graham settled in the view that *Brideshead Revisited* was Waugh's best novel.
He continued to admire *The Ordeal of Gilbert Pinfold*, remarking on it as Waugh's self-
examination: 'But in this strange book he has left out all his fine qualities: physical
courage, private generosity, loyalty to friends. *Pinfold*, I think, shows him technically
almost at his most perfect. How well he faces the problem of linking passages between
the scenes. There is almost a complete absence of the beastly adverb – far more dam-
aging to a writer than an adjective.' (*Ways of Escape*, 200)

69 Guy Burgess (1911–63) was a member of the Cambridge spy ring. In the late
1930s he joined the BBC as a talks producer and was mainly responsible for 'The
Week in Westminster'. In 1938, he was recruited to British intelligence and, after
Dunkirk, secured Kim Philby's entry to MI6. In 1951 he and Donald Maclean
defected. In Moscow, he worked for the Foreign Language Publishing House and
drank himself to death. (ODNB)

TO GILLIAN SUTRO

Greene-Park Ranch, | Box 123 Cochrane | Alberta. |
December 18 [1957]

Dearest Gillian,

How very sweet of you to write such a long letter. I'm feeling a bit
better now – more than a fortnight practically without drink
probably helps. I've done 21,000 words – but the quality isn't as good
as the quantity. I couldn't write your sort of book in that time. Don't
be scared about my meeting with Laffont. It's off until the spring!

You may be right about Catherine, but I have a feeling that as
she's a far better Catholic than I am – a remarkable one really –
providence has had a hand in the game & released her for a rather
better sort of life than she could lead with me. So to give up Anita
now would not only be a bit painful perhaps on both sides, but
wouldn't help. What you say about Stockholm is true – but it would
be worse to take her away from her own place & force her to give up
the theatre – even though she may think she wants to. One doesn't
want to start a relationship by imposing a sacrifice in the way of
career & friends. I'm much more a free agent, & can work anywhere,
& find reasons for mobility.

I'd love to have a dinner with Evelyn. I'm devoted to him & long
to see the ear trumpet.[70] As I've had only one card & one telegram
from Stockholm (she's back on a film) I don't know whether our
date for December 31 still stands. If it does I'll be home on the 5th
or 6th – otherwise earlier.

Lots of love to you both.

Graham

---

70 At this time Waugh was using an ear-trumpet to confound bores.

TO HERBERT GREENE

In the late 1950s and early 60s, Herbert conducted a very odd feud with Hugh. Repeatedly, Herbert complained about programming decisions Hugh had made as director of news and current affairs at the BBC, embarrassing him in front of the Director General, Sir Ian Jacob, who was grooming him as his successor.

10th February 1958

Dear Herbert,

I have just heard from Hugh that you are continuing to send these long absurd telegrams to the B. B. C., now directed towards the Director General. If any further telegrams of this kind are sent I shall assume that you no longer are in financial need of my allowance and will stop it forthwith, nor can you expect any presents financial or otherwise. You are making yourself a nuisance and holding yourself up to public ridicule. Can I have your assurance that this will stop otherwise I shall take the measures I mention.

Yours,
    Graham

Herbert was not persuaded and in 1960 led a protest against the BBC's cancellation of the 9 O'clock News, which had featured the booming of the chimes of Big Ben (Daily Mail, 17 October 1960). He claimed that his complaint was not with Hugh but with the BBC.

TO FRANCIS GREENE

26th March 1958

Dear Francis,

I enclose a carbon of my letter to you; as you see it didn't really contain anything in particular. The dinner I referred to should have come off last night but didn't as the man was ill with 'flu. I do hope you hear soon from Aldermaston. By the way our governess sent her greetings to you in a letter! You would probably have preferred greetings from the beautiful daughter of our other friend.

I've practically decided against Eyre & Spottiswoode now[71] and that is really all the news except that I enjoyed myself at Charlie Chaplin's and his autobiography is really extraordinarily good, what he has written of it so far. I also had an amusing lunch with the Queen of Spain and the Infanta and now I have to dash off to lunch with the Polish Ambassador – my contacts seem a bit mixed.

I was in Stockholm for the week-end and it took me 13½ hours to get back as the plane tried twice to get into London, the first time going back to Amsterdam and the second time dropping me in Manchester where I had to catch a train. I certainly seem to have a hoodoo on planes.

Is there any chance of your having leave[72] and being in London in the near future? We'd try and think up another amusement though not as fantastic I'm afraid as the Sagan ballet. *The Quiet American* comes on at the end of this week and you might like to look in at *The Potting Shed* sometime without me – it goes on until May 3.

Much love,
Graham

DAME EDITH SITWELL

Dame Edith Sitwell (1887–1964) was a fervent supporter of Graham Greene from his days in Oxford. In this letter he refers to her best-known work Façade, *a sequence of apparent nonsense poems set to music by William Walton.*

71 Graham was invited to become chairman of Eyre & Spottiswoode, by now much enlarged, but he turned down the offer in order to devote his time to writing.
72 Francis was then doing his National Service.

C.6 Albany | London, W.1. | 29th April 1958

Dear Edith,

I am off to Brighton today and my plans are a little bit uncertain as I may have to go across to Sweden for a few days soon, and I know you will soon be off to Oxford for *Façade*. I shall know my plans for certain in the course of the next few days and I will write you again suggesting some dates for lunch or dinner, whichever suits you best.

All good wishes to *Façade* and I wish I was there to hear it. I missed the original London production but I used to be an ardent player of the record until the blitz destroyed it. Can't you make them re-record on a long-playing?

Yours affectionately,

Graham Greene

TO R. K. NARAYAN

C.6 Albany, | London, W.1. | 2nd June 1958

My dear Narayan,

I too was overjoyed to see the *Lit. Supp.* article on your work which I thought was admirably done.[73] I sent the article the other day to my Swedish publisher who is staying in my cottage in Anacapri as I am anxious to see you published in Sweden as a possible Nobel prizewinner one day!

I have been very hard at work finishing a rather hack job, an Entertainment called *Our Man in Havana*. I am getting too old to boil the pot. Now it's finished and I'm going off for a month or two to Sweden and hope to do some more interesting work when I have settled down.

I wish you'd come to London again.

Affectionately,

Graham

---

73 The *TLS* (9 May 1958) contained a long article surveying RKN's career, judging that he 'has few equals among modern novelists'.

TO MURIEL SPARK

C.6 Albany, | London, W.1. | 27 June 1958

Dear Mrs. Spark,

It was very kind of you indeed to send me an inscribed copy of your new book. I read it on a dreary train ride up to Liverpool yesterday and the journey passed like lightning. I found *Robinson* fascinating and delightfully organised and written. It is a book which will certainly stick in one's memory. I am delighted that you have produced so worthy a successor to *The Comforters*.

Yours sincerely,
Graham Greene

6

A BURNT-OUT CASE

TO HANSI LAMBERT

A friend of Graham's, Hansi Lambert was the widow of Baron Lambert of the Belgian branch of the Rothschild family. She maintained a glamorous salon in Brussels, inviting scientists, artists, writers and politicians. When Greene decided to research a novel in the Congo, he turned to her for advice.

C.6 Albany, | London, W.1. | 15th September 1958

Dear Hansi,

I wonder if you can help me. I want for the purposes of a book to spend some weeks in a hospital of the Schweitzer kind in West Africa or Central Africa (because already I have a certain knowledge of the background), but run by a religious Order. I have found a leper hospital in Bamaco,[1] but this is the Sahara which I don't know and it is run by nuns and I wouldn't feel at ease with them! It occurred to me that there might be some place in the Belgian Congo. If you could help me I would be very grateful.

Love,
Graham

[1] In Mali.

TO MICHEL LECHAT

Lambert directed Graham to Dr Michel Lechat (b. 1927), who in 1950 had attended a dinner she gave in honour of the novelist. In 1951, he bicycled about the central part of the Belgian Congo distributing sulphone, the first drug effective against leprosy. By 1958, accompanied by his wife, the artist Edith Dasnoy, he was operating a leprosy clinic at a religious mission at Yonda. In the years that followed, Lechat became one of the world's pre-eminent authorities on the disease.[2]

C.6 Albany, | London, W.1. | 7th October 1958

Dear Docteur Lechat,

It was extraordinarily kind of you to write to me in such detail about Yonda and the other leprosy stations. Your letter contains all the information that I need. In principle what I should like to do would be to come out and stay at Yonda for some weeks towards the end of January if you would allow me to. Then if I had not got all that I required at Yonda I might be able to visit one of the other stations by the Mission boat. I am just off to Cuba so I hope you will forgive this hurried note. I will write to you again when I return and ask your advice as to what clothes to bring. I have never visited the Belgian Congo but I have always wanted to and was at one time nearly stationed there during the war. It would be a delight, too, to renew my acquaintance with you.

Again a thousand thanks for writing so fully and interestingly,

Yours sincerely,

Graham Greene

P.S. I will try and see Dr. Franck when I am passing through New York on my way back from Cuba. He sounds at any rate an interesting character.[3]

2 See *International Journal of Leprosy* 70:1 (March 2002), 49–50.

3 At Lechat's suggestion, Graham met in New York with Frederick Franck, an oral surgeon and artist who had visited Yonda in 1958. He had worked with Albert Schweitzer and written a book about him, which Graham reviewed warmly (see *Collected Essays*, 276–8). Deeply impressed by his drawings, Graham also wrote an introduction to his *African Sketchbook* (1961).

TO HUGH DELARGY, M.P.

24th October 1958.

Dear Hugh,

I sent you the rather cryptic message by Mrs Young because I don't think it is realised at all in England the feeling created amongst the Cubans by the British government's sale of jet planes to Batista. As you know I was there for some weeks last November and the change in Cuba between then and now is very striking. Castro has really succeeded in cutting communications inside the island to a minimum and his bands now are not only in control of the greater part of Oriente (capital Santiago) which is the largest state and from which a third of the revenue derives, but he also has stepped up operations throughout the island. For instance last November it was possible for me to motor to Cienfuegos, the naval port, and Trinidad, but now no car driver would take one more than a very few miles outside Havana itself. The murder of hostages by the government is an almost daily occurrence – bodies are found flung out by the way-side, and the activities of Captain Ventura,[4] the chief torturer of the Batista police, have been stepped up. Considering that Batista never came to power by constitutional means but by a coup d'état makes it all the more unreasonable, one would think, for the British government to supply planes for the bombing of his own population.

Two years ago Castro landed with a few men of whom only 8 survived to get into the mountains with him.[5] Last November conservative estimates of his forces were between 800 and 1200. This November his supporters would claim 15,000 and the sceptical would put the figure round 7,000. As one Cuban said to me, there is hardly a family in Havana who has not lost one member at the hands of the Secret Police.

4 The notorious Esteban Ventura was often photographed in a white linen suit as he went about his duties in Havana's fifth precinct. He fled to Miami when Castro took power and died there in 2001 at the age of eighty-seven. In *Our Man in Havana*, Graham portrays a police torturer to whom he gives the name Captain Segura.

5 Castro actually landed on 2 December 1956 with eighty-two men in Oriente province; all but twelve were killed. That group reached the mountains and launched the revolution (information from Bernard Diederich).

Under the circumstances if only to prevent anti-British feeling on the part of the man who is likely to be the next ruler of Cuba, cannot you raise some opposition to the sale of these planes in the House of Commons?

This is rather a hurried note as I only got back from Havana two hours ago.

Yours ever,

Graham

Delargy, the Labour MP for Thurrock, working on a tip from Graham's friends in Cuba, later challenged the Minister of State for Foreign Affairs about a rumoured shipment of 100 tons of rockets from a British port. The Minister hotly denied the claim.[6]

TO MICHEL LECHAT

C.6 Albany, | London, W.1. | 27th October 1958

Dear Dr. Lechat,

I hope you will excuse me writing to you again in English, but my French is too poor to write in that language. I have just got back from Havana and New York where I was able to see Dr. Franck. A fascinating study! I went also to two exhibitions of his pictures which turned out – a little to my surprise – to be of extraordinary interest. He spoke very warmly of you and of your station and confirmed my desire to visit you. My problem is when? I am just starting a film script of my last book with Carol Reed and I don't expect to finish it until early in the New Year. I gather from Dr. Franck that the time I proposed – the end of January – is about the worst period possible because of the rains. On the other hand I would like to see something of 'the worst period'. Ideally speaking for my purpose I would like to come a little before the end of the rains and stay on into the beginning of the dry weather. In all perhaps about six weeks, if this would enable me to visit also

6 *The Times*, 16 December 1958; *Ways of Escape*, 190.

Imbonga and Wafanya by boat. Would such a long period be asking too much of your hospitality and the hospitality of the other Missions? I warn you that I shall be a rather nervous observer as disease is always a little upsetting to me perhaps because I have been too lucky in my own health until now.

[. . .]

The book that I have in mind has a leper mission purely as a background and I have no intention, I promise you, of producing a roman à clef. Indeed the reason why I want to visit all three missions if that be possible is to produce some kind of composite picture which will not be a portrait of any one of them. Nor am I looking for any dramatic material. The more normal and routine-like that I can make the background the more effective it would be for my purpose.

I hope you are having a successful stay in Tokyo and I hope very much that I shall be meeting you at Yonda in the fairly near future.

Yours very sincerely,

Graham Greene

TO SAMUEL MARSHAK

Samuel Marshak (1887–1964) was a prominent children's writer and poet in the Soviet Union. In this letter addressed to Marshak at the Union of Writers, where it would have been opened by the authorities and its contents noted, Greene offers discreet advice to the Soviet leadership on the treatment of Boris Pasternak (1890–1960), who had been awarded the Nobel Prize five days earlier. He initially accepted the prize but under extreme pressure declined it on 29 October. Expelled from the Union of Writers, he became the object of persecution, and his last two years were spent in misery.

28th October 1958

Dear Mr. Marshak,

[. . .]

Oh dear, oh dear. I wish that some of your authorities – and perhaps not the most important authorities – had not behaved so impetuously over the award of the Nobel Prize to Mr. Pasternak. I have just finished reading *Dr Zhivago* and with all its faults as a novel it seems to me undoubtedly the work of a great writer. What a wonderful propaganda it would have been to the West if the award of the Prize had been welcomed in Russia, for surely the Revolution now is strong enough to recognize such work even though some of the ideas may not be welcome. For me the ideas were very welcome because it seemed to me a constructive and not a destructive book. So many of the speeches could have been put into the mouth of Father Zosima or Alyosha. I still hope this will turn out that it was only the minor functionaries who have turned against the award and that the Russian Government will put them in their place and welcome it.

Yours sincerely,
Graham Greene

TO MICHAEL MEYER

Hotel Metropole, | Brighton, | Nov. 15 [1958?]

Dear Michael,

[. . .]

Sorry you weren't able to see Anita. It's more than a month since I heard from her. She doesn't even acknowledge house payments from Switzerland – or the play. A strange girl. I won't ring up in case a stranger is now installed & I don't feel I can write again. I wrote very warmly & was quite prepared to work out an arrangement, but I can't *pester* the girl. If you see or write her, you can indicate that she's still, unfortunately, in the blood stream & I'm quite unable to look for a successor. If only she'd taken a week's holiday in London, but I expect she's found a satisfactory successor. Anyway she's one of the nicest people I've ever met, & my only regret is losing her.

[. . .]

TO DAME EDITH SITWELL

Sitwell wrote Graham a wildly enthusiastic letter about Our Man in
Havana *on 15 November 1958. She added: 'Osbert and I are horrified to
hear of your proposed sojourn among the lepers. But we feel you ought to
have a little preliminary experience, think of us as moral lepers, and come
here on your way.'*

C.6 Albany, | London, W.1. | 20th November 1958

Dear Edith,

Thank you very much for your long and encouraging letter. I am
so glad you liked the book – this is rather more than I can say
myself. I hope the film will be better. I have been working very hard
on it the last three weeks with Carol Reed and now we are off to
Spain to do the second draft in a more suitable atmosphere than
Brighton.

I will try and get hold of the book you mention[7] as very much
against my will I have got to read all I can stomach about lepers
before I go to the Congo. I will really try hard to come to
Montegufoni[8] on my way. I shouldn't be at all surprised if Sabena
comes down in Rome on the way to Leopoldville.

I have only been in one slight earthquake in the West Indies, but
I felt sick for the rest of the day. I hope it didn't affect you and
Osbert like that.

My love to both of you,

Graham

7 Sitwell had encouraged John Lehmann to publish the British edition of *The Miracle
at Carville* (1952) in which Betty Martin describes her recovery from leprosy through
the new sulphone treatment that had made the disease curable. References to that
treatment occur throughout *A Burnt-Out Case*.
8 A palace near Florence owned by the memoirist Sir Osbert Sitwell (1892–1969).

TO MICHEL LECHAT

15th December 1958

Dear Dr. Lechat,

You must forgive this rain of letters. I am not yet certain of when I can come to Yonda as it depends partly on a clean bill of health (I suspect that I may have a little ulcer trouble, though I think this is simply psychosomatic due to very heavy work during the last year). It also depends on when the rehearsals of a new play are likely to begin. It seems to me useless to come to the Belgian Congo for less than 6 weeks and therefore I have to await the right opportunity. But still in principle I want to make it by mid-February. Directly I know for certain I will write as you suggest to Monseigneur Vermeiren.[9]

Please don't worry at all about my comfort. I can assure you that after three months years ago in Liberia and fifteen months during a war in Sierra Leone and nearly a year in all acting as a correspondent in Indo-China I don't expect, while gathering material, to live in grand hotels! My only fear is that I will be a trouble to you and your wife and I will certainly be a trouble if you take any special measures for my comfort. I want to see things as they are.

I want to reassure you about the subject of the novel. The real subject of the novel is a theological and psychological argument, which, for reasons I can't go into for fear of destroying this still nebulous idea, should take place against a background of an African hospital settlement. If I can visit other stations besides Yonda there will be no danger of my composite picture being attributed to any one station.

Thank you so much for your advice about clothes etc. and I do

9 Hilaire Marie Vermeiren (1889–1967), a Belgian-born missionary of the Sacred Heart of Jesus who was by this time the titular Bishop of Gibba and would soon become Archbishop of Coquilhatville. Belgian missionaries play a significant role in the novel.

hope that I shall be on your doorstep in February. All my best wishes
for Christmas to you and your family.

Yours very sincerely,
Graham Greene

TO MARION GREENE

Yonda, | Feb. 4. [1959] | 7.30 a.m.

Dearest Mumma,

Thank you so much for your letter. I had rather a chequered
journey here. Held up for five hours by fog in London airport. Then
taken across country by bus to Gatwick, & arrived in Brussels six
hours late *without* my luggage. However it came the next day, but my
plane *from* Brussels was 22 hours late in leaving! Then a good
journey.

Leopoldville a dull modern city of apartment houses 14 storeys
high – not like Africa at all. I was met by a Government Official &
had a very crowded day. I tried to get a siesta during the afternoon,
but I had no sooner lain down naked than there was a knock on the
door. I put a towel round my waist & opened it to a young woman
with so bad a stammer & so nervous that it took several minutes
before I could find out what she wanted. Her husband wanted me to
come to a meal but was afraid of asking me, so he'd sent his wife.[10] I
lay down again: more knocks: a journalist this time: lay down – more
knocks – two journalists & a camera.[11] I got to bed finally at 12 &
was woken at 3.30 a.m. to catch my plane here.

Met by Dr. Lechat, a very nice & amusing young man with quite
a pretty wife who paints. I have some meals with them & some with
the Fathers in whose house I have a room. I get up at 6.45 for
breakfast, then walk down a little way to the bank of the Congo –

---

10 In the novel, Rycker sends his wife with an invitation for Querry.

11 There had been riots in Leopoldville two months earlier. The journalists supposed
that Greene had come to write about the political unrest (*In Search of a Character*, 14).

good for meditation: at 10 it begins to be too hot for much & stays so till about 5 p.m. when I get another stroll.

[. . .]

The Governor here very amiable, but his wife – a sweet old thing – has written a novel & published it at her own expense & wants me to read it. My siesta interrupted yesterday by a schoolmaster who had also written a novel. I think if I found myself washed up on a desert island with one inhabitant he would have a novel he wanted published.

Lovely young women passing my window in gay cottons carrying babies on their hips – all lepers of course, but the babies are born clean & when they develop leprosy they can be cured (& permanently) in a year. The Brazilians separate the children at birth & 70% die as a result, but the Brazilians consider that more hygienic!

Lots of love,

G.

TO LUCY CAROLINE GREENE

Box 1028 Coquilhatville Belgian Congo | Feb. 10 [1959]

Dearest Carol – Carol again now you are back in Canada. This is just a note to say Welcome to your own home & how lovely it was to see you in England again. I do hope you enjoyed your visit as much as all of us did. I'll do my very best to see that Mummy and/or me come out this year – we miss you. Write to me when you get back & tell me how things are. You know that in any crisis I'd get on a plane & come to you, glad of the excuse!

Here I'm getting quite used to living in a little garden village of 800 people, everybody being a leper, except the babies. It's better to let them stay because when they catch it after two or three years they can be cured quite easily in a year or so & don't catch it again. Of course there are some rather hideous cases without fingers or toes, but I'm already used to that. I'm surrounded now by workmen chattering or singing & you would never know they were lepers – &

all contagious ones too. The non-contagious aren't allowed here. Except sometimes a husband or wife of a contagious.

Tomorrow I set sail on the Bishop's boat – like a tiny Mississippi paddle steamer – down a tributary of the Congo to two other leproseries – Ibonga & Wafanya, the first in the heart of the forest. No letters or anything for a fortnight then – ought to be back then a week more here [?], back to Leopoldville, down [?] the Congo to Brazzaville in French Equatorial Africa, then Douala for a few days in the Cameroons. Then Paris. Home about March 15.

Look after yourself, dearest Carol. I so want you to have a happy life.

All love from your wandering but loving
     Daddy

TO CATHERINE WALSTON

Written over ten days (February 15–24) travelling in the Congo, this letter is one of Greene's longest; it includes observations made more gravely in his Congo Journal. Many details of the journey reappear in A Burnt-Out Case. *His handwriting is here at its worst and the transcription is at several points tentative.*

Sunday. | Feb. 15 [1959] 8.00 a.m.
On the river Momboyo.

Darling Catherine, I won't be able to post this letter till I get back. Mass at 6 o'clock in the little deck house where there's a slide-in altar on top of a cupboard with a panel of the Nativity behind. Since then breakfast & writing up my journal – which is also notes for the book. Then washed my brush & comb in soda water as the river water is a thick brown. Missed the sight of

(boat stopped for a man in a canoe with a large fish for sale) a particularly big crocodile. The captain, Père Georges, who looks more like an officer of the Foreign Legion than a priest, tried to shoot it – his first instinct with any wild thing.

You would love this boat, a tiny version unpainted & decrepit of a

Mississippi paddle steamer & very pretty. Apart from the crew with some wives & sweethearts – one very attractive – there is nobody on board but Père Georges, the captain, myself & Père Henri, a convalescent taking the trip for a rest, tall & cadaverous & a joker.[12] I have taught them to play 421. I have the Bishop's cabin which is quite roomy with a nostalgic photo of a church covered in snow over the bed. Yesterday we looked in at Flantria where there is an Englishman (ex-Indian army) in charge of the Lever palm estate. His little girl excited by an English voice stood on her head & was sick. He looked awful but turned out nice & intelligent: his wife very pretty & intelligent too. I may spend a night on the way back.

Now we are on the way to Imbonga, where there is a leproserie some miles in the forest: very primitive: no doctor: looked after by Sisters. I probably shall spend two days there & then on for another 3 days to Wafanya for my third leproserie – then home to Yonda.

You would love this boat, the river is narrowing now to less than half a mile, unchanging forest. Very restful. I'm reading *The Roots of Heaven* (the film is on in London) about a man who makes war on the side of the elephants in this – more or less – part of the world. It would have been a very good book if Conrad had never existed, but the echoes are too strong.[13] I've also got: *David Copperfield*, Tawney's new book, *Business & Politics under James I*, Belloc's *The Cruise of the Nona*, & the first volume of a complete Casanova.

Last night I had one of my awful dreams about you: jealousy. You told me you had slept with Douglas Jay[14] & three other men since leaving home, & what right had I to be jealous anyway? In revenge I started making love to someone – not a bit like the person she was supposed to be – in bed in front of you. Then you became angry & the third person was amused & malicious. In the end we almost had

---

12 Michel Lechat remembers Père Henri (Rik Vanderslaghmolen) dancing with Graham on the 'barza' or veranda at the Fathers' house, and also riding the tricycle of Lechat's three-year-old son, and on another occasion struggling comically with Graham to enter his room.

13 This novel by Romain Gary was made into a film directed by John Huston and starring Trevor Howard.

14 Douglas Jay (1907–96), later Baron Jay, a prominent Labour politician. Greene had once worked with him at *The Times* and Walston had recently had contact with him.

made it up, & you said something profound about real love being always on the border of domesticity.

Dear, dear, dear.

We got to Imbonga before dark. Tomorrow a four mile walk each way to the leproserie. I'm in better condition than for a long time. If you were an X ray, you wouldn't recognise my liver – 2 glasses of whisky at most after sundown, otherwise soda water. And I brought 10 bottles of whisky on this trip!

Feb. 18. 7.30 a.m.

We had two nights at Imbonga, & the first morning I walked over ten miles – good way in this climate. A far more primitive leproserie than Yonda, & I was glad to see around it alone without any white people. A nice leper brought me back through the forest carrying a dish of eggs – bad lesions on the face & one eye nearly gone, but chattered cheerfully in French. In spite of modern drugs there are still some horrors: an old man cheerily waving goodbye with hands & feet, but without fingers or toes. Half one hut was in complete darkness – one could just make out an enamel pot. My black companion called & one heard movements. Presently an old woman crawled into the half light like a dog out of a kennel – no fingers or toes or eyes of course & she couldn't even raise her head.

It was odd last night 500 kilometres in the bush hearing of the disturbances at Brazzaville. One rather feels the end of European Africa is coming quickly. A lot of the people in Coquilhatville where there are about 300 whites are very nervous & sleep with guns beside them, & that's the chief danger, that somebody in a panic will make an incident. Some of them are far more nervous than the lonely settlers were at the time of Mau Mau in Kenya. The French, after Algérie & Indo-China, a little laugh at them.

We should get to Wafanya tomorrow, stay a few days & then start back towards Paris & you. The current will be with us then & we'll move quicker.

[. . .]

3 p.m.

It really is *too* hot. The river's narrowed from about a mile & a half to fifty yards & there's no air at all. And of course we eat roast meat & lots of boiled potatoes!

5 p.m.

Started rereading *David Copperfield*. My goodness, the first two chapters are perfect. I don't believe there's been anything better in the novel – & that includes Proust & Tolstoy. One dreads the moment of failure, for Dickens always sooner or later fails.

Fr. Georges, the captain, sits stringing a rosary, & Fr. Henri plays Patience. He & I will have our whisky in an hour & then I shall be beaten at 421. Rather like the University of Notre Dame at football, their daily communions seem to ensure their victory at dice.

Feb. 19

We've been going up the river now for a week & it's about enough! We should arrive at journey's end tonight – 8 days. A lot of tsetse flies, but few white people get sleeping sickness.

[. . .]

The frontier has been closed between Leopoldville & Brazzaville on the other side of the Congo River because of the troubles, & unless it's opened again by March 5 I'll have to find a different route to Douala or leave it out & come to Paris Sabena via Rome. But I'll telegraph any change & I'll aim to keep to March 13 unless I hear from you.

Père Georges has just shot a beautiful fishing eagle. He always shoots a sitting target & even then it's only winged, so one of the crew swims ashore & finishes it off with the branch of a tree.

[. . .]

Feb. 21

So encouraged because I got through all I wanted & gained a day. We started back (for Paris!) after lunch – but then we hit a snag in the river, damaged the steering. We are tied up in the forest & Lord knows whether the thing can be mended. Frustrating! Too hot to write. All the more frustrating because I had a most erotic dream of you last night when I fell asleep in the middle of a tropical storm.

2 hours later – they've managed to get the rudder on shore & now they have to build a fire to bend it. No chance of getting on tonight.

Feb. 22. Sunday

They got the rudder straightened & on again – with a great deal of singing – just by dark. I was never so hot in my life as yesterday & it was wonderful when dark came, in spite of the big 'vampire' bats creaking away over the forest. This morning off again at 6 – towards Paris & you. At Mass I noticed that one of the crew, who had a prayer book, had a holy picture, when he was reading – but when I looked closer it was Tom Mix or another in a big cowboy hat!

[. . .]

9.15 a.m. It's too dark to write. There's going to be one hell of a storm in a few minutes.

There was!

Oh, how tired one gets of trying to speak French. Mine gets worse & worse. All the same I'm very well. Only I have to take a sleeping pill every night because otherwise it's too hot to sleep. For a holiday I'd prefer Tahiti.

Even in this remote spot one has to sign books. A young planter came down to the shore with a cargo of oil & brought with him a copy of *The Power & the G*.! I don't a bit mind signing in these remote places. He had had his first holiday in Europe after 12 years in the Congo & had visited Capri.

Feb. 23

We are making good time & I should be back in Yonda the day after tomorrow: tomorrow Imbonga. The day after Flandria where I'm spending the night with the English plantation manager & getting a lift next day by car.

Bad night last night owing to a cold, but in the middle of the night I woke up & wrote down the last sentences of the new novel. I wonder if I'll ever get that far. (I've abandoned four in my time).

[. . .]

TO NORA GREENE

Upon hearing of his mother's death, Graham immediately wrote to his aged aunt who had been dependent on her and indirectly upon him.

Hotels St James & D'Albany | Paris | Monday
[21 September 1959] 10.30 p.m.

Dearest Aunt Nono,

I have just been speaking to Raymond on the phone. I feel that this is far worse for you than for Mumma's children because it creates a greater gap for you. Perhaps as a Catholic I am more 'cold-blooded' because I believe there is a future & that she is probably happier at this moment than any of us. I'm glad that death came gently.

What I want to say now is hard to phrase. I want to be of any help I can & I want you to feel that anything I was able to do for Mumma at the end, I would like to transfer to you. Please between us of the School House days, between the favourite aunt & the most difficult nephew, don't let's have any shyness. I've told Raymond to speak to you about this. All of us feel an enormous debt of gratitude to you in these years – particularly the years since her accident. I know how much she depended on you & worried about you, so you *must* let me help.

[. . .]

So much love,
    Graham

TO LUCY CAROLINE GREENE

C.6 Albany, | London, W.1., | 26th October 1959

Dearest Carol,

I've just come back from my walk with Francis. We did about sixty miles, but the Roman Wall where we started in Carlisle was the worst end and most of the time it was a case of trying to identify which farm track was the wall or which pile of stones. We were also in deadly fear most of the time of bulls and bullocks and tore our clothes over barbed wire. In the end it rained so hard that we gave up altogether about two miles from where the wall became really interesting. Wet through, with blistered feet and Francis having lost his brief case containing his pyjamas, washing things and my whiskey flask, we got into a hired taxi and drove to the nearest comfortable inn. However it was fun in a way.

   [. . .]

TO MARIE BICHE

Biche reported that a man named 'Peters or something similar' had approached a young woman at the Hotel Prince de Galles in Paris and offered her a job as secretary to his friend and partner Graham Greene. Thinking this too good to be true, the young woman, who worked in a bookshop, checked first with Greene's French publisher, Robert Laffont, and then with Biche, who confirmed that it had nothing to do with the real Graham Greene. Biche suggested she keep an appointment with the man and find out more, but she refused in the belief that she was being scouted by a 'traite des blanches' gang. Greene believed he had at least one impersonator and longed to catch up with him.[15]

                    C.6 Albany, | London, W.1. | 18th December 1959
PERSONAL

Dear Marie,

   What a wonderful story and how I wish I had been in Paris to go along with your attractive young Frenchwoman. It would have been a wonderful scene. I narrowly missed the other Graham Greene once in Rome as I think you know and of course there was the character who was blackmailed in Paris and the gentleman who was in prison in Assam. Presumably this is the same character. I can't help feeling when he starts trying to get hold of secretaries that the Police ought to be informed, but I leave that to you. It's a curious coincidence

15 See *Ways of Escape*, 231–7.

that when I was on his track in Rome he was staying at the George the Vth. It might be worth enquiring whether Mr. Peters is staying there. Anyway I think you ought to introduce me to the heroine one day in Paris!

[. . .]

TO GILLIAN SUTRO (POSTCARD)

[Reno, Nevada] | Feb 4 [1960]

Hope to be with you in less than a fortnight.

Love to both,

G

Won our night's lodging on the slot machines.

TO MICHEL LECHAT

C.6 Albany, | London, W.1. | 23rd March 1960

Dear Michel,

I wonder if you are back from Abyssinia yet. I am struggling towards the end of my novel which is now called *A Burnt Out Case* and I am wondering if I don't as I am inclined to do put it in the fire whether you would allow me to dedicate it to you as a poor return for all your kindness. I have another request to make. If I sent you a roneo'd copy of the book in due course with pages turned down wherever there was some reference to leprosy do you think you could glance at these and correct any mistakes. Don't hesitate to say that you are far too busy because I know what a burden this could be.

If you will allow me to dedicate the book to you I shall do it in a form of a letter which will enable me to point out that the book is in no way a picture of one leproserie and that none of the characters are those of living people.

My affectionate regards to you both,

Graham

TO LUCY CAROLINE GREENE

C.6 Albany, | London, W.1. |
April 18 [1960]

Dearest Carol,

Thank you so much for your delightful Easter card. I'm afraid I can't come to you because I came back from Moscow awfully ill & the same night was put on a stretcher & carted by ambulance to hospital. Pneumonia! I'm still there after two weeks, but I'm leaving tomorrow. *This is TOP SECRET. Mummy & Francis don't know as yet.* I didn't want people to worry & I felt too tired for visits, so I kept the affair secret. Only about four people got to know. I feel very silly because I'm never ill.

Of course it rather spoilt Moscow because I was feeling pretty poorly. However I went to the Bolshoi & to the Circus & to *The Quiet American* (very bad, & speeches & I had to make a speech from the stage). I've become a capitalist there & opened a bank account! Guy Burgess rang me up & came & had a drink my last night, & I had supper in a Russian home for the first time – quite quietly *en famille* which made me feel quite accepted. I kept going on vodka & everybody was very kind. I only did the public things (Bolshoi, Circus & Brit Embassy with the party).

I must stop now because I'm rather tired. Off to Italy on May 1 where I hope to feel better.

Lots of love,
    Daddy.

TO EVELYN WAUGH

C.6 Albany, | London, W. 1. | 22nd June 1960

Dear Evelyn,

Thank you so much for your letter and telegram. I think you are wise not to come to the sale but I can't resist it. I admit that I shall be a little piqued if Nancy Mitford's manuscript or a poem written out by Mr. Betjeman fetch more than mine![16]

I also looked for you in the theatre the other night. I waited till the lights went on watching approximately a spot where I had seen you last but couldn't see you at all. I then went out and searched the pavements but I expect you had already gone. I agree with you about the second act – I'd really enjoyed the first, but when it turned serious the play went all to pieces. I couldn't understand all this business about the heroic little man that the papers spoke of – he was only heroic after he had done his best to turn into a rhinoceros and failed.[17]

I long to come down and see you. I've got into an awful jam with commitments because I went to hospital for two weeks with a pneumonia that I caught in Moscow and somehow those two weeks have not yet been caught up. I've also got to go back into hospital next month for a check up but would some time in August be a possibility? I know you wouldn't mind if I brought a film script of *The Living Room* to work on.

Yours ever

Graham

TO AUBERON WAUGH

The twenty-year-old Auberon Waugh's (1939–2001) first novel The Foxglove Saga *appeared in the summer of* 1960.

C.6 Albany, | London, W.1. | [July 1960]

Dear Auberon,

I hope my long friendship with your Father allows me to call you that. I have been reading your book in hospital – by a strange coincidence, I was, like Father Thomas, about to be given a

16 Christie's was holding a large sale of pictures and manuscripts on behalf of the London Library (Amory, 545).

17 Ionesco's *Rhinoceros* with Laurence Olivier directed by Orson Welles at the Royal Court Theatre.

bronchoscopy although I did not have an enema and the result was more satisfactory. I got to that bit half an hour before my sedative, so at that stage I was reading the book with mixed feelings.

Now my feelings are not mixed at all. Only once this fifty years, I think, has there been a first night like this – and that too was in the Waugh family. It is superb, your book, in its fun and deceptive ease. Lady Foxglove and Stoat are magnificent; even the baby Tarquin.

You are going to suffer a lot of irritation when every hack reviewer compares you to Evelyn, but *The Foxglove Saga* has only one parent and stands magnificently alone.

A thousand congratulations.

Graham Greene

TO LUCY CAROLINE GREENE (LATER BOURGET)

C.6 Albany, | London, W.1 | Jan. 3 [1961]

Dearest Lucy – I mean Carol,

I was so overjoyed at your news & the fact that you sounded so happy – it has quite made my new year. I thought John [*sic*] sounded very nice too.

I long for details. What does he do in oil? Will you have to find a house or an apartment? How old is he – rumour says 35 which sounds ideal? A photograph please. Mummy will be asking you all the necessary questions about the wedding. Full name please for an announcement in *The Times*. Any ideas for wedding presents? Do I, oh horror, have to get myself tails & a top hat? (I *hope* it's not the Canadian custom) What are *you* wearing? Can you find what you want in Calgary? Are you going to get the bishop? I shall come out on my way to Japan so let me know dates as soon as possible. How sad that Granny isn't alive to hear – she'd have been so excited.

[. . .]

Lucy Caroline Greene married Jean Bourget on 29 April 1961. They divorced in 1970.

TO EVELYN WAUGH

Waugh was distressed by A Burnt-Out Case, *which, on the heels of the bleak short story 'A Visit to Morin', suggested that Greene was finished as a Catholic. The book also struck Waugh as technically deficient, repeating the main character's predicament three times, once 'painfully' in a fairy story. He regarded Deo Gratia's attempted escape as poorly handled and the death of Querry as 'absurdly melodramatic'. On the whole, he thought Greene's skills were 'fading'.[18] He refused to review it and apologised for his own Rycker-like behaviour in promoting Greene as a Catholic author.[19]*

C.6 Albany, | London, W.1 | 4th January 1961

Dear Evelyn,

A typewritten letter always looks so formal, but I know you can't read my handwriting. I'm very sorry to hear that you won't be reviewing *A Burnt-Out Case* (I'm afraid I committed the indiscretion of suggesting that you should do so to Father Caraman),[20] but I quite understand your feelings in the matter. I was all the more anxious that you should review the book because I realize it will cause a certain amount of hostility in the Catholic press and, although I expected severe criticism from you, I felt sure that it would be at least founded on genuine unemotional principles. Whatever Querry may have felt about his Catholic critics, I have certainly not felt at any time about you. I have always found our points of disagreement – as in the case of *The Heart of the Matter* – refreshing and enlightening and miles away from the suburbia of *The Catholic Herald* or *The Universe*. I do really assure you that never once have you behaved like Rycker!

18 Waugh, 779.

19 See *Ways of Escape*, 195–8, and Amory, 557–60.

20 Philip Caraman, S.J. (1911–98), priest and historian, was, for a time, a close friend of both Greene and Waugh. He specialised in literary conversions, having brought into the church, among others, Edith Sitwell. He was not in a position to have Waugh review the book since he had been removed as editor of *The Month* in 1959. Graham came to despise him apparently for meddling in his relationship with Walston. See June Rockett, *A Gentle Jesuit: Philip Caraman, S.J.* (2004).

With a writer of your genius and insight I certainly would not attempt to hide behind the time-old gag that an author can never be identified with his characters. Of course in some of Querry's reactions there are reactions of mine, just as in some of Fowler's reactions in *The Quiet American* there were reactions of mine. I suppose the points where an author is in agreement with his character lend what force or warmth there is to the expression. At the same time I think one can say that the parallel must not be drawn all down the line and not necessarily to the conclusion of the line. Fowler, I hope, was a more jealous man than I am, and Querry, I fear, was a better man than I am. I wanted to give expression to various states or moods of belief and unbelief. The doctor, whom I like best as a realized character, represents a settled and easy atheism; the Father Superior a settled and easy belief (I use 'easy' as a term of praise and not as a term of reproach); Father Thomas an unsettled form of belief and Querry an unsettled form of disbelief. One could probably dig a little of the author also out of the doctor and Father Thomas!

Anyway whatever the rights and wrongs of this book I do want you to believe that never for a moment have I felt other than pleasure or an interested dismay at your criticisms and never for a moment anything other than affection for yourself. I do hope that we can meet some time in the not too distant future. I heard rumours of your presence in London the other day which happened to coincide with one of my rare presences. I wish you would ring me up when you do come to town, but I know your hatred of the telephone.

Yours with deepest affection,
Graham

Waugh found this letter pretentious and flimsy. On 5 January 1961 he wrote that he was not so dotty as to think Rycker only a portrait of himself, but that it was a caricature of a number of Graham's Catholic admirers including himself who had failed to recognise the broad hints that he had now amplified into 'a plain repudiation' of faith. He said that he found the notion of an easy and settled atheism meaningless since an atheist denied the central purpose of his life – to love and serve God. Graham would not

*encounter hostility from Catholics so much as regrets for a 'Lost Leader':
'God forbid I should pry into the secrets of your soul. It is simply your public
performance which grieves me.'*[21]

TO EVELYN WAUGH

C.6 Albany, | London, W.1 | 6th January 1961

My dear Evelyn,

This is rapidly becoming a Claudel–Gide correspondence![22] I
think you have carried your identification in this novel much too
far. Must a Catholic be forbidden to paint the portrait of a lapsed
Catholic? Undoubtedly if there is any realism in the character it
must come from the author experiencing some of the same moods as
Querry but surely, not necessarily, with the same intensity; I hope
you don't attribute to me Querry's suicided mistress! I suppose, if one
chose to draw the character of an atom-scientist traitor, there would
be an element in one's own character which would make the
description of his motives plausible, but I'm sure that you wouldn't
accuse me, as Dame Rebecca West did both of us, of having a
treasonable inclination.[23] I suggest that if you read the book again
you will find in the dialogue between the doctor and Querry at the
end the suggestion that Querry's lack of faith was a very superficial
one – far more superficial than the doctor's atheism. If people are so
impetuous as to regard this book as a recantation of faith, I cannot
help it. Perhaps they will be surprised to see me at Mass.

21 Amory, 557–60.
22 Selections from the monumental 1899–1926 correspondence of Paul Claudel and
André Gide had been published in English in 1952. One of the main themes is
Claudel's urging of Gide to become a Catholic.
23 Evelyn Waugh pursued libel suits as a means of raising tax-free money and as a
hobby. In 1956, he had pounced on an expanded edition of West's *The Meaning of
Treason*, which had first been published in 1947. She had added a new chapter on
Burgess, Maclean and the Korean War, observing that not all those who undermined
affection for the classic virtues were on the left, but that Waugh, Greene and Mauriac
had done their part. The edition was suppressed as part of the settlement. See Bonnie
Kime Scott, ed., *Selected Letters of Rebecca West* (New Haven and London: Yale
University Press, 2000), 316–17.

What I have disliked in some Catholic criticism of my work, particularly some of the books which have been written about it in France, is the confusion between the functions of a novelist and the functions of a moral teacher or theologian. I prefer the statement of Newman. 'I say, from the nature of the case, if Literature is to be made a study of human nature, you cannot have a Christian Literature. It is a contradiction in terms to attempt a sinless Literature of sinful man. You may gather together something very great and high, something higher than any Literature ever was; and when you have done so, you will find that it is not Literature at all.'

I will match you quotations from Browning with Bishop Blougram:

> All we have gained then by our unbelief
> Is a life of doubt diversified by faith,
> For one of faith diversified by doubt:
> We called the chess board white – we call it black.

Ever affectionately,
Graham

The quotations from Newman and Browning take Greene back to his exchange with Bowen and Pritchett (see pp. 147–58). However, Waugh seems to have made a deep impression on Greene, who wondered if he had gone too far in the expression of doubt.

TO JOSEPH MACLEOD

A poet and playwright, Joseph Macleod (pseud. Adam Drinan) (1903–84) was Greene's closest friend at university. He qualified as a barrister, but pursued careers in radio, film and theatre. Eventually, he settled in Florence.

C.6 Albany, | London, W.1. | 6th February 1961

Dear Joseph,

I've just come back to England for a couple of nights from France and found your night letter telegram. How it brought back the days when you would leave in my room a new poem for the *Oxford Outlook*. Even your writing hasn't changed very much. I'm proud and flattered after all these years to receive another even though I have no paper to publish it in.

Here I am talking on without even congratulating you and your wife on your son, but you had buried the news quite a number of lines down in the poem.[24] Did I really make a ground plan for the future one day in the meadows?! I am glad I don't remember, for how awful it would be to find it fulfilled.

I have put the night letter poem into my copy of the *Ecliptic*[25] which has survived all these years and the blitz.

Affectionately,
Graham

TO CATHERINE WALSTON

C.6 Albany, | London, W.1 | Feb.13 [1961] | 9.30 p.m.

Dearest Catherine,

The last two days I've been missing you more than usual – perhaps it's just the melancholy that comes from working over & over again on that stale subject, *The Living Room*, to satisfy Rex Harrison, but I don't think so.[26] Apart from loving you as I've never loved another human being, it's not really apart from that, you are the only person I can talk to – except for gossip or work. Tonight I'm very aware of how disorganized I am – but I feel as though I've come to the end of a long rope with *A Burnt-Out Case* & that I'll probably never succeed in getting any *further* from the Church. It's like, when one was younger, taking a long walk in the country & at a certain tree or a certain gate or the top of one more hill one stopped & thought 'Now I must start returning home.' One probably went on another mile to another hill or another tree, but all the same . . .
   [. . .]

24 Iain Antony Macleod was born 21 January 1961.
25 A volume of Macleod's poetry published by Faber in 1930.
26 Rex Harrison (1908–90) was to have starred in this abortive film project.

TO THOMAS ROE

Thomas Roe (b.1917) was a solicitor and tax consultant with Mafia con-
nections, who swindled Greene, Noël Coward and Charlie Chaplin. On his
advice, Greene and Heinemann entered a deal with Penguin for paperback
rights in ten of his novels, bringing Greene an advance of £33,750. This
was to be paid into Roe's company, Co-Productions Roturman S.A., which
would, in turn, agree to pay Greene an annuity, then transfer both rights
and obligations to Verdant S.A., Greene's holding company in Switzerland.
The object of the transaction, which came to involve more and more off-
shore companies, was to allow Greene to escape at least surtax and perhaps
other tax obligations.[27] *When Roe's operation came to the attention of the*
authorities, Greene found himself in a dispute with the Inland Revenue,
which ended in his becoming a tax exile from 1 January 1966.

C.6 Albany, | London, W.1. | 28th September 1961

Dear Tom,

I have now spoken to Laurence Pollinger and to Frere and there
seems no reason at all against my selling to Roturman's my
paperback rights on the basis which we discussed, i.e., that I should
receive in effect a pension beginning at the age of 60 in October
1964 of £1,500 a year for 15 years payable to myself or in the event
of my death to my next of kin or anyone to whom I assigned the sum
in my will. Perhaps now you would make a contract with me on
those terms.

Yours ever,
Graham

TO FLANN O'BRIEN

Flann O'Brien was the most famous of the pseudonyms of Brian O'Nolan
(1911–66), an Irish novelist and journalist renowned for his prose, his wit
and his consumption of whiskey.

27 See West, esp. 190–201.

25th October 1961

Dear Mr. O'Brien

I was delighted this morning to receive a copy of *The Hard Life* from your publishers and to find it dedicated to me. I'm a proud man! *At Swim Two Birds*[28] has remained to my mind ever since it first appeared one of the best books of our century. But my God what a long time it has been waiting for the next.

Yours
    Graham Greene

TO EVELYN WAUGH

C.6 Albany, | London, W.I. | 27th October 1961

Dear Evelyn,

I wish I could come with you to British Guiana[29] – it would really be a most rewarding experience. Would we remain friends at the end of it? It would be worth the risk if I were free to go, but now I have promised to remain in Europe this winter.

Thank you so much for your extremely generous review in *The Spectator*. I expect you saw that Miss Macaulay wrote in her letter that we always praised each other in writing.[30] I think I once reviewed a book of yours – *Campion* – and that well, but I can't remember any other review, oh yes, *Knox*! and as for you you have never hesitated to speak your mind, thank God, which makes the notice in *The Spectator* the more gratifying.

[. . .]
Love,
    Graham

28 Published in 1939.
29 Waugh and his daughter Margaret were sailing in November.
30 See Rose Macaulay, *Letters to a Friend 1950–1952* (London: Collins, 1961), 180.

Waugh's review of In Search of a Character *(Spectator, 27 October 1961) is a masterly mingling of kindness and correction. He praises Greene lavishly and draws attention to how expertly he created the setting for* A Burnt-Out Case *but does not praise the novel otherwise. He suggests that there is no spiritual state analogous to that of a burnt-out case of leprosy. At the end, he expresses the hope that Greene has ended 'his long exploration of the fever-country on the unmapped borders of superstition and apostasy' and that he is about to enter a serene and creative maturity.*

TO ZOË RICHMOND

An important figure from his youth, Zoë Richmond was the wife of Kenneth Richmond, who had psychoanalysed Graham in 1921.

13th November 1961

Dear Zoë,

How nice after all these years to hear from you. Terrible to think that it must be more than 40 years ago that you sheltered an unhappy schoolboy in your house! My stay with you and Kenneth remains among my happiest memories.

I was very interested to hear of Nigel's book which I will try to get hold of. I don't remember him, but only your two daughters whom I used to look after on Sunday evenings when you and Kenneth went to a rather strange church near Lancaster Gate. Nigel must have been born just after I left you.

All good wishes
    Yours sincerely,
        Graham

TO RALPH WRIGHT, OSB

A poet and literary scholar, this Benedictine monk, trained at Ampleforth Abbey but transferred to the St Louis Abbey in Missouri, detected hope at the end of A Burnt-Out Case. *Greene's response seems a coda on his exchange with Evelyn Waugh.*

C.6 Albany, | London, W.1. | 30th January 1962

Dear Brother Ralph,

Thank you very much indeed for your long and perceptive letter.
You have disinterred my intention – you notice that Querry even
makes a joke at the last moment which is also a sign of returning
health. However the first hundred and seventy four pages were not
intended in any way as a debunking. One must remember that
technically the book is written through the eyes of Querry and it is
Querry's irritation with the facile Father Thomas and the bogus
Rycker. These two are intended as a contrast to the really selfless and
practical work of the fathers in the mission. I think you would find
that if these two characters had been left out the book would
suddenly have become extraordinarily sentimental. On the one side
Querry rediscovering a bit of life, on the other a group of noble
priests. To make even their nobility plausible one has to put in the
shadows. After all even the everyday life of a Catholic is haunted by
the corruptio optimi.[31]

I don't know why, but this book was the hardest I have found to
write and left me in a state of exhaustion which still rather
continues. Perhaps one is getting a little old to procure one's
material the hard way. On the chance that it might interest you
I am sending you a copy of the journal which I wrote in the
Congo.

Thank you again for your very kind letter.

    Yours sincerely,

      Graham Greene

TO EVELYN WAUGH

*The critic F. R. Leavis (1895–1978) and the novelist C. P. Snow, later
Lord Snow (1905–80), conducted a feud at Cambridge in early 1962 over
Snow's theories on the separation of scientific and literary cultures. Various*

---

31 The full phrase *corruptio optimi pessima* means the corruption of the best is the worst
of all.

writers signed a public protest on behalf of Snow. Waugh supposed that Cambridge's award of an honorary doctorate to Greene was intended to purge the shame of the whole episode.[32]

C.6 Albany, | London, W.1. | March 26 [1962]

Dear Evelyn,

Thank you so much for your letter which pleased me at least as much as the degree; I also never saw it in the papers, but it never occurs to me to look at university news. I'm rather daunted by the thought of the actual day – the walk in procession with someone called Lefty Lewis,[33] who is presumably a character out of Damon Runyon.

The Snow–Leavis affair is rather like the Algerian War – no sympathy for either side, but I was rather horrified by the way Snow had improved on the Alroy Kear[34] technique. Only an Organization Man could have produced those pages of supporters.

I hate being photographed, but Catherine says they are inevitable, so I'll send you one. You & your family are always on my mantelpiece.

Yours,
    Graham

TO HUGH GREENE

C.6 Albany, | London, W.1. | 21st May 1962

Dear Hugh,

Having reached my present advanced age I began to think about my eventual burial and not wishing to be interred in some vast Catholic affair in the north of London it occurred to me to reserve a

---

32 See Amory, 583.

33 A maniacally devoted scholar, Wilmarth Sheldon 'Lefty' Lewis (1895–1979) was the editor of the 48-volume Yale Edition of *Horace Walpole's Correspondence*.

34 Alroy Kear was the thrustingly ambitious literary biographer depicted in Somerset Maugham's *Cakes and Ale*.

patch in Harston[35] churchyard as there is no objection from the Catholic point of view or from the Church of England. I therefore communicated with Mr. de Candole the vicar to see whether I could buy a small portion near the other Greene's and it may amuse you to see the difficulties in the way. I enclose a copy of his letter to me.[36]

It seemed to me a little bit extreme to put him to all this trouble for myself alone and I asked Raymond whether he had any feeling on the matter and Raymond seems to be rather inclined to be buried himself also in Harston – that I suppose includes Eleanor! Have you any views on the point? If we are all going to be buried there it will need more than a few feet of the vicarage garden, but on the other hand I would have less scruples in pressing the vicar, although as you see he is perfectly cooperative. One just wants to have a vague idea of the number of corpses or rather corpse space required. I don't like the idea of a kerb, even a temporary kerb, and I thought of suggesting that a memorial stone could already be set up minus the dates, but I feel that Mr. de Candole would feel that that suggestion was frivolous. I told him that I would be quite prepared to pay all legal expenses.

Love,

Graham

It is not surprising that the author of A Burnt-Out Case *considered erecting his own tombstone, but he lived another three decades and was buried in Corseaux, Switzerland.*

TO A. S. FRERE,

Short of capital, William Heinemann Ltd was bought by Thomas Tilling Ltd, of which Frere's friend Lionel Fraser, himself a former chairman of

35 Graham's uncle Sir Graham Greene and other relatives had lived in Harston, Cambridgeshire.

36 Rev. Donald de Candole advised that several steps were necessary: a legal process to incorporate a small part of the vicarage grounds into the churchyard, removal of an old and unsafe acacia tree, extension of the boundary wall, consecration of the new ground, issuing of a faculty and erection of a kerb to define a family plot. Death in Cambridgeshire evidently required a certain amount of paperwork and landscaping.

Heinemann, was the head. After seventeen years as chairman, Frere was promoted to president and so made irrelevant to the daily operations of the firm.

C.6 Albany, | London, W.1. | 16th October, 1962

Dear Frere,

I want to write to you to explain why I have, after a great deal of thought, come to a decision to leave Heinemann's. You have been my publisher for more than thirty years and my greatest friend for close on twenty years, and I owe you an explanation.

From the time the war ended until recently I have always had the sense that I was published by a friend who took a personal interest in my work. It is to you I owe the publication of my uniform edition; with each new book we have together discussed the problems of production and publication, and it isn't easy, therefore, for me to abandon all the past and to go with future books into an unfamiliar region. I want you to know the circumstances which arose last year and determined my decision.

An arrangement was discussed with Heinemann's and accepted in principle one Sunday afternoon in I forget what month by your Chairman Lionel Fraser that I and Max Reinhardt[37] should join the board of William Heinemann as part of a general reorganization which would have included The Bodley Head. On the Monday I received from Lionel Fraser a copy of the announcement he proposed to give to the Press and I approved it. On Tuesday I was informed that my presence on the board was considered undesirable by other members of the Heinemann group. This personal rebuff could have been laughed easily off if I had not become more and more aware of the fact that I no longer had any personal contact

37 Max Reinhardt (1915–2002) acquired the Bodley Head in 1956–7 and controlled it for thirty years. In 1973, he joined forces with Chatto and Windus and Jonathan Cape. In 1987, the group was taken over by Random House and he established a new firm under his own name (ODNB), where he continued to be Graham's publisher. Reinhardt and his wife Joan (née MacDonald) were among Graham's and Yvonne Cloetta's closest friends. Judith Adamson's forthcoming biography of Reinhardt is expected to contain much detail on Graham's friendship with him and their business dealings.

with anyone in the firm and that – to speak frankly – I could no longer depend on you to look after my work; from my agent and the rumours circulating in the publishing world I had learned that you were no longer in a position to do so.

I was therefore left as an author without any personal contact with the firm of Heinemann, apart from Alan Hill on the educational side. I have never disguised from you my lack of confidence in your managing director (on two occasions during my period at Heinemann's I very nearly left the firm because of the type of publicity he thought my books required). I have not even met Mr. Charles Pick, although he telephoned me yesterday morning just at the moment when I am leaving for the continent to suggest a meeting.[38]

Please believe me when I say that I am quite certain no responsibility whatever attaches to you – I have become only too aware of how powerless in the whole matter is the President of the company. Under these circumstances what was I to do? Leave myself in the hands of strangers who showed so little interest in my books? I have had many years' experience of publishing and I am a director of The Bodley Head and a personal friend of Max Reinhardt, so the decision to be taken seemed an obvious one. In spite of that after thirty-two years with Heinemann it has taken me many months to make up my mind, but a publishing firm to an author means a personal contact, a personal sense of confidence reciprocated, and this I can no longer find in a company of whom the directors are nearly all unknown to me. I am sure you will understand my motives and I am sure too that it won't interfere with the very great personal friendship we have for each other.

Yours affectionately,
   Graham

After several more years of awkward relations with Heinemann, Graham finally moved to The Bodley Head, but the firms collaborated on the collected edition of his works. Frere himself left Heinemann and became an adviser to The Bodley Head (ODNB).

38 Alan J. W. Hill was a Director of the company and Charles Pick the Managing Director.

TO EVELYN WAUGH (POSTCARD)

Waugh looked on the Second Vatican Council with sadness, as it promised, in his view, to canonise uncertainty and vulgarity. In 'The Same Again, Please' (Spectator, 23 November 1962) he remarked that the supposed 'voice of the laity' was usually equated with the views of a minority demanding reform. As one of the middle rank of the Church, he dissociated himself from them and, in a veiled reference to Graham Greene, from the 'doubting, defiant, despairing souls who perform so conspicuously in contemporary fiction and drama'.

[25 November 1962]

Do accept from one who has written about 'the doubting defiant despairing' my *complete* agreement with your 'middle rank' statement & my intense admiration for the lucidity with which you have made it. It's always my hope & my trust that we are not very far apart.

Affectionately,

Graham

And if you can't read this, don't ask my secretary to translate.

TO RALPH WRIGHT, O.S.B.

During three days of silence after taking his final vows at Ampleforth Abbey, Ralph Wright wrote to Greene assuring him of his prayers. Although Greene refers to him as 'Father' Wright, he was not ordained until 1970.

C.6 Albany, | London, W.1. | Sep. 28 [1963]

Dear Father Wright,

I have only just got your letter as I have been abroad. It moved & touched me a great deal & you can feel assured that I am always grateful for your prayers.

The end of the middle period of life is always a difficult one. If I am in a crisis, it is a continuing one – I doubt if I shall escape it much before death. But I feel encouraged by your friendly signal.

I do wish you all the happiness possible in your vocation – which is perhaps the only true one. Ours are [*sic*] a substitute for the real thing.

Yours, with affection,

Graham Greene

TO AUBERON WAUGH

C.6 Albany | London W. 1. | 8th November 1963

My dear Auberon,

Thank you so very much for sending me an inscribed copy of *Path of Dalliance*. I shall take it away with me tomorrow to read in what I hope will be the sun of Antibes. I feel sure that while being amused by your book I shall forget all those thousands of political prisoners in Cuba about whom you told me!

Yours ever,

Graham

TO KURT VONNEGUT[39]

10th February 1964

Dear Mr. Vonnegut,

How pleasant indeed it is to get a letter from you out of the blue. I first read *Cat's Cradle* when it was published over here by Gollancz and then searched second-hand booksellers' catalogues to find two other of your books, *Player Piano* and *The Sirens of Titan*. I've enjoyed them all immensely. Since Ray Bradbury turned whimsy and poetic you are the only writer of this genre whom I can admire. I hope that one day our paths may cross physically.

Yours sincerely,

Graham Greene

39 Kurt Vonnegut, jr. (b. 1922), prominent American author and graphic artist.

TO EVELYN WAUGH

At the request of Lord Birkenhead, chairman of the Royal Society of Literature, Waugh asked Greene to reconsider his refusal to become one of its Companions. He said he had himself once turned down a CBE as not good enough and now felt ashamed: 'Pocket pride & accept "C.Lit."' [40]

130 Boulevard Malesherbes, | Paris 17. | May 14 [1964]

My dear Evelyn,

Your letter has only just caught up on me. Really you old school prefect come off it. I share the view of Mr. T.S. Eliot & *The Times* leader-writer on the subject of these companionships, & why should I swallow my views – & my words frequently expressed – because half a dozen quite respectable people, including two good writers, think otherwise? I am not snubbing the society, for I have been a fellow now for nearly 20 years – like most writers – as a means of contributing to their charitable funds. The Fellows were not consulted before these companionships were founded & it seems to me pretentious nonsense that 'a body of well-intentioned people' should assume the right to separate ten authors from the multitude for special honour. This is less pride than principle – & sanity – a wish not to look absurd. Many people have expressed surprise to me at your acceptance & I have defended it as an outbreak of eccentricity.

I too have refused a C.B.E. & am not ashamed of the fact. From your letter now, I judge that you would accept an O.B.E. Kipling refused a knighthood. I prefer his attitude.

Come off it old warhorse. You have made yourself a little absurd by joining the octogenarians, but we love you for it.

Love,

Graham

Waugh responded by postcard that he knew it wouldn't work and signed himself 'Unamuno (Junior Prefect)'. [41]

40 Amory, 619–20.
41 Amory, 620.

TO FRANCIS GREENE

Graham describes as a 'pirate' the publisher and Labour MP Robert Maxwell (1923–91) who, of course, walked the plank near the Canary Islands on 5 November 1991. Francis was seeking work from Maxwell's firm, Pergamon Press, as a translator of Russian physics texts. There is a passing reference in the letter to Thomas Roe, a pirate whose practices were not so evident to Graham.

27 May 1964

Dear Francis,

Here is another pirate who would be interested if you got in touch with him. His name is Robert Maxwell (address: Headington Hill Hall, Oxford) and he is very interested in anyone with a background of physics who knows Russian. He is a very successful business man and his name disguises I think a Central European origin. I met him at Boy Hart's, the director of the Ansbacher Bank.[42] It would be worth sending him a note and having at any rate a word with him. He said himself of his own accord that he would like to meet you. Roe has several ideas which I suppose he will put out when we meet for dinner.

Love,
    Graham.

P.S. Not a very nice man I think, and a Labour politician, but you want piracy!

42 Hart was a business associate of Max Reinhardt.

7

THE COMEDIANS

TO CATHERINE WALSTON

Villa Rosaia | Aug. 4 [1964]

Dear dear Catherine,

I did 600 words my first morning – the highest, I think, I've done on this novel,[1] I suppose because I'm working somewhere far more familiar than Paris or Antibes. Perhaps the place where I've been happiest in my life. Everything is the same but a bit empty – the garden shabby with only the bougainvillea out. Not too hot – a nice breeze. In fact yesterday the wind was too strong for the helicopter & I took the slow boat. Last night dreamed of you.

The usual ceremony at landing, but driven up by Aniello's younger son who has a taxi which is put (rather embarrassingly) at our disposal, so the Dottoressa[2] & I went down to dinner & came up in it. Tonight we shall escape to the bus. The D. much the same – she tells me she is 79 – but I thought she was over 70 when we first knew her. I worked hard at Gemma's dispelling her melancholia – successfully. Gemma's husband a few days ago went temporarily berserk during dinner, shouted that Gemma was a whore, & tried to strangle the waiters. Last night all seemed as usual – with the husband & waiters both there & Gemma affectionately inquiring

1 *The Comedians* (1966).

2 Among the colurful residents of Anacapri was Elisabeth Moor (1885–1975), the 'Dottoressa', an eccentric and outspoken Austrian physician. Her practice included many of the ordinary people who sometimes paid for her services with fish. Something of her personality may be found in Aunt Augusta in *Travels with My Aunt*.

after you. Cavalcanti is also here – much improved. He has become a stage director & had a success in America & France.[3] Now I'm going out with the D. & her dog. The dog is causing much trouble by killing cats, & people are threatening the D. with the police.

Just finished *The Journal of Thomas Moore* (the poet). Fascinating. Do read it. Batsford paper back. 12/6. In the plane I read Galbraith's *The Liberal Hour* – he's my favourite American writer, but at least he was born in Canada. The essay on Henry Ford enthralling. In Penguin. I hear the dog barking up the road.

[. . .]

TO EVELYN WAUGH

In his autobiography A Little Learning (1964) *Waugh recalled how as a schoolboy he visited the house of W. W. Jacobs (1863–1943), author of 'The Monkey's Paw', in Berkhamsted. Waugh became close friends with Jacobs's daughter Barbara, who was engaged to his brother Alec. Her elder brother was a student at Berkhamsted School, but none of these early connections led to a meeting with Greene. At Oxford, the two were acquainted but not close, as they would later become, since Greene seemed to look down on his group as 'childish and ostentatious' (200). He noted with apparent amusement, that whenever Greene wished to portray an unpleasant character with a pathetic attachment to a minor public school, he made it Waugh's own school, Lancing (120).*

C.6 Albany, | London, W.1. | 10 September 1964

My dear Evelyn,

I was delighted to receive the autobiography which I have been anxiously awaiting. As always I have nothing but admiration for the style and content, though may I make two little personal corrections?

3 Greene had known the producer and director Alberto Cavalcanti since the mid-1930s, when he was an associate of John Grierson at the GPO Film Unit. In 1942 he directed *Went the Day Well*, a film based on Greene's story 'The Lieutenant Died Last'. See Adamson, 32–3 and Falk 25–6.

I never knew Jacobs's son at Berkhamsted as I was a boarder and he was a day-boy and as in so many schools a great gulf divided the two. Probably it was the same at Lancing! Or were you so buried in the depths of the country that you didn't have any day-boys? I think I began to use Lancing as my symbol of a minor public school after being given the life of one of the headmasters to review in very early days.[4] There seemed to be so much in common between Lancing and Berkhamsted that I thought I could safely depend on transferring impressions from one school to another!

I was not suffering from any adult superiority at Oxford to explain our paths not crossing, but I belonged to a rather rigorously Balliol group of perhaps boisterous heterosexuals, while your path temporarily took you into the other camp. Also for a considerable period of my time at Oxford I lived in a general haze of drink. I've never drunk so much in my life since! There was also in the last two years a would-be Oxford *Horizon* called the *Oxford Outlook* to keep me occupied. Harold used to contribute to this and Eddy Sackville-West and Edith Sitwell. Alas I had no chance of printing anything from you.

I've just been going through a horrible experience with a play which has determined me never again to write for the stage. In a few days the worst will be over and I depart to the peace of France.

Affectionately,

Graham

---

4 Greene's bibliographers have not recorded such a review. More likely, Greene had been teasing Waugh, as he did occasionally in his novels. For example, in *Our Man in Havana*, Dr. Hasselbacher refers to the hero of Waugh's first novel *Decline and Fall*: "'Now if my friend, Mr. Wormold here, had invented you, you would have been a happier man. He would have given you an Oxford education, a name like Penny-feather . . .'" Wormold and Waugh are both storytellers, but the parallel between them collapses as the reader tries to imagine the author of *The Loved One* selling vacuum cleaners. For his part, Waugh signalled to Greene's fictional world when Guy Crouchback sailed past Freetown at the same time as Scobie was 'demolishing partitions in native houses, still conscientiously interfering with neutral shipping'. See *Men at Arms* (Harmondsworth: Penguin, 1964), 233.

TO RALPH RICHARDSON

Greene's play Carving a Statue, *directed by Peter Wood, had its first performances in Brighton, then opened at the Theatre Royal Haymarket on 17 September 1964. It closed after a month and Graham believed that the biggest problem with the play was Ralph Richardson's humourless interpretation of the lead role as a man in search of God.*

14 September 1964

My dear Ralph,

I feel that in the last weeks I have been very patient, but my patience is now exhausted. Only once have I had an experience comparable to the last fortnight at Brighton, and on that occasion the leading actor had at least the excuse of drink.

You have been sacrificing the whole cast in order to build up – with a minimum of effort – your own idea of your own image. Peter Wood and I have done our best to enlighten you about your part, but you have consistently turned a deaf ear, though it seems reasonable to suppose that the author and the director understand a good deal more than you do about the play. Alas, you fancy yourself as a literary man, and I have as little faith in your literary ability as in your capacity to judge a play. I have found you – not for the first time – incapable of understanding even your own part. Last Friday in your dressing-room after a performance in which you had not shown the elementary courtesy of knowing or playing my lines, we agreed on a text together in the presence of Peter Wood and Binkie.[5] I now hear you have changed the dialogue agreed and introduced lines snatched out of context for your exit at the end of the first act, thus killing the curtain for your young and less experienced colleague. I am sure this should be attributed to stupidity and not to jealousy, but since you waited to break our agreement till I had left for France I cannot acquit you of cowardice.

The time has come to call an end to the selfishness, the laziness and

5 The theatrical producer Hugh Beaumont (1905–72), Managing Director of H. M. Tennent.

the obstinacy which has impeded nearly every rehearsal. In France there is a law which protects the author's rights. In England the author must defend himself, and I assure you that if you do not from now on speak the lines which I have written, I will see that the gist of this letter has a wide circulation – and I don't exclude the press. The vanity of an ageing 'star' can do far more damage to the living theatre than any censorship exercised by the Lord Chamberlain.

Yours sincerely,

Graham

Greene and Richardson quickly patched up their personal differences, but reviewers were appalled by the play. Greene continued to believe that the failure was due to Richardson's handling of his part. Reprintings contain his 'Epitaph for a Play', insisting that the work is farcical, not symbolic.

TO MAX REINHARDT

C.6 Albany, | London, W.1. [19 September 1964]

Dear Max,

A lunch yesterday with my friend, the Indian novelist R. K. Narayan plus this morning the appearance of one of his books *The Dark Room* published by Macmillan in 1938 in a Rare Book catalogue at the price of three guineas, has determined me to bring up his case to you.

He is at present under contract to Heinemann who published his last novel, which is still in print having sold between four and five thousand copies, *The Man-Eater of Malgudi*. They are also bringing out a book of his on Indian mythology, which hasn't the same interest as his novels, at the beginning of next year. He's about half way through a new novel, which he described to me and which sounds up to his best form, and this is contracted to Heinemann. Then his contract lapses.

I brought him to Heinemann myself when Frere was in charge and introduced him to Frere who has a high opinion of his work. He has become in his own way a minor classic already in England since Hamish Hamilton published his first book right back in the depression years. From Hamish Hamilton he went to Nelson and I wrote an introduction to his second novel *The Bachelor of Arts*. When I went to Eyre & Spottiswoode I took back the rights in his old books and reprinted them, except for this one published by Macmillan that I've just mentioned. I also published several new books including a very fine collection of short stories, humorous and sad, called *An Astrologer's Day*. All the books did reasonably well, but in those days there was a paper shortage and I saw to it that he had a proper allotment.

When I left Eyre & Spottiswoode, like all my favourite authors except Mauriac, he was cancelled out by Douglas Jerrold and then went to Methuen who had an extremely good press for *The Guide* (which has been filmed) but did very little with him, so that I was glad to transfer him under Frere's banner. David Higham has done nothing whatever about paperback rights and here I feel a great deal could be done by persuading one of the paperback firms to produce three of his best novels simultaneously. A great range of quotation could be used on the jackets from E.M. Forster to myself!

[. . .]

TO MARIE BICHE

Having weighed the matter 'seventy times seven' times, Biche suggested to Graham that he was now neglecting Catherine Walston, who was depressed after two surgeries and heavy medication to deal with a broken hip. From 1964 Graham spent more and more time in France with Yvonne Cloetta, who, despite being married, provided him through the last thirty-two years of his life with the happiness and stability he had not found in earlier relationships.

C.6 Albany, | London, W.1. | Dec. 5 1964

My dear Marie,

Thank you for your letter, but you don't really understand the character of either Catherine or myself. Since I arrived here a week ago I have written two (for me long) letters to C. & had intended to write a third today – but I choose to write to you instead & there are limits to what the old hand can write when one's trying to average more than

600 words a day of work. I can assure you there is no one (apart from dictated letters – I never dictate a letter to C.) to whom I write so much or so often as to Catherine. Far more than to Yvonne even during the summers of separation. It's not a duty, but I love Catherine dearly.

You must realise that what she says depends very much on her mood. One might have written six times in a month, but if at the moment she felt low she would say that she seldom got a letter. 'Buying books in Brighton' – I suppose we've done that once in 15 years – I know it's a symbol, & I try to arrange other symbolic things. I hoped that we could spend 2 weeks in Anacapri this last summer, but I realised how impossible it was when one thought of the bus rides, the jostling crowds in the piazza – she would have been a prisoner in Anacapri. Before I knew that she would have to have another operation, I was planning that this February we should both take a holiday in Vienna with the Dottoressa, but now . . . It's not poor Catherine's fault that rendezvous after rendezvous has had to be cancelled during the last 18 months – but nor is it mine – if anybody's it's the fault of a Dublin surgeon!

There is a geographical difficulty which Catherine does not easily admit. I have never been able to work in London since 1940 & I've confined my work to all intents to the two months' holiday we had together during a year. Now I spend I suppose 7 months of the year in France working – instead of 1 in Italy & 1 in the West Indies – but it means that the opportunity of seeing each other is reduced. I doubt if I could have continued to earn a living by working 2 months a year – & a few weeks at Brighton as an extra, & for that reason I planned a flat in France long before I knew Yvonne. . . . If Yvonne had never existed, I would have had to face a situation where less London, less Cambridge was essential if things were not going to go to pieces. I would love to retire & dangle around [?] & write more letters & less work – but the fact is I'm working harder now than during the last 16 years. This C. does not realise.

Love,

G.

I'll write the third letter in 10 days tomorrow when the shock of yours has worn off.

TO BERNARD DIEDERICH

One of the most important figures in Graham's later life, the journalist, biographer and historian Bernard Diederich[6] was born in New Zealand in 1926. He left school at sixteen and joined the crew of the four-masted barque the Pamir, the last of the great square-riggers, and finished the war in a modern ship of the United States merchant marine. He settled in Haiti from 1949, operating an English-language newspaper, the Haiti Sun. He was the resident correspondent for the New York Times and other international news organisations during the early years of François 'Papa Doc' Duvalier's dictatorship, reporting on killings, repression and corruption. In 1963 the regime determined to silence him; he was arrested by the Tonton Macoutes, imprisoned and finally exiled.

Diederich, whose memoir of Greene is eagerly anticipated, first met him when he visited Haiti in 1954 and got to know him better when he returned with Catherine Walston in 1956. After Greene's trip to Haiti in 1963, Diederich met him at the airport in Santo Domingo and acted as his guide in the Dominican Republic. In early January 1965, Diederich took him on a tour of the border between the Dominican Republic and Haiti, which became the setting for the climactic scene in The Comedians *(1966).*

C.6 Albany, | London, W.1 | 19 January 1965

Dear Bernard,

Thank you so much for sending me those publications. I have been meaning to write again and again to say how much I enjoyed our time together and how grateful I am to you [for] giving up two days to the trip. I always suspected that that tyre was no good. I tried to point out a hole in it to our friend the priest but he didn't seem to think it mattered![7]

---

6 For an engaging portrait of Diederich, see D. T. Max, 'The A-List Archive', *New Yorker* (11 and 18 June 2007), 68–71.

7 Father Jean-Claude Bajeux, who was working with Haitian refugees. 'Duvalier had killed his family and he was not talkative on our border trip.' (Bernard Diederich, e-mail to RG, 29 January 2006.)

I had already sent off a copy of the play to you when I got your letter. I hope you won't find it as boring as the critics did. All good wishes to both of you.

Affectionately,

Graham

TO JOHN SUTRO

In January 1965, John Sutro, deep in debt, tried to kill himself. His doctor set up a consultation with a psychiatrist for two weeks later, by which time there was a reasonable chance he would be dead. Gillian sent Graham an 'SOS'. With Raymond's help, he arranged John's admission to Holloway Sanatorium.

C.6 Albany, | London, W. 1. | Feb. 5 [1965]

Dear John,

Thank you so much for your letter. It gave me great pleasure to think that you were well enough to write it & I hope you are safely home by the time you get this.

For goodness sake stop flagellating yourself. We all make mistakes, we all make people we love suffer in one way or another – c'est la vie, & luckily people don't love us for our virtues or we'd be in a bad way. Only the saints are allowed to beat their chests & accuse themselves! So do forgive yourself because then we can all be at ease again & laugh again over a shepherd's pie.

[. . .]

TO EVELYN WAUGH

C.6 Albany, | London, W.1. | 4 March 1965

Dear Evelyn,

Rumours reach me from many sides that you are not well. I do hope these are false, but your friends are anxious to know. I hope that it's nothing worse than flu, forgetfulness and gout which are my own particular minor afflictions.

Affectionately,

Graham

TO RAYMOND GREENE

27th May, 1965

Dear Raymond,

Yesterday I had lunch with the wife of an old friend of mine Mervyn Peake, the writer and artist. It is rather a sad case and I wondered whether you could possibly give any advice in the matter.

Apparently Mervyn, who is about fifty-two years old, some ten years ago started Parkinson's disease. He had an operation on the brain in London and whether or not as a result of the case developed encephalitis. For the last eight years he has been completely incapable. He doesn't speak, he dribbles saliva and walks backwards. For a time he was put in a mental hospital but the mental hospital said in the end that he was not really a mental case, and the doctors thought it was bad for him to be in those surroundings. His wife has suggested to her own doctor that she take him back home and look after him, but the doctor has said that it would be highly dangerous both for herself and for Mervyn. There seems to be no National Health establishment for a case like his, and therefore his wife has had to put him in a private hospital for which she pays over £1000 a year. As she has three children and her income is only a little over £2000 it is becoming a burden impossible to bear. Is it really the case that there is no establishment run by the National Health for cases of this kind?

If you felt you could be of any help with advice I would be immensely grateful if you would see Maeve Peake.

Yours ever,

Graham

*Greene was not able to help Peake's situation. An effort at about this time
by John Brophy to establish a trust for his care also failed. From 1964,
Peake was a patient at The Priory in Roehampton and remained there until
the wing where he was accommodated was to be demolished. He was moved
to a smaller institution in Berkshire run by Maeve's brother, where he
received similar care. He died in November 1968.*[8]

TO LUCY CAROLINE BOURGET

Villa Rosaio, | Anacapri. | July 16 [1965]

Dearest Carol,

How are you & all the family? I am down here till July 22
finishing the revision of my novel *The Comedians*. I've just heard
that Hanoi has given me a visa, so I am off to North Vietnam at the
beginning of August for *The Sunday Times*.

At the beginning of this week I went up to Rome because the
Pope[9] had sent me a message that he would like to see me. It was all
very nice & informal – not a bit like the Vatican of Pius XII (when I
get home I'll send you a *horrible* photo of me & the Pope).

The Pope talked to me for twenty minutes about why he liked my
novels! He had read *The Power & the Glory*, *The Heart of the Matter*,
Brighton Rock, & *Stamboul Train*! He gave me a rosary in a nice little
case for Vivien, a medal of himself for me, & a beautiful leather
bound edition of The Gospels in an edition limited to 140 copies.
All the monsignori were very cordial, & the Pope didn't go in at all
for a talk about 'the duties' of a writer. He said there would be always
things in my books which offended some Catholics, but not to
bother about that!

Lots of love to all of you,
Daddy.

---

8 Information from Peter Winnington.

9 Pope Paul VI (Giovanni Battista Montini), who had earlier shielded Greene from
the Holy Office (see pp. 203–6).

TO JANET ADAM SMITH

Janet Adam Smith (later Carleton) (1905–99), the widow of the poet and anthologist Michael Roberts, was an old friend of Graham's and a biographer of his distant cousin, Robert Louis Stevenson. In this letter he describes an encounter with his old antagonist J. B. Priestley, a man equipped for bad weather.

12 November 1965

Dear Janet,

Will you forgive me? I came back from Paris specially, after celebrating Mauriac's eightieth birthday, to come to your party, and then it rained and it rained. I waited for a quarter of an hour in the shelter of Meakers[10] and no taxi came. Only the porter of Albany who was seeking a taxi for Mr. Priestley. Finally I went back into Albany and found Mr. Priestley who was sheltered under a great big hat. I don't possess a hat and rain on my head becomes more and more unbearable. Unfortunately I mentioned to Mr. Priestley that I didn't have a hat. Apparently he didn't get a taxi either, because later after I had had a snack at Bentley's I ran into him entering. He said I was a coward for avoiding the rain, and forgetting that I had already mentioned his hat I told him that I hadn't got a hat. He disappeared into the lavatory I suspect in umbrage. He must be proud of that hat. I don't suppose I would have had much chance of talking to you but all the same I feel a traitor. Will you let me come and see you one day when there is not a party, when it isn't raining so hard and when I don't have to feel an envy of Mr. Priestley's hat?

Affectionately,

Graham

10 Meakers was a now-vanished chain of men's outfitters in the West End. Their shop at 47 and 48 Piccadilly was on the north side of the street adjacent to the entrance to Albany (information from Bruce Hunter).

TO BERNARD DIEDERICH

C. 6 Albany, | London, W. 1. | 20 December 1965

Dear Bernard,

Thank you so much for your Christmas card. All the best wishes to you and your family. I was delighted to hear from you as I was afraid that something might have happened to one of you during the revolution – a revolution which alas I could not attend![11] I've got a novel about Haiti coming out at the end of January of which I am sending you a copy in the hope that it may arrive. I'm sure you will find a great many errors there, but perhaps you will be amused by the last chapter which reflects our visit to the Bauxite works! Forgive the errors for the sake of the intention.

[. . .]

TO EVELYN WAUGH

Having thought A Burnt-Out Case *both technically flawed and a confession of unbelief, Waugh judged Greene's new novel a return to form: 'I greatly admire* The Comedians. *What staying power you have. It might have been written 30 years ago and could be by no one but you.'*[12]

130 Boulevard Malesherbes, | Paris 17. | Jan. 6 [1966]

Dear Evelyn,

Thank you so much for your letter which encouraged me, not

---

11 In 1963 the constitutionalist president of the Dominican Republic was overthrown and replaced by a military-backed civilian Junta. In 1965 there was a rebellion to restore Bosch, but an American intervention in April, involving more than twenty thousand troops, left the government in the hands of Joaquín Balaguer, a close associate of the former dictator Rafael Trujillo. A conservative, he dominated the country's politics from 1966 until the 1990s. (E-mail from Bernard Diederich to RG, 25 February 2007)

12 Amory, 635. Waugh makes a similar remark to Diana Cooper; see *Mr Wu and Mrs Stitch: The Letters of Evelyn Waugh and Diana Cooper*, ed. Artemis Cooper (London: Hodder & Stoughton, 1991), 324.

only about *The Comedians*, but about the C.H.[13] which I felt
snobbish in accepting. You should have had it first & then I could
have happily followed in your footsteps, but you probably refused it.

1965 was bad for me too. Someone like Jones claiming a C.B.E.[14]
did away with half my savings, so I've had to leave England &
establish myself in France. Yes, & there were also deaths & the new
liturgy, but in my case no dentistry.

Love,
   Graham

TO BRIAN MOORE

*Along with Evelyn Waugh, R. K. Narayan and Muriel Spark, Brian Moore
(1921–99) was one of the few contemporary novelists in English whom
Graham regarded as a master. Born an Irish Catholic, Moore wrote often
about a lost faith. While the subject was close to Graham's heart, his real
interest in Moore was in his craftsmanship (see p. 343), as demonstrated in
The Emperor of Ice Cream (1965).*

28 January 1966

Dear Moore,

I was delighted to receive your new novel from the publishers and
I have read it with the usual pleasure and admiration. So many
writers claimed to be realists and trod[15] in the heavy hoof prints of
Zola. You are really the only realist writing whom I can read always
with a sense of pleasure and exhilaration.

It's sad that you have left Montreal because now as my daughter is
living there I make regular trips. I always remember our evening
together at the amusing striptease joint which has since been closed
down!

Yours ever,
   Graham Greene

13 Companion of Honour, announced in the New Year's Honours list.

14 Graham is comparing the con-man Jones in *The Comedians* with the charming
swindler Thomas Roe (see p. 256).

15 'clod' in the original seems to be a dictation error.

TO MICHEL LECHAT

130 Boulevard Malesherbes, | Paris 17. | 25 February 1966

Dear Michel,

I was so glad to get your letter and to hear that you found *The Comedians* readable. I am always rather apprehensive of the reactions from those who know Haiti as on the last occasion I spent far too little time there. I would have liked to have gone back two or three times before writing the book and I feel my lack of impressions in reading it.

[. . .]

I'm so sorry that you are feeling empty. Perhaps your menopause has come a little early. I went through a year or two of that in the 1950s, but I seem to have emerged and my melancholy now when it does rear its ugly head is quite bearable. I suppose that is one of the consolations of age.

My love to you and Edith,

Graham

TO R. K. NARAYAN

March 15 1966

My dear Narayan,

Do forgive a note dictated over the telephone and signed in absence, but I am heavily embroiled in the film script of *The Comedians*. I'm glad you liked the book. I am sure that Jones at least would have enjoyed Malgudi!

I read your book[16] a few days ago. I don't want to give a considered judgement until I have had time to read it a second time, as I have always found with your books that the second reading gives far more. To speak frankly I was a little disappointed with this one. The story line seemed to me to wander a bit and it needs a good deal

16 *The Vendor of Sweets.*

of editing as far as English is concerned. There's practically no changes required in the first fifty pages but after that it was as if you had grown a little tired and inattentive. I sound like a school-master in the Lawley Extensions! May I urge you to cut the last sentence of all on page 248. 'She was a good girl' seems to me the perfect ending. It might even provide you with a title?

Please don't be discouraged by my frankness. I am certain I shall like it far better at the second reading and when the little obstacles of English are corrected which at present impede a free reading. Nothing alters my opinion that you are one of the finest living novelists [. . .]

TO JOSEPH MACLEOD

Boulevard Malesherbes, | Paris 17. | March 30 [1966]

Dear Joseph,

Letters from you arrive miraculously – not only letters but once a night telegram poem – at five year intervals but always when one has a need of a friend, of a past. I'm in exile from England now like you, partly for 'sexual' reasons, partly because a C.B.E. stole half my savings & is now imprisoned (not by me) in Switzerland. Thank you for liking *The Comedians* – I half like it, but I find now that the effort of writing robs one of confidence, pleasure, everything. So the private life – as I hope you find – is the happiest.

'*The dust is laid & the wet sand is clean.*'

Do you recognise the line – my favourite in The Eclipse [*sic*]?[17] But it's not *my* sign. My sign produces only

'*Halfway between fidelity & adultery we enjoy our neutral dreams.*'

---

17 Macleod's volume of verse from 1930 was entitled *The Ecliptic*.

(It's 11:30 at night & I am a little drunk & I've only just opened your letter – with such pleasure. The pleasure I felt too when I read in 1924 'The Bank Clerk Drowned at Sea'. *That* I haven't got here with me – but I'm certain I'd still love it. I find the Meadows[18] stay.)

What has happened to the theatre? That I suppose belonged to the Meadows too. But I wish you'd tell me a little more of your life now. Do you see anything of poor Harold Acton – I say poor only because of his operation? Let's meet again – not at a Gaudy – but in Florence or Antibes where my life is mostly spent.

Love,

Graham

TO LAURA WAUGH

Evelyn Waugh died suddenly after attending Mass on Easter Sunday, 10 April 1966.

130 Boulevard Malesherbes, | Paris 17. | Easter Monday [1966]

Dear Laura,

I was shocked more than I can find it possible to write by the news of Evelyn's death. As a writer I admired him more than any other living novelist, & as a man I loved him. He was a very loyal & patient friend to me. What I loved most in him was that rare quality that he would say only the kind things behind one's back.

Please don't answer this letter, but do believe there is a real community of grief for him.

Yours with so much sympathy,

Graham

18 While students, Greene and Macleod had long talks in the meadows at Oxford. See p. 255.

TO VIVIEN GREENE

51 La Résidence des Fleurs, | Avenue Pasteur, | 06 Antibes. |
3 October 1966

Dear Vivien,

[. . .]

I've moved into this new flat in Antibes (thanks to the film company who are making *The Comedians*) and I have a problem which you would solve better than I. A small black cat has adopted me, coming from God knows where. She seems to have a home as she departs at night and only appears at the worst possible moment when I am beginning work in the morning and sits down firmly on my paper and sucks at my pen. I give her an occasional saucer of milk but she doesn't seem under-nourished. I have to go up to Paris in a fortnight's time and I wonder whether I shall lose her friendship in my absence. The greatest pleasure she has at the moment is an empty cardboard box which once contained a bottle of cognac into which she can just insert herself and pretend to be hidden. Obviously until I have got her under control I shan't progress much with the articles for the *Weekend Telegraph*!

Affectionately,
Graham

TO CATHERINE WALSTON

Please tell me how you are & how you are walking.

51 La Résidence des Fleurs, | Avenue Pasteur, | 06 Antibes. |
Oct. 3 [1966]

Dearest Catherine,

A line to wait for your return. Cuba was exhausting with heat & lack of sleep (I averaged about four hours a night over three weeks) but very rewarding. This time all the doors suddenly opened to me. I had a Cadillac & a French speaking chauffeur – & they wanted to put me into the grand house where they put heads of state with a butler, servants, swimming pool & a guard at the door, but I refused & stayed in a hotel. I came back loaded with presents (a crocodile brief case from the woman I met in hiding in 1957 who is now in charge of Latin American relations),[19] a Milian painting from Milian – a strange obsessed artist I like very much, & another one by him from Franqui who is writing Castro's autobiography,[20] a drawing by Portocarrero[21] from himself & a beautiful flowers painting by Portocarrero from Fidel who inscribed it to me at the back. My last night I spent from 11 p.m. to 2 a.m. with Fidel & we got on very very well. I liked him a lot & was very impressed. I was fetched away by a messenger from a private dinner with the British Ambassador who was quite jealous as he hasn't spoken more than two words to Castro yet.

I saw more of Cuba than ever before, driving all the way to Santiago & Guantanamo, & Raul Castro, Fidel's brother, gave me a military plane to take me to the Isle of Pines. Altogether it was quite a show [. . .]

TO SIR WILLIAM HALEY

Here Greene complains to Sir William Haley (1901–87), editor of The Times, *about the newspaper's failure to report the mysterious murder in Morocco of Yves Allain, who had fought in the French Resistance and was known to Greene through his work in intelligence.*

19 In 1957 Greene met Haydée Santamaria in Santiago. She was one of two women who had participated in the disastrous attack on the Moncada Army Barracks on 26 July 1953. She was captured and tortured, and she lost her brother and fiancé in the attack. She later ran Casa de las Américas, an artistic institution and publishing house. She committed suicide in 1980. (*Ways of Escape*, 190; further information from Bernard Diederich.)

20 Carlos Franqui (b. 1921) ran the official newspaper *Revolución* and was Castro's chief of propaganda; he went into exile and broke with the regime by 1968. He was the author of *The Twelve*.

21 Raul Milian (1914–86) and Rene Portocarrero (1912–85) were expressionist artists, and shared a house. Portocarrero wept at Greene's departure in 1966 (Greene to Michael Richey, 27 January 1986, Georgetown University).

21 November 1966

Dear Sir William,

I was a little surprised that up till now you were unable to publish even the small obituary paragraph which I wrote to you on the death of my friend Yves Allain, one of the most heroic resistants in Brittany who was decorated by the English and American governments. I cannot help feeling that he deserved more than Peter Baker!

Your obituary editor apparently was disturbed by my phrase 'brutal murder', and wanted documentary proof which I now attach, in the form of cuttings from the *Figaro* and *Le Monde*. I had assumed that *The Times* were aware of what goes on in the French Press.

I enclose also a card of his funeral service which lists Allain's decorations.

I would like to have these cuttings returned to me whether or not you publish the paragraph, but I would like also to know whether it is to be published as otherwise I would wish to write at greater length elsewhere – it seems to me deplorable that not a single English paper should even mention the murder of a man who rescued during the war more than a hundred allied airmen.

Yours sincerely,
Graham Greene

Greene's obituary of Allain was published on 24 November.

TO CATHERINE WALSTON

51 La Résidence des Fleurs, | Avenue Pasteur, | 06 Antibes. |
April 30 [1967]

Dearest Catherine,

[. . .]

Yesterday I went to the film of *Ulysses* – a deadly bore in spite of the verbal shocks which made people shout out 'dégôutant.' One came out depressed with a headache. I had tried to reread the book in preparation & found it a big bore like the film – really one of the most overrated classics. So instead I'm rereading Trollope's political novels.

[. . .]

TO BERNARD DIEDERICH

as from: 51 La Résidence des Fleurs | Avenue Pasteur | 06 Antibes. | 30 May 1967

Dear Bernard,

[. . .]

Baptiste, to whom you introduced me in the lunatic asylum at Santo Domingo, came down here during the last days of the filming of *The Comedians* with a man whom I did not take to much. He had been an officer in Duvalier's army until 1964 and I didn't trust him a yard. Poor Baptiste under his influence seriously thought that he could get some 80,000 dollars out of the film stars to – partly – finance an attack on Haiti. Unfortunately our director had lost some 50,000 dollars in giving mistaken support to Père Georges and the news had got around. I did my best to help them, writing personal letters to the Burtons and to Guinness, but there was no response. I sent Baptiste a small cheque to help him continue his search, but with my responsibilities I could do no more. I was also very suspicious of the other man. Perhaps I am learning suspicion from the Haitians themselves.

[. . .]

Fred Baptiste was born in the town of Jacmel. His brother Rénel (sometimes spelt Reneld) was also a rebel leader. Graham first met them in January 1965 in their camp at an abandoned insane asylum near Santo Domingo. In 1964 Fred Baptiste led a failed invasion of Haiti. In April 1965 he and his commando joined and fought beside the Constitutional forces in the Dominican civil war. In 1966 he left the Dominican Republic to travel in Europe and went as far as China seeking support for a new venture against Papa Doc. The brothers were captured in 1970 when they infiltrated into

Haiti. They then disappeared into Fort Dimanche, Duvalier's place of tor-
ture and execution. Graham made repeated inquiries on their behalf, but
Fred died, insane, of tuberculosis at the age of forty-one on 16 June 1974;
Rénel would die, at thirty-five, of the same disease on 19 July 1976.[22]

Father Jean-Baptiste Georges was a former Duvalierist who tried to
organise a small invasion from Florida. Peter Glenville gave him the
$50,000 donation. Georges obtained more money by selling documentary
rights to CBS for the hardly secret expedition. In early 1967, customs officials seized their equipment and arrested him. The episode came to be known
as 'The Bay of Piglets'.[23]

TO LUCY CAROLINE BOURGET

La Résidence des Fleurs, | Avenue Pasteur, | 06 Antibes. |
Aug. 22 [1967]

Dearest Carol,

[. . .]

I had a nice fortnight's holiday in Anacapri, doing no work at all,
but I arrived to find the island on fire, all the way along the
mountain. I wanted to go down to Capri for dinner but found the
road blocked, and we remained cut off for two days. I watched the
fire till midnight, then went to bed and was woken at 3 by the sound
of the flames which had spread to above my end of the village.
Water, fire brigades, Bersaglieri, American soldiers and Carabinieri
were sent from Naples and at last got the fire under control. Luckily
there was no wind or the village would have been wiped out. The
flames got to within 30 metres of a big hotel at the entrance, and all
the guests had to pack and be ready to evacuate in the middle of the
night. In Anacapri the priests brought out San Antonio to show him
the fire and in Capri his rival San Constanzo. People queued up to
kiss San Constanzo and wipe his face with their pocket
handkerchiefs. [. . .]

22 Bernard Diederich, *Le Prix du sang* (2005), 386 and passim.
23 Diederich and Burt, 363–5.

TO CHRISTOPHER SYKES

Graham wrote that many who dwelt on the cruelty of Evelyn Waugh's character had left out another side which was extraordinarily kind and seen him only 'as a sort of sacred monster'.[24] This has been Greene's own fate at the hands of some of his biographers. In this letter, he relates anecdotes about Waugh to Christopher Sykes (1907–86), whose Evelyn Waugh: A Biography *appeared in 1975.*

29 August 1967

Dear Christopher,

I was delighted by reading your broadcast programme on Evelyn in *The Listener* which could hardly have been better done. One or two points occur to me which may be of use to you as a biographer. Evelyn when he told me of the plane crash in Yugoslavia always said that he was flying to join Randolph. He remembered nothing of the crash, but after the crash found himself walking through a field and to his astonishment, because he had no idea where he was, saw Randolph walking towards him through the field carrying a drink! He never mentioned that Randolph was a fellow passenger. He also used to tell me that he found he was put off alcohol completely by sharing a hut with Randolph in Yugoslavia because the smell of Slivovitz coming from his companion was too strong for him.

Evelyn on Tito. Evelyn used always to say that Tito was a lesbian who had lived in Paris at the period when it was fashionable for lesbians to have their breasts removed!

I always disbelieved a little in the stories of Evelyn's rudeness at parties and used to deny such stories until one evening when Carol Reed invited Evelyn, myself and Korda, who was then living with Alexa, to dinner. Suddenly at table Evelyn developed an extreme anti-Semitic rudeness towards Korda. The next day I was with him in a taxi and I said, 'Why did you insult poor Alex like that?' He said, 'He had no right to bring his mistress to Carol Reed's house for dinner.' I said. 'But I had my mistress with me.' Evelyn's reply was, 'That is quite different. She is a married woman.'

24 *Ways of Escape*, 201.

It's only after a good lunch and reading *The Listener* that I send you these notes with affection.

　　Graham

TO THE SECRETARY, SOVIET UNION OF WRITERS

After their writings were smuggled abroad and published in the West the dissident satirists Andrei Sinyavsky (1925–97) and Yuliy Daniel (1925–88) were arrested in 1965 for anti-Soviet activities. Their widely publicised trial in the following year ended in sentences of hard labour.

　　　　　　　　　　　　　　　　　　1st September, 1967

Dear Sir,

　I would like all royalties due to me on my books, and any money deposited in my name for past royalties at the Grand Hotel, Moscow, to be paid over to Madame Sinyavsky and Madame Daniel to help in a small way [with] their support during the imprisonment of their husbands.

　　Yours very truly,

　　Graham Greene

TO GEORGE BARKER

The poet George Barker (1913–91) sent Graham a prayer candle and a sonnet.

　　　　　130 Boulevard Malesherbes, | Paris 17. | Sep. 13 [1967]

Dear Mr. Barker,

　Thank you very much for the candle. I half-believe myself in prayers & candles, & at least they do no harm – which cannot be said of many human activities. I like sonnets too – but rather as I like cheese. Not Roquefort, not Day-Lewis. Brie yes, & Hopkins – & sometimes Auden when mature.

I'm writing a small bit of autobiography myself. It's something to fall back on when the imagination begins to fail. No more disgusting to my mind than old age itself.

Thank you again for the candle.

Yours,

Graham Greene

TO MARIE BICHE

Four months after the Six Day War, Graham visited Israel. In the company of UN observers, he visited the area of Ismalia on 27 September, only to be caught in an exchange of fire, which spread from there along the length of the canal from Kantara to Suez.[25]

Dan Hotel | Tel Aviv | Sep. 29 1967

Dear Marie,

Returned here from the Canal to find your letter and C's two. Thank you so much. I came back from a battle! I do seem to have a nose because I stumbled on the worst point of the worst incident in two months. For more than two and a half hours in the sun I had to lie with my companion & our driver on the side of a sand dune with artillery (anti-tank guns), mortars, & small arms fire. Alas. I'd only had lemonade for two days – I could have done with a whisky. As we were within a hundred yards of the Israelite artillery who didn't know we were there & which was the Egyptian objective, I really thought I'd had my last game of roulette. However we survived! My companion had a small chip out of his cheek from shrapnel & I nothing worse than a sore on my elbow from all those hours on the sand!

Now I'm off to Jerusalem & the Syrian border. A ready made article on the Canal & the U.N. observers![26] Much cheered up.

Love

G.

25 See *Ways of Escape*, 211–19, and *New York Times*, 28 September 1967.
26 'An Incident in Sinai', *Sunday Telegraph* (25 October 1967), incorporated into *Ways of Escape*, 211–19.

TO PETER GLENVILLE (TELEGRAM)

The release of the film of The Comedians, *starring Richard Burton and Elizabeth Taylor, drew a noisy complaint from Duvalier's ambassador to the United States, who described it as 'A character assassination of an entire nation' presenting Haiti as a country of 'Voodoo worshippers and killers'. Its object, he claimed, was 'disgusting and scaring the American tourist at the beginning of the season. Haiti is one of the most beautiful, peaceful, and safe countries in the Caribbean.' The producer and director, Peter Glenville, looked to Greene for a response.*

[2 November 1967]

Suggest following: The ruler of Haiti, responsible for murder and exile of thousands of his countrymen, is really protesting against his own image in the looking glass. Like the ugly queen in Snow White he will have to destroy all the mirrors. But perhaps someone with a sense of humour drafted the official protest with its reference to 'one of the most peaceful and safe countries in the Caribbean' from which even his own family has fled.[27] I would like to challenge Duvalier to take a fortnight's holiday in the outside world away from the security of his Tonton.

   Love
      Graham

27 Papa Doc's war on the film of *The Comedians* followed soon after his scheme to kill Colonel Max Dominique, the husband of his eldest and favourite daughter, Marie-Denise. Her protests combined with those of his own wife, Simone, caused him to relent. The couple were exiled to Spain with his youngest daughter (also named Simone). However, Max was soon condemned to death *in absentia*; indeed, nineteen officers associated with him had already been shot. Two years later, the family patched things up with Papa Doc publicly embracing Max in a cheerful reunion scene on his return to Haiti. Both sisters were present when Papa Doc died in 1971. (Information from Bernard Diederich.)

8

THE HONORARY CONSUL

TO TREVOR WILSON

[Paris] | 11 October 1967

Dear Trevor,

Any news of Francis? Rumours reach me that he was shooed out of Laos. I hope he hasn't got you into any trouble like I used to! Is it true that he's in Hanoi? I hope all goes well with him.

Affectionately,

Graham

Francis Greene had become a documentary maker and photo-journalist. His impulse to travel equalled his father's, and in the summer of 1967 he set off for South-East Asia. In Laos he was, as he later wrote to his father, 'nabbed' for seeing too much of the Americans, 'who of course aren't there'. He was placed, naked, under 'protective custody' in a stockade in the Bolovens plateau where he contracted a specially virulent form of malaria. He believes he would have been shot but for the intervention of Trevor Wilson, then Cultural Attaché at the British Embassy in Vientiane, who had been tipped off by a midnight telephone call from an anonymous American radio operator.

TO LUCY CAROLINE BOURGET

51 La Résidence des Fleurs, | Avenue Pasteur, | 06 Antibes. |
Feb. 27 [1968]

Dearest Carol,

[. . .]

Francis I've been very anxious about, but say nothing to your
mother, as she doesn't read the papers. First he got a very bad dose of
malaria in Laos & when he was over that went on to Saigon & has
been around there ever since. For about ten days he was cut off in
the Delta & no one knew where he was – I could hardly sleep at
night & had telegrams flying everywhere. At last he reappeared, but
I do hope he leaves those parts soon.

[. . .]

*Like his father, Francis did not wish to be protected. After the episode of the
telegrams, which Graham sent to any English-speaking person who might
have information about his son, Francis told him to 'call off the hounds'.*

TO VALENTINA IVASHEVA

*A professor of English Studies at Moscow University, Ivasheva was one of
Graham's close friends in the Soviet Union. She wanted to interview him for
a profile she was writing. As a protest against the trials of Sinyavsky and
Daniel he was refusing to visit the Soviet Union.*

19 March 1968

My dear Valentina,

I am sorry about all this. A book usually is worse in translation
than in the original and to me Sinyavsky's books have great quality
and are not in any way an attack on the Soviet Union. I was glad to
see that my old friend Kim Philby in an interview agreed that the
trial had been a mistake! We Catholics have had a great experience
of literary censorship. The argument for the inquisition was that

there was only one true religion and it was the duty of every man to defend it. I can't help feeling that your censorship is rather like our censorship two hundred years ago. Now we realize there is no absolute truth and that people must be allowed to express their criticisms and opinions. The danger is suppression and not liberty of expression in the long run.

I agree, of course, that the Sinyavsky case is a very small thing compared with what the Americans are doing in Vietnam, but I think it is one's friendship for the Soviet Union that makes one criticize anything which seems to go against the constitution. As you know I am organizing a big protest by members of the American Academy of Letters against the Vietnam war,[1] and I would feel that I had less right to speak up on this point if I didn't speak up on the smaller case of Sinyavsky. There is a meeting of protest in London at the end of next week at which I intend to be present. No doubt this will offend some of my friends in the Soviet Union, but it does not mean that I have ceased to be on your side if the world has to choose between America and Russia. But I want my side free from any easy criticisms.

I am sure that I shall be coming and staying in your flat before long when we can treat this whole matter as a thing of the past.

Affectionately,

Graham

P.S. If only you would send me material on the case I would be happy. I have pre-judged nothing – except as my opinion S. is a very good writer.

TO MARIE BICHE

Gran Hotel del Paraguay | Asunción | Aug. 7 [1968]

Dear Marie,

I was delayed a fortnight in B. A. because the boats were full, & so I only got here on August 5 after five days on the river – an

1 Greene attempted to organise a mass resignation. See p. 308.

eccentric voyage. Does anyone want 2,000,000 plastic drinking straws because I know where to get them at a rock bottom price?![2] B.A. was a rather terrible experience – an author from Europe is treated like Elizabeth Taylor – I have an impression of clutching hands & hungry women of a certain age.

This is a dream town for anyone who has lost ambition – old colonial houses & the constant smell of orange blossom, syringa, camellias [?]. A lovely old hotel with jacaranda trees in blossom & five (good) courses at every meal. Not at all luxury.

After a first scurry of journalists on the boat when I arrived all is very peaceful after B. A. – exactly the place I wanted for 'my aunt'. The President has sent a message that he is 'gratified' that I have come in time for his third inauguration & expressing his desire to help me in any way! So I hope to get a lot of free travel at the expense of the air force.

[. . .]

TO AUBERON WAUGH

La Résidence des Fleurs, | Avenue Pasteur, | 06 Antibes. |
Oct. 25 [1968]

Dear Bron,

Without any personal experience of Biafra I feel quite unable to compose with any savagery a letter attacking these faceless politicians whom the people of England have elected to save their pockets & not their honour. But I will willingly sign any letter that you compose.[3]

Affectionately,
Graham

2 In *Travels with My Aunt* (1968) a Czech manufacturer of plastics offers Henry Pulling two million drinking straws for free (188).

3 Auberon Waugh was then the *Spectator*'s political correspondent. He wrote extensively against Britain's moral and material support of the Nigerian government in the Biafran war. In 1970 he campaigned on this issue in the Bridgwater by-election but withdrew in favour of the Liberal candidate. (Information from Alexander Waugh.) He and Graham Greene, along with Muriel Spark and V. S. Naipaul, signed a letter of protest published in *The Times* (13 November 1968).

I shall be at the Ritz to see a doctor from the 27th to the 31st (probably) if you had time for a drink. Your editor has failed to publish a letter of mine in reply to a faceless reviewer who said I had a 'repugnant mien.'![4]

TO JOSEF SKVORECKY

In 1968, the novelist Josef Skvorecky (b. 1924) left Czechoslovakia fearing for his wife, the novelist Zdena Salivarova, whose father, a bookseller, had already fled, and whose brother had been arrested. After the invasion of August 20–21, the couple returned, but left again by January. They settled in Canada, where Skvorecky became a professor of English in the University of Toronto and he and Salivarova established Sixty-Eight Publishers for works in the Czech language.

28 October 1968

Dear Mr. Skvorecky,

Thank you very much for your letter of October 19. I think it is very courageous of you to have made the decision to return and if at any time I can be of any help please let me know if it is possible. I suggest that if serious trouble occurs your wife should write to me asking permission to translate *The Man Within*. On receipt of such a letter I would try to get some agitation going.

I would very much like to come to Prague and to stay with you if this didn't increase your danger. I was one of the signatories of a protest made on the Russian service of the B.B.C. against the occupation. This too might prevent me getting a visa. What I would have most liked would have been to accompany you to Prague so that I would have been present at your reception, but again this might in fact only add to your risk.

If Faber and Faber turn down *Emöke* and *Bass Saxophone* would

---

4 In a review of Philby's *My Silent War* and Hugh Trevor-Roper's *The Philby Affair*, Charles Stuart recalled that Greene at SIS had discouraged conversation 'by rebarbative silence and repulsive demeanour'. (*Spectator*, 27 September 1968)

you let me try to arrange publication with my own publishers The Bodley Head?[5]

With my very best wishes,

Graham Greene

TO GILLIAN SUTRO

51 La Résidence des Fleurs, | Avenue Pasteur, | 06 Antibes. |
10 March 1969

Dearest Gillian,

Forgive a dictated letter. I was so glad to get a long one from you. I came back from Prague pretty tired as in the course of a week I had covered Prague and Bratislava and plunged myself into protests via television, radio, interviews, conferences etc. Unfortunately when I left, I left my passport behind in Bratislava! I think I'm the first person to have been able to leave Prague airport since 1948 without a passport![6]

I had three nights at Le Mas des Serres with Yvonne before collapsing into bed in Antibes. Now I'm feeling much better and I hope that the next analysis will show the bug has vanished. I had a very unpleasant radio of my kidneys but all was well. Poor Yvonne has had much the worse time. Whilst I was away the mother of her maid was dying slowly of cancer in hospital and she had to visit her every day and then I was no sooner out of my fever when her father went down with another heart attack in the hospital and she had to visit him every day. She's really tired out and we are trying to escape for two nights to St. Paul de Vence on Wednesday.

5 These novellas were not published in English until 1977 when a Canadian firm, Anson-Cartwright, in which Greene's niece Louise Dennys (b. 1948) was a partner, put out an edition. Dennys remained Skvorecky's publisher for a number of years in her new firm, Lester & Orpen Dennys.

6 Greene's trip was complicated by Skvorecky's being unexpectedly granted permission to leave the country. He sent his friend Jarmila Emmerova to the airport with a letter explaining the situation. She helped Graham through the early part of his visit, and he gave her what she supposes was a gift intended for Skvorecky's wife, three bottles of Chanel No. 5 (e-mail from Emmerova to RG, 13 March 2006).

In Prague I had an interesting time seeing Smrkovsky[7] among others who impressed me enormously.

Alas, there's no chance of my being in London on April 23. Yvonne returns from her fortnight in Africa on the 13th and I don't want to go and leave her so quickly after her return.

Yes I knew Michael Meyer had written a play – in fact it's been published and he sent it to me.[8] I can't say I was very enthusiastic. Over *Rosemary's Baby*[9] I disagree with you and agree with John. I found it repulsive and frightening but excellent.

Lots of love,

Graham

TO JOSEF SKVORECKY

The novelist Anatoly Kuznetsov (1929–79), author of Babi Yar, *had fled the Soviet Union and sought asylum in England on 30 July 1968. He was later murdered in London, probably on KGB orders. Greene wrote to* The Times *on 6 August asking his fellow novelists to refuse permission for their works to be published in the Soviet Union 'so long as work by Solzhenitsyn is suppressed and Daniel and Sinyavsky remain in their prison camps'. The secret police soon claimed to have found letters from Greene and others in Kuznetsov's apartment, a claim Greene denied in a letter of 15 August.[10]*

16th August 1969

Dear Skvorecky,

Thank you very much for your long and most interesting letter on the subject of Ginsberg's visit.[11] I feel a little guilty as you could

---

7 A socialist reformer, Josef Smrkovsky was President of the National Assembly under Dubcek and, like him, was arrested when the Soviets invaded.

8 *The Ortolan* (1967). The play was written in 1951 and had recently been revived. Its subject, the lot of the woman artist in northern Sweden, limited its appeal.

9 *Rosemary's Baby* (1968), a horror film directed by Roman Polanski and starring Mia Farrow.

10 *Yours etc*, 141–5.

11 The poet Allen Ginsberg (1926–97) had visited Prague in the mid-1960s. He and Skvorecky had a series of adventures until Ginsberg was expelled from the country by the police (Josef Skvorecky, e-mail to RG, 6 February 2006).

almost have written a short story in this space of time. And my letters are always so brief and dull. I am asking my secretary Miss Reid to enclose if she can two letters I have written to *The Times* about Kuznetsov's defection. I am afraid my honeymoon with the Russians is over! The raid on Kuznetsov's apartment in Tula and the announcement that a lot of letters from me had been discovered there – of course I didn't know Kuznetsov and have never once written to him – looks like a reply to my protest. If so it's a satisfactory one as they seem to have taken it a bit to heart. Forgive this very hurried note, but I am off for a fortnight to Finland – another frontier place!

Yours ever,

Graham Greene

TO PETER LESLIE

An earlier letter (pp. 61–2) tells how Greene and Peter Leslie, a British diplomat on his way to Estonia, struck up a friendship when they discovered they were both devotees of Henry James. Thirty-five years later Leslie wrote to offer Greene his collection of first editions of James.[12]

3 September 1969

My dear Leslie,

How very nice to hear from you after all these years. I always remember the moment in the plane between Riga and Tallinn when we saw that we were reading a volume of Henry James in the same pocket Macmillan edition. Alas you were never able to find for me that brothel in Tallinn recommended by Moura Budberg which had been in the same family for 500 years.[13]

It is very kind indeed of you to offer me those first editions. I have a number of James's firsts – including *In the Cage*, but not the ones

12 Ian Thomson, 'Our Man in Tallinn', *Articles of Faith*, 165–79.
13 In his letter of 16 October, Leslie remarked that Budberg's brothel no longer existed but had become a chemist's shop by his time.

you mention and I can assure you that they will have a good home. I am living in France now but I wonder if you wouldn't mind sending them to my secretary, Miss Reid, at 9 Bow Street, London, W.C.2., as I move around so much. I wonder whether there is any chance of your looking in on me in Paris one day? I am astonished to hear that you are eighty-six. I am just reaching sixty-five and I never realised there were so many years between us.

Yours sincerely,

Graham Greene

P.S. As a poor return for the Henry Jameses I am asking my secretary to send you the volume of *Collected Essays* which came out the other day.

TO MONICA MCCALL (TELEGRAM)

Since a disagreement over payments from the Literary Guild in February 1966, Greene had grown sceptical of his American publisher, the Viking Press. When it was suggested that he change the title of Travels with My Aunt *to something more saleable, he sent the following cable to his American agent in September 1969:*

Would rather change publisher than title.

Graham Greene

In August 1970, Graham left Viking for Simon & Schuster, where Michael Korda, the nephew of Alex Korda, became his new editor.[14]

---

14 The text of this telegram is taken from Korda's article, 'The Third Man', *New Yorker* (25 March 1996), 48. The original may be archived with files from the literary agency ICM at a warehouse in New Jersey (information from Mitch Douglas).

TO LUCY CAROLINE BOURGET

La Résidence des Fleurs, | Avenue Pasteur, | 06 Antibes. |
Nov. 22 [1969]

Dearest Carol,

Just a line to tell you that Herbert has died. It was, of course, a
release for him & Audrey from that ghastly Parkinson's disease, but
one feels sad for him all the same. He didn't have much luck in his
life – except Audrey.

Love,
Daddy
X X X

TO AUBERON WAUGH

La Résidence des Fleurs, | Avenue Pasteur, | 06 Antibes. |
25 November, 1969

My dear Auberon,

Thank you for your amusing review in *The Spectator*, but I must
protest against your statement that the CIA had employed a man
full-time for twenty years to track down a stolen Old Master. As far
as I can make out from reading the book he had been employed on
this job for less than a year. You were quite right to guess the
dénouement on page 16 – that was the page where I intended the
reader to guess. I wonder where you got that idea about the CIA
man.[15]

Affectionately,
Graham

P.S. Here is a technical point which may interest you as a novelist. I
had to choose whether Pulling's mother should be a mystery to him

15 Waugh specified these two points in his review (22 November 1969) as minor flaws
in *Travels with My Aunt*. Otherwise, it was 'a spanking good collection of short stories,
portrait-sketches and funny happenings'.

or to the reader or to both. I decided that there would be very little interest in the mystery, and it's not a very important part of the book, if it remained a mystery to the reader. Therefore I hoped that the reader would guess on page 16 and there would remain the minor interest of when Pulling would guess. Pulling, in fact, of course, guesses long before he refers to her as mother at the end. He begins to realize the situation after the scene with Miss Paterson and in the prison cell he is mainly checking up on the dates to see whether his impression is a true one or not. Perhaps he would never have disclosed his knowledge if he hadn't had the imperative desire to draw his mother's attention after the discovery of Wordsworth's death. Imagine how different the book would have had to have been if the mystery had been kept from the reader. The mystery would have loomed larger and larger and become much too important. Like in a murder story one would have had to have sown the tale with false clues. Unlike the detective story where the detective must be in advance of the reader, it was essential here that the reader should be in advance of the detective.

TO JULIAN MITCHELL

The dramatist and playwright Julian Mitchell (b. 1935), best known for Another Country (1981) *and numerous episodes of* Inspector Morse, *reviewed* Travels with My Aunt (New Statesman, 21 November 1969). *In a letter he asked whether the episode of the Doggies' Church (chapter 6) was based on Ronald Firbank's* The Eccentricities of Cardinal Pirelli (1926), *which opens with a canine baptism.*

1st December 1969

Dear Mr. Mitchell,

Thank you for your amiable letter as well as your amiable review! No, I hadn't been thinking of *Cardinal Pirelli* when I wrote about the doggies' church. It's a very long time since I read it. Of course it may have been in the unconscious. But these affairs still happen. I was sent the other day a leaflet for an animals' service in St. Paul's

Church, Covent Garden, where the world famous dog Goldie would speak to the congregation on biblical matters. The congregation were invited to bring their pets for blessing – dogs, cats, rabbits, goldfish, hamsters, tortoises and guinea-pigs. The service would include animal prayers and hymns with an address by Canon Clarence May,[16] 'The Lesser Brethren.' That is one of the sadnesses of writing, isn't it? One can't go too far. Life always goes further.

    Yours sincerely,

    Graham Greene

TO R. J. SPECTOR

This translator at the United Nations wrote to Greene, claiming that children were being kidnapped in Haiti and sent to a canning factory. He attributed this story at second hand to the Papal Nuncio.

130 Boulevard Malesherbes, | Paris 17. | 2 February 1970

Dear Mr. Spector,

    I find it a little difficult to swallow the canned children, though of course almost anything is possible in Haiti and one must remember that even Apostolic Delegates can be gullible. Unless the situation has changed there is no Nuncio in Haiti as the Nuncio was expelled by Duvalier and there is only a kind of chargé d'affaires. I am going to send your letter on to friends of mine who know more of the situation than I do, but I think it would be very dangerous to use such a story. Its apparent incredibility would only make people suspicious about stories of the very real massacres taking place there.

    Yours sincerely,

    Graham Greene

16 Prebendary of St Paul's and a devotional author.

TO MICHAEL RICHEY

130 Boulevard Malesherbes, | Paris 17. | 5 February 1970

Dear Michael,

It's true that Senghor[17] is probably the best living French poet,
but I doubt whether that would make your stay any more interesting.
I don't know anyone in Dakar which is a big modern city now. Why
don't you go further afield to Madagascar where at least you might
have the chance of seeing one of the dead bodies which are dug up
on their anniversaries, carted around in taxis and entertained by the
family?

Yours ever,

Graham

TO LUCY CAROLINE BOURGET

La Résidence des Fleurs, | Avenue Pasteur, | 06 Antibes. |
Feb. 10 '70

Dearest Caroline,

I hope you had a nice visit from your friend & that all goes well
with Jonathan. I feel a bit flat after Barbados & St. Kitts.

On the 13th (O dear, Friday the 13th!) I fly to London (Ritz) &
then on Monday I go into University College Hospital for the small
operation on my finger.[18] Back here with my arm in a sling on the
21st, & I have to keep the beastly hand up in the sling for nearly
two weeks & then back to London to have the stitches out. I never
imagined it would take so long. Paschoud[19] is coming here for a

---

17 Léopold Sédar Senghor (1906–2001), poet and philosopher who was the first president of Senegal.

18 Graham suffered from Dupuytren's contractures, which cause the fingers to stiffen.
Readers of Patrick O' Brian may recall that in *The Hundred Days* (1998) Stephen
Maturin acquires, as an anatomical specimen, a hand afflicted with this rare condition;
the sailors see it as a talisman and call it 'the hand of glory'.

19 Jean-Felix Paschoud, Greene's Swiss lawyer.

night on March 7. Is there anything you want me to discuss with him?
  Much love,
    Daddy.

TO CATHERINE WALSTON

La Résidence des Fleurs, | Avenue Pasteur, | 06 Antibes. |
May 9 [1970]

Dearest Catherine,

  [. . .]
  I hope you got my note from the Argentine. I spent four days with
Victoria[20] at Mar del Plata. The town is horrid but the house very
pretty and colonial with a lovely garden. We walked on the beach
and went to the movies every night and it was rather cold. Then I
went up to Corrientes near the Paraguay border which I'd seen from
the river boat on my way to Asuncion two years ago. Nobody could
understand why I was going there. It's very hot and humid, they said
(and that was true) and nothing ever happens there. (That wasn't). I
flew up in the same plane as the governor who passed a decree
making me the guest of the province so I paid for nothing . . . hotel,
drinks all free. In 8 days there was an archbishop under arrest, a
priest excommunicated (I liked him), a murdered man in a field (I
photographed the body), a bomb in a church, a consul kidnapped,
four churches closed by the archbishop, and a man who committed
suicide with his whole family by driving his car into the Parana river
just opposite my hotel. So I still seem to bring trouble . . .
  [. . .]
  Francis seems to be doing quite well. I like his girl friend and hope
he'll keep her. He does scientific films for the B.B.C. freelancing and
he's a scientific correspondent of *Time* Magazine. He has a reddish
beard, is very stylish and good-looking, and we occasionally smoke
pot together.
  [. . .]

20 Victoria Ocampo was Greene's South American publisher. They had first met in
1938 and were close friends.

TO THE AMERICAN ACADEMY AND INSTITUTE
OF ARTS AND LETTERS

130 Boulevard Malesherbes, | Paris 17. |
May 19 [1970]

Sir,

With regret I ask you to accept my resignation as an honorary foreign member of the American Academy-Institute of Arts and Letters. My reason – that the Academy has failed to take any position at all in relation to the undeclared war in Vietnam.

I have been in contact with all your foreign members in the hope of organising a mass resignation. A few have given me immediate support; two supported American action in Vietnam; a number considered that the war was not an affair with which a cultural body need concern itself; some were prepared to resign if a majority of honorary members were of the same opinion. I have small respect for those who wished to protect themselves by a majority opinion, and I disagree profoundly with the idea that the Academy is not concerned. I have tried to put myself in the position of a foreign honorary member of a German Academy of Arts and Letters at the time when Hitler was democratically elected Chancellor. Could I have continued to consider as an honour a membership conferred in happier days?

Yours very truly,
Graham Greene

TO SIR HUGH GREENE

3rd August 1970

Dear Hugh,

Carmelina is expecting you[21] on August 23 and I hope all will be in order. You may when you arrive prefer to live in the little house

21 In Capri.

and have the big bed to yourself – there is a single bed there also. You might feel yourself a bit cramped in the double bed in the big house. Neither bed I am afraid will be very comfortable for you.[22] Carmelina should come up and water the flowers in the evenings at least twice a week whilst you are there. She's a nice woman and I am sure you will get on well with her. If her husband Aniello invites you to go down to the Grande Marina for a meal jump at the opportunity. One has a very nice meal at a farmhouse near the Bagno di Tiberio kept by a man called Paoli. It's not really a restaurant – he just caters for his friends. Now for restaurants – we go very frequently to Gemma, up the steps by the Cathedral and turn right. Her food is not sensational but she's an extremely nice woman with a nice nephew who talks English.[23] She's expecting you so do introduce yourselves. Another restaurant which for fish is a little better than Gemma in Capri is the Settanni in a little street running off from the piazza by the post office.

One of the nicest restaurants and the only good one technically in Anacapri is Ricco's at the Grotta Azura. You can get a bus there from the little square in Caprili. Very good fish.

[. . .]

TO MURIEL SPARK

Villa Rosaio | Anacapri | Sat. [1970]

Dear Muriel,

Your book[24] arrived just as I was getting into a taxi in Paris to come here. Thank you so much for always sending me your books. Only Evelyn & Osbert have done that & they are both dead.

I read it last night in Naples & I think I like it better than any except *Memento Mori* – & perhaps *Brodie*, but I want to read all

22 Sir Hugh Greene was 6′ 6″; Graham was 6′ 2″.

23 Graham dined at Gemma's from the 1940s, and walked in her funeral procession in 1984 (Hazzard 34–5).

24 *The Driver's Seat* (London: Macmillan, 1970).

three again. One criticism – isn't the lavatory in tourist class always *behind*?? And a question – would it have been better if the idea had first consciously come to her on the plane when she smelt her man? Probably not: probably it's more grim as it is. Anyway I enjoyed it enormously, beginning it suitably in a restaurant crowded with old American couples on a cruise except for one solitary middle-aged woman who waited for me beside the lift & pounced – but I was warned by your book & saw the headlines 'American Hostess Found Strangled in Author's Bed' & left her coldly at her door – on the same floor as mine, a sinister Sparkian coincidence, & I finished your novel in my bed, safe.

Yours ever,

Graham.

I'm here for a week to see Aunt Augusta, 85 & going strong.[25]

TO LUCY CAROLINE BOURGET

La Résidence des Fleurs, | Avenue Pasteur, | 06 Antibes. |
Jan 9. 71

Dearest Carol,

That's fine. I look forward to seeing you here. Did you say the 20th of Feb.? If the Hotel Royal is booked, we'll get you somewhere in Juan-Les-Pins near to the Stratfords.[26]

One thing – I imagine you know I am not all alone here. I have a great friend, Yvonne – we have known each other for 12 years now – who lives at Juan. When you came here last time she was in Africa. She knows Elisabeth & Hugh & Francis, & she has always wanted to know you. She is a Catholic (she is the step grand-daughter of Madame Cloetta of Lausanne), about 45, & a very sweet person. She has done a great deal for me during the last 12 years & is a great

---

25 Elisabeth Moor. See pp. 268 and 331–2.

26 Presumably the Canadian scholar Philip Stratford, a friend of Greene's and an important critic of his works.

friend of all my friends – the Freres, the Reinhardts, the Sutros, Marie & Jean. Do you mind seeing her? I hope not because if you like her we can have fun together visiting places.

[. . .]

Both Caroline and Francis developed warm friendships with Yvonne Cloetta.

TO VICTORIA OCAMPO

As Greene was preparing for another journey to South America, he was visited by the Chilean poet Pablo Neruda (1904–73), who had been appointed ambassador to Paris by President Salvador Allende.

[Antibes] | 1st June 1971

Dear Victoria,

I hope by now you have received the letters in which I thanked you for your introduction to Neruda. I am never quite sure whether it is safest to send to you in San Isidro or to the office – I have a feeling that the office sometimes may suppress letters which are mere acknowledgements. Anyway I went and had lunch with Neruda and to my astonishment found myself rather liking him. Perhaps he was showing his best side. Within half an hour we were Graham and Pablo to each other. He has sent a telegram to Doctor Allende asking him to receive me and I expect I will hear the result in a few days.

My plans are beginning to form and I do hope you will be able to be part of them. I have to go to the States for a few days round about the second week of September and then I would propose to fly down to B.A. if you were there. I would rather like to get in touch again with those young would-be clandestine Catholics with whom I had spent an evening – do you remember? – on my first visit. They might be able to give me a contact or so in Montevideo because that is where I would like to go after seeing you for a short visit. Then I would like to fly over to Chile and spend three or four weeks there.

Neruda seems to think that by the beginning of October it would be warm enough to go down to the farmlands in the south which seems to be the trouble centre now. Of course if you were not around I might reconsider the whole programme because it is mainly an excuse to see you and San Isidro again.

    Love,

      Graham

It is surprising that there was no earlier friendship between Greene and Neruda as Neruda had spent 1952 as an exile in a house in Capri owned by Greene's friend the historian Edwin Cerio. The film Il Postino (1994) is based on this episode in Neruda's life.

TO ANDREW BOURGET (POSTCARD)

[Chile, 1971]

Try & find this place on the map. It's a very long & narrow country between the sea & mountains much higher than yours.

    Love,

      Grandpa.

TO JONATHAN BOURGET (POSTCARD)

[Chile, 1971]

I am going to the sea this weekend. It's called the Pacific Ocean – but the waves don't look pacific. I wonder if I shall see a cart like this.

    Love,

      Grandpa

TO ZOË RICHMOND

Richmond wrote that her husband, Kenneth, who had psychoanalysed Graham in 1921, had been a medium and that his spiritual activities had brought about a miraculous cure of alcoholism and psoriasis. His first activities as a medium around 1916 *led him into psychology. His early 'scripts' had just been published.*

27 August 1971

Dear Zoë,

Your letter caught me as I was passing through London on my way to South America and I was so pleased to hear from you and with such good news of your happiness. I am sending you a copy of the book so Anne[27] will have to find a different one for you for Christmas. I was most interested in all that you told me about Kenneth. How odd that I should have described him as having a head of a musician when I knew nothing of that start. Nor did I know anything about his psychic activities. I am very interested to see the pamphlet and if you don't mind I *will* keep it and your best wishes too.

It is quite true what I wrote that the six months I spent in the house with you and Kenneth were among the happiest in my life.

Yours affectionately,

Graham

In a subsequent letter she remarked that Graham was a repressed medium and that this sensitivity made him a great novelist.

TO SALVADOR ALLENDE

*Salvador Allende (*1908–73*) was the socialist President of Chile from* 1970 *to* 1973*. Greene met with him in mid-September* 1971*, and wrote 'Chile: The Dangerous Edge' for the* Observer Magazine *(*2 January 1972*; reprinted in* Reflections, 275–83*).*

27 Apparently, her daughter.

13 October 1971

Dear Doctor Allende,

I do want to thank you most warmly for all the help you gave me on my visit to Chile. I particularly enjoyed my visit to the north and I was very sorry that circumstances prevented our meeting again before I left. I was very glad that the Argentine affair ended satisfactorily, for it must have been a cause of great anxiety to you.[28]

I do hope that one day I may have the pleasure of revisiting Chile and meeting you again.

Yours very sincerely,

Graham Greene

TO AMANDA DENNYS (LATER SAUNDERS)

Amanda Dennys, the daughter of Elisabeth Dennys, was close to Graham, as were her sister, the publisher Louise Dennys, and her brother, the bookseller Nicholas Dennys. Although Graham here expresses a passing wish to meet Chris Todd, her first husband, this did not happen. He did, however, become friends with Ron Saunders, her second husband, and attended their wedding. Elisabeth Dennys had become Graham's personal secretary in 1975, but when she suffered a stroke in 1989 Amanda took over her work. After Graham's death, she and her brother oversaw the sale of his papers to the Burns Library at Boston College. She served as secretary of the literary estate until her untimely death on 14 February 2007.

15 November 1971

Dear Amanda.

I am sorry to have missed you in the south as I'd very much like to meet Chris. I also missed Louise who very sweetly left me a note and would you send her my love when you next write. I will certainly let you know when I'm next in London and we'll meet for dinner. I

28 An attempt had been made to overthrow General Alejandro Lanusse, the liberalising president of Argentina, while he was meeting Allende at Antofagasta (see *Reflections*, 275–6).

don't expect to be in London except in immediate passage to Barbados for some months though.

The difficulty of Capri in the spring or early summer is that that is the very time when Yvonne and I are likely to be going there. If you could make your visit in the later summer it would be easier. August or September. Even in August my end of Anacapri is very quiet as traffic cannot pass the door and there is generally a slight breeze in the afternoon. But of course from the point of view of swimming the sea is very crowded.

Love,

Graham

TO W. A. SAUNDERS

After the publication of A Sort of Life *in September 1971, Greene received many letters from people who had lived near Berkhamsted School and from people mentioned in the book. One old boy, W. A. Saunders, a former missionary to China who had settled in Ann Arbor, Michigan, wrote him a thumpingly cheerful letter, chiding him for melancholy and for various errors of fact.*

15 December 1971

Dear Mr Saunders,

Thank you very much for your long and interesting letter on the subject of Berkhamsted. It interested me a great deal. Who knows, one day I may be able to visit Ann Arbor, but I don't know that my 'melancholy would lighten a little'. Does anybody really want to change a little? A complete change, I suppose, one could accept, but not a small change – otherwise one would be losing one's thing.

I had forgotten about 'Tarzan of the Alps' and I wish I had remembered at the time I wrote the book.[29]

---

29 Saunders reminded him of an announcement Charles Greene had made: "'I have here a request from some boys who want to see the film "Tarzan of the *Alps*",' said Charles breathing over the note. Masters to right & left & rear lean toward him and gratingly whisper, "*Apes*".'

A strange thing happened after the publication. I had forgotten the name of the train boy who was caned in our class until I received a letter from a woman written from Berkhamsted where she was living with her husband saying that her father had had a traumatic experience of Berkhamsted. He was now in hospital and she would like to send him an autographed copy of the book. His name was Mayo and I suddenly realized that he was mentioned in it. I sent the book and I heard from her that he had just finished reading it when he died.[30]

Was Carter really the name of my tormentor? I thought that I had invented the name.[31]

It is you who have your wires crossed about Edmunds. Clodagh, the golden-haired daughter, was Clodagh O'Grady quite definitely. I knew her before her mother remarried.

David Copperfield was one of those blackouts. It has been corrected in later editions.[32]

Was Whitehead ever really housemaster of Adders? I thought Whitehead was the master who left the school to take up law and in fact became a K.C. It was quite a remarkable achievement.

Poor old Sunderland Taylor who lost his son in the war was the one who gave me my only prize for a short story and he was very distressed about doing it because it was atheist. I must have

---

30 Arthur Mayo suffered terribly at Berkhamsted School. It was his daughter, Hilary Rost, a county councillor and governor of the school in the 1970s, who contacted Graham about *A Sort of Life*. She says that her father spoke of one master in particular who 'would make the scholarship boys stand up, while he told the rest of the class that they must watch these characters carefully as their fathers were paying their fees and they should make sure that they were not wasting their money. They were verbally abused and most of the staff evidently condoned this. Graham Greene would make a point of coming up to my father after these sessions and would engage him in discussions about some academic subject, making it quite clear that he respected him and would have nothing to do with the invitation to bully' (Letter to RG, 12 March 2006).

31 Saunders remembered Carter: 'pale red hair, snake-like skull who curled the lip & distended the lip at the approach of buggy Saunders et al.'

32 Saunders noticed that Greene referred (152) to a meeting between David Copperfield and Mr Squeers, but Squeers actually appears in *Nicholas Nickleby*.

been one of the few people in the school who liked 'The Oily Duke'.[33]

Yours sincerely,

Graham Greene

TO MURIEL SPARK

La Résidence des Fleurs, | Avenue Pasteur, | 06 Antibes. |
Dec. 22 [1971]

Dear Muriel,

I only got your book[34] yesterday because it had been waiting for me in Paris – & first I was in Chile & then London & then here & never in Paris.

What fools the reviewers have been. It's a wonderful idea, brilliantly carried out, & to me your best book since *Memento Mori* – perhaps even better? I must reread M.M. I loved particularly the dialogue of Heloise & Pablo on page 95. All my congratulations. You have reached the point when all the little people become jealous.

Peter G.[35] promised to arrange a meeting in Rome – but then his film blew up & he forgot. I still hope it may happen before I die of old age.

Affectionately,

Graham

TO MALCOLM RENNIE

Malcolm Rennie of Suffolk named his brown two-year-old filly 'Aunt Augusta' and asked Graham if he would like to buy a third- or half-share.

---

33 Saunders recalled Whitehead as no gentleman for having encouraged boys to sneak. Sunderland Taylor assigned the boys to parse and analyse *The Rime of the Ancient Mariner* while he read a detective story. 'The Oily Duke', later called 'the Devil', was a master named Rawes who did not suffer fools.

34 *Not to Disturb.*

35 Glenville.

9 February [1972?]

Dear Mr Rennie,

Thank you very much for your letter of January 29 and for the honour you have done me in naming your filly after Aunt Augusta. I wish I could take a share in the filly, but I am afraid that it's not only out of my line altogether but there would be great difficulties in transferring money to England. The currency regulations here are almost as strict as at home. In any case I am afraid that with grandchildren to provide for it's not a gamble I would take. I've even given up roulette! However I shall follow the filly closely and back her whenever I get the chance!

Yours sincerely,
    Graham Greene

TO ETIENNE LEROUX

A leading Afrikaans writer, Etienne Leroux (pseudonym of S. P. D. le Roux, 1922–1989) was at this time best known for his novel Seven Days at the Silbersteins *(1962). Graham's evolving interest in South Africa had a direct influence on* The Human Factor.

Dear Etienne,

[. . .]

I can't reproach you with not having written for a long time, because I only write letters when I receive letters. I imagine that's a common fault with a writer who feels he's done enough when he's put his five hundred words on paper. About two hundred words now in my case.

We shall miss you after Easter. Yvonne is off with the children – if one can call them still children – to Brazzaville for her usual African Easter and I shall fill up the time in Paris, Switzerland with my daughter and London. Both of us back again in mid-April and then we shall lack your presence.

I can't remember whether the new port had been started when you were here last. It's now nearly finished except for the gardens which are going to be planted outside my windows. I hope the value of the apartment has risen to atone for all the dust and noise we have suffered for more than a year. The wife of the retired spy[36] still prepares a good omelette. I am not sure whether the whores are still in the Hotel Metropole. The bar has changed completely and become clean and a pizzeria. Brandade Nimois is still obtainable at the Liberacion, my telephone is still the same, the *Time* chap arrives at intervals to see his children, but I haven't seen any women leaving mysterious markings for about a year now. The beastly man with the dogs has left the little Hotel Belle Vue outside my window and now there's a big fat man from the Loire who cooks excellently and we call Silvertooth. The mysterious man with the Mercedes who used to turn up in the old days is now wanted by the police both in Italy and in France and is rumoured to have escaped to Morocco. We have our dramas. I expect you read about the boat which was chased and shot at from Villefranche nearly to Marseilles which was overloaded with heroin.

[. . .]

TO BERNARD DIEDERICH

La Résidence des Fleurs, | Avenue Pasteur, | 06 Antibes. | 12 October 1972

Dear Bernard,

Your letter written on my 68th birthday came to me as quite a shock. Thank goodness Ginette and the children came back safely from Haiti. What a brave girl she is to have attempted the visit. Your story of her being taken under guard to see Cambronne and Claude was terrifying. Haiti on that last visit was to me quite a traumatic experience and I still at intervals dream of the place. My dreams even keep up to date – so that the last one I had Baby Doc was in charge and not Papa Doc. I suppose there's still no news of our friends who may be in Fort Dimanche?

[. . .]

36 Graham's friend and neighbour in Antibes, R. Hudson-Smith.

With the death of Papa Doc on 21 April 1971, the presidency-for-life of
Haiti passed to the nineteen-year-old Jean-Claude 'Baby Doc' Duvalier
(b. 1951). Less paranoid than his father, he operated a regime that was
totally corrupt. Diederich's wife Ginette, then a medical student, thought
it reasonably safe to visit her family in Haiti. However, she was taken
by the police from her parents' home to see General Breton Claude, the
persecutor of suspected Communists. Their interview the next day
was interrupted by Luckner Cambronne, who declared that Bernard
Diederich could never return to the country. As Minister of the Interior,
National Defence and Police, Cambronne held a complicated portfolio of cruelties. Chiefly, however, he was the bagman for the Duvaliers.
Often attired in sharkskin suits, he made vast sums of money from the
export of cadavers and of blood plasma taken from impoverished
Haitians. He also enjoyed a lucrative monopoly on quickie divorces. By
15 November, Cambronne lost favour and took refuge in the Colombian
embassy.[37]

TO RAYMOND GREENE

Graham consulted his brother Raymond on the abduction of Charley
Fortnum in The Honorary Consul (1973).

La Résidence des Fleurs, | Avenue Pasteur, | 06 Antibes. |
24 October 1972

Dear Raymond,

Many thanks for your letter. I am glad that you had a good time in
Malta and Gozo and do hope you are feeling better for it.

I would prefer the knock on the head and morphia because of
what you told me about the effect of morphia on somebody with a
high alcoholic content. The man who would have given the
injection is an educated man and there have been weeks if not
months when his doctor friend could have given him practice. I

37 Bernard Diederich, unpublished second volume of his history of modern Haiti.

suppose there's something harmless one could use in practising. Anyway when proofs are ready I'll send a set to you and we can probably tinker about a little with the situation.

[. . .]

TO MICHAEL MEYER

as from Antibes | 13 November 1972

Dear Michael,

Many thanks for sending me your memories![38] I wish however your printer had not misprinted Orwell's letter to Fyvel and reversed the positions of France and England in the quotation. If you read it again you will see that it doesn't make sense as it stands if I am to be the first Catholic fellow-traveller. It should read 'A thing that doesn't exist in England but does in France.' I think too from page 131 it would have been fairer to say 'that Graham partly admired him'. The only book of his I've really liked is *Animal Farm* and I found later the selected letters in the book of essays published by Penguin in four volumes almost deplorable during the war period. His rumour-mongering at the time of the blitz I think was really despicable.

The meeting between Truffaut and Martine went very well and he told her he had seen her on television and thought at the time that it was a good face for the films. I think he is putting her in touch with some form of agent on the coast and Suzanne was also very kind. Yvonne and I went to a little cocktail party on Friday evening at a hotel to celebrate the end of his film, but we only stayed about a quarter of an hour as it was really too noisy. We had also had Truffaut and Suzanne to dinner at Félix.

[. . .]

38 'Memories of George Orwell', in *The World of George Orwell*, ed. Miriam Gross (1971); the essay is incorporated into Meyer's autobiography, *Not Prince Hamlet* (1989). Orwell's letter disputes the assertion that Greene is a Catholic reactionary, and describes him instead as mildly left-wing with Communist Party leanings – an accurate description.

I hope to see you in England in December when I'm feeling better after the operation.

Love,

Graham

In 1972, François Truffaut (1932–84) and his collaborator Suzanne Schiffman (1929–2001) shot La Nuit américaine (Day for Night), starring Jacqueline Bisset (b. 1944), in Nice. Yvonne's daughter Martine, an aspiring actress, wanted to discuss her prospects with the director. For Graham to help her, he needed to meet Truffaut. Michael Meyer took him, identified as 'Henry Graham', a retired businessman, to a party and proposed him for the tiny role of an insurance agent in the film. Schiffman decided he was perfect. Apparently, Truffaut did not know whom he had directed until the scene was shot. This was the first time Graham's face was seen in a film; his hand had already appeared in Mario Soldati's The Stranger's Hand (1954).[39]

TO PETER OWEN

In March 1972, having been asked by the publisher Peter Owen to provide an endorsement for Shusaku Endo's novel Sea and Poison, Greene had found himself unable to finish it as it made him ill to read about surgery. For much the same reason he had been unable to read Solzhenitsyn's Cancer Ward. Nonetheless, Greene was a staunch admirer of Endo and was willing to endorse his next work.

La Résidence des Fleurs | Avenue Pasteur, | 06 Antibes |
12 February 1973

Dear Mr. Owen,

I read *Wonderful Fool* in typescript and I would certainly be glad to comment on it. It was simply my squeamish stomach that made me refuse comment on the previous book of Endo's that you published. I still think it very sad that his best book about the Jesuit missionaries never had more than a paperback publication in England. Perhaps one day you could revive it in hardback. A marvellous book – so much better than my own *Power and the Glory*.[40]

Yours sincerely,
Graham Greene

TO BERNARD DIEDERICH

La Résidence des Fleurs, | Avenue Pasteur, | 06 Antibes. |
16 March 1973

Dear Bernard,

Thank you so much for your letter. I am glad the holidays went well in New Zealand, but I shall be sad to see you go so far off. I have always wanted to spend some time in Australia but I have always thought of New Zealand as the dullest of the countries in the old Commonwealth, although of course if you have a farm it can hardly be dull!

[. . .]

I'm very drawn towards Panama and have been for some years. Unfortunately my sole excuse for visiting South America has gone now that I've finished my three year old novel. It had become quite a habit to visit the Argentine and neighbouring countries in the summer. I wish we could have had another trip like our Dominican one before you shake the dust off your feet.

Personally I would very much like to read a book on May 30, 1961 – whether the great public would I don't know. I'd like to put the idea up to my publisher, but he's not very enterprising unless he can see certain commercial gains. I hope this time if you do it you

---

40 Endo's novel *Silence* has since been reprinted a number of times in William Johnston's translation.

will do it alone. I felt that the collaboration was the cause of a certain amount of disorder in Papa Doc. For [the] title what about *The Death of the Goat*?[41]

How amusing that the filming of James Bond was done at Ocho Rios.[42] I used to know Ocho Rios well and once I rented Ian Fleming's house from him for a month. He offered to let me have it rent free if I would write an Introduction to an omnibus volume of his novels for America, and I had rather tactfully to explain that I would prefer to pay rent. He had a villainous old housekeeper with the evil eye. He had told me to order all drink through her as she would get it at trade rates, but after a week or so I grew suspicious and asked for my bills. She was charging more for the drinks than one paid in the shops and there was a considerable row. She then started muttering curses on the doorstep and we found it better to depart before we were poisoned. A friend of Ian's was kind enough to take us in a house nearby and getting out of the swimming-pool I slipped and did something to my shoulder from which I suffered for some months, so that evil eye really worked. She must have disliked Ian for letting me go there because when he returned he had his stroke.

Have you any useful contacts, preferably English-speaking, in Panama as I really would rather like to visit that country perhaps in the summer or would it be a terrible climate then? I have managed to take Cuba in August without suffering too much.

My love to you and Ginette,

Graham Greene

---

41 Rafael Trujillo, the Dominican dictator, was shot to death on 30 May 1961. Diederich's *Trujillo: The Death of the Goat* appeared in 1978 and was republished in 2000 as *Trujillo: The Death of the Dictator*.

42 Part of *Live and Let Die* was filmed in December 1982 near Ocho Rios in Jamaica. One of the locations was a large crocodile farm.

TO LUCY CAROLINE BOURGET

51 La Résidence des Fleurs, | Avenue Pasteur, | o6 Antibes. |
23 March 1973

Dearest Carol,

It was a very nice visit! I look forward to the next and seeing the
house even more advanced. I've lost all my keys. I expect they fell
out of my sack when I broke a bottle of whisky in it at Orly airport
and tried to pour the liquid into an almost closed pot for cigarette
ends, but it's just possible it fell out in the boot of your car. You
remember my passport slipped out and we recovered it. Could you
have a look? Don't bother to send the keys if they should be there
but keep them for me as I'll have some copied.

    Much love,
      Daddy

TO GILLIAN SUTRO

La Résidence des Fleurs, | Avenue Pasteur, | o6 Antibes. |
23 March 1973

Dearest Gillian,

I returned from a short visit to Lucy in Switzerland to find your
letter. I must say my post was not an encouraging one. A young
American writer in Florida wrote to say how he had been held up at
the point of a black banana by a robber in his own house, a Czech
writer and old friend wrote to say that he was dying of cancer 'in
inconceivable pain', a nice South African writer and friend wrote to
say that he was about to be charged of manslaughter because one of
the horses on his immense farm had strayed on to the road and
caused a car accident in which a woman was killed and he had seen
her die.[43] Now poor John's breakdown.[44] It was quite a post.

43 Graham is referring to the American novelist Mike Mewshaw; the Czech novelist
is the émigré Egon Hostovsky who died in May 1973 (information from Jan Culik);
the South African is Etienne Leroux.
44 See p. 276.

I do feel so much for you and I do admire your courage and the way in which you manage to carry on. I know admiration doesn't help but it's there and it has to be expressed. When I think of the state John was in that time when I was present in the flat I can only wonder at his power of recuperation – he seemed so well on the last two times I've seen you.

[. . .]

All my love and sympathy

   Graham

TO CAROLINE BOURGET

Koffiefontein | Aug. 4 [1973]

Dearest Caroline,

[. . .]

I had ten very full days in the Transvaal – the most interesting a visit to the Rain Queen, who makes rain. One was not supposed to look at her directly & all conversation had to be directed through an intermediary. He wore a very good European suit & crawled over the floor like a snake & made notes on the palm of his hand with a ballpoint. The queen looked very kind & nice – but she's probably only got two more years before she's moved on – with the choice of a poison cup or starvation! Very Rider Haggard.

Now I'm resting on my friend Etienne Leroux's little farm of 60,000 acres. Tomorrow we move to Cape Town for a week.

   Lots of love,

   Graham.

P.S. The queen has a lot of wives!

'She' in Rider Haggard's novel is a Rain Queen of the Lovedu – the rain queens had wives as a form of property and were required at the age of about sixty to drink a poison made from the entrails of a crocodile.

TO JOSEF SKVORECKY

Skvorecky kept Greene informed about the literary scene in Czechoslovakia and about individual writers such as Ladislav Fuks (1923–94). He often included in his letters grimly amusing anecdotes, including the story of Comrade Balasova, the director of Prague television, who enforced a strict dress-code which, among other things, required women employees to be checked for bras.

15 October 1973

Dear Skvorecky,

[. . .]

As usual your descriptions of the literary scene in your poor country fill me with a mixture of amusement and despair. I particularly like the story of the horse Fuks. Considering the situation I was rather surprised to receive a letter from my publisher Vysehrad asking whether they could publish *The Honorary Consul* on the same terms as they had published *Travels with My Aunt*. I said yes. Am I still regarded as a safe author in Czechoslovakia? I also received a letter from my Russian translator of the past saying that now Russia had joined the Berne Convention could he get the publishers to approach me about the new novel, and I replied that I had already made my situation clear and this was not altered by any adhesion to the Berne Convention. As long as the situation of the dissident writers in Russia remained what it was I was not going to sign any contract for any book to be published in Russia. Am I wrong not to take up a similar attitude with Czechoslovakia? Other so-called democratic republics continue to publish my books – Rumania and Poland. I've done nothing in the case of Czechoslovakia because one feels that all the governments are acting under the tutelage of Big Brother, and it's only Big Brother that one should take the firm line with. I would like your opinion about all this.

Your description of Comrade Balasova amused me enormously. I wish you would allow me to write that I had received the story from a friend in Czechoslovakia and send it to *The Times*, naturally with quotation marks. Perhaps however this would somehow get back to its source. I do think that farce is the best way of attacking these people.[45]

I liked Allende very much and I liked the type of communists who were around him who belong much more to the school of Dubcek than to Moscow, and I was horrified but not surprised by the putsch.[46] It's an odd thing to be able to say that about two years ago one was at a lunch party – not a very big lunch party – of men only, of whom three have now died by violence. This was in Santiago and the dead men are Allende, his naval attaché Captain Araya[47] and his Minister of Finance at that moment Vuskovic[48] with whom I visited one of the taken-over factories and whom I liked very much. Another member of the lunch party is now in exile in France and two others I have no news of and may have been executed. The Chile affair was horribly efficient and far more murderous than the Prague putsch. But perhaps in the long run it was less corrupting. If there is anything I can do for your friend from Chile do let me know – not that I have influence with anyone on the right or the left.

Yours ever,

Graham Greene

TO ERIC QUAYLE

Eric Quayle, an expert on children's literature, sent Graham a copy of his Collector's Book of Boy's Stories *(1973).*

45 The letter appeared in the *New Statesman* (28 December 1973) and is reprinted in *Yours etc.*, 170–1.

46 On 11 September 1973 the Chilean military led by General Augusto Pinochet overthrew the government of President Salvador Allende, who was found dead shortly after.

47 Arturo Araya Peters was shot on the balcony of his house on 27 July 1973; the circumstances are disputed but it had the effect of further weakening Allende's hold on one branch of the military. See Nathaniel Davis, *The Last Two Years of Salvador Allende* (1985), 183. In the typed letter, this man's name is spelled Ayala.

48 Pedro Vuskovic Bravo initiated an aggressive programme of nationalisation and was held responsible for soaring inflation. He was removed from that portfolio in June 1972 but retained influence with Allende (Davis, *passim*). In the typed letter his name is spelled Buskovitch.

130 Boulevard Malesherbes, | Paris 17. | 6 December 1973

Dear Quayle,

A thousand thanks for the handsome *Collector's Book of Boys' Stories*. I have never collected them in a big way myself, although when I had more space[49] in England I used to collect the boys' stories which had had what I thought a formative influence on me! I am sorry for that reason you have rather scamped Captain Gilson! I must have read *The Pirate Aeroplane*[50] a dozen times and it had some effect on a book of mine called *England Made Me*. I look too in vain for Jack Harkaway,[51] though that was a later discovery. I had dealings at one time with Captain Gilson's son (a drop-out) who was arrested by the French police at Lyons and he told me fascinating stories about 'Herbert Strang' who were friends of his father. I can't remember which of the collaborators was an alcoholic and worse.[52] I suspect that a lot of these boys' writers led most extraordinary lives and I suggest you do a book on the oddities among them. Again many thanks.

Yours ever,

Graham Greene

---

49 Presumably a typing error, the word 'room' appears after 'space'.

50 '*The Pirate Aeroplane* [1913] made a specially deep impression with its amiable American villain. One episode, when the young hero who is to be shot at dawn for trying to sabotage the pirate plane, plays rummy with his merciless and benevolent captor was much in my mind when I wrote about a poker game in *England Made Me*' (*A Sort of Life*, 40). Oddly enough, when the whisky priest is awaiting execution in *The Power and the Glory*, he too plays with a deck of cards while talking to the Lieutenant (192–7). Gilson may also have influenced the conclusion of *The Captain and the Enemy* (1988), which dwells both on pirates and small planes.

51 A series from the penny-dreadful mill of Edwin John Brett (1828–1895).

52 Herbert Strang was a pseudonym used by the collaborators Charles L'Estrange (d. 1947) and George Herbert Ely (d.1958) (*Who's Who of Children's Literature* (1968), 255–6). They were extremely prolific; one of their most popular works was *Round the World in Seven Days* (1910).

TO R. K. NARAYAN

La Résidence des Fleurs, | Avenue Pasteur, | 06 Antibes. |
23 March 1974

Dear Narayan,

Marshall Best[53] sent me the proof of *My Days* and I've read the
book with enormous pleasure. I almost begin to believe in
horoscopes! We are both Libra, we both write novels, we have both
published an autobiography, and both our fathers were headmasters.
One can even see a parallel between us when we both left college
and were trying unsuccessfully to settle down to a job.

I was fascinated by your adventures with the Prime Minister (of
Mysore: Sir Mirza Ismail). Would it be possible for me somehow to
buy a copy of your *Mysore*? I want to add it to the collection of your
books on my shelves.[54]

With all my affection,
Graham

TO FRANCIS STEEGMULLER AND SHIRLEY HAZZARD

The journalist Bernard Levin (1928–2004) wrote in The Times *(31 May
1974) that while President Nixon might be guilty of all that he was accused
of in the Watergate scandal and so be unfit for office, many of his pursuers
in the liberal establishment were motivated by desire to undo the election of
1972 and 'shove that landslide back up the mountain'.*

53 Editor-in-chief of the Viking Press and a good friend of Narayan's. He once
remarked of Narayan's disorganised papers that he needed a curator rather than a secretary (RKN, 178).

54 A story possibly invented or exaggerated by Kit Purna: when Somerset Maugham
visited Mysore as a state guest in 1938, he asked to see Narayan. A British administrator said that there was no novelist in Mysore, so Maugham declared his visit had
been a waste. Word of this reached the *diwan* Sir Mirza Ismail (1883–1959), who
invited Narayan to visit him and commissioned him to write a book about Mysore.
Narayan travelled extensively and wrote quickly only to have the bureaucracy dispute
his payment. (RKN, 115–24).

La Résidence des Fleurs, | Avenue Pasteur, | 06 Antibes. |
May 31 [1974]

Dear Francis & Shirley,

Forgive the address on the envelope. I have no other.

Certainly you have seen this piece absurd even for barrow-boy
Bernard. It doesn't merit a reply in words, but haven't you some
friend in Washington who would collaborate with a plausible address
perhaps for a reply in a telegram?

'The President has much appreciated the stand you have taken
in the London Times of May 31 & he would like to invite you to
be the guest of the government in Washington on June 15–22.
During that week the President will be making an important
statement off the record. A room has been booked for you at . . .
Hotel. Only if you are unable to be present please reply to . . .
White House.'

You can draft this much better than I can. My experience in life
assures me that the big lie always comes off & the barrow-boy will
turn up in Washington.

Our love to you both from rainy Antibes.

Graham.

TO MICHAEL KORDA

130 Boulevard Malesherbes, | Paris 17. | 24 June 1974

Dear Michael,

[. . .]

I've finished the first complete draft of my ghosting book – *An
Impossible Woman: The Memoirs of Doctor Elisabeth Moor of Capri*.
I don't know whether you will be in the market for it? It's a
curious book, not like many others. Based on tape recordings
translated from German into English and then altered again to
suit the Dottoressa's very individual style, plus large insertions by
myself in her style, plus an epilogue by myself, you may find it a
bit of a ragbag. Old Elisabeth is a bit of a combination of

Chaucer's Good Wife of Bath and Mrs Bloom. She lost her last lover at the age of 70 and is now approaching 90. Her last feeling was that she didn't want the book published while she was alive, but I suspect she will outlive all of us and I think she might be open to persuasion. Max and Polak of Zsolnay have the world rights. Anyway by September I may have something to show you.

> Affectionately,
> > Graham

Korda declined the manuscript, which was published in America by the Viking Press.

TO MURIEL SPARK

La Résidence des Fleurs, | Avenue Pasteur, | 06 Antibes. |
Dec. 17 [1974]

Dear Muriel,

I've just received The Abbess[55] with an undignified crow of delight. Thank you so much. I've been bookstarved by the postal strike & here's 2 hours – no, an hour & a half – of pleasure before Christmas drops its melancholy pall. Don't make your books any shorter, please, or you'll disappear like Beckett.

> Love,
> > Graham

I receive news of you from the Steegmullers. Why don't you come & see us all in Capri?

---

55 The Abbess of Crewe (1974).

TO RAYMOND GREENE

In 1975, Raymond was suffering from throat cancer, requiring treatment with radioactive gold pellets, then cryogenic therapy, to get rid of tissue that would not heal.[56]

La Résidence des Fleurs, | Avenue Pasteur, | 06600 Antibes | Jan. 30 [1975]

Dear Raymond,

I was so very sorry to hear from Elisabeth that you had to go back to hospital – by an odd coincidence I dreamed of you very vividly that night & woke worried & meant to write. It seems so awful that you now have to face yet another season of pain. I pray – literally – that this one will be shorter & you'll feel the progression. You are the real heart of the Greene family & we have always depended on you more than you know.

Don't bother to answer this. I wish I were in London & not so far away.

Love
Graham

TO MARIO SOLDATI

La Résidence des Fleurs, | Avenue Pasteur, | 06600 Antibes | March 21[57]

Dear Mario,

Thank you so much for *The Malacca Cane* (you had given it me in Italian & I didn't know it had appeared in English). It's come at the best moment because no books are being published & I am being

---

56 Information from Oliver Greene. Raymond seems to have had a lifetime of throat trouble; see p. 35.

57 No year is indicated. Gwyn Morris's translation of *The Malacca Cane* appeared in 1973, but Greene did not use letterhead with the longer postal code until 1975.

driven to reread Proust – with less pleasure than 20 years ago & some impatience.

We long to see you.

Love,

Graham

TO ANITA BJÖRK

La Résidence des Fleurs, | Avenue Pasteur, | 06600 Antibes. |
[31 December 1975]

You are quite wrong. I've never tried to avoid seeing you – I would love to see you. But you are most of the time in Stockholm. I am most of the time – say 8/12ths – in Antibes. I go to London for a week perhaps four times a year, to Paris for a week perhaps six times, & in the summer – which was when you came here – I go away – for three years to South America, another year to South Africa – because this flat is impossible to live in during the summer because of the noise. So it is that the odds are all against us being within reach at the same time. But avoid seeing you – never. Whenever I'm in Paris – that is to say the colder North – I drink Swedish akvavit out of the little silver beaker you gave me & always with thoughts of you.

Love,

Graham

TO ELISABETH DENNYS (NÉE GREENE)

Ritz Hotel, | London | June 1 [no year]

Dear Elisabeth,

My plans for June remain rather uncertain – but I think I will be burying myself in Brighton* to fight through a writer's block, & an American professor wouldn't help, especially one who brackets me with the Murdoch & the Amis whom I consider two of the worst novelists of the period! I'd love to see *you* – but somehow Biles of Georgia[58] – I doubt if it would be advisable.

    Love,
        Graham

* Royal Albion from the 14th.

TO MURIEL SPARK

La Résidence des Fleurs, | Avenue Pasteur, | 06600 Antibes | Aug. 2 [1976]

Dear Muriel,

    I got your book yesterday & finished it avidly today. The reason I didn't get it earlier was because I was driving 3,500 kilometres in Spain in a tiny Renault with a priest & a student & two large boxes of wine. Now my back aches – but your book was good for it. Beware though of the whos & whoms & whiches – first sentence on p. 217![59]

    Affectionately,
        Graham

58 Professor Jack I. Biles of Georgia State University wrote about twentieth-century British literature and conducted interviews with various authors, including William Golding and Iris Murdoch.

59 On p. 217 of *The Takeover* (London: Macmillan, 1976), Spark describes: '. . . a Swedish patient who had no relations who bothered with him, no friends, but who was apparently cured of the drug addiction which had landed him in that place two summers ago.' Greene thought that good prose writers should conduct 'which hunts'.

9

THE HUMAN FACTOR

TO BERNARD DIEDERICH

Since early 1973, Graham had been discussing with Diederich the possibility of a visit to Panama. After a good deal of quiet negotiation by Diederich, who, as a journalist, preferred to keep a low profile, Graham finally received an invitation on 9 September 1976 from General Omar Torrijos (1929–81), the 'Chief of Government' of Panama.

La Résidence des Fleurs, | Avenue Pasteur, | 06600 Antibes |
15th September 1976

Dear Bernard,

I have at last had the telegram from Velarde[1] and I have replied that the earliest I can go is December. There is a K.L.M. flight from Amsterdam which I would propose to take, arriving in Panama on Dec 4. I wanted to avoid passing by way of New York. Is there any chance of your being able to come up for a few days anyway and see me? I suppose in due course Velarde will be booking me in a hotel etc. Have you any idea whether the Government plan to pay my passage or only for my stay in the country? If all goes well I would plan to stay the best part of three weeks. It would be lovely to see you. I doubt if the C.I.A. will enjoy having me around! They didn't like it in Chile.

Affectionately

Graham

---

1 Fabian Velarde was an adviser of Torrijos's. Greene thought him comic and sinister, but felt guilty for teasing him when he dropped dead after one of his visits.

TO AUBERON WAUGH

La Résidence des Fleurs, | Avenue Pasteur, | 06600 Antibes. |
29th November 1976

Dear Bron,

Have you read the first of two reviews in *Motor Sport*[2] of Evelyn's
Diaries? It's a wonderful achievement and is to be followed by a
second article. The author deals only with the motorbicycles and
cars mentioned in the *Diaries* and shows immense motoring
scholarship in identifying them. It really is a prize piece and I
wonder if your press cuttings have sent it to you.

I do hope you are better now. I would like to have news of you.

Affectionately

Graham

TO BERNARD DIEDERICH

*This letter draws a portrait of José de Jesús Martinez (1929–91), called
'Chuchu' (the diminutive of Jesús). He held the rank of Sergeant and was
the most trusted member of Torrijos's security guard. He was also a poet and
a professor of mathematics. Graham spent far more time in his company
than with Torrijos, and he becomes the central figure in* Getting to Know
the General *(1984).*

La Résidence des Fleurs, | Avenue Pasteur, | 06600 Antibes |
30 December 1976

Dear Bernard,

I am writing after my return from one of the most charming
countries I have visited! I was very grateful for your support those
first days and as you can imagine we had a running struggle with Mr.
Velarde. He told Chuchu to report at every Guardia Nacional on the
routes we took so that he could know where I was, but Chuchu

2 See issues for November and December.

completely disobeyed instructions. In any case the General on, I think, our second meeting had told us to do the opposite of anything Mr. Velarde required. The downfall of Mr. Velarde occurred just before I left when the General was having one of his Saturday binges, which I began at 5 o'clock and ended at 10.00 and Mr. Velarde may have begun earlier. Anyway, Velarde was quite incapable and when he left me at my hotel he just managed to get out that he hoped I would have a cup of tea with him and the General next day, which seemed something of an improbability.

Chuchu was a tower of strength though, unlike what you thought, he always carried a revolver in his pocket! In fact his car had been blown up by a bomb a little before my arrival and so we travelled always in one of the General's cars. I saw a great deal of the General and liked him more all the time. He soon came to realise that I was not an intellectual! I got involved even in his private life as well as Chuchu's. Altogether it was a complete holiday and, apart from Mr. Velarde and that fat translator, I liked everybody. My only dislikes seemed to have been shared with the General. I even got an idea for a novel when I was in the country with Chuchu and, if it does seem to take root, I shall go back to Panama in July.

I was very touched by the little note left under my door and I was sorry to be out when you telephoned. With the help of Chuchu I tried to telephone Mexico several times but without success. I do hope you have had a nice holiday with your family in New Zealand, and perhaps we can meet again next summer. Everybody appreciated your piece in *Time* magazine, which occurred at psychologically the right moment, because of Mr. Bunker's arrival with the negotiators.

Affectionately
   Graham

All good wishes for the New Year.

The new Carter administration would place a greater importance on concluding the stop–start negotiations conducted, on the American side, by Ambassador Ellsworth Bunker (1894–1984) and other diplomats. Greene distrusted Bunker, who had led a six-year mission to Vietnam and been a hawkish adviser to President Johnson. He had also handled negotiations in the Dominican Republic following the crisis of 1965–66. The agreements announced on 10 August 1977 ended the existence of the Canal Zone but allowed Americans to retain military bases until 2000. There was also a large aid package for Panama to supplement operating revenues from the canal.[3]

TO JOSÉ DE JESÚS MARTINEZ (CHUCHU)

30th Dec. 1976

My dear Chuchu,

I had a nightmare journey home! All the Dutch were going back from Curacao for Christmas and so I had no seat beside me to stretch out on and when we got to Frankfurt we were parked on the tarmac for a couple of hours because of fog in Amsterdam. I transferred to an Air France plane at a few minutes notice and got off to Paris and my flat, but of course all my luggage had to go on to Amsterdam and it was some days before I recovered it. It wasn't such a happy journey as the one I had coming to Panama.

I miss you a great deal and our daily talks. I have no one to recite Rilke to me! And nobody here needs my sun glasses! I promise myself that I shall return next July and find you all as you were, but you know the kind of fears I have for the future. Are you still thinking of going up into the mountains? You must at any rate come down from them to find me. Do remember to send me your play and speaking all at random give my love to the three children I met!

I started writing an article and in fact have done about 1,700 words. I hope the *New York Review of Books* will publish it in America.[4] I hope the general won't find my portrait too personal – though naturally I have left out the story of his wife and father-in-law. I keep on remembering him with greater and greater affection. I have tried to make his portrait a little bit of a warning to the

3 See *Getting to Know the General*, 29, 91, and Howard B. Schaffer, *Ellsworth Bunker: Global Troubleshooter, Vietnam Hawk* (Chapel Hill: University of North Carolina Press, 2003).

4 'The Country with Five Frontiers', *NYRB* (17 February 1977).

Americans – the portrait of a man with a sense of desperation who is prudent against his own will. He needn't be afraid of any lack of charisma – I said that unlike the charisma of rhetoric (in the case of Churchill and Fidel) he has the charisma of desperation. I hope you find that true and it won't offend him. Anyway, I write what I think.

Do keep on at the General over those awful Walt Disney signs and also persuade him just for the sake of interest to probe into the history of the haunted house.[5]

I even miss Doctor Velarde. It was fun escaping from him. Now the routine of life is a little bit difficult to bear. Some books are going off to you and of course I'll send you any news of any articles which may appear. I know you thought I ought to write the novel[6] and not write the articles, but I prefer to put in a blow quickly. Who knows what the situation may be by the time a novel is finished?

Do give messages of friendship to all those I like, the architect, the Communist, etc. etc.

Affectionately,
Graham

TO THE SUNDAY TIMES

Presumably a joint effort, this letter is in Graham's hand, but the return address is that of the Sutros.

A.311 Château Périgord | Monte Carlo | [January 1977]

Sir,

Although I am an old lady (past 70 alas!) & living in enforced retirement here because of the abominable taxes I would still like to

5 Graham and Chuchu had stopped at a house said to be haunted by a screaming woman. Graham was not able to get into the house until his next visit when he was presented as a medium on his way to a spiritualist conference in Australia (*Getting to Know the General*, 86–7).

6 Graham's unfinished novel *On the Way Back*, based on his travels with Chuchu, is described in *Getting to Know the General*, 49–50. Part of *The Captain and the Enemy* (1988) is set in Panama and the character of Pablo has a remote resemblance to Chuchu.

make the acquaintance of your Mr Peter Conrad who writes that 'for Isolde death is as easy, & as infinitely repeatable, as an orgasm.' He must be some boy! I have led a somewhat rackety life & prided myself on not being what people call 'a cold fish' – but 'infinitely repeatable' – he must be some man or his girl friend's out of my class.

Forgive a rather flippant letter, but all the same . . .

Mary Procter

The letter was returned with a form-letter citing limitations of space.

TO AUBERON WAUGH

La Résidence des Fleurs, | Avenue Pasteur, | 06600 Antibes | Feb. 4 [1977]

Dear Bron,

I much enjoyed 'Stand up & Be Counted' & I'm glad to hear that your Diaries pleased Martin Amis – they certainly pleased me.[7] But I wish you had taken the opportunity to mention that Amis Père had made an advertisement for W. H. Smug naming it (& photo of himself) his favourite bookshop. I suppose the poor man needed money, but some of us would rather live abroad (though we still pay taxes) than fall to that level.

Evelyn could never read my handwriting so I always dictated letters to him – so forgive me inflicting it on you.

How are you? With Evelyn, Grossmith, George Birmingham & P.G.W.[8] dead, we have only you to depend on when life is grey.

Affectionately,

Graham

7 *Four Crowded Years: The Diaries of Auberon Waugh, 1972–1976*, ed. N. R. Galli (London : Private Eye Productions, André Deutsch, 1976).

8 Evelyn Waugh; George Grossmith, author of *Diary of a Nobody* (1892); George Birmingham (pseudonym of James Hannay), a prolific novelist from whose works Greene drew the title for *The Captain and the Enemy* (1988); P. G. Wodehouse.

TO VICTORIA OCAMPO

15th February 1977

Dear Victoria,

Thank you so much for your letter. Don't be angry with me because I liked General Torrijos. He is a very different type to Perón and I doubt whether he got on with him. Tito is more his type and Fidel. However I shall ask him all about Perón when I next see him!

[. . .]

Malraux: I knew him slightly soon after the war when we were on the same committee judging translations from English into French. I never took to him very much and I wrote an open letter to him in *Le Monde* at the time of the atrocities in Algiers. He probably did not like that. It was at the time when he was a Minister in De Gaulle's government. I don't like his rhetorical style and when I re-read *La Condition humaine*, because somebody asked me to do a film script of it, I was deeply disappointed. I remembered liking it very much when I was young. I dislike too his mythomania. The pretence that he had been in China during the Chinese revolution, the way in which he almost swallowed up the Resistance in France although he was a Resistant of the last moment, his exaggeration of his achievements in Spain during the Civil War. Oh well, I am speaking of a friend of yours but you asked me to tell you.

Lots of love
Graham

TO GLORIA EMERSON

Greene admired the gallantry and insight of Gloria Emerson (1929–2004), a foreign correspondent who reported on the Vietnam war for the New York Times.

La Résidence des Fleurs, | Avenue Pasteur, | 06600 Antibes |
6th April 1977

Dear Gloria Emerson,

Of course I would be delighted to see you. I wouldn't regard
meeting you as being an interview! You won't however find me at
Cap d'Antibes where the millionaires live. I am only three minutes
walk from the station on the edge of the Port. I can't promise to be
in Antibes at the end of April as I may have to be in Paris, but I am
almost certain to be here in early May. I quite agree that *Rolling
Stone* would be more amusing than *Atlantic Monthly*.

Yours sincerely

Graham Greene

The interview appeared in the Rolling Stone (9 March 1978). *Their meeting on this occasion and subsequent correspondence inspired Emerson to
write* Loving Graham Greene (2000), *a novel in which a character
haunted by her friendship with him attempts to protect the freedom of
writers in Algeria.*

TO PETER THORSLEV

*Brian Moore had held a visiting part-time appointment teaching creative
writing at the University of California at Los Angeles and was applying for
a permanent position. The chairman wrote to Greene for a letter of reference.*

22 April 1977

Dear Mr. Thorslev,

All I can say in reply to your letter of 11 April is that I consider Mr.
Brian Moore one of [the] three or four best novelists in the English
language at the moment and I think that the University would be
lucky to have him. In my opinion his style has the simplicity and
depth only equalled in my generation by Evelyn Waugh.

Yours

Graham Greene

TO RAGNAR SVANSTRÖM

Svanström was Greene's publisher in Sweden. His wife Greta had recently suffered a recurrence of breast cancer.

13th May 1977

My dear Ragnar,

I am terribly sad to hear the news of poor Greta. I had thought after twenty years she was safe. It must in a way be even worse for you. I shan't tell Yvonne about it because it will awaken fears for her daughter who had a dangerous cancer of the leg four years ago and who we hope is out of trouble. But with cancer one can never be certain. I thought at the time four years ago that Yvonne was going to have a nervous breakdown from her anxiety but I think she forgets about it a lot now. She and her daughter are very close.

For Greta I shall continue to hope as long as possible. The human body is mysterious and one knows of cases like the one in Scotland the other day when the body seems to react even at the last moment and win. The case in Scotland was of a man who was not expected to survive the night with a cancer which had spread very much throughout his body. They talk of a miracle of course and a priest is being canonized who was killed in their religious persecution and to whom the village were praying.[9] I prefer to be an agnostic and think that the body itself produces its own miracle.

[. . .]

TO LEE GOERNER

An editor at Knopf, Lee Goerner (1947–95) sent Graham a copy of Michael Herr's Dispatches *(1977), a memoir of the Vietnam war that reads like a rock-and-roll dithyramb.*

9 This is the case of John Fagan, a Glasgow dockworker whose sudden recovery from stomach cancer in 1967 was scrutinised by various physicians. In February 1977, Pope Paul VI concluded that a miracle had occurred at the intercession of the Blessed John Ogilvie (d. 1614). Ogilvie was then canonised.

La Résidence des Fleurs, | Avenue Pasteur, | 06600 Antibes |
9th July 1977

Dear Mr. Goerner,

I read *Dispatches* naturally with great interest. I was rather put off
by the opening part which seemed to me too excitable, but Herr
calmed down a bit later. I think when one is dealing with horrors
one should write very coldly. Otherwise it reads like hidden
boasting – 'just see what a brave chap I am to have voluntarily put
myself in the way of such experiences.' To adapt Wordsworth, horror
should be remembered in tranquillity.

Yours sincerely
Graham Greene

TO MARIA NEWALL

*Now in her mid-eighties, Pistol Mary from Kenya was living in Sintra,
Portugal, where Graham and Father Leopoldo Durán, a Spanish literary
scholar, would visit her in the course of their Quixotic journeys.*

1st August 1977

Dearest Maria,

I am dictating this letter to Elisabeth because I know how difficult
my handwriting is. The Holy Father, myself and Michael[10] got safely
back to Madrid via a monastery in Badajoz and a parador in
Guadalupe. I was nearly suffocated in the monastery in Badajoz by
the Holy Father who inadvertently turned on in that very hot city
the heating in my room and I didn't realise it until I had undressed
and had to wander the corridors of the monastery seeking help
because there seemed to be no way of turning off the heating. In the
parador I was startled to receive a call from the Holy Father carrying
his toothpaste and toothbrush and soap because he wanted to clean
his teeth and wash his hair in my bathroom. I said surely you have

10 Presumably, Miguel Fernandez, the driver or 'third man' in the party. He is identified in a photograph in Durán's memoir of Greene.

got a bathroom and he admitted he had, but of course then he couldn't talk. All the same I love him dearly and he is immensely fond of you after those three days. I am sure he would fly off at a moment's word to see you.

From Madrid we made two excursions without Michael. The first to Cuenca which was quite sensational and the other to El Toboso which I hadn't realised existed apart from the imagination of Cervantes until I happened to be reading an essay of Unamuno in Madrid. El Toboso was completely unspoilt except of course there was a little library containing translations of Don Quixote signed by all the heads of state including Hitler – the copy signed by Stalin had mysteriously disappeared. The English copy was signed by Ramsay MacDonald.[11] We were the only tourists in the village.

Father Durán was delighted by the story I started writing in my head – asking for his aid in technical matters – of a book to be called *Monsignor Don Quixote*. We added to the adventures of the Monsignor as we went along the road. Chuchu in Panama is going to be worried as I have now got another character to play with.[12]

All this is nonsense, but what is not nonsense is how much we all of us enjoyed our stay with you and I wish it had been longer.

Much love,
Graham

TO MARIE BICHE

51 La Résidence des Fleurs, | Avenue Pasteur, | 06 Antibes. |
Oct. 26 . 77

Dear Marie,

I know this letter will annoy you, but be patient with me & try to understand. After all we have been friends for nearly thirty years & I know how much you've done for me during that time, so be reasonable

---

11 Such a 'Museum of Signatures' is described in *Monsignor Quixote*, 17.
12 *Monsignor Quixote* effectively took over the structure of the abortive Panamanian novel; in both stories, two characters travel by road and eventually one is killed.

& do something – which will hurt you – to please me. I'm scared of your reaction & afraid you'll disappoint me, but please say Yes & allow me this year for Christmas to give you instead of a classic shirt from the Faubourg unsuitable for country wear, allow me – I ask it with trembling voice – to give you a small car – Volkswagen or what you like. This year I've earned an absurd amount of money & I hate to save all of it for not very long a future. Please say Yes & please me.

Love,

Graham

Astonished, Biche replied that 'no present could make me happier! It makes me sad tho' to realise what a bitch I am that you should have to go to such verbal pains to offer me this precious gift.' She compared her excitement to that which she felt on getting her first bicycle. With his next letter, Graham enclosed a cheque to pay for a new Citroën.

TO BERNARD DIEDERICH

La Résidence des Fleurs, | Avenue Pasteur, | 06600 Antibes | 30 November 1977

Dear Bernard,

I hope you had luck this time with the General. Chuchu did tell me that he was hoping to have a holiday with his ex-wife from America and I'm glad to hear he got it. I have done a piece about the signing of the Treaty for *The New York Review of Books*[13] and *The Spectator* over here and I'll send you a copy in due course when it appears.

Yes, I had had a news report that the Baptistes were dead. Maybe my challenge put an end to their misery.[14]

All good wishes to the two of you for Christmas.

Affectionately

Graham

---

13 'The Great Spectacular', *NYRB* (26 January 1978).

14 Graham had issued a public appeal, largely composed by the journalist Greg Chamberlain, on behalf of the Baptistes in the *Guardian* (15 March 1976). See pp. 288–9.

TO FATHER LEOPOLDO DURÁN

6 April 1978

My dear Leopoldo,

Thank you for various letters which have come in – I begin to lose count of what I have written and what you have written. I am so glad that you and Laszlo Robert[15] got on so well together and I liked very much his drunken letter. Why is it that you are not drinking a little bit of whisky even these days? You won't be able to qualify as one of my whisky priests. Thank you too for sending me Maria's letter. She certainly loves you deeply and your letter must have given her great pleasure and confidence. It was very good of you to send it to me but I return it to you because it belongs to you. Perhaps you should indicate to her that we shall have a different chauffeur this time! I have an idea that she was a little bored by our friend and she will probably welcome our new conductor. I hope to bring you for your amusement the first chapter of Monsignor Quixote – the first and the last chapter because I doubt that the book will ever go on.

[. . .]

TO EVA KEARNEY

Greene received an enormous amount of mail from his readers. He took a surprising concern for these strangers, including a Dublin grandmother who confessed to having had 'scruples' when she first read his works. Scruples are, of course, an affliction of the devout, now thought to have been eradicated like polio.

28 April 1978

Dear Mrs. Kearney,

Thank you for what you say about my books and I am sorry that twenty years ago you had scruples! Perhaps I ought to tell you what

15 A Hungarian documentary maker.

Pope Paul said to me in a private interview when I pointed out to him that among the books of mine he had read was *The Power and the Glory* which had been condemned by the Holy Office. His reply was 'Parts of all your books will always offend some Catholics and you shouldn't pay any attention to that.'[16]

As for your husband's question I must admit that I don't go to Mass every Sunday. I go once or twice a month probably on the average but no more. It always seemed to me an absurdity of the Church teaching to miss Mass without proper reason was a mortal sin. Luckily I have met many priests who admit that in all their years in the confessional they have never even heard a mortal sin confessed. A mortal sin in theology is a sin done in conscious defiance of God and I should imagine that is a very, very rare event. I think in Ireland you have always been rather black Catholics if you will excuse my saying so.

For that reason perhaps I don't take as seriously as you do the question of your children – your grandchildren are hardly your responsibility. I think it was Saint Thomas Aquinas who attributed a sense of humour to God and I am sure that your children's peccadilloes will probably please him as much as your children pleased you when they disobeyed a rule of the household. Even if you smacked one of them you were probably pleased by a certain independence and I see no reason why God *should* not be pleased by a certain independence on our side. Surely, or rather perhaps, the only important rule one should try not to break is that of charity and if there is a God he must be charitable too.

When I rather hastily said that if I was young today I would not become a Catholic I think I meant that the differences between the Christian beliefs were becoming less and less. For example I doubt if there would be a quarrel today between a Catholic and an Anglican on the subject of transubstantiation. Our idea of transubstantiation has become far less physical and more philosophical.[17] I dislike the

16 See p. 278.

17 Dr Priscilla Chadwick, the current principal of Berkhamsted Collegiate School, suggests that Greene's comments reflect a reading of the reports of the Anglican-Roman Catholic International Commission (ARCIC), of which her father the theologian Professor Henry Chadwick was a member. According to The Windsor

new liturgy, but that is partly because I no longer feel at home in a church, especially abroad. If a new liturgy was required I don't understand why a model should not have been made and translated into the various languages instead of allowing many priests to put in fancy prayers, sometimes of a rather sentimental kind, before the canon. In a foreign language these make one lose one's place entirely! I think today I would be just as at home in an Anglican church and the English of the traditional Anglican service is rather better than the English of the new liturgy. This may sound a purely aesthetic criticism, but it's not. Words have a certain holiness; they should be able to represent truthfully a certain emotion as well as a certain belief and I do think the language of the 17th century succeeded in this better than the language of the 20th century which is apt to date from one year to another. The language of the 17th century is a little bit like Latin – it doesn't change its meaning.

Again many thanks for your letter.

Yours sincerely

Graham Greene

TO MICHAEL KORDA

La Résidence des Fleurs, | Avenue Pasteur, | 06600 Antibes |
13 May 1978

Dear Michael,

[. . .]

Certainly you can say No to the David Frost Show! If you could make the No a bit insulting so much the better. Perhaps you could put it that Mr. Greene wouldn't dream of appearing on a David Frost Show!

Affectionately

Graham

Statement of 1971 on Eucharistic Doctrine, 'The Word transubstantiation is commonly used in the Roman Catholic Church to indicate that God acting in the eucharist effects a change in the inner reality of the elements. The term should be seen as affirming the fact of Christ's presence and of the mysterious and radical change which takes place. In contemporary Roman Catholic theology it is not understood as explaining how the change takes place.'

TO CATHERINE WALSTON

10th July 1978

Dearest Catherine,

I find at 74 that one is apt to forget present things though one remembers clearly the past and I don't think I ever thanked you for your very nice long letter. Forgive this being dictated to Elisabeth, but I am off to Spain to spend my yearly fortnight with my only priest, Father Durán. (He has written a book in Spanish on my theology!) We do a trip each year to include Portugal and my Kenya friend, Maria Newall, who must be now 86 and is continually falling down and breaking bits of herself, but she remains in spirit younger than I am. Then in mid-August I am off for my yearly visit to Panama and my pal General Torrijos. This will be the third visit and I don't quite know why I make it except to escape from the Côte in the summer. Perhaps one day a novel will come out of it. In between Spain and Panama I hope to be in England for some days and I'll telephone and see if I can come down and see you. That poor Norman Sherry[18] who has been trying to follow in my footsteps in Mexico, Haiti, and Paraguay has returned to England very unwell. I do hope I'm not going to be the death of him.

Much love
Graham

TO ANITA BJÖRK

La Résidence des Fleurs, | Avenue Pasteur, | 06600 Antibes. |
Sep. 9. '78

Dearest Anita,

I was so happy to receive your postcard just as I returned from my third visit to Panamá (I don't think I want to go a fourth time as I feel exhausted – 18-hour flights are too much at 74!)

18 Greene had authorised the Conrad scholar Norman Sherry (b. 1925) to write his biography.

My God, how you work! Play in Stockholm, film in Oslo! I wish I knew what play & what film. I too would like to see you in this life – do keep me posted about your movements if you come southwest. I always leave here mid-July to September & in October I go to Capri, but otherwise I can always get to Paris with a little notice. I still feel life is very long & sometimes I feel a hundred years old & that I ought to grow a white beard.

[. . .]

Much love,

Graham

TO GLORIA EMERSON

La Résidence des Fleurs, | Avenue Pasteur, | 06600 Antibes | 9th January 1979

Dear Gloria,

Thank you so much for your postcard from Los Angeles, that sink of iniquity, where I once had a very good Chinese meal and accompanied that fat actor, Robert Morley, to the equivalent in those days of strip-tease. I have forgotten what it was called then, it's so long ago. Thirty years ago.[19]

I have just begun re-reading *Moby Dick* in celebration of starting a new book which I thought I would never do. I suppose Nantucket is already spoilt and not worth visiting? A summer resort? At the moment, under the influence of *Moby Dick* which I never thought to read twice, it's the only place in North America which I want to visit. Do tell me about it. What has become of it?

Affectionately

Graham

Emerson immediately began making firm arrangements for Graham to stay in Nantucket. He was amused at this response to his whim and wrote on 5th February 1979: 'What an impulsive girl you are! You are positively dangerous!'

19 Robert Morley (1908–92) played the part of Dreuther in *Loser Takes All* (1956).

TO VIVIEN GREENE

La Résidence des Fleurs, | Avenue Pasteur, | 06600 Antibes |
5th February 1979

Dear Vivien,

The explanation why I keep my ship in the lavatory is that there
is no other place available and also if I turn on the music the waves
rise and fall and the ship wallows among them making one think of
the seasick passengers on board. That is why it seems to me suitably
placed. On another wall is a hurricane notice from Belize telling
people what to do when the siren blows.

Affectionately
Graham

TO LUCY CAROLINE BOURGET

The Ritz, | Piccadilly, | Feb. 20 [1979].

Dearest Caroline,

Alas! I have to go into the King Edward VII Hospital this
afternoon for an operation on the intestines – not serious but
disagreeable. After lunch today no more food till after the operation
on Friday. Then 4 days of intravenous. I should be out in 12 days. I
only tell you this in case you try to get hold of me for some reason &
can't.

Lots of love,
Graham

Graham was suffering from cancer of the intestines, but his surgery was successful.

TO ANDREW BOYLE

The journalist and historian Andrew Boyle sent Greene portions of the manuscript of The Climate of Treason: Five Who Spied for Russia (1979) *dealing with Philby's progress through the ranks at MI6. Felix Cowgill was head of Section V when Philby arrived in 1941; when a new Section IX was established in late 1944 to study Soviet and Communist activity, Philby was given charge of it rather than Cowgill, who resigned.*

6th March 1979

Dear Mr. Boyle,

I don't at all like you having me say that 'I might have guessed there was something fishy about his rise'. I saw nothing fishy in Kim Philby's rise – he was a very able man. What I think I have written somewhere is that I was glad to discover years later that his supplanting of Cowgill was not simply the desire for personal power.[20] I would never use such a phrase as 'blurted out the truth' and it was a thing that could never possibly have happened. During the years that I knew him I never once saw him the worse for drink. Frankly I would much rather you left me out of your book entirely.

Yours sincerely

Graham Greene

Although Boyle removed the passages Greene objected to and referred to this letter in the published version, he remained critical of Greene's account of Philby as a Communist true-believer. In addition to Philby, Burgess, Maclean and Blunt, the book discusses Greene's friend the translator and literary scholar John Cairncross as the 'fifth man'.

20 Greene had written in the introduction to Philby's book, My Silent War (1968): 'I saw the beginning of this affair – indeed I resigned rather than accept the promotion which was one tiny cog in the machinery of his intrigue. I attributed it then to a personal drive for power, the only characteristic in Philby which I thought disagreeable. I am glad now that I was wrong. He was serving a cause and not himself, and so my old liking for him comes back . . .' (rpt in Collected Essays, 313).

TO DR. ELLEN RIVIÈRE

This Parisian dentist noted the number of characters from her profession who appeared in Greene's novels and asked if this indicated a repressed vocation.

16th May 1979

Dear Doctor Rivière,

Many thanks for your letter and the nice things you say about my books. Yes, I am a little aware of dentists creeping in. The dentist in *The Power and the Glory* can be found also in *The Lawless Roads* and was actually a man I travelled up with to Villahermosa from Frontera.[21] I don't think a repressed vocation is the explanation, but I am certainly aware of very unpleasant childhood memories. As a child I went to a very bad local dentist who caused me agonies. This has made me always associate stained-glass doorways and windows with the old-fashioned dentists. I am glad to say now I have an admirable dentist and friend who is also Greek Consul in Cannes. He has never caused me a moment's agony!

Yours sincerely
Graham Greene

P.S. I think there are more general doctors in my books than dentists, but perhaps that is due to having an elder brother who is a doctor.

TO MURIEL SPARK,

La Résidence des Fleurs, | Avenue Pasteur, | 06600 Antibes |
May 26 '79

Dear Muriel,

How kind you are! *Territorial Rights* arrived today, just after I had

21 See *The Lawless Roads*, 108–27. The dentist in *The Power and the Glory* is an extremely important character. As an Englishman viewing the persecution, he seems to stand in for the author and is given the name Tench, a variation on Greene's pseudonym Hilary Trench.

been reading in the *Nice-Matin* that our mail is being discovered in plastic bags off Cap d'Antibes by skin-divers.

I took the almost unreadable *New Statesman* out to lunch & saw that a woman called Elizabeth Berridge is advertised as saying of you 'She is back in spanking form' – that's going to bring you quite a new class of reader. In the same number of the N.S. I read that 'Fortunately a "little pat" is far from an adequate summing-up of Miss Redgrave.' What are we coming to?

Tonight I shall read *Territorial Rights*. If I am disappointed (which I'm sure I shan't be) it will prove that I am a typical N.S. reader seeking a spanking or a pat.

Love,

Graham

TO MURIEL SPARK

La Résidence des Fleurs, | Avenue Pasteur, | 06600 Antibes |
June 5 '79

Dear Muriel,

It's your best, your very best. I thought you'd never top *Memento Mori*, but you have. I've been reading it all day in one gulp. Written with excitement at 9.35 p.m.

Love,

Graham

The post office is on strike here & I doubt whether this will ever reach you. It's like throwing a message in a bottle into the sea.

TO CHARLES RYCROFT

A London psychoanalyst and author, Rycroft was a critic of the theories of Sigmund Freud. His best-known work is A Critical Dictionary of Psychoanalysis *(1973). Greene found himself enthralled by* The Innocence of Dreams *(1979).*

18th June 1979

Dear Dr. Rycroft,

I am only writing this letter on the distinct understanding that you won't bother to reply to it. As a writer myself I know how irritating it can be to receive letters from strangers however appreciative. I am at the moment reading your book *The Innocence of Dreams* and the fact that I am not yet half way through is a measure of my interest because I am a quick reader as a rule.

There are one or two questions not to be answered but which may be relevant to your own ideas.

1. I am unhappy by the use of message in referring to the unconscious dreamer. This surely supposes a conscious purpose in the dreamer which I find difficult to believe in.
2. This brings in the theory of the censor which you partly accept. Today is there anything in the world of morals that one cannot imagine oneself offending, so what room is there for a censor in our unconscious if we haven't got one in our conscious self? Perhaps this is why the students reported by Calvin Hall did not report any dreams which referred to the dropping of the atomic bomb.[22] It was something they could perfectly well accept in their working life. The censor had nothing to do.

My interest in dreams dates from the age of 16 when I went to a psychoanalyst of no known school. Since then at intervals especially in the 60's and early 70's I have kept dream diaries when I have no work on hand if only to keep my hand in at writing.[23] My experience bears out the fact that one dreams at least four or five times a night when once one has disciplined oneself to have a pencil

22 Rycroft (63) notes that the psychologist Calvin Hall was collecting dreams from American students in the last few days of the war and did not find one that referred to the dropping of the atomic bomb on Hiroshima. From this, Rycroft concludes that dreaming is an egotistic activity just as sleep is.
23 On his deathbed, Greene asked Yvonne Cloetta to organise the publication of selections from the diaries. *A World of My Own* appeared in 1992.

and paper beside one in bed! Is it possible (I repeat that I am not asking for an answer but only putting a question for you to consider) that a writer's profession influences his dreams? I have had two or three dreams which have gone straight into short stories without any great change. I have also found that many dreams are serial going on for periods of more than three days.

One curious experience, or what seems to me curious, came to me in one novel where I was completely blocked and didn't know how to continue the book. It was like coming to a river bank and finding no bridge. I knew what would happen on the other side of the bridge but I couldn't get there. I then had a dream which seemed to me to belong entirely to the character in the book rather than to myself and I was able to insert it in the novel and bridge the river.[24]

Perhaps my questions will be answered by your own book as I have only reached the half-way mark and am looking forward with great enthusiasm to finishing it. I repeat – please do not bother to reply to this letter. It is simply an expression of interest, even of enthusiasm, which needs no reply.

Yours sincerely,

Graham Greene

P.S. Perhaps you have answered my question about the message on page 66.[25]

24 'Querry's dream in A *Burnt-Out Case*, dealing with a lost priesthood and the search for sacramental wine, is an exact reproduction of one of my own dreams which occurred while I was writing the novel at the precise moment when I needed it. I wrote it in the next morning. My novel, *It's a Battlefield*, had its origin in a dream.' (*In Search of a Character*, 75; A *Burnt-out Case*, 42–3).

25 Rycroft writes, somewhat enigmatically: 'The dream agent is some thing that is part of oneself but also more than oneself, that is personally impersonal and impersonally personal, that sends messages without ever willing or deciding to do so but only because it cannot not do so.'

TO JOHN HARRIS

This reader of the The Human Factor *suspected the character Daintry of being a sinister foreign agent because he did not know what Maltesers were, which the reader recalled as having been available at cinemas in his childhood.*

31st July 1979

Dear Mr Harris,

I would defend the maltesers in this way: when the first draft of the book was ready my secretary told me that maltesers no longer existed and I very nearly took them out. However my wife to prove that they could be obtained sent me a packet, but apparently they are much rarer than they used to be. Daintry was a young man when the war came and perhaps he hadn't moved in malteser cinema circles. Anyway they wouldn't have been available in the war and when the war was over so many years later he may have forgotten all about them or perhaps he was confused by the conversation in the Club. As a matter of fact I had forgotten that he hadn't heard of them.

Yours sincerely
Graham Greene

TO HARRIET OLIVERI

This woman in Holbrook, New York, asked Greene to comment on a disagreement she was having with her grandson over the morality of the bombings of Hiroshima and Nagasaki.

15th September 1979

Dear Mrs Oliveri,

Thank you for your letter. I half agree with your grandson, John Gillen. I still remember the shock we felt in Europe at the news. But even if it were a crime I think we owe to the bombing the peace which so far has not been broken between the great powers. It might be argued that a demonstration of the bomb in a desert would have been sufficient to induce the Japanese to surrender, but I doubt whether it would have had the effect on the imagination of the actual bombing. Because of that bombing both great powers are afraid of atomic war. Whether in the long run this will prevent a war remains to be seen.

   Yours sincerely

    Graham Greene

TO ANTHONY BURGESS

Anthony Burgess (1917–93) shared with Greene a fascination with Catholic subjects. According to his biographer Andrew Biswell, Burgess was corresponding regularly with Greene by 1961, when he dedicated the novel The Devil of a State *to him.*[26] *Few of their letters have come to light; it is possible that most were disposed of following their public row in 1988. Here, Greene refers to a radio lecture Burgess gave on the occasion of his seventy-fifth birthday. At the time, the two were caught in a disagreement between their French publisher Robert Laffont and their translators Georges Belmont and Hortense Chabrier.*

9th October 1979

Dear Burgess – or can I say Anthony or should I say Tony?

   Just to put the record straight about your very generous broadcast: it was not *The Heart of the Matter* which was condemned by the Holy Office but *The Power and the Glory* and it was *The Power and the Glory* that Paul VI had read. It does make a good deal of difference because in my opinion *The Heart of the Matter* would be quite rightly condemnable but not *The Power and the Glory*. I do hope you are going to come and see me one day without Georges. I am faced at the moment with a difficult job of writing a letter to Robert Laffont

26 See Andrew Biswell, *The Real Life of Anthony Burgess* (London: Picador, 2005), esp. 379–84.

to say that I am leaving him and following Georges. One of those things one postpones until the last moment.

Yours ever

Graham

TO ANTHONY BURGESS

31st October 1979

Dear Anthony,

I don't envy you your American trip. I have managed to avoid going there now for about 15 years except for my few days in Washington with the Panamanians.

I can't imagine what kind of contract you signed to give Laffont four new novels before you go. In the bad old days in England fifty years ago one had to offer an option on two novels if one was a first novelist but today no options are required. I realise that things are rather different in France but all the same . . . Laffont has no options on my novels. All the same after discussions I am staying with him if Georges continues to translate me. I think there were certain faults on both sides and anyway Georges told me that he and Hortense did not wish me to come to them. It was hitting Laffont too hard and of course I have known him since around 1946.

I am going off to Paris for about a week next week, but after that do ring me up at 33.71.80 and suggest a date for meeting.

Graham

In the background of this letter is a problem Yvonne Cloetta was handling for Graham. Even after many years in France, he had no great command of the language and no basis on which to judge the quality of translations. Cloetta, who moved expertly between French and English, made the final judgement on these questions – usually placing her trust in the distinguished Belmont. The point has a broader significance, since Cloetta is sometimes spoken of as lacking the intelligence to be an equal companion with Graham.[27]

27 See Cloetta, 87–8.

TO AUBERON WAUGH

La Résidence des Fleurs, | Avenue Pasteur, | 06600 Antibes. |
Jan. 29. 80

Dear Bron,

I got your letter today with great relief (letters between England
& France take at least seven days) because I thought my radio talk –
which wasn't scripted but done impromptu – might have hurt.[28] I
prepared myself for the ordeal in the King Edward VII Hospital by
rereading almost every book of Evelyn's. I look back with nostalgia
to that time of peace. Oh, for another operation. But, thank God,
you weren't hurt anyway by the shortened version. I was responsible
for the absurd mistake – that's what comes of speaking without a
script – of 'the cross-Channel' instead of 'trans-Atlantic' love affair.
No one to my horror seems to have noticed it.

[. . .]

TO NICHOLAS DENNYS

*This letter to Graham's nephew, a bookseller, refers to Nelson
Sevenpennies, which Graham and Hugh collected, a series of casebound volumes once published by the Scottish firm Thomas Nelson and Sons, priced
at 7d. The letter mentions David Low, a bookseller whom Graham had
known for many years; their 'bibliophilic correspondence' was published as
Dear David, Dear Graham (1989).*

2nd February 1980

Dear Nick,

Many thanks for your letter. I am glad you had such a good day
with David Low. He's a very nice man. He wrote to me that he had
enjoyed it too. Of course you should sell my letter for what it will
fetch and any future ones!

28 'Graham Greene on Evelyn Waugh as a Novelist', BBC Three, 4 October 1979.

Nelson Sevenpennies: I would like *Major Vigoreux* of Q. and also *In Kedah's Tents* of Merryman and *Born in Exile* of Gissing. Ask Elisabeth to pay you what you ask out of petty cash! Of course I will sign your book for you. Why not leave it with Elisabeth.

I am afraid I don't know anybody but Hugh and I who collect Nelsons. I have none in dust-wrappers but we saw a number in dust-wrappers and a good collection in a bookshop in Leicester once. As I am going there for my play I shall look in again.

Which days are you visible in the Portobello Road? I'd like to call on your stall one day.

Love

Graham

TO MALCOLM MUGGERIDGE

Muggeridge reminded Graham of a compact they had made in Galilee to go on television together when they were eighty and asked him to 'put this rendez-vous forward a year or so'.

La Résidence des Fleurs, | Avenue Pasteur, | 06600 Antibes | 26th March 1980

Dear Malcolm,

I am afraid my decision is a fixed one. I won't appear on television. As for the 80th birthday that is still quite a long way off and I hope to escape having to break my promise!

I have found in writing autobiographical pieces how often memories of even things long past fail or are altered. I noticed a small alteration in your memories in a cutting I received the other day from was it *The Daily Mirror*? I was already installed at SIS when you were recruited, so I can't have asked my sister to put our names up on the top of the In Basket. I had been destined for Monrovia but the Liberians refused to have me and when I was appointed to Freetown I learnt that they needed a man in Lourenço Marques and suggested you in order that you should escape those wintry rides on a motor-cycle.

My love to Kitty
Affectionately
    Graham

TO FATHER LEOPOLDO DURÁN

Martine Cloetta, the daughter of Yvonne and Jacques, found herself bullied
and harassed by her estranged husband, a man with underworld connections
that kept him safe from the law. Greene concluded that Nice was being run
by crooks. He wrote a pamphlet J'Accuse (1982), which some, including
his friend Michael Korda, who decided against publishing it in the United
States, regarded as an old man's eccentricity.[29] Perhaps a case of domestic
abuse would be harder to trivialise a quarter of a century later; feminism has
won that argument.

                                                          9th April 1980

Dearest Leopoldo,

   Thank you for your letter of March 28. I do hope that you had a
happy rest in Galicia at your village and also in our monastery. I am
afraid that when I came back from England things were in a rather
more violent situation than they had been before. Last week the
fiend tried to break into the house of Yvonne and the police had to
be called. The next day when Martine was returning to her
apartment with her children he was waiting and attacked Jacques[30]
who was saved by Martine with the help of a tear-gas bomb. The
authorities seem hopeless in this affair, but now my friend Pierre
who is the Honorary Consul-General for Ireland[31] has written to the
Préfet enclosing a letter which I have proposed to write to *The Times*
about the conditions of the law here. A kind of blackmail.[32] I have
to go to England now for my medical check up and then to see my
daughter in Switzerland but I shall be back on April 16. I hope

29 Michael Korda, 'The Third Man', *New Yorker* (25 March 1996), 49.
30 Jacques Cloetta, Yvonne's husband with whom Graham had an amicable relationship.
31 Pierre Joannon was Honorary Consul General for Ireland in Antibes.
32 Such a letter appeared in *The Times* (25 January 1982); rpt. *Yours etc.*, 207–8.

through this intervention of the Préfet something can be done. The law seems powerless.

I have also had a letter from General Salan in reply to one of mine which definitely establishes that whatever he may say he never belonged to the OAS – the secret army that he always claims was the cause of his imprisonment.[33]

About the end of May, God and not I know whether it would be a good thing. If only we could get a period of peace it might well be the only time when Yvonne and I could go off to Capri and I would be able to do a little bit of work in tranquillity. I want very much to see you and to discuss certain things with you, but we also need a short period of rest. England was a very short period and only led to the drama when he assaulted the house and assaulted Jacques.

When I come back from Switzerland I will write to you again and tell you what the situation is. Certainly we have need of all your prayers. I do hope you had a happy time with the Trappists and I really long to be there again with you. All three of us send our love.

Graham

TO COUNTESS STRACHWITZ (BARBARA GREENE)

La Résidence des Fleurs, | Avenue Pasteur, | 06600 Antibes |
April 17. 80

My dear Barbara,

[. . .]

This is only to explain how impossible it is to be sure when I'll be in England again (I shall have to be there for a medical in October – *my* birthday month!). Gozo is a dream,[34] but if we can get this man

---

33 General Raoul-Albert-Louis Salan (1899-1984) had been head of the OAS, the secret army opposed to Algerian independence. A death sentence for his part in the attempted coup against de Gaulle was commuted to life imprisonment and he was released in 1968. Graham first knew him in Vietnam (*Ways of Escape*, 126 and 139).

34 After the death of her husband, Barbara Greene, who had accompanied Graham on his trek through Liberia in 1934, bought a house around 1970 on the Maltese island of Gozo and spent four to six months there every year (information from Rupert Graf Strachwitz).

behind bars (my writing becomes unreadable) we *have* to go to
Anacapri to see my little house (I am now an honorary citizen) in
the spring – God knows if it will be possible. Impossible even to
work at the moment. Anyway let's keep in touch – this comic
nightmare must end before long either in blood or a laugh. Today I
discussed the matter with the mayor of Antibes who is at least
alerting his police & he said, 'But you are living one of your own
books.'

Anyway, a lot of love,
    Graham

TO LOUISE DENNYS

*In his last decade, Graham relied on his niece as the editor of his works.
Here he discusses drafts of* Ways of Escape, *his second volume of memoirs,
which she knitted together out of his articles and his introductions to the
novels.*

17th June 1980

Dear Louise,

Thank you so much for your letter of June 7 with the enclosures. I
wish I could have been at the party and discovered with you the
secret stair and eaten – however is it made? – the caviar pie. I do
think you are a wonderful publisher – apart from Frere much the
best that I have known. If I have been able to give you a little help it
was worth all the work on the book. Don't worry about letting me
know about all these subsidiary rights. I have absolute trust in you as
a publisher.

Love
    Graham

TO VALENTINA IVASHEVA

A professor of English studies, Ivasheva was one of Graham's closest friends in Russia. Here he responds to the news that her husband has committed suicide by throwing himself from the balcony of their seventh-floor apartment in Moscow.

17th June 1980

My dear Valentina,

Your letter was a great shock. I can't begin to tell you how sorry I am. How terrible it must be for you – much more so than a death in bed. I am quite sure you have nothing to blame yourself for. In his condition it was almost certain that your husband would kill himself one day but now at any rate he is at peace. I don't believe myself that death is the end of everything, or rather my faith tells me that death is not the end of everything and when my belief wavers I tell myself that I am wrong. One can't believe 365 days a year, but my faith tells me that my reasoning is wrong. There is a mystery which we won't be able to solve as long as we are alive. Personally even when I doubt I go on praying at night my own kind of prayers. Why not try at night talking to your husband and telling him all you think. Who knows whether he mightn't be able to hear you and now with a mind unclouded?

[. . .]

TO FRANCIS GREENE

Greene was twice called upon as intermediary in kidnappings by Salvadoran rebels. In the first case, two bankers were released upon payment of a $5,000,000 ransom by their employer, a branch of Lloyd's. The second case involved Ambassador Dunne of South Africa. Graham's contact with the guerrillas was through the novelist Gabriel García Márquez in Mexico City.

130 Boulevard Malesherbes, | Paris 17. | Sep. 11 1980

Dear Francis,

This 'happy birthday' will arrive a bit late I'm afraid. I'm back from Panama (again the guest of Omar Torrijos) & three days in Nicaragua (the guest of Borge – most equal among the equal Sandinista junta) & meeting in Panama the rather creepy little head of the San Salvador rebels ('pen name' Marcial) & putting in a word for the poor South African ambassador who has been in their captivity for about 9 months. My fifth trip to Central America! Why? I suppose anything to get away from Antibes in August.

[. . .]

The Popular Liberation Front (FLP) led by Salvador Cayetano ('Marcial') was one of the groups that combined into the Farabundo Marti National Liberation Front (FMLN). Greene had met with Cayetano c. 20 August 1980 and provided the names of two South African millionaires who might pay the ransom. His mediation proved vain. Ambassador Dunne died in captivity several months later.[35]

TO JOHN MICHAEL GIBSON

John Michael Gibson approached Greene to provide a preface to A Bibliography of A. Conan Doyle (1983). He had compiled this book in collaboration with Richard Lancelyn Green, whose bizarre suicide in 2004 was said to have been modelled on 'The Problem of Thor Bridge'.

20th October 1980

Dear Mr. Gibson,

Thank you very much for your letter of October 4. It is very kind of you to invite me to write a preface to your bibliography of Doyle's writings and if you didn't mind a very unscholarly and short one I would be pleased to do it. One point I would like to make is how

35 *Getting to Know the General*, 134–41.

good a writer he was apart from [the] Sherlock Holmes works. I can reread him as I find myself unable to reread Virginia Woolf and Forster, but then I am not a literary man.

    Yours sincerely
      Graham Greene

TO ANNE AND FRANCIS GREENE

51 La Résidence des Fleurs, | Avenue Pasteur, | 06 Antibes. | Jan. 16. '81

My dear Anne & Francis,

The splendid box of goodies arrived today (the box worthy of the contents). Thank you so much. I hastened to unpack it before Yvonne arrived in case it contained a bomb. One lives a strange life here. A week ago an anonymous type rang me up & asked whether I would receive 3 Brigades Rouges. I said, 'No!' He said, 'Why?' I said, 'Because I would have to leave France if I did.'

There have been other dramas. Daniel, the ex-husband, attacked his mistress with such violence her nose was broken & she came to Yvonne & 'told all' (his corruption of the police & even a member of the procureur's office. Also his obsession with murdering Yvonne by putting some explosive substance in the oil of her car.) I thought that at last we had to go to the top. So I sent a letter to the Chancellor of the Legion returning my insignia & saying that I wanted to be free to speak out against the corruption of justice on the Côte. I sent a copy with another letter to Alain Peyrefitte, the Minister of Justice.[36] Immediate action. The Grand Boissieu[37] returned my insignia & Peyrefitte wrote & spoke to me on the telephone, saying he was sending his Inspector General & a colleague down the next day. Two extremely nice men. He had expected to stay 24 hours & stayed four days – he was quite

36 Alain Peyrefitte (1925–99), historian and Minister of Justice under President Valéry Giscard d'Estaing.
37 General Alain de Boissieu was then the Grand Chancellor. He returned the insignia with the observation that Greene might find it useful in his campaign.

overwhelmed by what he found. Now I think action will not be long delayed. Light at last at the end of the tunnel.

Love from us both,

Graham

TO SHIRLEY HAZZARD

Alicja Wesolowska, who had been a doctoral student in New York, was on her way to a UN posting in Outer Mongolia when she was arrested on 10 August 1979 in Poland on an espionage charge, something that often happened to returning exiles. Despite protests on her behalf, she was imprisoned until 1984.

La Résidence des Fleurs, | Avenue Pasteur, | 06600 Antibes |
17th January 1981

Dear Shirley,

It was nice hearing your voice on the telephone. Perhaps by this time you have received my letter about cancelling my Polish visit. Apparently it did go off safely from London! In April I am getting something called the Jerusalem Prize which is given for the defence of the individual. I shall have to make a short speech apparently and if our hunger striker has survived and nothing has been done about her case I would like to introduce it into my speech. It might catch the attention of journalists. Could you send me not a lot of documents but a brief resumé of the whole affair in your own words. I would have to receive it before I leave for Israel on April 2. Do include in your resumé the attempts to get that awful man at the head of the United Nations to take action.

Our love to both of you

Graham

P.S. I notice that Kurt Waldheim omits from *Who's Who* whatever career he had between 1939 and 1945. Can you give me details? Why does he omit all this from *Who's Who* which is always provided by the character himself?

P.P.S. This morning January 17 I have received the following telegram from Waldheim:

'Dear Mr Greene. Your telegram of 13 January raises the problem of United Nations employees under detention. Particularly Ms. Alicja Wesolowska. I can assure you I have personally followed this problem very closely and expressed my concern both privately and publicly. As recently as 13 January 1981 I reiterated my appeal to the government of Poland to exercise clemency in Ms. Wesolowska's case and requested access to her by a United Nations representative. My efforts will continue as long as necessary. Yours sincerely (Kurt Waldheim – General United Nations).'

One would like to know what reply he received to his appeal of January 13. The telegram is addressed to me at Résidence des Pleurs. Somewhat symbolic?

Graham's remarks about Waldheim's war years anticipated the revelations during his 1986 campaign for the Austrian Presidency that he had served in a German army unit guilty of atrocities in Yugoslavia. A prominent novelist, Hazzard wrote two books and a number of articles on the failures of the UN, most importantly The Countenance of Truth: The United Nations and the Waldheim Case *(1990).*

TO AUBERON WAUGH

In Private Eye *(13 February 1981) Waugh claimed that Patrick Jenkins had lied in the claim that there was an epidemic of alcoholism in Britain. Rather, figures from the World Health Organisation showed that drunkenness was at a dangerously low level. He suggested that Jenkins be thrown into a duckpond according to the old method of testing whether a man with three nipples is a witch.*

17th February 1981

Dear Bron,

I was painfully reminded by your Diary in the 500th issue of *Private Eye* of the fact that I have four nipples. A doctor when I was examined medically at the beginning of World War II made the same remark that in the Middle Ages I would have been regarded as a witch. I haven't addressed this letter to *Private Eye* because I would hate to think that 150,000 people who buy the paper might want to investigate my four nipples.

    Affectionately
    Graham

TO MICHAEL MEYER

La Résidence des Fleurs, | Avenue Pasteur, | 06600 Antibes |
13th April 1981

Dear Michael,

Forgive the delay in answering your letter as I have been away for a week in Jerusalem and was faced with a big mail when I returned. I am delighted to hear [of] the success of your Strindberg.[38] I am coming to London on Monday April 20. Would there be any possibility of seeing it that night? I shall be alone and it would be nice if you would come with me but perhaps you have seen it too often now.

I did see *Kagemusha*[39] and I am afraid beautiful though it was visually I was awfully bored by it. I seem to have been the only person to have had this reaction. No, I have great doubts about the Roger Hollis story and Mr. Chapman Pincher.[40] It looks to me like a classical piece of disinformation and destabilization – perhaps engineered, who knows, by Kim.

    Love to you and your daughter
    Graham

38 Meyer's *Lunatic and Lover*, a play about Strindberg, had been produced both on stage and radio.

39 A Kurosawa film set in sixteenth-century Japan.

40 In *Their Trade is Treachery* (1981), the journalist and novelist Chapman Pincher named Sir Roger Hollis (1905–73), the former head of MI5, as a member of the Cambridge spy-ring.

TO AVITAL SCHARANSKY

Writing to the wife of Anatoly (Natan) Scharansky, the Ukrainian mathe-
matician and dissident imprisoned for treason, Graham expressed concern
that if he accepted an invitation to the Soviet Union he might find his visit
used by the government for propaganda purposes.

22nd April 1981

Dear Mrs Scharansky,

Thank you for the documents you sent me. Alas, I hadn't got your address in Paris or in London where I hope you had a useful visit. I have telegraphed as follows to the man[41] who had invited me to Moscow and Georgia:

'Having met Mrs Anatoly Scharansky in Jerusalem and heard full details of her husband's tragic case feel unable to visit USSR. With great regret and affection.'

I don't know who was really behind the invitation which must have had some sort of object, but whoever he might be he will certainly have seen the telegram. It's a small effort, but one never knows – it may be of some use.

I hope we shall be able to meet again one day and that soon there will be good news for you.

Yours sincerely
Graham Greene

TO MICHAEL KORDA

La Résidence des Fleurs, | Avenue Pasteur, | 06600 Antibes |
30th May 1981

Dear Michael,

I have always been meaning to ask you whether it would be possible for you to get my dossier from the FBI under the Freedom of

41 A translator named Boris Izakov.

Information procedure. I would be quite ready to pay all expenses. It might even make an amusing article with my comments if there is sufficient material. I suspect with Vietnam etc. there might be sufficient material.

   Affectionately
      Graham

Graham received a dossier of forty-five pages, of which sixteen were blacked out. The rest were mainly press clippings, including a two-page gossip piece by Walter Winchell. Amidst various inaccuracies, Graham was pleased to note that they got his weight right at 180 pounds.[42] *Twenty years later Rob Evans and David Hencke, two journalists, made a new application under the Freedom of Information Act with better results: they learned that the FBI had indeed monitored Graham's activities over a forty-year period (Guardian, 2 December 2002). However, while the release of the thicker dossier merited a headline, it contained little that Graham had not already made public in his own writings. The FBI could have saved its money.*

TO JOSÉ DE JESÚS MARTINEZ (CHUCHU)

As Graham was preparing to leave for a visit to Panama, he received word that Omar Torrijos had died in the crash of a small plane.

7 August 1981

Dear Chuchu,

   It's difficult to write about Omar's death. I really loved that man. What an extraordinary thing it was that a tiny country like Panama produced one of the great men of our time. Perhaps the Panamanians will miss him the least. I can imagine what a catastrophe his death will seem in Nicaragua, and San Salvador, and Belize – as far anyway as Price is concerned.[43] I had already

42 'Freedom of Information', *Spectator*, 7 April 1984, rpt. *Reflections*, 303–5.
43 George Price, a former seminarian, was the first prime minister of Belize. Greene admired him as a man of principle, and Diederich recalls his frugality with his nation's money was such that when he visited Miami he would take a bus downtown rather than a taxi (e-mail to RG, 5 February 2005).

packed my bags to come to you last Wednesday and the shock left
me staggered.

I have an idea in which perhaps you will be able to help me when
the time comes. I have a short novel about a Spanish priest
Monsignor Quixote which I hope to finish before the end of the
year. After that I want to write a short fiction book called simply *The
General*. I have so many records of him in the three or four diaries
which I kept in Panama with a lot of his conversation and I will try
to draw a good portrait of him. I am sure I can depend on you to
criticize the draft when once it has been made and to make
suggestions.

You must feel terribly lost. Are you going to leave the National
Guard and concentrate on the University? Please when your mind
has settled a bit write me a few words to say how you are. Yvonne
will want to add her love to mine even though she has never met
you, but she always says that your voice sounded exactly on the
telephone as she had always imagined it.

My love again
Graham

*Chuchu was convinced that there had been a bomb aboard the plane, a posi-
tion Graham advanced in* Getting to Know the General. *The plane's
manufacturers concluded that the crash was accidental, the result of bad
weather. Bernard Diederich conducted his own thorough investigation and
reached the same conclusion.*

TO COUNTESS STRACHWITZ (BARBARA GREENE)

La Résidence des Fleurs, | Avenue Pasteur, | 06600 Antibes. |
22nd June 1982

Dear Barbara,

Thank you so much for your letter and your kind thoughts. Yes,
this war has been going on a long time; we are now in our fourth
year and I hope we are reaching a crisis. Anyway I have four writs
against me, three of which have to be tried in Paris and I hope will

procure some publicity against our enemies. All the same it's a tiring affair. I am asking Elisabeth to send you a copy of the pamphlet which will give you the whole story. Last week the Nice judges decided that the pamphlet in France was to be seized because it intruded on the private life of our enemy Guy. I knew nothing about the hearing because I was in Paris. The Bodley Head who are also concerned had received no warning nor my advocate. He is appealing against the procedure which is typical of Nice. When will the end come? Who knows? One hopes by the end of the year at least.

    [. . .]

The battle went on for two more years, but the litigation eventually turned in Martine Cloetta's favour. She won clear custody of the children by the summer of 1984 and moved to Switzerland. As a test of Graham's character, the episode has important implications. Nearly eighty years old, he was willing to risk, on the one hand, violence, on the other, mockery and condescension, to protect a person he loved. Part of his sacrifice was that after Monsignor Quixote *(1982) he had the stamina to finish only one more novel,* The Captain and the Enemy, *which he had begun in the mid-1970s.*

TO ——

A woman (her name withheld here) who had recently read The End of the Affair *wrote to Graham about her own dilemma. She was married to a civil servant who permitted her to conduct an affair with a writer. She said that she loved both men and they loved her. Unlike Sarah, she did not have faith to fall back on and she had no intention of dying. She asked what she should do.*

2nd August 1982

Dear Mrs. ——,

    You ask me a question impossible for a stranger to answer. I can only suggest that you do nothing hurriedly and let the situation continue as it is for as long as possible. Perhaps you are too bored with security, but I can tell you from my own experience that insecurity can be very boring too. Companionship is not something to throw over lightly, but of course nor is love – if it lasts.

All this is no answer, but I can hardly be expected to find one.

Yours sincerely

Graham Greene

TO MALCOLM MUGGERIDGE

The following letter was written on the occasion of Muggeridge's reception into the Roman Catholic Church.

La Résidence des Fleurs, | Avenue Pasteur, | 06600 Antibes |
Nov. 3 82

My dear Malcolm,

I don't know whether to congratulate you or to commiserate with you on making your decision, but I can sincerely wish you good luck & I can also hope that you will make a better Catholic than I have done. Anyway you will both be in my thoughts at 12.30 (French time!) on Nov. 27.

My love to Kitty & yourself,

Graham

TO MR. COREY[44]

15th December 1982

Dear Mr. Corey,

Thank you for your letter and the nice things you write about my work. I think you have a little misread the opening chapter of *The Quiet American*. Fowler records the conversation with Vigot, which,

44 Not otherwise identified.

of course, is a very carefully phrased one, to guard himself. But until Vigot's questions show him that Pyle is dead he is not certain of it. Although he has signalled to the Vietminh an indication of Pyle's movements that night he hopes against hope that Pyle will have escaped.

So in a sense he is still waiting for Pyle, hoping that he may after all turn up. You have to remember that the point of view throughout is Fowler's and Fowler's motives are mixed. Jealousy of Pyle over Phuong is one motive and his horror at the bomb outside the Continental in which Pyle is obviously concerned is another motive. The telegram from his wife [is] a cruel irony at the end. I wouldn't describe his remark at the end as being a demand for forgiveness. It's only a regret that he has no religious faith and therefore he can't ask for forgiveness.

Yours sincerely

Graham Greene

TO VIVIEN GREENE

La Résidence des Fleurs, | Avenue Pasteur, | 06600 Antibes | Dec. 30 82.

Dear Vivien,

Many thanks for the fire extinguisher! I realise that I have lit a fire in Nice, but I don't want to put it out!

The Christmas holiday was a little shadowed by the death of poor Raffles.[45] Now I'm off to Nicaragua (as the guest of the Sandinista government) to light a small fire under the fool Reagan.

Affectionately,

Graham

---

45 Raffles, Caroline's coffee-coloured miniature poodle, was struck by a car on Boxing Day.

TO BERNARD DIEDERICH

La Résidence des Fleurs, | Avenue Pasteur, | 06600 Antibes |
2nd February 1983

Dear Bernard,

I did a piece on regional television about that hatchet job in *Time*.[46] It struck me too as completely unconvincing and I said on screen that I did not believe a word of it and that it read like the attempt of a young deserter to please his new friends. I also showed on screen photographs of some of the unpleasant bombs being used from the United States including the Micky Mouse. I was very surprised *Time* printed it as they have been on the whole quite good about San Salvador and previously about Nicaragua. And they don't either seem to be very pleased with the Washington administration.

I had an amusing meeting with Fidel in my twenty-four hours in Cuba. He looked to me much younger than he had done in 1966 and much more relaxed.

Affectionately
Graham
[. . .]

TO FIDEL CASTRO

Although he admired Castro, Greene was aware of the denial of human rights in Cuba. He cooperated closely with the Writers in Prison Committee of International PEN, which supplied him with information on detainees. The committee arranged for this letter to be translated and delivered.

46 In an interview with James Willmerth (*Time*, 24 January 1983), Roberto Guillén claimed that he had left the counter-intelligence service of the Defence Ministry and joined the defector Eden Pastora's guerrillas in Costa Rica because of the Sandinistas' use of torture and disappearances against their political foes. He claimed that he himself had been asked to organise the slaughter of eight hundred Miskito Indians.

[14 February 1983]

Dear Mr. President,

It was a great pleasure for me to meet you again after sixteen years, and I am grateful to Colonel Diaz and Colonel Noriega[47] who made my journey possible. You and I had a great mutual friend in General Torrijos whom I had grown to love almost as a brother, but I was happy and encouraged to feel that his line was being followed in Panama in spite of superficial difficulties.

Will you forgive me if as a writer and a member of International PEN I put in a plea for two writers Angel Cuadra Landrove and Jorge Valls Arango. I know nothing of their offences, but I feel that an amnesty would have a good and useful effect in Europe at this time when we are suffering from the stubborn policies of President Reagan.

Yours in most sincere friendship

Graham Greene

Angel Cuadra Landrove (b. 1931) was a poet and activist released in May 1982 after fifteen years in prison; he was refused an exit visa and required to report weekly to the police. It was feared that he would be re-arrested. In 1984, he was finally allowed to leave. At the time of this letter, the poet Jorge Valls Arango was being confined incommunicado and had had no family visits in two years. He is now in exile in the United States.

TO RICHARD INGRAMS

One of the founders of Private Eye *and for many years its editor, Ingrams (b. 1937) has become the world's authority on pseuds.*

47 After the death of Omar Torrijos, the politically flatfooted General Ruben Dario Paredes took over, but Colonel Diaz Herrera and Colonel Manuel Noriega (soon to promote himself to General) were locked in a struggle for power. Greene was sympathetic to Diaz, who later succumbed to a mental illness and went into exile (e-mail Bernard Diederich to RG 19 February 2005). Although Greene speaks well of him here, he came to distrust Noriega and by 1988 believed that Noriega might kill him and blame it on the CIA if he returned to Panama (see p. 400).

La Résidence des Fleurs, | Avenue Pasteur, | 06600 Antibes |
Sep. 27 '83

Dear Richard Ingrams,

No letters are being accepted for 'abroad' at this moment, so I must send very tardy thanks for the *Oxford Book of Pseuds* which you have so kindly sent me. I was delighted by it a) for the binding, b) for the exposure of poor Burgess & (I won't say *poor*) Levin, c) for the confirmation of my belief that the true home of the Pseuds is in the so-called 'quality' press. *The Sunday Times*, as one would have expected, narrowly beats *The Observer*: S. T. 16 entries, *Observer* 15 – *The Times* takes a close third place with 14 examples & *The Guardian* unexpectedly lags behind with only 10. I'm rather sorry to see that the *New Statesman* with 5 has been beaten by *The Spectator* (whom I am sure we both love) with nine.

Anyway I hope that this research shows my appreciation of your present. Only one complaint: you have given T. S. Eliot one L too many.

Yours ever,

Graham Greene

TO ED ROLLMAN

Having read The Power and the Glory, *Ed Rollman of Bremerton, Washington, wrote to Greene on 24 October 1983: 'What troubles me and so I would like to ask you is do you really believe in Marxism? Because to me that is really scary. I mean to be a Marxist is to be communist isn't it?'*

9th November 1983

Dear Mr. Rollman,

No, I am not a communist nor am I a Marxist. Perhaps you will find my position best expressed in a novel called *Monsignor Quixote*. Personally I find *Das Kapital* unreadable, though I have struggled with it. The trouble is that your rulers are apt to consider anyone who is left of centre, even Social Democrats, Marxist. The word has become completely misused.

Yours sincerely

Graham Greene

TO EDWARD GREENE

In a letter of 26 December 1983, Graham's cousin Edward (1904–90), known as 'Tooter', recalled how in his two years as a coffee trader he had visited Nicaragua and El Salvador and seen traders living in luxury, children starving and governments propped up solely because they were not Communist.

2nd January 1984

My dear Tooter,

Forgive a dictated letter, but my hand is not very good at writing. I agree with every word you write in your letter. I have been to Nicaragua twice since the revolution, in 1980 and 1983, and I am very impressed by what they are doing. They had the brilliant idea of sending school children who had reached the higher class for several months into the countryside to live with the peasants and to work with them and in the evening to teach them to read and write. In this period they reduced illiteracy from I think it was 30% to 13%. Five of the school children were murdered by Somozista guerillas and a number died of sickness, but they had a huge national greeting when they returned to Managua.

I know Tomas Borge the Minister of the Interior, Umberto Ortega the Head of Defence, Daniel Ortega the chief man in the Junta, Father Cardenale the Minister of Culture and Lenin Cerna the Chief of Security. I have just met Father Escoto the Foreign Minister. Of course there are Marxists in the Government –Tomas Borge in particular, but the presence of the two Catholic priests as Ministers and the fact that health and education are in the hands of a Jesuit guarantees that this will not be a conventional Communist government.

[. . .]

TO ELISABETH DENNYS (NÉE GREENE)

La Résidence des Fleurs, | Avenue Pasteur, | 06600 Antibes. |
March 19 '84

Dearest Elisabeth,

We only really got to know each other at the time of Munich, but how much I have owed to you since to the present day. A very happy birthday to you, & this is a totally inadequate present. Buy something stupid & pretty, or perhaps it will help with a holiday.

All my love & Yvonne sends hers too.

Graham

TO BERNARD DIEDERICH

La Résidence des Fleurs, | Avenue Pasteur, | 06600 Antibes. |
3rd April 1984

Dear Bernard,

Many thanks for your letter. Your spelling of Espriella[48] has gone rather astray! Chuchu arrived safely and corrected many misspellings of mine. I would have liked you to have seen the book before publication but we are anxious to get it out before the American elections – Chuchu is especially anxious. He likes it better than I do. His character really overshadows Omar in the book and I feel it an uneasy falling between two stools of memoirs and autobiography. However I will follow Chuchu's advice and publish.

I have hopes that Hart will beat both Mondale and Reagan. I don't feel it likely somehow that Reagan will go whole-hog on an invasion of Nicaragua. After all the Pentagon decided that it would need a hundred thousand troops to guard the Canal so I should imagine it would need close to half a million to do anything in Nicaragua.

---

48 Ricardo de la Espriella had resigned the presidency of Panama under duress on 13 February.

I begin to feel old and tired, so though Chuchu brought me letters from Colonel Diaz, Noriega and Espriella, who sent me a picture also, I doubt whether I shall take off again for Central America. I shall probably go no further than Spain this year.

Affectionately
Graham

TO JONATHAN BOURGET

La Résidence des Fleurs, | Avenue Pasteur, | 06600 Antibes |
Oct. 23 '84

My dear Jonathan,

I'm afraid that in my fleeting visits we have little time to talk, but I am so glad to hear that you called on Martine & the children. They were all delighted with you, & want to see you again.

I know that life for you at this stage is not very easy (it's not all that easy at my stage!), but I do want you to feel that you can write to me in confidence & if there is any way that I can help I'll do my best. We are too alike to remain strangers!

Love,
Graham

TO JOCELYN RICKARDS (DONNER)

La Résidence des Fleurs, | Avenue Pasteur, | 06600 Antibes |
5th November 1984

My dear Jocelyn,

I haven't read Freddie's autobiography, but next time I am in Hatchards I'll look in the index and find what he says! Of course write what you like. I'm no more ashamed of our affair than you are. It will probably bring my biographer Norman Sherry on your heels, but he's a nice man and I don't think that he is going to bother much about the private life.

    Much love

      Graham

Rickards had had a long affair with the sceptical philosopher A. J. Ayer and a short one with Graham c. 1953. Ayer's second volume of autobiography More of My Life *was published in 1984. Greene's* The End of the Affair *was, in some respects, a dispute with the ideas of Ayer.*

TO MAHAUT COSTE

13th March 1985

Dear Mlle Coste,

    I first used the distinction between entertainment and novels because I thought some of my books were more adventure stories and less serious than the others. I found more and more that the distinction was a bad one and that the two types of book came closer and closer to each other. I abandoned the distinction altogether in the case of *Travels with My Aunt*, which I thought was on one side quite a funny book and could be described as an entertainment but on the other hand it was a book that described old age and death. The difficulty began with *Brighton Rock*. *Brighton Rock* was published under the category of entertainment in the United States but I dropped that distinction in England where it was published under the heading of novel. The whole idea of distinguishing between the two genres was a mistake from the beginning and I am glad that I have abandoned it.

    Yours sincerely

      Graham Greene

P.S. I think the first time that I distinguished a book as entertainment was *A Gun for Sale* where I wanted my publisher to issue it under an assumed name[49] but I found that if I did so I would

49 Hilary Tench. See p. 71.

have a very small advance which I couldn't afford to accept so instead of the assumed name I used the word entertainment.

TO ROALD DAHL

Roald Dahl (1916–90), the author of James and the Giant Peach *and* Charlie and the Chocolate Factory, *wrote a memoir* Boy: Tales of Childhood *(1984), which recounted odd episodes of school fagging, such as having been forced by an older boy to warm a frost-covered toilet seat with his buttocks.*

13th May 1985

Dear Roald Dahl,

I have just finished reading *Boy* with immense pleasure and great horror. It's extraordinary to me that you had an operation for removing the adenoids without an anaesthetic in those past days when in 1910 I remember having a total anaesthetic at home and my tonsils and adenoids removed. I was shocked too by all the beatings and I realize now even more what an advanced man my father was as Headmaster of Berkhamsted. No prefects or fagging there. I look forward immensely to the sequel and I look forward too to a visit again from you here.

Yours ever

Graham Greene

10

THE LAST WORD

TO KIM PHILBY

In a letter of 10 October 1985 Philby thanked Greene for the gift of The
Tenth Man *and remarked that if it and not* The Third Man *had been
filmed he might have been spared some personal notoriety. He joked about
Graham's numeric titles, remarking that seven and thirteen would have a
cabbalistic significance: 'you seem to prefer ordinals to cardinals'. He wished
that the Pope would not talk about birth control and that 'the White House
phoney wouldn't talk, period'.*

24th October 1985

My Dear Kim,

Many thanks for your note of October 10. I am glad *The Tenth
Man* reached you safely – not that it was a very valuable gift! You
know how much I share your views not only about a man in
Washington but about a man in Rome. He is the most political Pope
we have suffered for many generations.

I am just back from Washington where I went for a question and
answer session at Georgetown University. I had hoped that there
would be some questions about the man in Washington and his
policy in Central America above all, but unfortunately no questions
emerged, although through a question on the Pope I was able to give
my views in a small way about Nicaragua.

I wish I was a fly on the wall when there is a meeting between your man and the B-Film actor.[1]

Yours ever
   Graham

TO MALCOLM MUGGERIDGE

La Résidence des Fleurs, | Avenue Pasteur, | 06600 Antibes
[November 1985]

My dear Malcolm,

Thank you many times for your letter. *Night & Day* has brought many memories back to me too.[2] Including 'Dream Land'. I think some of the best things in it were your voyages with Hugh Kingsmill – perhaps best of all the Wordsworth interview.

I'm so sorry about the deafness (even though part a blessing). And near blindness I couldn't take with your courage. I had the Reagan cancer six years ago which alas! means that he may survive it as long as I have done.[3] You have a blessing in Kitty (to whom all my love) & I for the last 26 years have had a blessing in Yvonne. Alas! that I can't take her with me next week to Panama & Nicaragua.[4] I wish you could come with me to laugh in another Dreamland.

Anyway all my affection while we march almost shoulder to shoulder towards what end?
   Graham

1 Mikhail Gorbachev had taken over as Secretary General of the Communist Party on 11 March 1985. His first summit with Ronald Reagan was set for November.

2 Christopher Hawtree's edition of the magazine *Night and Day* had recently appeared with a preface by Greene.

3 Ronald Reagan had a portion of his colon removed on 13 July 1985.

4 Greene arrived in Panama on 30 November.

TO ALBERTO HUERTA, S. J.

Now an Associate Professor in the Department of Modern and Classical Languages at the University of San Francisco, Alberto Huerta's scholarly interests include Miguel de Unamuno and Cervantes, both of whose works loom large in Monsignor Quixote. *Huerta wrote to Greene about the novel in 1982 and the two struck up a close friendship. Unlike the conservative Father Durán, whom Greene admired and relied on for other reasons, Huerta belonged to the Jesuit order and shared his opinions about politics in Central America.*

La Résidence des Fleurs, | Avenue Pasteur, | 06600 Antibes |
15 February 1986

Dear Alberto,

Many thanks for your letter. Of course I would like to make a second visit to San Francisco, but it all depends what I am doing and what I am feeling like! About Unamuno whom I read of course in translation: I have read *Our Lord Don Quixote, The Agony of Christianity, The Tragic Sense of Life, Ficciones* and *Novela.*[5] I think I have attempted *Don Quixote* several times in the far past but never succeeded in getting right through. The first was in the translation by a contemporary English writer, I mean contemporary with Cervantes, and finally when I was planning my book I managed to get through Cohen's translation. I do find the Interludes very boring.

Forgive a hasty note, but I have only just come back from abroad.

Affectionately
Graham

TO JOCELYN RICKARDS

Perhaps embarrassed by A. J. Ayer's woefully indiscreet memoirs, Rickards wrote her own autobiography, The Painted Banquet: My Life and Loves *(1987).*

5 See Alberto Huerta, 'El lugar de Don Quijote: Miguel de Unamuno, Graham Greene y Carlos Fuentes', in *Religion y Cultura* (Julio–Agosto 1986).

La Résidence des Fleurs, | Avenue Pasteur, | 06600 Antibes |
21.2.86

Dearest Jocelyn,

Thank you so much for your letter – one of the few out of about
100 which has given me real pleasure.[6]

I'm so glad your book is ready. I long to read it – not because of
what Freddie says. I have read his two volumes – the only thing I
liked in the second was your photograph. He seemed to have no idea
of what to leave out & I found it hard to finish. Names dropped like
rain on a windless day – I longed for a mistral to chase them away.
Poor Freddie – you mustn't wear yourself out with boosting his
morale as you nearly did with Chandler.[7]

Much love to you & affectionate greetings to Clive.

Graham

[*On envelope flap:*] I always return with pleasure to your two paintings
in Anacapri – especially the nuns. Are you painting still? I hope so.

TO LADY DIANA COOPER

La Résidence des Fleurs, | Avenue Pasteur, | 06600 Antibes |
28.2.86

Dear Diana,

Only yesterday did I get your letter of the 12th (French post or
English post or the horrible weather). Thank you so much, but I find
myself depressed, even though pleased, by the award. It's like writing
Finis at the end of a book.

I wish I could say that I was the Graham who sent you the
Christmas message. At that season I close the doors & the windows –
no Christmas cards, no replies to Christmas cards. It's a season I

6 Congratulating him on being awarded the Order of Merit.
7 She had been one of a number of friends who attempted to support Raymond
Chandler in times of depression. (Obituary of Rickards, *Guardian*, 14 July 2005)

hate – good for the shops, good for Harrods. I want to be alone. But that doesn't mean that I don't think of my friends – & of you.

Affectionately,

Graham

I wish that dear Evelyn had got that O.M. I would rather have followed in his footsteps than those of Jolly Jack Priestley.[8]

TO JOCELYN RICKARDS

La Résidence des Fleurs, | Avenue Pasteur, | 06600 Antibes | May 23 86

Very dear Jocelyn,

Thank you so much for sending me the autobiography which I read in one gulp as I'm off to Switzerland tomorrow. I was glad at the happy ending, though a little sad earlier. How much simpler & easier things seemed in the fifties – the early fifties. I found myself remembering a disappointment in Battersea Park during the Festival of Britain & a strange train journey from Southend.[9] Why should remembering happy times make one sad?

Very Affectionately

Graham

TO RUFA AND KIM PHILBY

In a letter of 24 September 1986, Kim Philby wrote to thank Graham and Yvonne for their visit. He was himself suffering from 'an acute attack of the esprit d'escalier' and Rufa, his fourth wife, felt that the three days they had spent on and off together were among the happiest of her life. In a PS he noted that after Graham and Yvonne had left the flat, he found that Yvonne had left half her whisky-and-soda: 'Naturally, I drank it.'

8 J. B. Priestley received his OM in 1977.

9 They made love in a first-class carriage. See obituary of Jocelyn Rickards, *Telegraph* (12 July 2005).

La Résidence des Fleurs, | Avenue Pasteur, | 06600 Antibes |
Oct. 6. 86

Dear Rufa & Kim,

Thank you so much for your letter. We loved our visit to you &
the strong feeling of how our friendship has survived all these years
untouched. It was a great dividend too to see you twice more.
Yvonne tells everyone that her visit to Russia was the greatest
adventure of her life.

I was so happy to meet Rufa & to feel her fondness for you. A
party of four fond people is a rare [?] experience. I do hope the
opportunity of seeing you both will come again before too long.
Yvonne is glad that you finished her whisky.

With great affection from us both
Graham

[*Yvonne adds a postscript calling their gathering* 'une soirée
inoubliable'.]

TO JOCELYN RICKARDS

La Résidence des Fleurs, | Avenue Pasteur, | 06600 Antibes |
5th November 1986

Dearest Jocelyn,

Your letter took 9 days to arrive! The posts here are really
dreadful or is it in England? Thank you so much for it. Forgive a
dictated letter on a beastly new machine to which I am slowly
becoming accustomed but Yvonne and I returned a bit exhausted by
Russian hospitality. All the same it was a wonderful journey and full
of interest. We even met the cosmonaut who had made the record
time of three months in space and he presented me with his marked
copy of a Penguin of *Our Man in Havana* which he had taken with
him into space!

I sent off a few lines to John Curtis[10] for his cover and I hope they are suitable.

Yvonne sends her love and so do I.

Graham

TO JAMES GREENE

Upon hearing that Hugh was near death, Graham hurried back from Moscow and reached the King Edward Hospital shortly before his 'favourite brother' died from cancer on 19 February 1987.[11] This letter to James Greene (b. 1938), Hugh's son by his first wife, refers to Sarah (née Grahame), Hugh's fourth wife, and to James's brother and two half-brothers.

Antibes | Feb. 26 '87

Dear James,

I don't need to tell you how shattered I was by Hugh's death. I tried to return more quickly from Moscow, but there was no plane. It was terrible sitting beside him the day I returned, in his coma, and when you rang me up at Bentley's it was a sort of relief, knowing he wouldn't have to struggle any more with his breath.

I'm sorry I couldn't come to the funeral, but Moscow and Hugh's death had knocked me out. I still find it difficult to do anything – the last sight of his face comes between the lines when I read.

Elisabeth tells me how splendidly you spoke at the church. It was more than I could have done. Please forgive me for not being there. I couldn't bear the thought of all the strangers.

I found Sarah wonderful.

Lots of love to you – and your family.

Graham

10 A cover endorsement for *The Painted Banquet*, published by Weidenfeld & Nicolson in 1987.

11 Durán, 268–9; ODNB.

I've tried to telephone you, but I seem to have got the number wrong. I can't write (bad hand) to all four of you so would you convey my sympathy to the other three?

TO JAMES GREENE

10th March 1987

Dear James,

I think our letters crossed. Thank you very much for sending me Hugh's little poem which I think is rather good.[12] Many congratulations on the birth of the little girl. I hope she won't take after Hugh in height.

Yes, the death was a bad shock. We had shared a great many experiences including the war in Malaya. I had also interested him in pirates and read aloud to him when he was six years old. I found the sight of him very painful, and the breathing was so heavy and strained. I find it difficult to get it out of my mind.

Love to you both
    Graham

TO HON. JULIA CAMOYS STONOR

Jeanne Stonor (Lady Camoys) was enraged by a passage in Anne Sebba's biography Enid Bagnold (1986) *suggesting that she had once had an affair with the novelist's husband Sir Roderick Jones. Her daughter thought the threat of a lawsuit foolish and destructive and so sought Graham's advice. Curiously enough, the book turned Graham's thoughts to an old friend, Count von Bernstorff, the diplomat who had financed his trip to the Ruhr in 1924.*

12 James Greene is himself a distinguished poet and translator. See *Woman, Child, Alphabet* (forthcoming) and other works already in print.

La Résidence des Fleurs, | Avenue Pasteur, | 06600 Antibes |
30th March 1987

My dear Julia,

Thank you very much for sending me the life of Enid Bagnold and kindly pointing out the dangerous page! It is quite absurd to start a libel action on such tiny grounds. Your mother will lose a lot of money in fees and not gain in anything. I do hope you can persuade Thomas[13] to call in John Mortimer[14] to advise her.

You can be quite assured that my mail is not opened. Things haven't gone as far as that in the Nice war yet. I wouldn't entirely trust my telephone. That is all.

I was glancing at the book and was amused to read about Enid's love for Bernstorff. I knew him too in the early 20s and later had a last meeting with him in a hotel in Berlin after Hitler had come to power. I liked him but he was such a complete homosexual and haunter of homosexual clubs that it is difficult to believe that a woman would take to him. He was, of course, a very brave man and died in Dachau[15] after saving a number of Jewish lives.

Don't hesitate to write to me.

Love

Graham

TO FATHER FRANCIS J. MURPHY, S. J.

On 16 February 1987, Graham gave a widely reported impromptu speech at the Moscow Peace Forum, where he shared a podium with Mikhail Gorbachev. Father Murphy, a historian at Boston College, wrote asking for the text of his remarks.

13 Julia Camoys Stonor's brother, the 7th Lord Camoys.
14 The playwright and memoirist John Mortimer (b. 1923) is a leading barrister.
15 He was, in fact, held at Ravensbrück concentration camp and shot in Berlin (see p. 59).

9th April 1987

Dear Father Murphy,

Thank you very much for your letter. I am afraid that my very short speech (about 4 minutes) at the Kremlin was not prepared and was more or less spontaneous so that it is difficult for me to give you any details of it. The main point was that I hoped the hundred year suspicion between Catholics and Communists was being buried in Central America by our co-operation in fighting against the Contras, the death-squads and Pinochet. I ended up with saying that it was my hope that there would be an Ambassador from the USSR to the Vatican, a hope not altogether improbable as the Pope had sent representatives to the Forum. I also pointed out that Marx had criticised Henry VIII and condemned him for the closing of the monasteries which at that period was the only resource for the poor. Alas I can't give you the text of the speech because I had not prepared it.[16]

With all good wishes.

Yours sincerely

Graham Greene

TO MICHAEL MEYER

Meyer's autobiography Not Prince Hamlet *was published in* 1989.

La Résidence des Fleurs, | Avenue Pasteur, | 06600 Antibes |
17 October 1987

Dear Michael,

I've only just got your typescript as I have been away in Budapest. Of course you may quote from my letters. What an extraordinary memory you have even without them. A few minor points.

16 The text is now available in *Reflections*, 316–17.

Page 148.

Trevor Wilson belonged to MI6. I don't think I've ever had a friend in MI5, thank God. Harold Lee was at Oxford but after my time. I didn't know him there. I got to know him during my frequent visits to Hong Kong [going] to and from Vietnam.

Page 187.

I don't know what this letter really means. I don't remember ever making payments to Anita. Perhaps it was a mortgage on the house. It gives the impression that I used to pay her as my mistress which was quite untrue. She was and I am sure is an extremely independent girl. She even used to insist on paying for my lunches when I came to visit her in Stockholm. As these generally contained caviar I at last persuaded her to drop it. The final agreement to part came on the eve of one of my usual departures from Stockholm when we had friends of hers to dinner. After dinner I happened to say that I had enjoyed the Blitz, and the Swedes, not Anita, were deeply shocked by this. It was then I realized that it would be impossible for me to settle at all in Sweden and we discussed it in a friendly way afterwards. The next morning we made love before I caught the plane. By the way she has been down here recently with her friend Mrs Lam and we all had a meal together. She and Yvonne got on extremely well together.

[. . .]

TO KIM PHILBY

In late 1987 Graham and Yvonne Cloetta made another trip through the Soviet Union, which included a visit with Kim Philby. Upon returning to England he sent, as Philby requested, a copy of Peter Wright's Spycatcher, *the publication of which caused a controversy in 1987.*

2nd December 1987

My dear Kim,

I am so glad that *Spycatcher* arrived safely even if it was two months late. I wonder where it spent the two months. The

Minehead postmark doesn't mean that Elisabeth has changed her address. Elisabeth was on holiday and so my cassette went to my old secretary Josephine Reid who lives in Minehead to be typed. They both of them have stocks of my signed notepaper because I find it impossible to cope myself without dictating onto a cassette as I find I get on an average about 180 letters a month to deal with even though a lot of them go into the wastepaper basket.

Yvonne and I both protest against your apology for Aragvi's[17] meal. We both enjoyed it immensely. Perhaps you mistook my lack of great appetite which is perpetual with me for a criticism!

We both hope that we shall be meeting again before too long and we both send our love to you and Rufa.

   Graham

TO RODERICK YOUNG

Roderick Young was researching the figure of the Jew in twentieth-century English literature and had noticed that the uses of the word 'Jew' had been sharply reduced in later editions of Stamboul Train *and* Brighton Rock. *He also told Graham a story about a poetry reading in the 1950s, at which Emmanuel Litvinoff praised T. S. Eliot, who was in attendance, as a modern prophet but attacked him for his use of the Jew as a symbol of decadence.*

28th March 1988

Dear Mr. Young,

Yes, the changes in *Brighton Rock* and *Stamboul Train* and if there is one in *A Gun for Sale* were made by myself. After the holocaust one couldn't use the word Jew in the loose way one used it before the war. Myatt in fact is one of the nicest characters in *Stamboul Train*, both brave and sympathetic. In the case of Colleoni I think I was wrong to have made him a Jew in the first place with such an Italian name. The casual references to Jews at one particular hotel is

17 A Georgian restaurant in Moscow; it is referred to in *The Human Factor*, 248.

a sign of those times when one regarded the word Jew as almost a synonym for capitalist. Big business seemed our enemy and such men who happened to be Jewish as Zaharoff[18] who indulged in the private sale of arms. Now we know that governments sell arms as recklessly as private individuals.[19]

I liked your Litvinoff story and wish I had his poem to read.

Yours sincerely

 Graham Greene

TO MURIEL SPARK

La Résidence des Fleurs, | Avenue Pasteur, | 06600 Antibes |
April 10 '88

Dear Muriel,

I have just returned to find your new book[20] – no present could have given me greater pleasure. I write at once, because after the first three pages, I know that this will prove to be one of your finest novels since my previous favourite *Memento Mori*.

I have a great sense of guilt. You have sent me so many of your books & I don't believe I have sent you mine. My last, I mean final, (& I don't much care for it) I will be sending you in September. (I abandoned it 15 years ago). A poor return.[21]

---

18 Sir Basil Zaharoff (1849–1936), the director and chairman of the munitions firm Vickers-Armstrong during World War I. He is very likely the model for Sir Marcus in *A Gun For Sale* (see Mockler, 118).

19 In a letter to *The Times* (15 September 1980) Greene referred to the Prime Minister as 'Zaharoff–Thatcher' over the sale of arms to the Pinochet regime in Chile. See *Yours etc.*, 196–8.

20 *A Far Cry from Kensington*.

21 Greene's dislike for his own books is not to be taken seriously. *The Captain and the Enemy*, though on a smaller scale than the great works of his mid-career, may be an unnoticed masterpiece. It is at the very least a scouring of the rag and bone shop of the heart, bringing together with absolute narrative precision, material from his school-days, his six-month truancy with the Richmonds and his sojourns in Panama. The opening paragraph about a boy won in a game of backgammon is certainly one of the most memorable in modern fiction.

I wish we could have met after all these years more than one brief encounter.[22]

Yours admiringly,
    Graham Greene

P.S. I'm glad that the Russians are appreciating your books.

TO BERNARD DIEDERICH

La Résidence des Fleurs, | Avenue Pasteur, | 06600 Antibes |
13th April 1988

Dear Bernard,

Many thanks for your letter. Chuchu has still been ringing up at intervals and claims that he is in no danger. Noriega has now become a patriot in his eyes and I must admit that if I have to choose between a drug dealer and United States imperialism I prefer the drug dealer. I never much cared for him but Omar at least would have appreciated the way he is hanging on. I was delighted by the news from Honduras. I don't feel much like returning to Panama at this moment. It would be so easy for the CIA to bump me off and blame it on Noriega and, vice versa, though I doubt if Noriega would do it. I seem to spend a lot of my time now going to and fro to Russia. I have been four times in the last two years and we are probably going again towards the end of May. [. . .]

TO RUFA PHILBY

Kim Philby died in Moscow on 11 May 1988.

22 They met again in early May 1989.

La Résidence des Fleurs | Avenue Pasteur | 06600 Antibes |
May 15 '88

Dearest Rufa,

We have been deeply distressed by the news of Kim's death & we think of you with love and sadness. It was always the high point of our visits to Moscow when we saw you and Kim together. To me he was a good and loyal friend.

I do hope that the three of us will meet again before very long & please, please believe in our love for you.

Graham & Yvonne

[*Yvonne adds a similar message in French.*]

TO ANTHONY BURGESS

According to Andrew Biswell, the quarrel between Greene and Burgess was rooted in Burgess's belief that Greene, whom he had venerated, did not take him very seriously. Burgess reviewed most of Greene's work from 1961, and, as he said in April 1991, 'never gave him a review less than almost fawningly laudatory'. Greene did not reciprocate, and by 1988 Burgess was conscious of the slight.[23] His public outbursts were soon reported to Greene, who wrote two letters on the same day ending the friendship. It is interesting that apart from personal and literary matters, the first of Greene's letters contains what appears to be a public declaration that his correspondence with Philby was vetted by security agencies on both sides – in fact, his correspondence with Philby was passed on to MI6 though his brother-in-law Rodney Dennys.

23 See Burgess's obituary in the *Daily Telegraph* reprinted as 'Graham Greene: A Reminiscence' in *One Man's Chorus*, ed. Ben Forkner (New York: Carroll & Graf, 1998), 252–6.

La Résidence des Fleurs | Avenue Pasteur | 06600 Antibes
| June 13 '88

My dear Anthony Burgess,

I hear you have been attacking me rather severely on the French television programme *Apostrophes* because of my great age & in the French magazine *Lire* because of my correspondence with my friend Kim Philby.

I know how difficult it is to avoid inaccuracies when one becomes involved in journalism, but as you thought it relevant to attack me because of my age (I don't see the point) you should have checked your facts. I happen to be 83 not 86 & I trust that you will safely reach that age too.

In *Lire* you seem to have been quoted as writing that I had been in almost daily correspondence with Philby before his death. In fact I received ten letters from him in the course of nearly 20 years. You must be very naïf if you believe our letters were clandestine on either side. Were you misinformed or have you caught the common disease in journalism of dramatizing at the cost of truth?

Never mind. I admired your three earliest novels & I remember with pleasure your essay on my work in your collection *Urgent Copy*, your article on me last May in the *Sunday Telegraph* & the novel (not one of your best) which you dedicated to me.

Yours,

Graham Greene

TO ANTHONY BURGESS

La Résidence des Fleurs | Avenue Pasteur | 06600 Antibes
[June 13, 1988]

Dear Burgess,

I have now received another cutting in which you claim I told you of an aggrieved husband shouting through my window (difficult as I live on the fourth floor.) You are either a liar or you are unbalanced and should see a doctor. I prefer to think that.

Graham Greene

TO IAN THOMSON

Ian Thomson (b.1961), the biographer of Primo Levi and editor of Greene's Tablet *articles, writes: 'In 1988, The Independent Magazine sent me to the Estonian capital of Tallinn to write an article about my Baltic roots . . . To my astonishment, Graham Greene had visited Tallinn in the mid-1930s when my mother was a child there.' As a result of the trip and his time with the diplomat Peter Leslie, Greene conceived 'a film sketch, "Nobody to Blame", about a British sales representative in Tallinn for Singer Sewing Machines, who is a spy. The film was never made yet it contained the bare bones of what was originally "Our Man in Tallinn", later* Our Man in Havana. *Anticipating my visit to Tallinn, I wrote to Greene asking why he had moved his Cuban "entertainment" from Estonia in the 1930s to Cuba in the 1950s; I was also keen to know of his 50-year-old impressions of my mother's native land.'[24]*

La Résidence des Fleurs, | Avenue Pasteur, | 06600 Antibes |
18th August 1988

Dear Ian Thomson,

The reason why I changed from Estonia to Cuba for *Our Man in Havana* was that one could hardly sympathise with the main character if he was to be involved with the Hitler war. I already knew Cuba and my sympathies were with the Fidelistas in the mountains. Nothing came of the suggested meeting with Grieg.[25] I tried to track the famous brothel but failed. I think the hotel was called the Ambassadors but I am not sure. I am afraid I saw very little of Estonia apart from Tallinn and have very little memories of the place except that it had a great charm for me.

Yours sincerely
Graham Greene

24 E-mail to RG, 3 March 2006. See 'Our Man in Tallinn', *Articles of Faith*, 165–79.
25 Graham's friend, the Norwegian poet Nordahl Grieg.

TO JOCELYN RICKARDS

La Résidence des Fleurs, | Avenue Pasteur, | 06600 Antibes |
29th October 1988

Dearest Jocelyn,

Thank you so much for your letter. I do commiserate with you about having Freddy so much on your hands. I read about his four [minutes][26] of death which he wrote [about,] but one thing I could not understand. How does he know that the experience he had during those four minutes was not an experience he had immediately his heart began to beat again and before he became fully conscious. I don't see that there is any proof there of the memory existing for a while after death. Do get him to explain that.

Lots of love

Graham

In 1988, Freddie Ayer choked on a piece of smoked salmon and his heart stopped. He reported that in the four minutes before he was revived, he saw a red light responsible for the government of the universe but it was not doing its job well, 'with the result that space, like a badly fitting jigsaw, was slightly out of joint'. Ayer died again without being revived on 27 June 1989.

Greene was actually very interested in near-death experiences, and in his late years seemed to debate with himself the possibility of an afterlife, finding it marginally easier to believe in the existence of a God than in the survival of the soul. In Cloetta's view, he decided the matter a few days before his death, remarking: 'If we human beings come on this earth only in order to spend about eighty years here, that makes no sense. What is eighty years compared to eternity? So there must be something else.' Earlier, he had written, '. . . perhaps in Paradise we are given the power to help the living. I picture Paradise as a place of activity. Sometimes I pray not for the dead friends but to dead friends, asking their help.'[27]

26 An obvious error, Greene writes 'days'.

27 See A. J. Ayer, 'What I Saw when I was Dead', *National Review* (14 October 1988); NS 3: 793; Cloetta, 186–7; and p. 367 of this volume.

TO ROBERT CECIL

*Robert Cecil (b.1913) was a historian and the biographer of the defector
Donald Maclean.*

14th February 1989

Dear Robert Cecil,

Thank you so much for getting your publisher to send me your
book which I found fascinating reading. It was a change to have a
well-written book on the subject and not the usual journalistic type.
I never knew Maclean and I only met Burgess twice, once over
coffee with David Footman[28] during the war and once when he
forced himself on me on my visit to Moscow as a guest of British
Airways in 1961. I don't know why he particularly wished to see me
as I didn't like him. I was leaving early the next morning and I had
begun a serious attack of pneumonia. However curiosity won and I
asked him in for a drink. He drove away my very nice translator
saying that he wished to be alone with me but the only thing that he
asked of me was to thank Harold Nicolson for a letter and on my
return to give Baroness Budberg a bottle of gin!

One thing strikes me as odd. On page 138 you speak of his
telephone call to Stephen Spender to ask for Auden's address in
Ischia which 'falls into the same pattern of deception.' I wonder why
he was playing the same deception all those years later in 1961 when
he told me in the course of our meeting that he had intended to split
from Maclean in Paris and go on to stay with Auden in Ischia. I
remember he said that he was caught up in the arrangements which
had been made for them and had to go on to Prague with Maclean.
Perhaps he thought I would write an article about our meeting, but
why persist with the Ischia story after so many years?

Again thank you so much for this excellent book.

Yours ever

Graham Greene

28 David Footman was an MI6 officer, a friend of Maclean's, and the author of various works on the Soviet Union. See Cecil's *A Divided Life: A Biography of Donald
Maclean* (London: The Bodley Head, 1988), 146.

P.S. I see that you have answered my question about Burgess in your final pages!

Before his escape to the Soviet Union, Burgess tried to create a cover-story by calling Stephen Spender and asking for Auden's address in Ischia. Cecil notes that the KGB sought to surround the British defectors in as much disinformation as possible to avoid giving credibility to the revelations in 1955 of the Soviet defector Vladimir Petrov. Burgess himself entertained hopes of returning to England.[29]

TO MICHAEL MEYER

La Résidence des Fleurs, | Avenue Pasteur, | 06600 Antibes
| 24th May 1989

Dear Michael,

Poor Anita is suffering from a bombardment of letters from Norman Sherry. I have told her to put them all in the wastepaper-basket. He will probably get onto you and I do hope you will refuse to give him any information about Anita. She has a right to her private life.

Love,

Graham

TO SHABBIR AKHTAR

Born in Pakistan but having lived many years in Bradford, Akhtar led protests against Salman Rushdie's Satanic Verses. *He opposed violence, but helped organise a ritual burning of the book. His own book entitled* Be Careful with Muhammad: The Salman Rushdie Affair *was published in 1989. In the midst of the controversy he wrote to Greene, asking for advice.*

29 See *A Divided Life*, 138 and 167.

3 July 1989

Dear Dr. Akhtar,

I sympathise with you over this silly Rushdie affair. I doubt
whether I can be of much help however. I haven't read Rushdie's
book and have no desire to. I can sympathise with anyone who loses
his faith altogether, but then there is no need to preach disbelief.
One should allow others to believe what one has ceased to believe
oneself. On the other hand I disapprove equally of death
sentences.[30]

As a very doubting Catholic (that is to say I very much doubt the
infallibility of the Pope) I would be on Rushdie's side perhaps if he
hadn't apparently made a mock of all believers. I have occasionally
mocked the Pope but that is quite different from mocking those who
believe in the existence of Christ. I respect their belief and
sometimes share it. I think your articles are excellent and I think
you should persist in what you are doing.

Yours sincerely,

Graham Greene

PS Without having read his book and judging by reports I would say
that Rushdie was guilty of shocking bad taste but that hardly justifies
violence and death.

*Greene never admired Islamic culture. His first direct encounter with it was
in Liberia in 1935, where, as he remarked in old age, one offensive
Mandingo porter aroused in him 'a few prejudices reinforced today by that
horrible old man Khomeini'. Throughout his life Greene took the side of the
Israelis against the Arabs. A particular admirer of Moshe Dayan, the hero
of the Six Day War, he feared nonetheless that Menachem Begin and the
Likud Party might fail to take the steps necessary for peace. See Allain,
107–16.*

30 Greene signed several petitions protesting against the fatwa.

TO REV. RALPH WRIGHT, O.S.B.

La Résidence des Fleurs | Avenue Pasteur | 06600 Antibes |
28th July 1989

Dear Ralph,

It was very nice seeing you the other day and I hope you are safely
home now. I have read your book with great pleasure. I have a habit
of marking with a little tick poems I particularly like and I find I
have marked thirteen – a good score. The three I particularly liked
were O *Hidden God, Jericho* and *Distance*.

Yvonne and I send our love,

Graham

*Even when the author was someone as close to him as Ralph Wright,
Graham Greene was incapable of praising thirteen poems he did not like.
This 'good score' is a remarkable endorsement of Wright's little-known col-
lection,* Seamless *(1988).*

TO ALBERTO HUERTA, S.J.

*Huerta said he was 'plowing' through the recently published first volume of
Sherry's biography. He had also heard rumours that Graham had left the
Church.*

La Résidence des Fleurs, | Avenue Pasteur, | 06600 Antibes |
1st August 1989

Dear Fr. Huerta,

Leopoldo[31] has just spent a few days here but I have too much
work, too much age.

Reviewers have been rather kind to Sherry's first volume, but I
found it far too long and full of unnecessary details. Anyway I hate

31 Durán.

being written about and there is another man Mockler[32] coming on the scene shortly. At least Sherry writes well but Mockler doesn't.

Your rumour is not quite correct. I usually go to Mass on a Sunday but sometimes I have too many people to see or too much work to do. I disagree with a good deal that the Pope has said and done but that doesn't mean that I have left the Church. I would call myself at the worst a Catholic agnostic!

All good wishes,

Yours ever,

Graham Greene

TO HANS KÜNG

The Swiss theologian Hans Küng (b. 1928) served with his friend and colleague Joseph Ratzinger (later Pope Benedict XVI) as a theological consultant to the Second Vatican Council. Whereas Ratzinger turned to the right after 1968, Küng became a dissident within the Church. Largely in response to his Infallible? An Inquiry *(1971), Pope John Paul II stripped him of his licence to teach theology.*

La Résidence des Fleurs, | Avenue Pasteur, | 06600 Antibes |
Oct. 24 89

Dear Hans Küng,

I was delighted to get your essay[33] with its generous & undeserved dédicace. The admiration is all on my side & the gratitude, for helping me to keep one foot in the Catholic church. It's a delight to add this essay to the five books of yours I have on my shelves.

Yours with gratitude, admiration and friendship.

Graham Greene

---

32 See Anthony Mockler, *Graham Greene: Three Lives* (1994). After seeing extracts in the *Sunday Telegraph*, Greene refused Mockler permission to quote from his works.
33 Professor Küng has no recollection of which essay he sent to Greene.

TO TOM BURNS

It is no small task to interview an ironist. Typically, Greene was both defensive and provocative when he spoke with journalists. In an interview with John Cornwell that was published as 'Why I am still a Catholic' in The Tablet (23 September 1989), he debunked eucharistic doctrine and natural law, compared Gorbachev to John XXIII and the curia to the politburo, and he talked about the taste of Trappists for gossip. He also hinted that he only received the sacraments to make Father Durán happy.

25 October 1989

Dear Tom,

I rather rashly gave permission to *The Tablet* to syndicate the interview because I thought that Cornwell's book on the death of John Paul I was excellent. I regretted it later when it all appeared again in *The Times*, *Telegraph*, *Observer* and *Independent*. Because of the silly personal paragraph *Vogue* have now asked for it from America but Wilkins[34] I am glad to say is cutting out that paragraph. How could I possibly refer to somebody I have known for thirty years as a girlfriend? I think I must have thought the interview was over and we were talking vaguely but not as vaguely as that. There were other minor errors. I have two armchairs and not one and I have never drunk a vodka cocktail in my life. It would have been pure virgin vodka!

I am so glad that Wilkins is keeping *The Tablet* on the liberal lines which you instituted after your very conservative predecessor.[35] It remains a monument to your work. I can't help wondering whether Newman was not welcoming a compromise rather than welcoming the idea of infallibility at all. I don't see why the church – a very vague term which includes you and I – can be any more infallible than the Pope. I disbelieve in infallibility anywhere in this world.

Love

Graham

34 John Wilkins was the editor of *The Tablet* 1982–2004.
35 Burns, who had been involved with the ownership of the magazine since the 1930s, had taken over as editor from Douglas Woodruff in 1967.

At the First Vatican Council in 1870, John Henry Newman opposed the Ultramontane party which argued for a very strongly worded definition of papal infallibility, but he did accept the more moderate definition that was passed; still, he would have preferred to wait.[36]

TO THE EDITOR, BALLIOL COLLEGE MAGAZINE

Anthony Powell reviewed Sherry's first volume in the Balliol College Record (1989). He complained about the amount of paraphrase of published works and described the whole as 'interminable'. He disputed Sherry's description of Greene's personality as private, since some of the information he had supplied, especially about sex, 'borders on the exhibitionist'.

[*Note in Greene's hand: Don't* send the letter to Balliol!]

7 November 1989

Dear Sir,

I am no defender of Norman Sherry's biography, perhaps I can defend myself a little. I accepted him as biographer because I had a great admiration for his two books on Conrad. I would certainly have cut massively his biography of me if I had had an opportunity. However I received no galley-proofs of the book, only the final proofs. I would have reduced it if I had had galley-proofs by at least 60 or so pages and I have insisted that for the second volume I must receive the necessary galley-proofs. To have cut as I wished the first volume would have meant reprinting the whole book which I could not expect the publisher to do.

Yours truly,

Graham Greene

---

36 See Ian Ker, *John Henry Newman: A Biography* (Oxford: Clarendon Press, 1988), 652–84.

TO MARIE-FRANCOISE ALLAIN ('SOIZIC')

The daughter of Greene's murdered friend Yves Allain, Marie-Françoise
Allain was a literary journalist who compiled volumes of interviews with both
Greene and Cloetta.

January 1, 1990

My dear Soizic,

[. . .] Your question about Cambridge is difficult to answer. All the
five concerned were at Cambridge long after I was at Oxford.
Generations at university go in three years. I belong to the 1922
generation and Kim and the others belonged to a much later one –
at the beginning of the thirties. It was then apparent that Germany
was the main threat and the hunger marchers were busy. It was more
natural in the early thirties to side with our possible ally Russia.
Years later after I had left the Service I received a letter from an
authority asking the same question as you. What about Oxford?
They named one man whom I had known but who I am convinced
had not the making of a double agent. An obvious candidate would
have been my friend Claud Cockburn, but he was so openly a
communist that he would not have made a very good double.

Your second question about Kim. I had grown to like Kim
immensely during the period when I worked with him in 1942–3
and later after he had left for Moscow he wrote to me supporting my
action in asking for my books no longer to be published in Russia
because of the imprisonment of two people whose names I
temporarily forget.[37] He said this was an honorable action and he
hoped it would have an effect. He also wrote to me on the subject of
the Afghan war saying that he was against it and he knew nobody
there who was for it – in other words he indicated that the KGB had
been against the war. In the last years of his life I saw a lot of him on
my four or five visits to Russia. As you may have read [in] my speech
at Hamburg published under the title *The Virtue of Disloyalty* I never

37 Daniel and Sinyavsky (see p. 291).

believed in the prime importance of loyalty to one's country. Loyalty to individuals seems to me to be far more important.

I hope the time won't be long off when we can meet again and discuss things more closely perhaps also with Bernard Violet.[38]

Much love,

Graham

PS It may amuse you to hear that when I published *Our Man in Havana* MI5 rang up the head of MI6 to say that I should be prosecuted under the Official Secrets Act. The head of MI6 laughed.

TO BERNARD DIEDERICH

La Résidence des Fleurs, | Avenue Pasteur, | 06600 Antibes | May 14, 1990

Dear Bernard,

Many thanks for your letter. My sickness is not a painful one only boring because one sees no end to it.[39] I do hope you will get back to Haiti for the Pope's visit. I was astonished to read that Fidel had sent him an invitation!

Yvonne and I send our love to you and Ginette and Jean-Bernard and I look forward to his photographs.

Affectionately,

Graham

TO KENNETH L. WOODWARD

Simon & Schuster asked Greene to provide a blurb for Kenneth L. Woodward's book Making Saints: How the Catholic Church Determines Who Becomes a Saint, Who Doesn't and Why. *Greene complied, but wrote a separate letter to Woodward about his own encounters*

---

38 French investigative journalist.
39 Greene's final illness was a form of leukaemia.

with two saints, the stigmatic Padre Pio, whose picture Greene as an old
man still carried in his wallet,[40] *and Pope Pius XII. Woodward, a religious*
affairs specialist with Newsweek, *responded to musing by David Lodge on*
whether Greene was actually a believer at the end of his life by offering the
letter not as conclusive proof but as evidence that Catholicism was still of
interest to Greene in his last months.[41]

September 11, 1990

Dear Mr. Woodward,

I've been reading your book *Making Saints* with great interest. I
thought you might be interested in your turn by my own experience
at a Mass of Padre Pio in a village in Southern Italy. He was a friend
of a great friend of mine, the Marquess Patrizi,[42] and I went to the
village with a woman friend[43] of mine. I was invited to see him that
night in the monastery, but I made excuses not to go as neither of us
wanted our lives changed! We were both Catholics. However the
next morning we went to his Mass. He was not allowed to say Mass
at the high altar but only at a small side altar and he had to say his
Mass at 5.30 in the morning. There were only a few women outside
the monastery gates waiting for them to open, and during the Mass
we were only about six feet away from him. The women had all
immediately gone to the confessional box as directly his Mass was
over he went into the confessional until lunch time.

Throughout the Mass he tried to hide the stigmata by pulling his
sleeves halfway down his hands, but of course they kept on slipping.
He was presumably not allowed to wear gloves. I had been warned
that his Mass was a very long one so I was surprised to find it of
average length, except that it was spoken clearly and without, as
some Italians do, gabbling. I was even more surprised when we left

40 John Cornwell, 'Why I am Still a Catholic: Graham Greene on God, Sex and
Death', *Articles of Faith*, 131.

41 See *NYRB* 2 Dec. 2004 and 10 Feb. 2005.

42 Marchese Bernardo Patrizi, a member of the papal nobility with an estate at
Gerneto near Monza. The 'meeting' with Padre Pio took place at San Giovanni
Rotondo near Foggia in southern Italy.

43 Catherine Walston.

the church to find that it was seven o'clock and I had no idea where this long period of time had been lost.[44]

In Rome I was told by a Monsignor of the Vatican that Padre Pio was a 'pious old fraud', a view which I did not share. I also felt that I had said the wrong thing when I met Pius XIII – or was it the XII (this was in the early fifties) when I told the Pope that the two Masses which had most impressed me in my life were his own double Mass on the anniversary of his becoming a priest at Saint Peter's[45] and the Mass Padre Pio had said in his village. My interview with the Pope became rather a stiff one.

Yours sincerely,

Graham Greene

P.S. You might tell your publisher that I have never in my long life seen such bad page proofs circulated. Whole pages and lines missing sometimes in the most interesting places.[46]

TO VÁCLAV HAVEL

An old friend of Greene's, the playwright Václav Havel (b. 1936) was gaoled three times for political activities under the Communists. He became president of Czechoslovakia in 1989.

October 5, 1990

Dear President Havel (It gives me great pleasure to address you thus formally!)

I hope you got my note thanking you for your kind enquiry after my health. Alas it's such that much as I want to come to Prague I

---

44 For more on Padre Pio, see Allain, 156–7.

45 On p. 206 Graham refers to his audience with Pius XII occurring in 1950. The fiftieth anniversary of the Pope's ordination to the priesthood occurred on 2 April 1949.

46 Woodward notes: 'the only section of proofs where a whole page was missing was the chapter entitled "Sanctity and Sexuality." For all his interest in Padre Pio, I like to think that is the chapter Greene turned to first.'

can't make the journey. I live between blood transfusions! If you see her do give Mrs. Temple also my regrets.[47]

I often remember the evening we spent together in 1969 with a suspicious character in the old town the night that you had discovered a listening apparatus in your ceiling!

All my best wishes for you and for your country.

> Yours very sincerely,
> Graham Greene

TO GLORIA EMERSON

With the Gulf War imminent, Gloria Emerson was considering a visit to Baghdad.

> Résidence le Chêne, | Chemin du Châno 26, | 1802 Corseaux,
> | Switzerland | November 20, 1990

Dear Gloria,

You are a courageous woman. Do take care of yourself. You would certainly be in grave danger if war does break out. My only feeling is that Bush is afraid to take that step. What I don't understand is that America could elect a former head of the CIA to the White House. After all he has been brought up in an atmosphere where lies are not only permitted but necessary as well as all the other tricks of the trade. One expects a President to have a rather more moral training.

I am glad you like *The Honorary Consul*. At one time I also thought it my best book.

> Affectionately,
> Graham

47 Shirley Temple was appointed ambassador to Prague by the elder George Bush. Far removed from the libel case of 1938 (see p. 83), she had struck up a late friendship with the novelist.

TO BERNARD DIEDERICH

Résidence le Chêne, | Chemin du Châno 26, | 1802 Corseaux,
| Switzerland | November 20, 1990

Dear Bernard

Many thanks for your letter. The *Daily Express*, as you could
assume, have got things entirely wrong. Yvonne and I have taken
this flat to escape from the noise and dirt that has developed in
Antibes. I haven't given up Antibes and I am not living with my
daughter. I expect to spend most of the year here except perhaps a
month or two in the winter when we will go back to Antibes. I sold
my house in Capri to pay for the flat which is a very nice one with a
beautiful view.

[. . .]

TO JOHN CAIRNCROSS

*Widely believed to be the fifth man in the Cambridge spy ring, Cairncross,
a translator and literary scholar, passed on to the Soviets important information from intercepts at Bletchley Park that helped them to defeat
German tank divisions at the battle of Kursk. He denied that he had passed
on information that allowed Stalin to develop an atomic bomb. Greene had
known Cairncross, a Scot, from his days with the SIS, when he dubbed him
'Claymore'. In the 1980s Greene advised Cairncross on many matters,
including his efforts to secure a carte de séjour in France. When various
researchers, including the Cambridge historian Christopher Andrew, identified him as the fifth man, Greene was unconvinced and advised him on the
writing of* The Enigma Spy: An Autobiography, *published posthumously
in 1997. Another friend of Greene's, Colonel Ronald Challoner, an intelligence officer who had been British consul in Nice, also assisted Cairncross
over many years; he eventually edited his manuscript and provided an introduction summarising the evidence in his favour.*

January 22, 1991

Dear Claymore,

I have dictated this letter because I am really too ill to write.
However my secretary is a complete safety box. And also
incidentally my niece![48] She will send your letter back to me. Or
rather I am not sending your letter to her as I keep all your other
letters.

I would gladly write to my own publisher, Max Reinhardt, about
your book and if necessary show him the testament, but I wouldn't
do either of these things without your consent. He is not now a very
large publisher but all the same he might be very interested. The
trouble is that your book should come after the new Andrew book if
it contains material which you wish to attack, and a controversy of
the two books might well sell each other. The other point is secrecy.
I can't absolutely guarantee anybody's secrecy except my own. My
own feeling is that you should remain in the dark for a period as
Challoner suggested, unless certain circumstances broke. This would
make your reappearance on the scene in your own book all the more
important. Do get on with that and let me know when it is finished.

I'm glad Gayle is doing well.

> Yours ever,
> Graham

TO ALBERTO HUERTA, S.J.

La Résidence des Fleurs, | Avenue Pasteur, | 06600 Antibes |
January 22, 1991

Dear Fr. Alberto,

Your two little presents arrived very happily to raise my morale a
bit as this Christmas has been exactly like the last one – a history of
hospitals and transfusions. I thought your sermon on the dead Jesuits

48 Amanda Saunders.

was absolutely first-class. I wish somebody could insert it into the reading matter of Bush. Anyway I shall treasure it always.

Really the only link I feel I have with the Catholic Church now is with the Jesuit Order. I can't bear the present Pope!

With much affection.

> Yours ever,
> Graham

One gift was a photograph of several religious in Roman collars kneeling and saying the rosary in front of the Federal Building in San Francisco as a protest against military involvement in Central America. In front of them is a line of helmeted and baton-bearing police officers. The other gift was the text of a rousing sermon Huerta had delivered on 15 November 1990, the first anniversary of the murders of six Jesuit priests and two laywomen at the University of Central America in El Salvador.

TO GLORIA EMERSON

Résidence le Chêne, | Chemin du Châno 26, | 1802 Corseaux, | Switzerland | February 25, 1991

Dear Gloria,

Many thanks for the magazine and your letter. I'm sorry about the trip to Baghdad in one way and glad in another as I wouldn't like to think of you being bombed. The whole affair seems a flurry of nonsense due to Mr. Bush.

I was interested in the dream articles but I have never been a Freudian or a Jungian. Two things never seemed pointed out by these scientific giants. One is, as I can prove from my diaries, that Dunne's experiment with time is reliable and that dreams take incidents from the future as well as from the past.[49] The other interesting point is that it's the dreams which refresh and not the

---

49 Greene had long believed in J. W. Dunne's theory, expounded in *An Experiment with Time* (1927), that dreams could provide glimpses of the future. Greene also absorbed Dunne's fascination with 'serial' dreams.

sleep. This has been pretty well proved. However here we're in the realm of facts and not theories.

I'm in the same state of bad health which is likely to continue to the bitter end.

Affectionately,

Graham

TO NORMAN SHERRY

Philby had described the results of Greene's intelligence work in Sierra Leone during the war as meagre. Sherry planned to dispute this claim.

February 27, 1991

Dear Norman,

I begin to regret my decision that you should not come here because tired as I am I think it is going to be more tiring answering your letter than meeting face to face. My daughter I am sure would have put you up for a couple of nights but unfortunately she is going to be away the whole of April. Please believe that I liked your book except for what I thought was an excess of sentimental love letters at the beginning when one would have been sufficient.[50] A face to face interview would perhaps have been less tiring than a long letter.

Philby's assessment of my work in Freetown is not a bit bleak to my mind. It's absolutely correct and he is defending me rather than criticising. I didn't at that time know that he was my boss in London. All I knew was that I was under control of a man in Lagos whom I disliked very much and who disliked me. We quarrelled incessantly and finally London withdrew me from his care and I worked direct with London though little knew that it was Kim. I was overworked though I have no memory of the day to day stuff which filled my time. I was sufficiently overworked for them to send me a secretary, a young woman who unfortunately was very bad at coding

---

50 Despite the mollifying tone, Greene's position is unchanged from p. 411.

which only added to our work. Too many telegrams were sent back asking for a repeat.

One of the things which I disliked in my job was that it seemed to be taking over the duties of MI5. All Portuguese boats had to be searched for commercial diamonds and information. In the papers on one boat I learnt that my friend and literary agent Denyse Clairouin had been arrested by the Germans as a member of the Resistance. One interrogation that I had to make of a prisoner disgusted me so much that I never made another. It was a great relief to join Kim and his outfit when I returned.

My two plans which were turned down. An African intellectual, a friend of Victor Gollancz, had been put in prison under the iniquitous 18B regulation which also imprisoned my cousin Ben.[51] My idea was that he should be rescued from his prison by two purported communists and in return for getting him out he would have to agree to send some harmless economic information from French Guinea. When we had sufficient of this we would blackmail him and threaten to show it to the French if he did not provide more interesting material. The Commissioner of Police was ready to work with me on this, but London wasn't. Their objection was that a question would be asked in Parliament.

My other rather wild plan was to open a brothel on a Portuguese island (Bissau?) just off the coast from Dakar where the *Richelieu* was stationed. The French were apt to take holidays on the Portuguese island. I had found an admirable Madame, French by origin but very patriotic, who was ready, given the money, to open the brothel. I felt that valuable information could be obtained from many of her visitors. The reply to that was that all brothels were very strictly under French intelligence control which seemed to me dubious in the case of a Portuguese brothel. Anyway I was fed up.

My visits inland [in] Sierra Leone were I suppose in search of some form of information but I can't in the least remember what.

51 Ben Greene, one of the 'rich Greenes' of Berkhamsted, was held under this wartime regulation that allowed the Home Secretary to have anyone of hostile origin or association detained (Shelden, 20). Jeremy Lewis, who is writing a book about the whole Greene family, will present further information about Ben Greene's incarceration.

These are very inadequate replies to your questions but perhaps after all we can meet one day.

   Yours ever,
    Graham

TO NORMAN SHERRY

March 20, 1991

Dear Norman,

   I have been thinking over again your letter of queries. I think you should pay more attention to the background of the war at that point. The importance of Freetown was this. The Mediterranean was completely closed and all convoys military or otherwise had to go to Egypt and North Africa via the Atlantic and the West Coast, and Freetown was the main port of call. After de Gaulle had attacked Dakar unsuccessfully we were militarily at war with Vichy France and Freetown was more than half bordered by French Guinea in Vichy hands. We had to be prepared at any time for a military assault. I had to have agents near the border on the look out for any possible movements by the French. I imagine this was why I was travelling a number of times in the interior to find agents and to check with them.

   My final quarrel with the man in Lagos was when he refused permission for me to go up to the border of French Guinea where I had made an appointment with the English Commissioner because a Portuguese boat was arriving at the same time in Freetown. The search was perfectly competently done by the police and didn't need me, but I had to cancel my appointment with the Commissioner which angered him and caused trouble. The quarrel reached a point where Lagos cut me off my pay which used to come by diplomatic bag. I had to borrow money from the Commissioner of Police who luckily became a great friend, although it must have been embarrassing for him.[52] Because of my cover all my telegrams came

---

52 NS 2: 117 and Shelden, 294, identify this man as Captain Brodie.

in to the police station in a code unknown to the police and I had to send all my telegrams out from the police station in a code unknown to them. Anyway this was the end of my relations with Lagos and I was allowed in future to deal direct with London.

[. . .]

'All I do is go from one room to another,' said Graham Greene on 12 February 1991. His health continued to decline and, exhausted, he entered Providence Hospital in Vevey, where Yvonne Cloetta and Caroline Bourget were in constant attendance. On 2 April he received the last sacraments from Father Durán, who was following an arrangement for his death made years earlier. On 3 April at 11.40 a.m. he died. He was buried in the village cemetery at Corseaux. Of his life's work, he remarked to Martine Cloetta on 1 April, 'A few, yes, are good books. Perhaps people will think of me from time to time as they think of Flaubert.'[53]

52 Durán, 91 and 340; Cloetta, 188.

Abbreviations

Adamson	Judith Adamson, *Graham Greene and Cinema* (Norman, OK: Pilgrim Books, 1984)
Allain	Marie-Françoise Allain, *The Other Man: Conversations with Graham Greene*, trans. Guido Waldman (London: The Bodley Head, 1983)
Amory	Mark Amory, ed., *The Letters of Evelyn Waugh* (London: George Weidenfeld and Nicolson, 1980)
Articles of Faith	Ian Thomson, ed., *Articles of Faith: The Collected Tablet Journalism of Graham Greene* (Oxford: Signal Books, 2006)
Cash	William Cash, *The Third Woman* (London: Little, Brown, 2000)
Cloetta	Yvonne Cloetta and Marie-Françoise Allain, *In Search of a Beginning: My Life with Graham Greene*, trans. Euan Cameron (London: Bloomsbury, 2004)
Diederich and Burt	Bernard Diederich and Al Burt, *Papa Doc: Haiti and its Dictator* (Harmondsworth: Penguin, 1972)
Durán	Leopoldo Durán, *Graham Greene: Friend and Brother*, trans. Euan Cameron (London: Harper Collins, 1994)
Falk	Quentin Falk, *Travels in Greeneland: The Cinema of Graham Greene* (London: Quartet Books, 1984)
Hazzard	Shirley Hazzard, *Greene on Capri: A Memoir* (London: Virago, 2000)
Mockler	Anthony Mockler, *Graham Greene: Three Lives* (Angus: Hunter Mackay, 1994)
NS	Norman Sherry, *The Life of Graham Greene*, 3 vols (London: Jonathan Cape, 1989–2004)
ODNB	*Oxford Dictionary of National Biography*
RKN	R. K. Narayan, *My Days* (1973; London: Picador, 2001)
Shelden	Michael Shelden, *Graham Greene: The Man Within* (London: William Heinemann, 1994)

St John   John St John, *William Heinemann: A Century of Publishing, 1890–1990* (London: William Heinemann, 1990)

Tracey   Michael Tracey, *A Variety of Lives: A Biography of Sir Hugh Greene* (London: The Bodley Head, 1983)

Waugh   Michael Davie, ed., *The Diaries of Evelyn Waugh* (London: Weidenfeld & Nicolson, 1976)

West   W. J. West, *The Quest for Graham Greene* (London : Weidenfeld & Nicolson, 1997)

Yours etc.   Christopher Hawtree, ed., *Yours etc.: Letters to the Press* (London and New York: Reinhardt in Association with Viking, 1989)

Acknowledgements and Sources

I am grateful, above all, to Francis Greene and Caroline Bourget, who encouraged me to undertake this work and then patiently answered literally thousands of my queries over a period of five years. I note with great sadness the passing of Amanda Saunders (née Dennys), who was involved in every stage of the preparation of this book apart from its appearance. As Graham Greene's secretary, she was very close to her uncle while he lived and then devoted an enormous effort to the affairs of his literary estate, sacrificing time that she might have given to her own work as a photographer and painter. Her sister Louise Dennys of Knopf Canada has devoted a great effort to this project in the very painful time of her sister's illness and death.

I have likewise enjoyed the extraordinary kindness and good counsel of other members of Graham Greene's family including Nicholas Dennys, James Greene, Oliver Greene and Rupert Graf Strachwitz. I would like to make special note of my debt to two of Graham Greene's surviving close friends, Bernard Diederich and Professeur Michel Lechat, who lavished their time on my concerns. Bruce Hunter of David Higham Associates has advised me and watched out for my interests over a period of almost twenty years. Richard Beswick of Little, Brown has exercised great patience with a slow author and keen insight over his manuscript.

The list of people who lent their time and assistance to this project is long and my sense of obligation to them is great: Judith Adamson, Nobuko Albery, Marie Françoise Allain, Christopher Andrew, Verity Andrews, John Atteberry, John Baird, Lisa Bankoff, Shelley Barber, Jill Bialosky, Andrew Biswell, Anita Björk, Mike Bott, Carol Bowie, Bill Burns, Euan Cameron, Priscilla Chadwick, Greg Chamberlain, Giles Clark, Chérie Collins, Rowan Cope, Jan Culik, Barry Day, Hugo de

Quehen, Kildare Dobbs, Linda Dobbs, Mitch Douglas, Richard Eder, Jarmila Emmerova, Patrice Fox, Miranda France, Frederick Franck, Alan Friedman, Paul Goring, Deirdre Greene, Dustin Griffin, Peter Grogan, Molly O'Hagan Hardy, Selina Hastings, Christopher Hawtree, James Hodkinson SJ, Alberto Huerta, Ian Hunter, Dom Philip Jebb, Pierre Joannon, the late Aubelin Jolicoeur, David Knight, James Knox, Michael Korda, Hans Küng, Jørgen Leth, Jeremy Lewis, Harold Love, Iain Antony Macleod, John Maddicott, Diane Martin, Lucy McCann, Michael Mewshaw, Michael Millman, Janet Moat, Anthony Mockler, Gilles Mongeau SJ, the late John Muggeridge, Karl Orend, David Pearce, Rolando Pieraccini, Joan Reinhardt, Timothy Rogers, Jean Rose, Hilary Rost, Nicholas Scheetz, Ken Sherwood, Rosemary Shipton, the late Francis Sitwell, Josef Skvorecky, Sam Solecki, Thomas Staley, Hon. Mrs Julia Camoys Stonor, Nicholas and Margaret Swarbrick, Ian Thomson, Robert Vilain, James Watson, Alexander Waugh, Lady Teresa Waugh, Tara Wenger, Peter Winnington and Ralph Wright OSB.

I am for ever in the debt of my wife, Marianne Marusic, and my children Sarah and Samuel Greene for their constant encouragement and their forbearance.

OWNERS OF LETTERS

I am extremely grateful for the kindness and cooperativeness of owners of letters written by Graham Greene that appear in this book. The following list indicates page numbers on which a letter begins; where there is more than one on a page they are distinguished as a, b and c:

Lucy Caroline Bourget: 239, 245b, 248a, 250, 278, 285a, 289, 295a, 303a, 306b, 310, 312a, 312b, 325a, 353b, 378, 384a.
David Higham Associates for the estate of Michael Meyer: 220, 235, 321, 372, 396, 406a.
David Higham Associates for the estate of Anthony Powell: 105, 162.
Louise Dennys: 68, 69, 73, 75, 78, 84, 95a, 97, 132a, 202b, 207a, 228, 272, 330a.
Nicholas Dennys: 6, 120, 128b, 192, 245a, 334b, 383a, 384b, 389b,

391a, 392b, 404.

Francis Greene: 1, 3, 4, 5, 31, 37, 38, 40, 41, 48a, 55, 65, 70, 77, 93a, 93b, 104, 107b, 108, 111, 114, 115, 121, 177, 181, 184a, 193, 195a, 200a, 222, 238, 246, 273, 292, 296, 326, 343b, 346, 352, 353a, 366, 367b, 369, 411, 416, 419, 420, 422.

Oliver Greene: 32, 35, 89b, 117, 122, 320, 333a.

Alberto Huerta: 389a, 408b, 418.

Richard Ingrams: 380.

Michael Korda: 331, 350, 373b.

Hans Küng: 409.

Rolando Pieraccini: 328, 333b.

Hon Julia Camoys Stonor: 394b.

Rupert Graf Strachwitz: 365, 375.

Ian Thomson: 403.

Alexander Waugh: 249, 265a, 297, 303, 337a, 341, 362a, 371.

Ralph Wright, OSB: 264b, 408a.

Beinecke Library, Yale University: 36a, 63.

Bibliothèque Jacques Doucet : 164.

Bodleian Library, Oxford: 14a, 51, 54, 60, 99, 100, 107b, 126, 128a, 133, 158, 215b, 219, 221a, 225, 247a, 276a, 299, 325b, 340.

British Library: 132b, 139a, 160, 175, 178, 179b, 186, 190, 191a, 191b, 199, 203b, 207b, 215a, 224, 248b, 251, 253, 257, 259, 264a, 266, 269, 276b, 280b, 284.

Burns Library, Boston College: 131, 136, 140b, 163b, 176, 195b, 198, 200, 204, 210, 212, 213, 214, 226b, 232, 234, 256b, 258a, 258b, 265b, 267, 271, 277, 279, 281, 282b, 286, 290, 291a, 291b, 293, 294, 295b, 301, 304, 305, 308a, 311, 312c, 313, 314, 315, 317b, 318a, 318b, 322, 339, 342a, 343, 344a, 344b, 345, 348a, 348b, 364, 354, 355a, 356b, 359a, 359b, 361, 362b, 363, 364, 367a, 368, 373a, 374, 376, 377a, 377b, 379b, 381, 382, 385, 386, 387, 393, 394a, 395, 397, 398, 405, 406b, 410, 412, 413b, 415, 417b.

Ekstrom Library, University of Louisville: 49.

Eton College Library: 179a, 196, 203a, 390b.

Fischer Library, University of Toronto: 298, 300, 327.

Huntington Library: 9, 33a.

Harry Ransom Center, University of Texas at Austin: 10, 11b, 12, 13,

14b, 15, 16, 17, 18, 20, 21, 23, 24, 25, 26, 27, 28, 43a, 43b, 44, 48b, 50, 72, 85, 88, 90, 91, 96b, 98, 102, 103, 124, 172, 184b, 227, 230, 231, 233, 236, 237, 247b, 256a, 261, 275, 280a, 282a, 288, 319, 323, 336, 337b, 347, 360, 379a, 383b, 400a, 401, 402, 413a, 417a.

Houghton Library, Harvard University: 11a.

Courtesy of the Director and University Librarian, John Rylands University Library of Manchester: 69.

King's College, Cambridge: 100.

Lauinger Library, Georgetown University: 8, 29, 33b, 34, 36b, 39, 42, 46, 47a, 47b, 53, 57, 59, 64, 66, 71, 79, 80, 82a, 86, 88, 89a, 96a, 118, 137, 138, 139b, 140a, 141, 142, 143a, 143b, 144, 145, 146, 147a, 161, 163a, 165a, 165b, 166, 168, 169, 170, 180, 182, 187, 188, 194, 208, 217, 221b, 226a, 240, 255, 260, 268, 285b, 287, 306a, 307, 308b, 330b, 334a, 351a, 351b, 370, 391b, 392a, 400b.

McPherson Library, University of Victoria: 83, 95b, 109, 135.

National Library of Scotland: 216, 229, 254, 283, 309, 317a, 332, 335, 355b, 356a, 399.

National Library of Wales: 202a.

Penguin Group USA (Viking): 107a.

The Pierpont Morgan Library: 28, 197.

Random House Group Archive and Library (Rushden, Northants): 127.

Reading University Library: 52, 82b.

University College, London: 129, 134.

Wheaton College Library: 388.

Appendix: The Comma and the Applecart

The so-called 'deathbed letter' has become notorious in recent years. Its place in this volume is questionable, since Greene did not actually write it although he did contribute a signature and a comma. In fact, it is not, strictly speaking, a letter. Still, an editor of Graham Greene's letters, whatever his preference, cannot pass over it in silence.

Greene's decision to accept Norman Sherry as his biographer was based on assurances that the work would focus on Greene's writings in the context of his travels and that it would not be a sexual exposé. Sherry wrote to him on 3 July 1975: 'Understanding your fears, I will try to keep away from the personal, where this is irrelevant to my work. I will try to work in the manner of my Conrad but if the work begins to move in a biographical direction you will be free to censor it.' And again: 'If I seem to be moving into the more private sphere I'll consult with you hurriedly.' When the book appeared, Greene was shocked to discover that a quarter of it was devoted to a paraphrase of his courtship letters to Vivien, including a great many direct quotations of copyright material for which he had not given permission and which he wanted cut (p. 411). At the end of 1989, the two met in a fraught session at Antibes, which left the biographer 'contrite'.[1] Greene did not meet again with Sherry and considered withdrawing from the project, but he gradually accepted that other biographers might make a worse job of his life. For his part, Sherry's contrition was short-lived; once the novelist was dead, he stooped to the keyhole again in volumes two and three, eventually declaring: 'you can't help but admire him for having sex with everything in sight'.[2]

1 Yvonne Cloetta's contemporaneous account of this meeting may be found in the Sutro papers at the Bodleian Library.

2 *New York Times*, 4 November 2004.

In the meantime, however, Sherry needed to get copyright clearance for his future work and to secure his position against rival biographers. He wrote to Greene on 25 March 1991, that is, ten days before the novelist's death: 'After 17 years as your authorized biographer (and how many more years will be needed and how many more volumes before I complete my work?), I should like your blessing to quote – I promise to be sensitive. We must avoid the possibility of Mockler and Grub Street wallahs (and Grub Street wallahs are everywhere) coming along and upsetting the applecart.' Greene accepted Sherry's renewed assurances, and a document was drawn up:

I, Graham Greene grant permission to Norman Sherry, my Authorized Biographer, excluding any other, to quote from my copyright material published or unpublished.

Executed on April 2nd 1991.

Signed

Graham Greene

Witnessed:

Caroline Bourget

Y. Cloetta

Greene signed this document on the day before he died, carefully adding the comma that appears after the word 'other', thus restricting the permission that was granted. Without the comma, Sherry was the only person permitted to quote from the works. With the addition of the comma, he was given permission to quote but could not prevent anyone else from doing so.

Undeterred by niceties of punctuation, Sherry persevered in the belief that he alone was permitted to quote from Greene's works, and he construed this letter as granting something more than quotation rights.[3] In his public statements Sherry, who in 1975 had suggested that Greene could 'censor' his work, has held up the letter as the

---

3 In a public lecture at Berkhamsted on 29 September 2004, Sherry paraphrased the letter substituting the word 'publish' for 'quote.'

guarantee of his intellectual freedom. However, he has also used it in an effort to silence another scholar. William Cash obtained the permission of Greene's literary estate to quote from copyright materials in *The Third Woman*, a book on Greene's relationship with Catherine Walston. Sherry's lawyer, Robert M. Callagy, wrote to the publisher on 13 December 1999: 'The purpose of this letter is to put Little Brown and its author, Cash, on notice that it has no right to quote or closely paraphrase any of Graham Greene's unpublished letters, diaries or other materials.'

Francis Greene, the novelist's son and literary executor, objected to this lawyer's letter on the grounds that it attempted to wrest control of Greene's copyrights from his heirs and give it to the biographer, a situation made more complicated by Sherry's plans to edit and publish copyright materials from various archives. A legal opinion obtained by Little, Brown made short work of Sherry's position. In addition to the comma, Martin Soames, a copyright specialist, noted another problem with the letter which addressed the use of published and unpublished material in the same way: 'Such an agreement is on the face of it invalid. At that date [2 April 1991] all Greene's published works were already under various exclusive licences to major publishers around the world and it would have been impossible to grant exclusive rights in them again, separately, to Norman Sherry, so it seems highly unlikely that this is what Greene's letter means. If it did have the meaning which Sherry has adopted it would be legally unenforceable.'[4]

The episode of the deathbed letter has provided an interesting object lesson on the uses of the comma in Lynn Truss's bestseller *Eats, Shoots & Leaves* (2003), 101–2. For a full discussion of the context and significance of the deathbed letter, see Richard Greene, 'Owning Graham Greene: The Norman Sherry Project', *University of Toronto Quarterly* 75:4 (Fall 2006), 957–70.

---

4 Soames's opinion is quoted in a letter of 16 December 1999 from Richard Beswick, editorial director at Little, Brown, to William Cash. Copies of all letters quoted are in the files of the literary estate.

Index

Achill 140, 141, 143, 146, 171, 218
Ackerley, J. R. 58
Ackland, Rodney 66, 67
Acton, Harold xxi, 8, 178, 197, 270, 284
Adam Smith, Janet (later Carleton) 279
Akhtar, Shabbir 406
Alberta xxix, 215
Allain, Marie-Françoise ('Soizic') xxxiii, 412
Allain, Yves 286, 287, 412
Allende, Salvador 311, 313, 328
American Academy and Institute of Arts and Letters 296, 308
Amis, Kingsley 334, 341
Amis, Martin 341
Anacapri: Catherine's visits 171, 188, 274; fire 289; GG's house xxviii, 171n, 197, 366, 390, 417; GG's life in xxx, 268–9; residents 268n; restaurants 309; visitors 228, 309, 315
Andrew, Christopher 417, 418
Anglican-Roman Catholic International Commission (ARCIC) 349n
'Anthony Sant' 13–14, 16–17, 18
Antibes: in August 368; GG's description of 318–19; GG's home 285, 343; GG's life in 265, 284, 299, 334, 417; GG's move to xxx, 268; mail 356; mayor 366; residents 319n, 364n; Sherry's visit 428
Apostrophes 402
Aquinas, Thomas 349
Araya Peters, Arturo 328
Argentina xxxi, 307, 314, 323
Ash, Henry (pseudonym) 99
Aspinall-Oglander, Cecil Faber 58
Attenborough, Richard 124, 136, 147
Auden, W. H. 53n, 80, 291, 405, 406
Authors' Club 162
Ayer, A. J. (Freddie) xvi, 384–5, 389, 390, 404

Babbling April xxi, 13, 63, 178n
Baddeley, Hermione 124, 125
Bagnold, Enid 394, 395
Bajeux, Father Jean-Claude 275
Baker, Peter 287
Balaguer, Joaquín 280
Balasova, Comrade 327
Balfour, Patrick (Lord Kinross) 9
Balliol College Record 411
Baptiste, Fred xiv, 288–9, 347
Baptiste, Rénel xiv, 288–9, 347
Barker, George 291
'Basement Room, The' 142
Batista, Fulgencio 232
BBC: Director General xviii; Film Unit 71; Francis's work 307; GG's scripts 107; Herbert's protests 226; poetry reading xxi, 8–9; Russian Service 298; short stories 58; Third Programme discussion 147
'Bear Fell Free, The' 65n
Beaumont, Hugh ('Binkie') 271
Begin, Menachem 407
Bell, Adrian 82
Bell, Kenneth xxi, 43
Belloc, Hilaire 34, 48, 241
Belmont, Georges 360, 361
Benson, Theodora 82
Berkhamsted School: GG's education xviii–xix, 54n, 183, 270; headmastership xviii, 29n, 349n, 386; pupils 183, 269, 315–16
Berkman, Edward O. 75
Bernstorff, Count Albrecht von 17, 59, 394, 395
Berridge, Elizabeth 356
Bertillon, Suzanne 56, 57
Best, Marshall 330
Betjeman, John xxi, 83, 95, 109, 135, 249
Biche, Marie (Schebeko): African contacts 166, 167; letters to 177, 181, 246, 273, 292, 296, 346; relationship with GG xiv–xv, 177; view of Catherine 168, 273; view of Yvonne 311

Biche, Jean 177, 311
Biles, Jack I. 335
Birkenfeld, Guenther 44
Birkenhead, Lord 266
Birmingham, George (James Hannay) 341
Bisset, Jacqueline 322
Biswell, Andrew 360, 401
Björk, Anita: husband's death 221; letters from Sherry 406; letters to 334, 351; relationship with GG xxix, 221–2, 225, 235, 397
Blackwell, Basil 10, 13
Bloy, Léon 187
Blunden, Edmund 52
Bodley Head, The 262, 263, 299, 376
Boissieu, Alain de 369
Boothby, Guy 134
Borge, Tomas 368, 382
Borrow, George 45
Bost, Pierre 195
Boulting, John 136, 147
Boulting, Roy 136
Bourget, Andrew (grandson) 312
Bourget, Jean 214, 250
Bourget, Jonathan (grandson) 306, 312, 384
Bourget, (Lucy) Caroline (Greene, daughter of GG): babyhood 60, 62; birth xxi, 55n; childhood 77, 93, 104, 171; children xxix, 214; dedication of *The Heart of the Matter* 158n; GG's last illness xxxii, 423, 429; letters to 239, 245, 248, 250, 278, 289, 295, 303, 306, 310, 325, 326, 353; marriage xxix, 214, 250; ranching in Canada xxix, 214, 218, 222–3; Swiss home xxxii, 364, 417, 420
Bowen, Elizabeth x, 53n, 91, 147, 254
Boyle, Andrew 354
Bradbury, Ray 265
Brandt, Johanna 215n
Brecht, Bertolt 54n
Brett, Edwin John 329n
Brighton Rock: changes to text 398; film 147; film script xxvii, 136–7; material for 80, 90; origins xxiv; play 124–5; publication 35n, 385; readership 278; sales 95; success 96; writing of 89
Brodie, Captain 422n
Brontë, Charlotte 148, 153
Brook, Natasha xxix, 207, 210, 212
Brook, Peter xxix, 195, 207, 210
Brophy, John 278

Browning, Robert 152n, 189, 254
Bruce, William S. xxiii
Budberg, Moura, Baroness 60, 301, 405
Bunker, Ellsworth 338
Burgess, Anthony 360, 361, 381, 401, 402
Burgess, Guy 224, 253n, 354, 405–6
Burns, Tom 88, 216, 410
Burns Oates 216
Burnt-Out Case, A: material for xxx, 17n, 236n, 240, 247, 358n; religious stance xxii, xxx, 255, 259; responses to 251, 258–9, 280; writing of xxii, 247, 261
Burton, Richard 293
Bush, George 416, 419
Byng, Douglas 100
Byron, Robert 9

Cagney, James 54n
Cairncross, John 354, 417
Calcutta Statesman 73
Calder-Marshall, Arthur 57–8
Callagy, Robert M. 430
Cambronne, Luckner 319, 320
Cameron, Alan Charles 53, 71, 72
Cameroon xxx
Camoys, Jeanne Stonor, Lady 176, 394
Camoys, Lord (Thomas Stonor) 395
Cannan, Denis 195
Capote, Truman xxix, 209–10
Captain and the Enemy, The xxxii, 329n, 340n, 376, 399n
Caraman, Father Philip 251
Cardenale, Father 382
Carter, Jimmy 338
Carter, Lionel xix, 183, 316
Cartmell, Canon Joseph 160, 161
Carving a Statue xxviii, 271
Cash, William 430
Castro, Fidel 232, 286, 340, 342, 379, 413
Castro, Raul 286
Catholic Herald, The 251
Cavalcanti, Alberto 269
Cayetano, Salvador ('Marcial') 368
Cecil, Robert 405
Cedillo, General Saturnino 90
Cerio, Edwin 312
Cerna, Lenin 382
Cervantes, Miguel de 389
Chabrier, Hortense 360, 361
Chadwick, Priscilla 349n
Challoner, Ronald 417, 418
Chamberlain, Greg 347n
Chandler, Raymond 390
Chaplin, Charlie 166, 199, 227, 256

Chatto & Windus 52, 129, 262n
Chekhov, Anton 155
Chile: CIA 336; GG's view of
    government xi; GG's visit xxi,
    311–12, 313–14, 317, 336;
    overthrow of Allende 328; Pinochet
    regime 328n, 399n
'Chile: The Dangerous Edge' 313
Christie, Agatha xiv
Chuchu (José de Jesús Martinez):
    Getting to Know the General xxxii,
    337, 340n, 375, 383; holiday 347;
    letters to 339, 374; relationship with
    GG xxxi, 337–8, 346, 383–4, 400
'Church Militant' 214
Churchill, Randolph 221, 290
Churchill, Winston 3, 123, 340
Cibber, Colley 90
Clair, René 47
Clairouin, Denyse: death 40, 177, 421;
    letters to 40, 41, 48, 55, 65, 70, 93;
    relationship with GG 40, 56, 57
Clare, John 155
Claude, General Breton 319, 320
Claudel, Paul 253
Cloetta, Jacques xxxiii, 364, 365
Cloetta, Martine: career 321, 322;
    dispute with ex-husband xxxii, 364,
    369, 376; GG's last illness 423;
    illness 344; Swiss home 376, 384
Cloetta, Yvonne: daughter's career 321;
    daughter's dispute with ex-husband
    xxxii, 364, 365, 369; family
    problems 299; friendships 262n;
    GG's last illness and death 404, 423,
    429; letters to xxxiii; life with GG
    299, 315; marriage 273; publication
    of GG's diaries 357n; relationship
    with GG xxx, 273–4, 310–11, 361,
    388, 417; relationship with GG's
    children 311; Sherry biography
    issues 428, 429; Soviet Union visits
    391–2, 397, 398; travels 300, 318
Cockburn, Claud xviii, 17, 87, 412
Cocteau, Jean 166
Colette (Sidonie-Gabrielle Colette)
    207–8
Collier's Magazine 96
Comedians, The: film 285, 288, 293; film
    script xxvii; political impact xxxi,
    293; publication xxxi, 280–1, 282;
    responses to xxxi, 280–1, 282;
    setting 34n, 275; writing of 278
Communist Party xxviii, 198, 210,
    321n, 388n
Complaisant Lover, The xxviii

Confidential Agent, The xxiv, 96
Congo: GG's plans for visit 230–1, 236,
    237; GG's visit x, xv, xxx, 238–44,
    259; Leopold II's rule 64n; lepers xv,
    xxx, 231, 236, 239–40, 241–2
Congo Journal 240, 259
Connolly, Cyril 190
Conrad, Joseph 42, 163–4, 411
Conrad, Peter 341
Cooper, Duff 196–7, 203
Cooper, Lady Diana 196, 203, 280n,
    390
Corey, Mr 377
Cornford, John 410
Coste, Mahaut 385
Coward, Noël 256
Cowgill, Felix 354
Cowper, William 155
'Creation of Beauty, The' 5
Cuadra Landrove, Angel 380
Cuba: Batista government 232–3;
    Castro government xi, 379; Castro
    revolution 232–3; GG's description
    of Havana 211; GG's visits x, xxxi,
    231, 285–6, 324; *Our Man in
    Havana* 403; political prisoners 265,
    379–80
Curtis, John 393

Dagerman, Stig 221
Dahl, Roald 386
Daily Express 98, 417
Daily Mail 72
Daily Mirror 363
Daily Telegraph 42, 87n, 410
Daily Worker 87
Dalrymple, Ian 201
Dane, Clemence (Winifred Ashton) 31
Daniel, Yuli xiv, 291, 295, 300, 412n
D'Arcy, Martin 176
Dasnoy, Edith 231
'Day at the General's, A' 91
Day-Lewis, Cecil 291
Dayan, Moshe 407
Dayrell-Browning, Muriel (mother-in-
    law) 49
Dayrell-Browning, Patrick (brother-in-
    law) 100
de Candole, Donald 261
de Gaulle, Charles 365, 422
de la Mare, Walter xxii, 5, 6n, 14, 44n
de Lattre, General Jean 185, 186
de Valera, Eamon 2
Dean, Basil 74, 78, 78, 166–8
'Dear Dr Falkenheim' 216
Delannoy, Jean 175

Delargy, Hugh 232, 233
Denmark xxiii
Dennys, Amanda (later Saunders, niece) 314, 418n
Dennys, Elisabeth (Greene, sister): brother Hugh's funeral 393; brother Raymond's illness 333; childhood 30; father's death 122, 123; husband's career xxvi; illness 314; letters to xvi, 6, 7, 113, 120, 128, 192, 334, 383; marriage 119; relationship with GG xviii, 314, 345, 351, 363, 376, 398; relationship with Yvonne 310; SIS career xxv, 108–9, 113n; war preparations 94
Dennys, Louise (niece) 299, 314, 366
Dennys, Nicholas (nephew) 314, 362
Dennys, Rodney (brother-in-law) xxvi, 119n, 120, 401
Des Vallées, Marie 174
Devonshire, Duchess of 35
Diaz Herrera, Colonel 380, 384
Dickens, Charles 155, 243
Diederich, Bernard: career 275; Cuban information 232n; investigation of Torrijos' death 375; letters to 275, 280, 288, 319, 323, 336, 337, 347, 379, 383, 400, 413, 417; relationship with GG xxxi, 275
Diederich, Ginette 319, 320, 413
Dietrich, Marlene 166
Dieu Vivant 172, 187
Dominique, Marie-Denise (Duvalier) 293n
Dominique, Max 293n
Donne, John 36
Doran, George 31, 32
Dostoevski, Feodor 155, 164
Doubleday, Doran xxii, 31–2, 35, 80, 86
Douglas, Mitch 55
Doyle, Arthur Conan xii, 368–9
Dubcek, Alexander 300n, 328
Dunn, Ambassador Archibald 367, 368
Dunne, J. W. 419
Durán, Father Leopoldo: GG's death 423; letters to 348, 364; relationship with GG 389, 408, 410, 423; travels with GG xxxi, 345–6, 351
Duvalier, François 'Papa Doc': death 320; expulsion of Nuncio 305; regime xxx–xxxi, 275, 319; response to *The Comedians* xxxi, 293, 324; treatment of opposition 288–9
Duvalier, Jean-Claude ('Baby Doc') 319–20

Duvalier, Simone, 293n

Eliot, T. S.: friendships 101; GG's view of xxviii; GG's writing on 53, 58; view of Jews 398; views on honours 266
Emerson, Gloria 342, 352, 416, 419
Emmerova, Jarmila 299
Endo, Shusaku xiii, 322–3
End of the Affair, The: ideas in 385; material for xxvi, 137–8, 139, 187n, 190n; responses to 376; setting xxv
'End of the Party, The' 48
England Made Me (The Shipwrecked): material for xxiii, 28, 51, 62n; publication 71; title, 65n; writing of 65, 66
Espriella, Ricardo de la 383, 384
Essex, 2nd Earl of (Robert Devereux) 154
Estonia xxiii, 60–2, 301, 403
Evans, Charles 31, 64, 85n, 97, 127, 128
Evans, Rob 374
Everyman 42
Eyre & Spottiswoode: Century Library 134; GG's career xxvi, 129, 132, 227, 273; GG's departure xxvi, 162; Iddesleigh at 82

Faber and Faber 255n, 298
Fagan, John 344n
Fallen Idol, The xxvii, xxviii, 142
Faulkner, William 178n
FBI 373–4
Fenby, Charles 38
Fernandez, Miguel (Michael) 345, 346
Figaro, Le 164, 287
Firbank, Ronald 304
Flaubert, Gustave 423
Fleming, Ian 324
Fleming, Peter 53, 82
Fonteyn, Margot 192
Footman, David 405
Ford, Ford Madox xxii
Ford, Henry 269
Ford, John 241n
Forster, E. M. 149, 273, 369
Fortnightly Review, The 72
Franck, Frederick 231, 233
Franqui, Carlos 286
Fraser, Lionel 261–2
Freetown, *see* Sierra Leone
Frere, A. S.: career 85n, 263, 366; friendship with GG 311, 366; at Heinemann 85, 88, 97, 256, 262, 272; letter to 261
Freud, Sigmund xix, 356, 419

Frost, David 350
Fuks, Ladislav 327

Galbraith, J. K. 269
Galsworthy, John 74, 77, 78, 85n
Gandhi, Mahatma 207
Garnett, David 82
Gary, Romain 241n
Gaskell, Elizabeth 114, 148
Gauguin, Paul 150
George, W. L. 134
Georges, Father Jean-Baptiste 289
Georges, Père 240–1, 243
Germany xxiii, 17, 37–8, 54, 66, 412
Getting to Know the General xxxii, 337,
    340, 375, 383
Gibson, John Michael 368
Gide, André 175, 253
Giffey, Major 62
Gilby, Thomas 188, 190, 191
Gillen, John 359
Ginsberg, Allen 300
Gish, Lillian 221
Glenville, Peter 288, 289, 293, 317
Glover, Dorothy: appearance and
    character 102; career 103, 119;
    relationship with GG xxv, xxvii,
    96n, 102, 124, 126, 138, 145–6;
    relationship with Hugh 118, 119
Goering, Hermann 61
Goerner, Lee 344
Gogol 155
Golding, William 335n
Goll, Yvan 93
Gollancz, Victor 421
Gorbachev, Mikhail 388n, 395, 410
Gordon, John 219–21
Gould, Gerald 44, 45, 46
Grand Conférence Catholique 164
Graves, Robert 55
Grayson 65
'Great Spectacular, The' 347
Green, Richard Lancelyn 368
Green-Armytage, R. N. 44, 49
Green-Armytage, Vivian 49–50
Green Cockatoo, The 75, 80
Greene, Alice Marion (Molly, sister)
    xviii, xix
Greene, Anne (daughter-in-law) 369
Greene, Audrey (sister-in-law) 28, 29,
    303
Greene, Ave (cousin) 3
Greene, Barbara, Countess Strachwitz
    (cousin) xxiii, 64, 65n, 365, 375
Greene, Ben (cousin) 421
Greene, Charles (father): career xviii,

xix, 29n, 315n, 386; death xxv,
    121–2; family xviii; health 115, 117,
    121
Greene, Charlotte (sister-in-law) 29,
    32, 35
Greene, Edward (cousin, 'Tooter') 17,
    382
Greene, Edward (uncle) xviii, 1
Greene, Eleanor, (sister-in-law) 55, 90,
    93–4, 261
Greene, Elisabeth (sister), *see* Dennys
Greene, Eva (aunt) 1, 2, 3
Greene, Felix (cousin) 58
Greene, Francis (son): appearance 307;
    birth xxi, 77; career 267, 294, 307;
    childhood 93, 104, 171, 218;
    dedication of *The Heart of the Matter*
    158n; GG's estate 42n, 430; GG's
    illness 248; illness 294, 295; letters
    to 184, 193, 195, 226, 267, 367,
    369; National Service 227n;
    relationship with Yvonne 310, 311;
    travels 294, 295; walk with GG
    245–6
Greene, Graham: birth xviii; childhood
    xviii–xx, xxix; education xviii–xix,
    xxi, xxix, 5–6, 183, 315–17;
    marriage xxi–xxii, xxv, 10, 128;
    early career xii, xxii, 23, 25, 63; full-
    time writer 52–3; fatherhood xxi,
    55n, 77; writing career xxiii–xxiv;
    Night and Day 82–3; wartime career
    xxv–xxvi, 94, 101–2, 106, 107, 109,
    111, 124, 363, 420–3; affair with
    Dorothy Glover xxv, 102–3, 145;
    father's death 121; at Eyre &
    Spottiswoode xxvi, 129, 162; affair
    with Catherine Walston xxvi–xxvii,
    xix, 128, 137–8; affair with Anita
    Björk xxix, 221; mother's death 245;
    relationship with Yvonne Cloetta
    xxx, 273–4; film appearances 322;
    death xxxii, 423, 429; tomb 260–1,
    423
    FINANCES: advances 32, 35, 88;
    difficulties 46, 48, 53; generosity
    xiv–xv, 28, 217, 291, 347; income
    from films 66; swindled by Roe
    xxx, 256, 267, 281, 283; tax exile
    xxx, 256; wartime 93–4, 106, 109
    HEALTH: appendectomy 27, 90; boils
    79; bronchitis 110; bronchoscopy
    250; eyesight 61; finger operation
    306; hemorrhage 161; illness in
    Antibes 299; intestinal cancer
    xxxii, 353, 362, 388;

Greene, Graham: HEALTH – contd
last illness xxxii, 413, 423; liver
cure 215; manic depression
(bipolar illness) xx, xxvi, xxix,
xxx, 20, 159; nipples 90, 371–2;
pneumonia 248; psychoanalysis
xix–xx, 1; tonsillectomy 386;
treatment by Strauss xxix
HOMES: Albany flat xxviii, 279;
Anacapri house xxviii, 171n, 197,
366, 390, 417; Antibes xxx, 285,
343; Chipping Campden xxii, 41;
Clapham Common xxiii–xxiv,
xxv, 93, 104–5, 106; Gower Street
mews flat 105n, 106; house
hunting 139; Oxford 52; Paris xv,
xxx, 339; St James's Street flat
xxviii; Vevey xxxii, 417
HONOURS AND PRIZES: attitude
to honours 266; collecting xxx;
Companion of Honour xxx, 281;
Hawthornden Prize xxv, 115–16;
Jerusalem Prize 370; Légion
d'Honneur 369; Nobel candidate
178; Order of Merit 390–1
INTERESTS: afterlife xv, xxxii, 404;
dream diary xix, 357–8, 419–20;
stamp collecting 5
POLITICS: attitude to Soviet Union
xi, xxix, 234–5, 295, 300, 327,
373, 412; attitude to United
States xi, xxviii–xxix, 198–9, 221,
296, 308, 338–9, 378–9, 383, 416;
Biafra protest 297; Communist
Party membership xxviii, 198,
210, 321n; Cuba 233, 379–80; FBI
dossier 373–4; fighting injustices
xi–xii; mediation in kidnappings
367–8; mid-left xi, 321n; Moscow
Peace Forum speech 395–6;
Nicaragua 382, 383; Sinyavsky
and Daniel campaign xiv, 291,
295–6, 300, 412n; view of
Marxism xi, 381–2; views on the
writer and the state 153–8
RELIGION: account of Padre Pio
414–15; attitudes to Church
teaching xv–xvi, 407; burial plans
260–1; A Burnt-Out Case 251–4,
258–9; Catholicism and
communism xxiv–xxv, 396;
conversion to Catholicism
xxi–xxii, 21, 23; correspondence
with Waugh 251–4, 264;
godfather to Catherine xxvi,
137–8; meeting with Pope 278,

349; in old age xxii, 407; The
Power and the Glory controversy
203–6; relationship with
Catherine 189–90; statement of
position in 1978 348–9; views on
papal infallibility xi, 407, 409,
410–11; views on being a
Catholic writer 151–3, 253–4
TRAVELS: ix–xi, xxii–xxiv,
xxviii–xxix, xxx, xxx–xxxi, see
also under names of countries, e.g.
Mexico, Sierra Leone, Vietnam
WRITINGS: biography of Rochester
39, 43–4; film scripts xxvii, 74–5,
80–2, 136, see also under individual
titles; first novel 16; first published
novel 31, 63; first thriller 17; plays
xxvii–xxviii, see also under
individual titles; poetry xxi, 8, 13;
reviews xxvii, 53, 59, 80;
translations of works 40, 48, 67n,
204, 206, 298, 327, 360–1; views
of his own work xiii–xiv, 31, 38–9,
63, 172–5, 377–8, 385, 399, 416
Greene, Sir Graham (uncle) 261
Greene, Graham Carleton (nephew) 81
Greene, Helga (sister-in-law) 68, 81, 87
Greene, Herbert (brother) xviii, 87,
226, 303; letters to 28, 197, 226
Greene, Sir Hugh (brother): birth xviii;
career xviii, xxviii, 180, 226;
childhood 5, 6, 30; death 393, 394;
letters to 8, 29, 33, 34, 36, 39, 42,
46, 47, 53, 57, 59, 64, 66, 71, 79, 80,
82, 86, 89, 96, 118, 187, 260, 308;
in Malaya 180, 182; marriages 68n,
393; relationship with brother
Herbert 226; relationship with
Yvonne 310; travels with GG 51–2
Greene, James (nephew) 115n, 393, 394
Greene, Lucy Caroline (daughter) see
Bourget
Greene, Marion (mother);
Crowborough home 29n; death 245;
family xviii; health 72, 218;
husband's death 121–2, 123; letters
to 1, 3, 4, 5, 31, 37, 38, 77, 93, 104,
107, 108, 111, 114, 115, 121, 222,
238
Greene, Nora (Aunt Nono, aunt) 4, 8,
245
Greene, Raymond (brother): birth xviii;
career xviii, 3n, 117n, 276;
friendships 3n, 38n; gun story xx,
67n; health 333; home 55; letters to
32, 35, 89, 117, 122, 140, 277, 320,

333; marriages 29, 55; mother's
death 245; tomb 261
Greene, Sarah (sister-in-law) 393
Greene, Vivien (Vivienne Dayrell-
Browning, wife): character xxi, 10;
children 49–50, 55n, 77; courtship
by GG xxi, xxii, 10, 428; dedication
of *The Heart of the Matter* 158n;
father-in-law's death 123; finances
106n, 171; furniture xxi, xxiv, 105,
107; GG's illness 248; on *Gun for
Sale* film 115; health 78, 95; letters
to 10, 11, 12, 14, 15, 18, 20, 21, 23,
24, 25, 26, 27, 51, 54, 60, 99, 100,
126, 128, 133, 158, 214, 285, 353,
378, 428; mother's death 49–50;
relationship with GG 124, 126, 128,
139, 141, 142, 143–4, 145, 170;
religion xxi, xxvii, 10, 128, 278;
separation from GG xxi, xxvii, 126,
128, 170, 171; theatricals 30n;
travels with GG 89, 145; war
preparations 93–4; wartime home
xxv, 104, 126, 127
Greenwood, Walter 50n
Gretchko, B. I. xxxii
Grieg, Nordahl 57, 60, 67, 403
Grierson, John 71
Griffin, Cardinal Bernard 204n, 205
Grigson, Geoffrey 80
Grossmith, George 341
Grydzewski, Mieczyslaw 163
Guardian, The 381
Guest, Eric 4
Guillén, Roberto 379n
Gun for Sale, A: changes to text 398;
film 78n, 115; material for 399n;
publication xxiv, 385–6; sales 78;
writing of 71
Gyde, Arnold 103

Haggard, Rider 186
Haig, 1st Earl (Douglas Haig) 3, 4
Haiti: *The Comedians* 275, 280, 282,
293; Duvalier regime xxx–xxxi,
288–9, 293, 319–20; Ginette
Diederich's visit 319–20; GG's
interest in 34; GG's visits xxix,
xxx–xxxi, 207–9, 212, 275, 319;
human rights xiv, xxxi, 305,
319–20; insurgencies xi, 288–9;
Pope's visit 413; Sherry's visit 351;
US policy xxviii; voodoo ceremony
208–9
Haiti Sun 275
Haley, Sir William 286

Hall, Calvin 357
Hamish Hamilton: Narayan's work xxiv,
69, 70, 73, 76, 79, 84, 273; Spark's
work 216
Hardy, Thomas 151
Harper's 69
Harrington, Wilfred 176
Harris, John 359
Harris, Sir John 64, 67n
Harrison, Rex 255
Hart, Boy 267
Hart, Gary 383
Harvey, Frank 125n
Havel, Václav 415
Hawthornden Prize xxv, 115
Hawtree, Christopher xxxiii, 388n
Hayward, John 101
Hazzard, Shirley 330–1, 332, 370, 371
Heart of the Matter, The: film 200–1;
material for 5n, 80n, 111, 128,
140n; play 166; publication 158;
religious dimensions 160, 172–5,
360; responses to xxvii, 160, 251,
278, 360; setting ix–x, 111
Heinemann: advances to GG xxii, 35,
53, 256; *The Confidential Agent* 96,
97; Frere's career 85n, 216, 262;
GG's departure 262–3; *A Gun for
Sale* 71; *Journey Without Maps* 65,
71; *Lord Rochester's Monkey* 44; *The
Man Within* xxii, 31, 35; *The Name
of Action* xxii, 37; Narayan's work
272; *Refugee Ship* 98; *Rumour at
Nightfall* xxii, 42; *Stamboul Train* 47,
48; Thomas Tilling purchase
261–2
Hemingway, Ernest 87
Hencke, David 374
Henri, Père (Rik Vanderslaghmolen)
241, 243
Henry VIII, King 396
Henson, Leslie 8
Hergesheimer, Joseph 34, 37n
Herr, Michael 344–5
Higham, David: career 79n; letters to
85, 88, 96; Narayan's work 79, 84,
97, 273; Powell relations 162;
Refugee Ship 98
Hill, Alan J. W. 263
Hitchcock, Alfred 79
Hitler, Adolf 154, 308, 346, 395
Ho Chi Minh 187
Hollis, Sir Roger 372
Honorary Consul, The xxxi, 85n, 192n,
320, 327, 416
Hood, Thomas 153, 155

Hopkins, Gerard Manley 291 *
Hornung, E. W. 134, 378n
Hostovsky, Egon 325n
Housman, A. E. 216
Howard, Brian 8, 9
Howard, Trevor 200, 201, 241n
Hudson-Smith, R. 319n
Huerta, Alberto 389, 408, 418–19
Hughes, Emmet 184
Hugo, Victor 185, 186
Human Factor, The xxxi, 318
Huxley, Aldous 34, 39

Iddesleigh, 3rd Earl of (Henry Stafford
    Northcote) 82
In Search of a Character 258
Independent, The 410
Ingrams, Richard 380
International PEN 379–80
Ionesco, Eugène 249n
Ireland: Catherine in 138, 144, 208,
    217, 218; GG considers living in
    139; GG's holiday with Catherine
    xxvi–xxvii, 140; GG's journey
    (1923) xxiii, 2n; GG's plans 145,
    146; religion 349
Isherwood, Christopher xviii, 33
Ismail, Sir Mirza 330
It's a Battlefield xxii, 39, 67n, 74n, 358n
Ivasheva, Valentina 295, 367
Izakov, Boris 373n

J'Accuse xxxii, 364
Jacob, Sir Ian 226
Jacobs, Barbara 269
Jacobs, W. W. 269, 270
James, Henry xxviii, 61, 151, 301
Jarrett, Bede 54, 59
Jay, Douglas 241
Jenkins, Patrick 371
Jerrold, Douglas xxvi, 129, 162, 273
Jerusalem Prize 370
Jesse, F. Tennyson 32
Joannon, Pierre 364
John XXIII, Pope 410
John Paul I, Pope 410
John Paul II, Pope xvi, 387, 409, 413,
    419
Johnson, Lyndon B. 338
Jonathan Cape 53, 216, 262
Jones, David 202
Jones, Sir Roderick 394
Journey Without Maps xxiii, 65n, 71, 80,
    81
Joyce, James xiii
Jung, Carl Gustav xix, 419

Kavanagh, Patrick 109, 110
Kearney, Eva 348
Kenya: GG's visit x, xxix, 213–14;
    Maria from 345, 351; Mau Mau
    insurgency xi, xxix, 213, 242
Khomeini, Ayatollah 407
Kincaid, Dennis 69
King, Cecil 166
Kingsmill, Hugh 388
Kipling, Rudyard 6, 35, 266
Knoblock, Edward 58
Knox, James 9
Knox, Ronald 190, 191
Korda, Alexander: *The Fallen Idol* xxvii,
    142; GG's work for xxvii, 80, 106n,
    166; *The Green Cockatoo* 80–1, 82;
    letter to 200; nephew 302; *The
    Third Man* xxvii, 142, 158; Waugh's
    rudeness to 290; yacht 192
Korda, Michael 302, 331, 332, 350, 364,
    373
Kreuger, Ivar 51
Kuhnelt–Leddihn, Erik von 70
Küng, Hans xxii, 409
Kurath, Mrs 63
Kuznetsov, Anatoly 300, 301

Laffont, Robert 225, 246, 360, 361
Lambert, Hansi 230, 231
Lancaster, Osbert 85
Lanusse, Alejandro 314n
Latvia xxiii, 60, 61n
Lawless Roads xxiv, 77, 91n, 96, 183,
    355
Lawrence, D. H. 39, 86, 186
Le Huu Tu, Bishop of Phat Diem 184,
    185, 187
Leavis, F. R. 259–60
Lechat, Michel: career 231; Congo
    leproserie xxx; GG's visit xxx,
    238–9, 241n; letters to 231, 233,
    237, 247, 282
Lee, Harold 397
Lee, Nathaniel 155
Lehmann, John 236
Lehmann, Rosamond 80
Leigh, Vivien 74, 192
Leningrad Union of Writers 152
Leonard, Mary, *see* Pritchett
Leroux, Etienne (S. P. D. le Roux) xxxi,
    318, 325n, 326
Leroy, Colonel Jean 184, 185
Leslie, Peter 61–2, 64, 301, 403
Levin, Bernard 330, 331, 381
Lewis, Jeremy 421
Lewis, Wilmarth Sheldon ('Lefty') 260

Liberia: GG's plans for journey 64, 65, 66–7, 68; GG's trek xxiii, 65n, 237, 322, 365n, 407; GG's wartime plans 106, 363; GG's wartime visit 112; *Journey Without Maps* xxiii, 71

Lie, Nils 67

'Lieutenant Died Last, The' 269

Life 192

Life and Letters 53, 57

Linnit, Bill 124, 125

Lire 402

Listener, The 290, 291

Literary Guild 302

Little, Brown 430

Litvinoff, Emmanuel 398, 399

Living Room, The xxvii, 249, 255

Lloyd George, David 4

Lockwood, Roy 66, 67

Lodge, David 414

Longman 86, 88, 89

Lord Rochester's Monkey 43–4

Loser Takes All xxvii, 192n, 352n

Low, David xxxiii, 362

Lowe, Thomas 28

Lowell, Amy 11

Lowndes, Frederick 48

Lowndes, Marie Belloc 48, 50

Lundkvist, Artur 178n

Macaulay, Rose 257

McCall, Monica 55, 302

McCarran Internal Security Act (1950) xxviii, 198

McClintock, Robert 198

MacDonald, Ramsay 346

MacGregor-Cheers, Major Joey 180

Maclean, Donald 224, 253n, 354, 405

Macleod, Ian Antony 255

Macleod, Joseph 8, 254, 283

Macmillan 84, 95, 216, 272, 273

Malaya: GG's plans for visit 178, 179; GG's visit xix, xxviii, xxix, 180–4, 185, 186, 394; insurgency xi, 180–4, 394

Malraux, André 342

Man Within, The: dramatisation of 58; film, xxvii, 66, 67n; GG's opinion of 31, 38–9; publication 31; responses to 36; success xxii, 43; translations of 40, 67n, 298; writing of 63

Maritain, Jacques 40, 41, 42n

Márquez, Gabriel García 367

Marsh, Richard 134

Marshak, Samuel 234

Marx, Karl 396

Mathew, David 204

Maugham, Somerset 330n

Mauriac, François: on dilemma for Christian writers 151; eightieth birthday 279; English publisher xxvi, 273; letter and telegram to 164, 200; Nobel Prize 200; West on 253n

Maxwell, Robert 267

May, Canon Clarence 305

Mayo, Arthur xviii, 316

Menzies, William Cameron 80–1, 82

Methuen 207n, 273

Mewshaw, Mike 325n

Mexico: government xi; GG's contact with Márquez 367; GG's interest in 34n; GG's plans for visit 77, 78, 79, 86, 88, 89; GG's visit x, xxiv, 21, 90–2, 126; *Lawless Roads* xxiv, 77; *The Power and the Glory* xxiv, 34n, 77, 206; Sherry's visit 351

Meyer, Michael: friendship with GG 220; letters to 220, 235, 321, 372, 396, 406; Truffaut contact 322; works 300, 396

MI5 372n, 397, 413, 421

Milian, Raul 286

Mills, John 80

Ministry of Fear, The xxv, 111, 129

Ministry of Information: emergency dressing station 108; GG's view of 102, 107; GG's work xxv, 105–6, 107; Spender's work 99

MI6: Footman's work 405n; GG's correspondence with Philby xi, 401–2; GG's work xxv–xxvi; Philby's career 224n, 354; Philby's treachery xi, xxv–xxvi; view of GG 413; Wilson's work 397

Mitchell, Julian 304

Mitford, Nancy 249

Mockler, Anthony 409, 429

Mondale, Walter 383

Monde, Le 287, 342

Monkhouse, Patrick 8

Monsignor Quixote: GG's political stance in 381; material for xxxi, 346, 389; planning 3, 346; writing of 348, 375, 376

Month, The 178, 179, 251

Montini, Giovanni Battista, *see* Paul VI

Moor, Elisabeth (Dottoressa) 268, 269, 274, 310, 331–2

Moore, Brian xiii, 281, 343

Moore, George 34

Moore, Sir John 2

Moore, Thomas 269

Moré, Marcel 172, 187

Morgan, Charles 115, 163
Morley, Robert 352
Morrell, Lady Ottoline 39, 43
Mortimer, John 395
Moscow Peace Forum 395
Motor Sport 337
Muggeridge, Malcolm: *Calcutta Statesman* position 73; correspondence 105; GG collaboration proposal 86, 129; letters to 363, 377, 388; religion 377; SIS recruitment 109, 363; view of Narayan's work 73
Murdoch, Iris 334
Murphy, Father Francis J. 395
Murry, John Middleton 42n

Nabokov, Vladimir 219
Naipaul, V. S. 297n
Name of Action, The xxii, xxiii, 17, 37, 38–9, 58
Narayan, R. K.: career xxiv, 272–3; influence on GG xxxi, 281; letters to 68, 69, 73, 75, 78, 84, 95, 97, 132, 202, 207, 228, 282, 330; relationship with GG xiii, xxiv, xxvi; wife's death 97–8
Narayan, Rajam 97, 98
Nelson 75, 76, 84, 273
Nelson Sevenpennies 362–3
Neruda, Pablo 311, 312
New Statesman 42, 91, 328n, 356, 381
New York Review of Books 339, 347
New York Times 275, 342
Newall, Maria ('Pistol Mary') 213, 345, 348, 351
Newman, John Henry 152, 254, 410, 411
Nicaragua: death of Torrijos 374; government xi; GG's visits xxxi, 368, 378, 382, 388; *Time* articles 379; US policy 378, 383, 387
Nice 322, 364, 376, 378, 395, 417
Nice-Matin 356
Nicoll, Maurice xix
Nicolson, Harold 44, 45, 46, 405
Night and Day xxiv, 82–3, 86, 388
'Nightmare Republic, The' 209n
Nixon, Richard M. 330
Nobel Prize xxvii, 178, 200, 234–5
'Nobody to Blame' 403
Norfolk, 4th Duke of (Thomas Howard) 154
Nottingham Guardian 42
Nottingham Journal xxii, 23
Novarro, Ramon 62

O'Brien, Flann (Brian O'Nolan) 256
Observer, The 43, 44, 313, 381, 410
Ocampo, Victoria 307, 311, 342
O'Ferrall, George More 200, 201
Ogilvie, John 344n
O'Grady, Mrs (at Berkhamsted) 4
Old School, The 53, 65
Oliveri, Harriet 359
Olivier, Laurence 74, 166, 192, 249
On the Way Back 340n
Ortega, Daniel 382
Ortega, Umberto 382
Orwell, George 134, 321
'Other Side of the Border, The' 28
Our Man in Havana: cosmonaut's copy xxxii, 392; film xxvii, xxviii, 142; material for xxiii, 60, 87, 232n, 270n, 403; responses to 236, 413; writing of xxix, 223n, 228
Owen, Peter xiii, 322
Oxford Chronicle 9
Oxford Mail 38
Oxford Outlook 10, 255, 270

Pain, Barry 134
Paine, Thomas 154
Panama: *The Captain and the Enemy* 340n; death of Torrijos 374–5, 380; *Getting to Know the General* 375; GG's plans for visits 323, 324, 336, 374, 400; GG's visits x, xxxi–xxxii, 337–8, 339, 351, 368, 388, 399n; *On the Way Back* 340n, 346; presidency, 383n; US policy 338–9
Paraguay x, xxxi, 85, 296–7, 307, 351
Paredes, Ruben Dario 380n
Paris: appreciation of GG's work xiv, 67, 163, 164; Chilean ambassador 311; Colette's funeral 208n; GG impersonator in 246; GG's agent 177; GG's flat xv, 339; GG's life in xxx, 268, 302, 318, 334; GG's plans to visit 96, 197, 222, 242, 243, 244; GG's visits xxiii, 54, 56–7, 93, 168, 172, 240, 279, 285, 309, 317, 343, 352, 361; litigation 376; Tito in 290
Paris Match 184, 187
Parker, Geoff and Pearl 223
Parkinson Keyes, Frances 135
Parsons, Ian 52
Partisan Review 147
Paschoud, Jean-Felix 306
Pasternak, Boris 234–5
Pastora, Eden 379n
Patrizi, Marchese Bernardo 414
Paul VI, Pope (Giovanni Battista

Montini): canonization of Ogilvie 344n; defence of *The Power and the Glory* 205, 349, 360; GG's meeting with 278, 349; letter to 204; readership of GG's novels xvi, 278, 360

Peake, Maeve 133, 277, 278
Peake, Mervyn xii, xiv, xxvi, 129, 133, 277–8
Pearce, David 183
Pearn, Nancy 72, 79n, 90, 98
Pearn, Pollinger and Higham 75, 79n
'People's Pilgrimage, The' 72n
Pergamon Press 267
Perón, Eva 322
Perón, Juan 322, 342
Pershing, General John 3, 4
Peters, A. D. 13, 16, 17, 106
Petrov, Vladimir 406
Peyrefitte, Alain 369
Philby, Kim: career xxv–xxvi, 224n, 354, 420–1; correspondence with GG xi, 402; death 400–1; disinformation techniques 372; GG's visits xxxii, 391–2, 397, 401; letters to 387, 391, 397; *My Silent War* 298n, 354n; relationship with GG xi, xxv–xxvi, 412, 420–1; on Sinyavsky trial 295
Philby, Rufa 391–2, 398, 400
Pick, Charles 263
Pick, Frank 105, 106
Pincher, Chapman 372
Pink, Dr 78
Pinochet, Augusto 328n, 396, 399n
Pio, Padre xvi, 414–15
Piper, John 96
Pius XII, Pope 204, 278, 414, 415
Pizzardo, Cardinal Giuseppe 203, 205
Plon 40, 41
Pollinger, Laurence 79n, 102, 124, 132, 256
Portocarrero, Rene 286
Portugal xxxi
'Postcard from San Antonio, A' 91
Potting Shed, The xxvii, 227
Pound, Ezra xxii, xxviii, 11, 155
Powell, Anthony: education xxi, 53n; letters to 105, 162; relationship with GG xxvi, 162, 411; works xxvi, 53n, 82, 162
Power and the Glory, The: dentist character 355; Hawthornden Prize 115; influences 34n, 329n; material for xxiv, 77, 83, 91; play 166, 195–6; responses to 53n, 103–4, 203–6,

244, 278, 349, 360, 381; themes xxiv–xxv, xxxi, 164n
Price, George 374
Priestley, J. B. 46, 47, 135, 279, 391
Pritchett, Mary (Leonard) 55, 88, 96, 97, 107, 198
Pritchett, V. S. x, xxii, 147, 148, 149, 153
Private Eye 371–2, 380n
Proust, Marcel 179, 334
Pulling, Henry ix
Purna, Kit (Krishna Raghavendra) 68, 70, 74, 330

Quayle, Eric 328
Quennell, Peter xviii
Quiet American, The: film xxvii, 227, 248; material for xxviii, 193, 194, 252; responses to 377–8

Raffalovich, Andre Sebastian 59
Random House 262n
Rattigan, Terence xxvii, 136–7
Ratzinger, Joseph (later Pope Benedict XVI) 409
Reade, Charles 155
Reagan, Ronald 378, 380, 383, 388n
Reed, Carol: dinner party 290; *The Fallen Idol* xxvii, 142; GG's view of 142; GG's work with 166; *Our Man in Havana* 233, 236; *The Third Man* xxvii, 142, 158
Rees, Goronwy 99
Refugee Ship 98
Reid, Josephine 301, 302
Reinhardt, Joan 262, 311
Reinhardt, Max 262, 272, 311, 418
Reiniger, Lotte 71
Rennie, Malcolm 317
Return of A. J. Raffles, The (play) 135, 378
Richardson, Sir Ralph xxviii, 271, 272
Richey, Michael 103, 306
Richmond, Bruce 20
Richmond, Kenneth: friendships 5, 31n; GG's memories of xxxii, 258, 399n; spiritualist views xix, 312–13; treatment of GG xix, 1, 258; treatment of GG's cousin 3
Richmond, Zoë xxxii, 5, 258, 312–13, 399n
Rickards, Jocelyn (Donner) xvi, 384–5, 389, 391, 392, 404
Rilke, Rainer Maria 339
Rivière, Ellen 355
Robert, Laszlo 348
Roberts, Michael 279

Robey, George 81, 82
Rochester, 2nd Earl of (John Wilmot) xxii, 21, 39, 43–4, 45, 101
Roe, Thomas xxx, 256, 267, 281n, 283
Rolling Stone 343
Rollman, Ed 381
Ross, Noel 182
Rossetti, Dante Gabriel 207
Rost, Hilary 316
Rowse, A. L. 8
Royal Society of Literature 266
Royde-Smith, Naomi 5n
Royden, Maude 149
Ruhr xxiii, 17, 59n, 394
Rumour at Nightfall xxii, 42, 44, 48
Rushdie, Salman 406–7
Russell, Bertrand 149, 178n
Rycroft, Charles 356, 358n

Sackville-West, Eddy 270
Sadleir, Michael 38
St Joan xxvii
Salan, General Raoul-Albert-Louis 365
Salivarova, Zdena 298
Salvador, El: death of Torrijos 374; Edward Greene's experiences 382; rebels xi, 367, 368; religious murders 419; *Time* position 379
Santamaria, Haydée 286n
Saunders, Ron 314
Saunders, W. A. 315, 317n
Scharansky, Anatoly (Natan) 373
Scharansky, Avital 373
Schebeko, Marie, *see* Biche
Schelling family 51
Schiffman, Suzanne 321, 322
Schweitzer, Albert 231
Scofield, Paul 195
Sebba, Anne 394
Selznick, David O. 175
Senghor, Léopold Sédar 306
Shakespeare, William 36, 154
Sheed & Ward 77, 86
Shelden, Michael 98
Sherry, Norman: GG's views on biography 408–9, 411, 428; legal position on quotations from GG's writings 429–30; letters to 420, 422; researches for biography of GG 351, 384–5, 406
Shipwrecked, The, see England Made Me
Shorrocks, Dr 55
Shuckburgh, Evelyn 217n
Sierra Leone: governor 112n; GG's description of Freetown ix–x; GG's intelligence work ix, xxv, 40, 111,

121, 363, 420–2; GG's jungle trek xxiii, 65, 68; *Journey Without Maps* 81; GG's visit (1949) 166, 167; GG's wartime experiences 112–19, 121, 122–3, 126, 141, 237
Simon, Dame Kathleen 67
Simon & Schuster 302, 413
Sinyavsky, Andrei xiv, 291, 295–6, 300, 412n
SIS (Secret Intelligence Service) xxv, 108–9, 363
Sitwell, Edith xxvii, xxx, 227–8, 236, 251, 270
Sitwell, Sir Osbert 179, 236, 309
Six Day War x, 292, 407
Skvorecky, Josef 298, 299, 300, 327
Smart, Christopher 155
Smith, Lady Eleanor 44, 45
Smrkovsky, Josef 300
Snow, C. P. 259–60
Soames, Martin 430
Soldati, Mario 322, 333
Solzhenitsyn, Alexander 300, 322
Sort of Life, A xvi, xix, xxix, 183, 315, 316n
South Africa xxxi, 318, 326, 334, 367
Soviet Union: Baltic policy 60, 62n; dissidents xi, xiv, 373; GG's attitude to xxix; GG's plans to visit 57, 373; GG's visits xxxii, 248, 393, 395–6, 397, 401, 405; Philby's defection xi, xxv; trials 295; writers 155–6, 234–5, 291, 295–6, 300–1
Soviet Union of Writers 291
Spain xxxi, 236, 335, 342, 351, 384
Spark, Muriel: Biafra protest 297n; career xiii; GG's view of her work 281; on her books xiv; letters to 216, 229, 309, 317, 332, 335, 355, 356, 399; relationship with GG xiii, 217
Speaight, Robert 186
Spectator, The: Auberon Waugh's work 297n, 303; Centenary edition 29; Evelyn Waugh's work 257, 258; GG's work 53, 56, 59, 91, 93, 95, 106, 110, 347; Narayan's stories 76, 78; pseuds 381; wartime plans 99
Spector, R. J. 305
Spender, Stephen 80, 99, 405, 406
Stalin, Joseph 346, 417
Stamboul Train: changes to text 398; film 47; material for xxiii, 59n; publication 47; responses to 49, 278; sales xxii, 48, 49, 53; style 71; writing of xxii
Stavisky, Sacha xxiii, 55–6

Steegmuller, Francis 330–1, 332
Sten, Anna 54
Stevenson, Adlai 221
Stevenson, Sir Hubert Craddock 112
Stevenson, Robert Louis 279
Stone, Louis T. 175
Stonor, Julia Camoys 394
Straight, Belinda ('Binny') 170
Strang, Herbert 329
Stratford, Philip 310n
Strauss, Eric xx, xxix
Strauss, Ralph 44
Strong, L. A. G. 76
Sudakoff, Colonel 61
Sunday Express 219, 220
Sunday Telegraph 402
Sunday Times 43, 213, 278, 340, 381
Surin, Jean-Joseph 173
Sutro, Gillian: husband's nervous
    breakdown 276; letters and cards to
    215, 225, 247, 299, 325;
    relationship with Yvonne 311
Sutro, John: education xxi, 215; John
    Gordon Society 219, 220; letters to
    221, 276; nervous breakdown xiv,
    276, 325–6; relationship with
    Yvonne 311
Svanström, Greta 344
Svanström, Ragnar 344
Swami and Friends xxiv
Sweden: GG's publisher 344; GG's
    relationship with Anita xxix, 222,
    225, 334, 352, 397; GG's visits
    177–8, 227, 228; research for
    England Made Me xxiii, 51
Swinburne, Algernon 149
Switzerland: Anita in 235; Catherine in
    217, 218; GG's business
    arrangements 256, 283; GG's
    daughter's home xxxii, 214, 318;
    GG's flat xxxii, 417; GG's grave
    261; GG's visits 318, 325, 364, 391;
    Martine Cloetta's home xxxii, 376
Sykes, Christopher 290
Synge, J. M. 146n

Tablet, The 88, 403, 410
Tallinn 60–2, 301, 403
Tawney, Richard Henry 241
Taylor, Elizabeth 293, 297
Taylor, Sunderland 316, 317n
Temple, Shirley xxiv, 83, 87, 92, 416
Tenth Man, The 387
Third Man, The xiii, xxvii, 142, 158,
    176–7, 387
Thomson, Ian 403

Thorsley, Peter 343
Tidy, Marge 58
Time, 190, 198, 307, 379
Time & Tide 91
Times, The: Allain's death 286, 287;
    appeal letters 149; Balasova story
    327; GG's letters 300, 364n; GG's
    work xxii, 21, 25, 63, 410; leaders
    266; pseuds 381; report on Sudakoff
    61n; reviews of GG's work 38; staff,
    48; Watergate scandal 330; wedding
    announcements 250
Times Literary Supplement 20, 21, 41–2,
    43, 228
Tito (Josip Broz) 290, 342
Todd, Chris 314
Tolstoy, Leo 155
Tomlinson, H. M. 35
Torrijos, General Omar: bodyguard
    337–8; death xxxii, 374–5; GG's
    Diederich's contact 347; GG's
    portrait of 339–40, 383; invitation
    to GG 336; Noriega's career 400;
    relationship with GG xxxi–xxxii,
    338, 342, 351, 368
Travels with My Aunt: GG's view of
    xxxi, 385; material for xxxi, 85n,
    268n, 297n; publication in
    Czechoslovakia 327; quotation from
    ix; responses to 303–4; title xii, 302
Trench, Hilary (pseudonym) 71, 355n
Trollope, Anthony 114, 288
Trollope, Father George 23
Truffaut, François 321, 322
Trujillo, Rafael 280, 324n
Truman, Harry S. xxviii
Truss, Lynne 430
Turgenev, Ivan 155
Turner, G. D. 74
Turner, W. J. 110
Twenty-One Days 74–5

Ulmanis, Guntis 60
Unamuno, Miguel de 389
Universe, The 251
Updegraff, Allan 56

Valls Arango, Jorge 380
Velarde, Fabian 336, 337–8, 340
Ventura, Esteban 232
Vermeiren, Hilaire Marie 237
Verschoyle, Derek 59, 99
Vietnam: GG's visits x, 184–6, 187n,
    193–4, 278, 365n; insurgency xi,
    185–6; US policy xxviii, 296, 308,
    338, 374, 397; war 296, 342, 344

Viking Press: GG's move from 302;
    GG's move to 80, 86; GG's work 89;
    An Impossible Woman 89; Journey
    Without Maps 80; Narayan's work
    330n; Travels with My Aunt xii, 302
Violet, Bernard 413
'Virtue of Disloyalty, The' (lecture) 148,
    412–13
'Visit to Morin, A' 251
Vogue 410
Vonnegut, Kurt 265
Vuskovic Bravo, Pedro 328

Waldheim, Kurt 370–1
Walker, Royston 27–8
Wallace, Nellie 100
Walpole, Hugh 102
Walston, Catherine: in Anacapri 199;
    Caraman's meddling 251n; in Haiti
    275; health 199, 273; in Ireland
    with GG 140n, 143; letters and
    cards to xiii–xiv, xxii, 137, 138, 139,
    140, 141, 142, 143, 144, 145, 146,
    161, 163, 165, 166, 168, 169, 170,
    180, 182, 188, 194, 208, 217, 221,
    240, 255, 268, 285, 287, 307, 351;
    marriage 137; Padre Pio visit 414n;
    on photographs 260; relationship
    with GG xxii, xxvi–xxvii, xxix,
    128, 137–8, 273–4, 430;
    relationship with Shuckburgh 217n;
    religion 137, 161n, 225; The Third
    Woman 430; travel plans 190, 191,
    197
Walston, Harry xxvi, 137, 163, 165,
    169–70
Walton, William 227
Waugh, Alec 269
Waugh, Auberon: letters to xiii, 249,
    265, 297, 303, 337, 341, 362, 371;
    political campaigns 297n; on Travels
    with My Aunt 303
Waugh, Evelyn: Brideshead film project
    175–6; on A Burnt-Out Case xxx,
    251–3, 254, 258, 280; on The
    Comedians 280; death 284, 341; ear-
    trumpet 225; education xxi, 269;
    friendships 9, 196; GG's memories
    of 290; GG's radio talk on 362; on
    The Heart of the Matter 160, 163n;
    letters to xiii, xxi, 132, 139, 160,
    175, 178, 179, 186, 190, 191, 199,

203, 207, 215, 224, 248, 251, 253,
    257, 259, 264, 266, 269, 276, 280;
    Night and Day contributions 82;
    portrait of Lady Ottoline Morrell
    39; relationship with GG 270n,
    281, 284, 309, 343; response to The
    Power and the Glory controversy
    204; view of Colette's funeral 208n
Waugh, Laura 284
Waugh, Septimus 175n
Ways of Escape xvi, xx, 57, 180, 366
Webber, William H. 131
Weekend Telegraph 285
Weekly Westminster Gazette 5, 9, 12
Welles, Orson 166, 249n
Wells, H. G. 60, 149
Wescott, Glenway 36
Wesolowska, Alicja 370–1
West, Mae 52
West, Dame Rebecca 253
Westwood, H. R. 72
Wheeler, Augustus xix, 183
Why Do I Write? xxxiii, 147
Wiadamosci 163
Wilkins, John 410
William Heinemann, see Heinemann
Willmerth, James 379n
Wilson, Margaret 74
Wilson, Trevor 187, 294, 397
Winchell, Walter 374
Wodehouse, P. G. 210, 341
Wolfe, Charles 2
Wood, Peter 271
Woodruff, Douglas 410n
Woodward, Kenneth L. 413–14
Woolf, Virginia 149, 164, 369
Wordsworth, William xxviii, 345
World Health Organisation 371
World of My Own, A xx, 357n
Wright, Peter 397
Wright, Ralph 258, 264, 408
Wyatt, Sir Thomas 154
Wyndham Lewis, D. B. 34

Yeats, W. B. 151
Young, Mrs (secretary) 191, 224,
    232
Young, Roderick 398

Zaharoff, Sir Basil 399
Zola, Emile 281